# THEORY AND PRACTICE OF SOCIAL PLANNING

# THEORY AND PRACTICE OF SOCIAL PLANNING

*Companion Volume to* STUDIES IN
SOCIAL POLICY AND PLANNING

**ALFRED J. KAHN**
*Columbia University*
*School of Social Work*

RUSSELL SAGE FOUNDATION

NEW YORK 1969

## PUBLICATIONS OF RUSSELL SAGE FOUNDATION

*Russell Sage Foundation was established in 1907 by Mrs. Russell Sage for the improvement of social and living conditions in the United States. In carrying out its purpose the Foundation conducts research under the direction of members of the staff or in close collaboration with other institutions, and supports programs designed to improve the utilization of social science knowledge. As an integral part of its operations, the Foundation from time to time publishes books or pamphlets resulting from these activities. Publication under the imprint of the Foundation does not necessarily imply agreement by the Foundation, its Trustees, or its staff with the interpretations or conclusions of the authors.*

Russell Sage Foundation
230 Park Avenue, New York, N.Y. 10017

© 1969
RUSSELL SAGE FOUNDATION
*Printed in the United States of America*
*Library of Congress Catalog Card Number: 79–81406*
ISBN: 0–87154–340–X

Fifth Printing, May 1979

for NANCY VALERIE KAHN

# PREFACE

USE OF the word "planning" immediately conjures up images of comprehensive rationality, of fitting all means to predetermined ends. And the student of the community, observing that decision-making is frequently a political process, asks whether planning is relevant to what actually occurs. A plan may emerge, he notes, but what does it do beyond occupying shelf space?

Thus, two alternatives to rational planning have been offered: interest-group politics and community organization. The first focuses on power struggles and bargaining, while the community organization tradition has concerned itself with involvement of community members in decision-making, with spelling out of the role of the professional worker as "enabler," with processes for determining social priorities in resource allocation in the light of community consensus. Both of these approaches have underplayed criteria and rationale. They raise more questions about power structure than about policy parameters.

Yet community organization or interest-group politics alone are obviously not adequate approaches to the public interest. Hard questions are not answered completely by trade-offs, consensus, or vote-counting, no matter how satisfied the participants are with the process en route. People—at least on occasion—do seek to enhance rationality in decision-making in the public arena. They ask whether there cannot be analysis before some choices—even interest-group dictation of choices.

Where does one go?

This volume takes the stance that there is point to a rational model for planning—as long as there is recognition that more than analysis and report-writing is involved in the total planning process. Modern science, the professions, and public administration are concerned with maximizing rational control over elements which are and should be under control. There is need, therefore, for concepts, theories, approaches to procedure. How does one *think* about long-range decisions? What elements go into the logic of policy development? What order of intellectual steps is necessary? How does one proceed from policy to program?

But the developer of rational models must recognize that his work does not encompass the entire process. Rational strategies may be on a continuum from the comprehensive to the segmented—as subsequent chapters will illustrate. Whether on the level of national government or national voluntary agency, local community or common-interest group, city or state, functional field or problem-solving organization, the planning process represents a constant shuttling between the comprehensive and the modest, between systematic, logical, empirical activity and that decision-making which is in the broadest sense political. He who would enhance planning must therefore concern himself with optimum understanding of and organization for both the rational undertaking and for the interpersonal, intergroup, and interorganizational process, which is often called community organization in some domains and politics in others. Under either label it is intertwined with the planning process and essential to it.

A rational model for the social planning process is here offered in this spirit. Much has been said and written about politics, participation, community decision-making, and the development of consensus and very little about *how to think* about planning issues. Therefore, while we attempt to relate rationality to the total process, our particular purpose is to encourage concern on the part of some people with the deliberative phases of the whole. Obviously it would be a naïve practitioner who would consider the mission accomplished if intellectual aspects of a problem were "solved," or who would not to some degree seek to prepare himself personally to cope with all phases of the process. Much can be said for the growing view that in many contexts the planner should also become "advocate."

We begin by clarifying the problems to which social planning is addressed and then offer a vocabulary of concepts relating to aspects of planning. Some viewpoints are developed about their interrelationships. Thus, this is a theory of planning only in the sense of Paul Davidoff and Thomas Reiner: it is a theory of how planning can, should, and sometimes does take place.* Or it could be viewed as a chain of interrelated hypotheses about how rational planning might be enhanced.

The chapters in the first volume are additive. The framework which emerges, admittedly tentative and incomplete, is summarized in Chapter XII. The chapters in the companion volume, STUDIES IN SOCIAL POLICY AND PLANNING, being published simultaneously, are perhaps better characterized as long essays, and are somewhat more autonomous. Taking the framework

---

* Paul Davidoff and Thomas A. Reiner, "A Choice Theory of Planning," *Journal of the American Institute of Planners*, XXVIII, No. 2 (May, 1962), 103–115.

as point of departure, each chapter in the latter work is employed to deepen the exposition of one or more major concepts and to introduce the specific problems of planning of a given type or planning in one field. Inevitably such an undertaking tends to accent problems and issues more than achievements.

Both the earlier chapters, which present the outlines of the process, and the subsequent illustrations of work in different fields share an overall purpose. They would spell out by exposition, argument, and demonstration how fact-finding, scientific perspective, and hard analysis, when combined with conscious efforts to consider how the values and preferences of the various publics concerned may be affected and when subjected to interest-group pressures and democratic decision-making, may place us somewhat closer to where we want to be in coping with social aspects of our complex environment.

The scope of social planning is a subject for exploration and debate, as is demonstrated subsequently. The need to talk specifically and separately of planning within social fields and of social aspects of physical and economic plans in itself signifies that planning in the United States is hardly centralized in concept or administration. The choice of a mode for the social planning of the future is also within the scope of a planning process.

The author is in very special debt to the Russell Sage Foundation, sponsor and publisher of this work. Strong encouragement, considerable laissez faire, and generous financial aid permitted part-time preliminary work over several years and the commitment of a full sabbatical year to the writing. Numerous governmental bureaus, foundations, social agencies, educational institutions, and citizen groups here and abroad—not specifically mentioned, for they certainly are in no sense accountable for the outcome—have served as the laboratories and forums in which these notions have been developed and tested. I am grateful to them all.

My debt to colleagues, readers, critics, and students is considerable. At certain points, at least, concept development is an interactional process. And only others who have assayed extensive projects of this sort will understand the portion of the costs carried by members of my family and the major contribution of my secretary, Mrs. Edna Thelwell.

ALFRED J. KAHN

*Columbia University*
*New York, 1969*

# CONTENTS

# WHAT IS
# SOCIAL PLANNING?

PLANNING as a process is in evolution. The word conjures up varied images. To some, it is as all-inclusive as thinking. To others, it is as delineated as specific time-phased programming. When the word "social" is prefixed, the range of imagery increases even further: from planning an entire "social system" to evolving the specifics of a project in a social service agency.

Formal definitions, although essential, connote different things to different people, particularly in a realm in which many professions and academic disciplines converge and compete and in which language tends to be imprecise. This volume, therefore, begins with illustrations rather than attempts at definitions, hoping thereby to clarify its concerns operationally. As a consequence, the initial listing is discrete and the order somewhat arbitrary; a more systematic classification is postponed for the final part of this chapter.

The basic questions of whether Americans are willing to plan and to meet the requirements imposed by democratic values upon the planning process are confronted in the next chapter.

## WHERE PLANNING BEGINS

*Translating social goals into effective programs*

In a period of general social reform or innovation, the planner's assignment is often "packaged" as one of translating social goals into effective programs. At the conclusion of the work of the Joint Commission on Mental Illness and Health,[1] for example, the leadership of the National Institute of Mental Health was called upon to suggest strategic legislation to President John F. Kennedy. Such legislation was to advance the objective of improving treatment of the severely mentally ill by creating a service system which

---

[1] Joint Commission on Mental Illness and Health, *Action for Mental Health* (New York: Basic Books, 1961, paperback).

maximized community-based treatment and sped up the return to the community of those who must be hospitalized.

Shortly thereafter authorities in each state had access to considerable planning funds, general federal guidelines, and the task of carrying through a planning process which would tie specifically to the general national objectives: What would they do to decrease long-term stays in the very large and essentially custodial state hospitals? How could they interrelate community and hospital treatment systems? What could be done to decrease or eliminate the artificial and dysfunctional barriers between psychiatry and general medicine?

These were by no means all the issues. They do, however, serve to illustrate a planning context relatively common in the nineteen-sixties. Americans are increasingly willing to formulate and to accept new goals and then to seek their programmatic, organizational, manpower, and fiscal implications. Sometimes the responsibility for planning is completely in the hands of those who write the federal legislation or of the bureaus to which programs are assigned. More often, as illustrated by legislation in the nineteen-sixties in such fields as mental health, mental retardation, delinquency, poverty, housing and renewal, local health services, heart-cancer-stroke demonstrations, education, the aged—to present an incomplete list—the federal legislation calls for and often finances a state or local planning process which is prerequisite to maximum funding.

In 1961, to illustrate further,[2] the President's Committee on Delinquency and Youth Crime sought to shift the focus of public anti-delinquency programs from control and treatment to prevention. Sixteen communities received federal funding over the next few years to plan experimental ways of "opening opportunity" to young people and to test the theory that this, in turn, would decrease antisocial outbreaks.

President Lyndon Johnson's "Great Society" offers many illustrations and, indeed, was itself a general illustration: what does one do to achieve a "great society" in this day? More specifically, how can federal sanctions and funding upgrade the education available to poor children and to those discriminated against because of race? And if one accepts the goal of the abolition of poverty, what are the means? What should one do? Similarly, what combination of federal leadership and direct action plus assistance to states

---

[2] Alfred J. Kahn, "Trends and Problems in Community Organization," in National Conference on Social Welfare, *Social Work Practice, 1964* (New York: Columbia University Press, 1964), 3–27; Peter Marris and Martin Rein, *Dilemmas of Social Reform* (New York: Atherton Press, 1967).

and localities could contribute to the humanization of the urban environment?

Again, these are illustrative and incomplete formulations, but they are only a few of the instances in which various elements in our society have begun to converge in the formulation of general social goals and have had to face the difficult task of moving from goals on a generalized level toward more specific goals, policies, laws, programs, division of responsibility, administrative structuring, manpower decisions, funding decisions and plans for evaluation, and monitoring. In short, the general goal formulations serve as the points of departure for planning at some level.

*Coping with major social problems*

This point of departure is sometimes indistinguishable from the first but it is worthy of special attention. Frequently it is the social problem that is in focus; even a generalized goal statement is not available as a point of departure:

□ How shall we cope with increasing crime?
□ What can be done about social disorganization and pathology at the core of many cities?
□ What should be done about the high rates of mental retardation?

At times the planning process is permitted to begin with a situation as open as that offered by these and similar questions. More often, as indicated above, earlier investigation, experience, or the policy of political leadership add some statement of goal to facts about the problem: "let us strengthen law enforcement"; "the heart of the city is to be rebuilt"; "retardation due to birth defects must be decreased."

Lloyd Ohlin has argued that it is useful occasionally to return deliberately to the problem afresh and to see it as the point of departure.[3] One thus wins at least temporary respite from the usual "grooves" of thinking in some fields and has an opportunity for innovation. Institutional change is an occasional outcome, policy change a frequent one.

*Introducing social (nonmarket) considerations*

The goals are not always given to the planner as a point of departure. He increasingly confronts the opportunity to formulate them either in their

---

[3] Lloyd Ohlin, "Prospects for Planning in American Social Welfare," in Robert Morris, Editor, *Centrally Planned Change: Prospects and Concepts* (New York: National Association of Social Workers, 1964, paperback), 125–146.

generalized or their more specific aspects. One type of activity of this kind, once almost non-existent, becomes quite important as the society seeks to extrapolate from its values and to bring nonmarket considerations to bear even in realms of activity previously dominated by market or economic considerations.

Tariff policy is no longer merely a matter of protecting an industry. It relates to the country's general economic (balance of payments) and political (effect on the economy and independence of other countries) objectives. Now another series of issues enters: how does one tie these considerations to the interests of given population groups, their levels of skill and their places in society?

To pursue questions of this sort is to note that all major matters of fiscal and monetary policy have *social aspects*. In effect it is the increasing importance of the social aspects of such policy matters in the welfare state that makes urgent the provision of social planning competence at the highest governmental levels.

One might illustrate with tax policy, where decisions taken may provide incentives or deterrents to women's entering into the labor market, to children's leaving school, to older people's retiring, and so on. While economic and narrowly political considerations may have been dominant in the past, a society which begins to conquer productivity, as ours has done, finds itself able to relate decisions of this kind to broader values. A tendency has developed to regard taxation as a realm in which social planning has a part— if sometimes a minor one.[4] One might predict continued expansion of the role.

The housing field provides a prime example. It was once an activity of the market place and nothing more. Governmental regulation, zoning, and standards proved necessary as the market permitted abuse and defeated some market values (land prices). Gradually, as it was noted that for some people this created and maintained living conditions below the level of community tolerance, it was social objectives which guided new standards and regulations. At first these, too, were protective only of the larger community (to prevent a health menace which might spread "across the tracks," for example). Then, whether in response to political pressure from below or out of humanitarian impulses, the desire to assure certain minimum living conditions for even the poorest residents became significant.

The process has been gradual and is far from complete, but we now devote

---

[4] Harold M. Groves, *Federal Tax Treatment of the Family* (Washington, D.C.: The Brookings Institution, 1963).

considerable research to the question of the price we pay for given lacks and defects in our housing stock and the payoffs of given types of reform.[5] All major federal programs for renewal, city rebuilding, and public housing demand comprehensive planning, which includes provision to assure that what will be achieved will be more than buildings—the possibility of a better social milieu.

Area redevelopment programs offer a prime illustration of how purely economic or largely social considerations may clash, offering the option of *economic determinations alone* ("One should not invest in this area; it would be more economical to invest elsewhere and to move the excess labor force"), an emphasis on *social considerations* ("If necessary, we should subsidize public works to guarantee jobs where the private sector does not find it possible to do so"), or the sort of attempt at *balanced evaluation* represented by the Appalachia or other regional programs.

It is clear that political considerations have intervened in the planning so that none of the interests may feel that its contributions has been optimized. Thus the early Appalachia programs concentrated expenditures on road building and brought in much of the needed skilled labor force from outside the depressed area. However, plans and programs in general involve large-scale efforts to interrelate the several dimensions, creating a viable economy based on investment in the people concerned and aimed at enriching their lives. The challenge to expand such contributions is one of the most difficult ones for those involved with the "social aspects" of planning.[6]

There are other types of illustration; in fact, the range expands as a society becomes increasingly concerned with the well-being of its people. Legislation at a national level for "truth in packaging" and local or national legislation to protect consumers making installment purchases may serve to suggest the area. It is no small step to move from the decision that consumer well-being justifies some intervention into these market relationships to the design of specific policies and programs which will achieve their objectives and not generate intolerable side-effects.

To those who work in this field, especially on an international basis, the separation of economic and social planning, or (in housing) of social, economic, and physical planning, soon ceases to have validity. As will be seen later in this book, the strands are closely intertwined and mutually interde-

---

[5] Alvin Schorr, *Slums and Insecurity* (Washington, D.C.: Government Printing Office, 1963, paperback); Nathan Glazer, "Housing Problems and Housing Policies," *The Public Interest*, 7 (Spring, 1967), 21–51.

[6] Sar A. Levitan, *Federal Aid to Depressed Areas* (Baltimore: The Johns Hopkins Press, 1964).

pendent. The discovery that this was so led the United Nations to propose the concept of "balanced development."[7] Thus, while we shall from time to time have occasion to talk of the social *aspects* of economic or physical planning, our orientation will be towards the notion of balanced development.

## Responding to gaps, fragmentation, and other failures in service programs

At first blush, this might appear as a less imaginative and more constricted approach to social planning than the ones already listed, and it often is just that. On the other hand, a very considerable portion of all social planning does originate in an attempt to reform or tinker with existing services. It was possible to show, in a previous work,[8] that if one looked at the total effort of agencies and organizations serving children in trouble in an urban area one had to conclude that:

- ☐ Cases are found, but opportunities are lost.
- ☐ Resources are allocated to cases through competition and uneconomical "shopping."
- ☐ Dispositions are often arrived at through inadequate case evaluation.
- ☐ Policy and plans of divers agencies are uncoordinated and services offered are, therefore, inadequate or in conflict.
- ☐ Services of divers agencies, which concurrently affect a given case or family or which affect a given case sequentially, are not meshed.

To cite another illustration, a social welfare expert recently reported that, in the fifteen or twenty cities which he knows well, most of the youth-serving agencies are unrelated to the needs and aspirations of their "clientele."

In one sense, we might describe this entire group of circumstances occasioning social planning as *situations in which the gap between the idealized service model and the operational reality becomes so large as to demand reform.*

One might seek improvement of individual agencies to correct such a situation (and this is often the task). One might also quite profitably reform professional training and augment the sense of professional responsibility. But the social planning might instead introduce and develop the concept of a

---

[7] United Nations, *Towards a Dynamic Development Policy for Latin America* (New York: 1963, E/CN.12/680 Rev. 1); United Nations Department of Economic and Social Affairs, *Planning for Balanced Social and Economic Development: Six Country Case Studies* (New York, 1964); United Nations, *Report on the World Social Situation* (New York, 1961).

[8] Alfred J. Kahn, *Planning Community Services for Children in Trouble* (New York: Columbia University Press, 1963).

service network, characterized by general accountability, program and policy coordination, and case integration. The consequences are then far reaching.

As the social circumstances and the definition of issues permit, one either moves away from the treatment network toward a contribution to prevention, or one seeks to guarantee prevention activities and basic services while continuing to meet the needs of those individuals already in difficulty. These, too, are planning questions, to be resolved in the light of ends chosen.

### Redesigning services to meet the intended "target population"

To describe a significant occasion for social planning, overlapping conceptually with several of the earlier illustrations but corresponding to a real-life perspective, we here borrow one of the favorite phrases of the anti-poverty effort, which began in 1964.

Service agencies have been known to lose their constituencies or to serve only part of the potential group. It is quite common, for example, to find one settlement house or community center full to the point of overflowing, while another, with a similar constituency—on paper at least—is virtually deserted. Or a center may "draw" well in one sector of its territory while failing to attract people in another sector.

In the family counseling field, it has been charged that professional, bureaucratic, and funding factors have led to a systematic "disengagement" of agencies from adequate service to the poor.[9]

On the larger stage, evidence has been assembled to demonstrate that the services of the welfare state or the "Great Society" may in fact be unequally distributed, with the middle class making good use of what is offered while the very poor fail to get a proportionate share or—where relevant—to benefit through a significant redistribution.[10]

Here, too, is a challenging point of departure for the planner. It is clear from the very beginning that his work cannot be done unless means are found to make choices with reference to very critical aspects of social policy.

### Reviewing the viability of specific fields

Even under narrow definitions, "social welfare" covers such diverse fields as social insurance, public assistance, child welfare, family services, special services for delinquents, group services, programs for the aged, and so on.

---

[9] Richard A. Cloward, "Private Social Welfare's Adjustment Agencies," in Mayer N. Zald, Editor, *Social Welfare Institutions* (New York: John Wiley & Sons, 1965), 623–643.

[10] Richard M. Titmuss, "The Role of Redistribution in Social Policy," *Social Security Bulletin*, 28, No. 6, (June, 1965), 14–20.

Outside the United States, education and health services are usually included.

The boundaries of a field or a system of service (or "intervention system," as we suggest calling it) are the product of historical accident, vested interest, professional assessment, conceptualization of problems at a given moment— and a host of other factors both rational and irrational. Periodically the march of events or the accumulation of problems in a given network generates a readiness to review boundaries and to rethink a system of service. Here, too, is an arena for social planning.

At this writing, for example, there is need for careful thinking about the viability of child welfare as a system of service and its relationship to family services or social services generally.[11] The general reform of income security programs and a determination to wipe out traces of "poor law" occasion broad re-examination of the relationship of income security programs and social services. An emphasis on comprehensive, community-based medical care calls for a review of the connection between general medicine and psychiatry.

Although these matters will be elaborated upon later, it is clear for present purposes that they carry considerable significance for social welfare and that a disciplined approach to their resolution is required.

## Responding to inconsistencies and diffuseness in service strategies

Juvenile courts nationally tend to dismiss about half of all the matters brought to them. Yet the range may be from 3 to 4 percent in one area to 90 percent in another. It is clear after brief investigation that the differences are not attributable to a range as great as this in the problems or needs faced by those served in the courts. At stake is the very concept of the juvenile court.

To illustrate from another field, comparison between two cities in the same region of the country discloses that one retains its schizophrenics on an ambulatory basis in the community at about four times the rate of the other. Very much involved here are both the concept of the illness and the balance of resources, in-patient and out-patient, within the total service system.

Similarly, there are great discrepancies among states or among cities within the same states, in the relative balance between institutional care and foster home care in child welfare, or in service in the child's own home as contrasted with services in substitute care.

---

[11] Alfred J. Kahn, "Planning for the Welfare of Children," in National Conference on Social Welfare, *Social Welfare Forum* (New York: Columbia University Press, 1966), 165–187; Chapter VII, in the companion volume, STUDIES IN SOCIAL POLICY AND PLANNING.

In a sense these illustrations refer to a subcase of the general situation described above as discrepancies between service models and operational realities. Here what is in question is *the service model itself*. What is the norm? What should the pattern look like in action? Social welfare planning often begins at this point.

## Allocating scarce resources

A recent goals study concludes that, even given a relatively modest conception of social welfare, current projections of costs of existing national goals will demand a substantially increased portion of the gross national product by 1975. In fact, expenditures for social welfare will be exceeded only by projected goals for consumer expenditures, urban development, private plant and equipment. Given the likelihood of new social welfare goals and competing demands from other sectors, careful choices will have to be made.[12] In one sense at least all planning may be seen as a process of resource allocation, and much of the time it is quite profitably viewed as just that.

Although we shall hold that more is involved, at least at certain points, there is little doubt that much planning is occasioned by the need to make allocation decisions. Generally, budget committees of community welfare councils and budget authorities on all levels of government are responsive to a variety of political factors and precedent in making financial allocations. To a small degree almost all the time, and to a considerable degree on some rare occasions, however, policy-makers and executives offer the budgeter more than this. A planning process is set into motion and intellectual tools are developed for making decisions in the light of other factors, which are consciously introduced.

With increasing frequency we must budget scarce professional and technical manpower as carefully as funds. Here the planner faces new questions such as: What "mix" of professional, preprofessional, nonprofessional, and volunteer staffing will best achieve the goals of the respective services? What training, recruitment, salary, and general personnel policies are needed to advance the long-term manpower goals? What interrelationships among manpower programs in different fields will increase efficiency and protect the respective goals?

More recently, in the context of the anti-poverty effort, attention has been drawn to the possibility of absorbing and upgrading in human services the

---

[12] Leonard A. Lecht, *Goals, Priorities, and Dollars* (New York: The Free Press, 1966), 120–121.

marketable skills of large numbers of untrained "poor" people.[13] New questions are opened up for investigation and planning, with prior need to determine whether the emphasis is job creation or optimized service delivery. While these are not necessarily incompatible goals, and may even happily prove to be mutually reinforcing, the task of discovering the facts and developing their implications is important.

### Promoting the migration of concepts from one field of social welfare to another

It is doubtful that any social planner will be hired and charged with this task, yet it is often his point of departure. No matter what is done to encourage exchange among fields or to educate professional workers to identify, not with a particular program but with their professions or their expertise, or better still with the task that needs to be accomplished, the experience is that one copes with complexity by reducing one's environment to manageable dimensions. For most workers in social welfare, this means that they concentrate on the client at hand, the office to which they are assigned, the specialized literature which they know to be immediately relevant to their current problems.

These are inevitable, normal processes and must be generally supported. At the same time, there are the facts that many people in need of help are not served, many who are served are not helped, and prevention activity is generally minimal. One possible source of breakthrough and reform derives from the migration of concepts from one field of practice to another. The planner, whose starting point may be any of the situations listed earlier, may make his most significant contribution by encouraging much migration. To do this his perspective must be broader than that of the particular field in which he is currently engaged, or he must be supported by collaborators who have different perspectives.

To illustrate, the community mental health field developed the concept of continuity of care. Adequate application to traditional child welfare and delinquency services offers the possibility of making a significant difference in those fields. Similarly, it was the adult psychiatric clinic and the family service agency which, out of their experience, insisted that the family as a whole be seen as the treatment unit. While implications of the approach are as yet only partially realized in the originating sources, it is already obvious that child welfare services or family courts, to select only two obvious illus-

---

[13] Arthur Pearl and Frank Riessman, *New Careers for the Poor* (New York: The Free Press, 1965).

trations, could benefit much from "migration" and consideration of implications. Otto Pollak has written two books designed to encourage the "migration" of social science concepts to child guidance work.[14] Systems analysts are moving into many territories.[15]

## Absorbing new technology

This last planning context or occasion for planning in our listing is by no means rare. The development of computers, and their use by airlines to allocate seats, for example, raises the obvious question of whether computers might not help solve the problem of maintaining a current and visible inventory of institutional space available to child welfare workers and, at the same time, rationalize the criteria used and make them visible.

Or, in a field in which cases are so often "lost" between and among agencies, to a point where community purposes are often forgotten in child welfare and community protection sacrificed in community mental health, the question arises as to whether a computer system could not provide the technological base for a system of case accountability.

Similarly, the Pentagon's success with its system of program budgeting known as Planning Programming and Budgeting System (PPBS), and its subsequent adoption as a tool for all federal departments on directive from President Lyndon Johnson,[16] poses new challenges to city and state agencies as well. The essence of the system is goal clarification, priority choice, effectiveness measurement, grouping of like things together, and constant feedback.

Both of these subjects are explored further in this volume. Each requires social planning personnel to maximize the gains from the new technological developments. One might cite similar illustrations from fields as diverse as the application of television to the new methods of teaching reading, from discoveries in the psychology of learning to house-cleaning technology. Knowledge and technology are important ingredients in planning and a conscious process may speed up and increase payoff.[17]

These, then, are situations occasioning planning. Planning is often con-

---

[14] Otto Pollak, *Social Science and Psychotherapy for Children*, and *Integrating Sociological and Psychoanalytic Concepts* (New York: Russell Sage Foundation, 1952 and 1956).

[15] Robert Boguslaw, *The New Utopians* (Englewood Cliffs, N.J.: Prentice-Hall, 1965).

[16] Charles J. Hitch, *Decision-Making for Defense* (Berkeley and Los Angeles: University of California Press, 1965).

[17] However, it is man's apparent inability to predict major technological innovation that imposes permanent limitations on comprehensive planning. See Chapters II and III.

cerned with priorities and resource allocation. However, it may go beyond these into the domains of policy change, institutional change, and power transfer as well. The listing contains overlapping categories, but does serve as an initial introduction to our areas of concern as well as documentation of the fact that the social welfare establishment, broadly defined, cannot operate successfully without a well-developed planning function.

Later, after a more systematic effort to define planning, it may be possible to order these situations a bit more logically.

## APPROACHES TO A DEFINITION

This volume's conception of social planning derives from the efforts of many workers in the field and from experience with a diversity of approaches. It is best understood if developed inductively in the guise of comments on and reservations about a series of earlier definitions and systematic borrowing from them.

First, however, it may be useful to distinguish pre-planning, or planning instigators, from planning. Planning begins with a problem, a widely-felt need, major dissatisfaction, or crisis. Or it begins with a transfer of power and the decisions of new leadership to systematize their activities. Or it begins with urgent need to allocate scarce resources or personnel. Or it begins with a demand from a source of funds or of power that planning be done to qualify for continued subsidy. Or it begins with the access to considerable new resources (from unprecedented economic growth or the assignment of revenues from new sources, for example). Or, finally, it is undertaken because "everybody is doing it."

The decision to plan is made, but then the right to plan must be accomplished. Here one enters the realms of politics and community organization, complex and critical processes to be considerably, but not completely, neglected in the present volume. Law, sanction, political action may all be involved before a department, a unit, a staff, or a commission has the right to plan. There may be considerable gap between the formal right and the achievement through exercise of power and bargaining of the actual right. Only then does meaningful planning begin.

But even the intellectual aspects of the planning process are never free of concern with sanction, preference, and power—as we shall see shortly. First, however, we turn to definitions.

### Elements for a definition

We begin with a view of planning as: *"a method of determining policy under which developments may take place in a balanced, orderly fashion for* the best interests of *the people in a given* area."[18] (Emphasis added.) The notion that planning focuses, first, on *policy determination* is a central one, to which we return constantly. But social planning is a particular way of approaching policy, just as legislative bargaining is another. Nor is a geographic area always the planning locus; as we have seen, planning may address a functional field, a problem, a group.

Planning is often described, as Joseph Bunzel describes it, as "a process where, because of faith in the *ability to influence the future,* one uses foresight to achieve *predetermined goals.*"[19] (Emphasis added.) Here again is a central notion: one could not plan if one could not to some degree at least project and predict. But we must note that the formulation here as to predetermined goals is over-rigid and unreal. Goals are a dynamic and developmental phenomenon in planning; rather than predetermined, they, too, are the product of a complex series of interactions. The scientist predicts and checks predictions as a means of testing theory. The planner looks at the future "to give meaning and worth to present choices."[20]

A large group of scholars applies a generalized "how-we-think" model to the planning process—and with considerable validity. To them, planning is a process of: clarifying objectives, pointing up alternative solutions and their positive or negative consequences, continuous evaluation to improve strategy and programs.[21] One does not merely project facts or trends. One tries to project *consequences* of different choices, which might be made as a basis for final selection. Also, planning is concerned with monitoring and feedback because it is a *continuous process,* not a single act. Programs and strategies may still be improved as a plan moves from drawing board to operations.

The items above begin to round out the elements of a definition but they, too, require supplementation. For one thing, much more emphasis needs to be placed on the analysis of the problem, need, or tension that occasions the planning. As we shall stress repeatedly, such analysis must be undertaken consciously, since it does so much to shape the objective.

Nor does the formulation as yet stress adequately the need to inventory

---

[18] Joseph Bunzel, "Planning for Aging," *Journal of the American Geriatrics Society,* 9, No. 1 (January, 1961).

[19] *Ibid.*

[20] A. Kaplan, "On the Strategy of Social Planning" (Unpublished paper, mimeographed, 1958).

[21] For example, Nelson N. Foote and Leonard S. Cottrell, Jr., *Identity and Interpersonal Competence* (Chicago: University of Chicago Press, 1955), Chap. V.

the knowledge, resources, and skill—what we might call the total interventive repertoire—available for consideration. George M. Foster has noted that one aspect of planning is to consider marshaling particular kinds of knowledge in order to meet specific problems or needs. In fact, Harvey Perloff has commented that "a well-developed scheme of broad-scale planning can serve as a *knowledge organizing measure*."[22]

No mention has been made as yet in this section of the subject of *coordination*. Gunnar Myrdal pointed out in *Beyond the Welfare State*[23] that the industrialized countries of the Western world began their separate interventions into the economy in response to discrete, specific crises or problems. There was no overall plan or strategy. The growth of the number and scope of acts of intervention gradually created the need to see them in some relationship to one another; in short, coordination became necessary. In Myrdal's formulation:

> Coordination leads to planning, or rather, it *is* planning as this term has come to be understood in the Western world. Coordination of measures of intervention implies a reconsideration of them all from the point of view of how they combine to serve the development goals of the entire national community, as these goals become determined by the political process that provides the basis of power.[24]

When planning began, historically, it was "pragmatic and piecemeal." Now to sum up Myrdal's views, it consists of:

> Conscious attempts by the government of a country—usually with participation of other collective bodies—to coordinate public policies more rationally in order to reach more fully and rapidly the desirable ends for future development which are determined by the political process as it evolves.[25]

Of course not all planning is governmental or national, nor would Myrdal argue that it is. Local bodies and the voluntary sector may also plan. A department may be the unit. However, coordination is an urgent motivation for planning on all levels; provision for coordination is a significant objective of planning; and coordination is an important outcome of planning. Indeed,

---

[22] George M. Foster, "Problems in Intercultural Health Programs" (New York: Social Science Research Council Pamphlet Series, No. 12, 1958); Harvey Perloff, "Social Planning in the Metropolis," in Leonard J. Duhl, Editor, *The Urban Condition* (New York: Basic Books, 1963), 334.

[23] Gunnar Myrdal, *Beyond the Welfare State* (New Haven: Yale University Press, 1960).

[24] *Ibid.*, 63.

[25] *Ibid.*, 23.

several of the illustrations, in the previous section, of situations occasioning planning might, in fact, be summed up as programs and policies in need of coordination. However, all planning is no longer adequately described in this fashion—at least in some views. Myrdal's later work illustrates added perspectives.[26]

More specifically, planning at times addresses new problems and needs, not limiting itself to the accumulation of interventions and responses. What is more, the affluence of the modern state permits a "take-off" from values and goals and an assignment to invent new measures to enhance our lives.

The Myrdal definition adds yet another element to the listing: the determination of goals "by the political process." The concept may be stretched a bit to note that there must be at the very heart of the planning process room for and provision for choices by those affected. Sometimes this will be as formal or systematic as a referendum or a parliamentary vote. At other times, it is a matter of analyzing values or seeking informal indicators of preference. Almost always there is a struggle for the right to specify choices. Planning thus partakes both of technology and of politics; it has elements both of knowing and of choosing.

### The inventory of elements

In summary, social planning involves a sequence of means-ends relationships. It is a process of policy determination for orderly development to achieve given objectives. As put by Preston LeBreton and Dale Henning, *"Policies are standing plans."* (Emphasis added.) To Harvey Wheeler, a "social plan must assume a status somewhat more detailed than an ideology but short of a legislative program."[27] From this perspective, the central goal of planning is not a blueprint but a series of generalized guides to future decisions and actions. It demands:

☐ *selection of objectives* in the light of assessment of interests, trends or problems, social goals or values, and awareness of their broader implications

☐ *a willingness to act in foresight,* based on more or less faith and rigorous projections

---

[26] Gunnar Myrdal, *Challenge to Affluence* (New York: Pantheon Books, 1963); and *Asian Drama*, 3 volumes (New York: Twentieth Century Fund and Pantheon Books [paperback edition], 1968).

[27] Preston P. LeBreton and Dale A. Henning, *Planning Theory* (Englewood Cliffs, N.J.: Prentice-Hall, 1961), 3; Harvey Wheeler, "The Restoration of Politics" (Santa Barbara, California: Center for the Study of Democratic Institutions, 1965, pamphlet).

   □ *constant translation of policies into implications for specific objectives and for programs and action*
   □ *constant evaluation and feedback.*

Successful implementation of the process would, therefore, seem to call for steps to:

   □ clarify goals, priorities, interests
   □ ascertain the facts, the social realities, the trends
   □ inventory the knowledge, skills, and resources available or obtainable
   □ analyze the alternatives and the predictable outcomes of choices among them
   □ formalize the expressions of preference and the process of choice
   □ translate policies into implications for program on different levels ("objectives")
   □ measure the outcome of the programs.

In social planning what may be sought as outcome is one or more of the following:

   □ new policies (standing plans)
   □ program and policy coordination
   □ service integration
   □ innovations in program
   □ choice of priorities in any of the above categories or for allocation of resources
   □ administrative decisions.

In effect, in focusing on the nature of the planning process per se (not on achievement of the right to determine or implement plans), we have described an essentially intellectual undertaking. Some of the component parts call for "action" in the form of surveys, fact-gathering, struggling, bargaining, and development of consensus around preferences. The central concern here nonetheless remains, *how does one think about planning*—that is, an intellectual endeavor.

All short definitions leave some of the components ambiguous, but the above discussion now permits the presentation of several, on the assumption that their implications will be somewhat clearer. Of course, much of the volume represents an effort to specify and elaborate the concepts and to suggest the relationship between the intellectual and political tasks which meet in planning endeavors.

## Definitions

Melvin Webber's formulation succeeds in stating the nature of the interrelationships of the elements here identified as residing at the core of the planning:

Planning is that process of making rational decisions about future goals and future courses of action which relies upon explicit tracings of the repercussions and the value implications associated with alternative courses of action and, in turn, requires explicit evaluation and choice among the alternative matching goal-action sets.[28]

Webber specifies that planning is "intrinsically normative," a theme to which we have already alluded and to which we shall return repeatedly.

Our own brief definition, to sum up all the components identified, may be stated as follows:

*Planning is policy choice and programming in the light of facts, projections, and application of values.*

Policies, we have already noted, are "standing plans." They are "general guides to future decision making that are intended to shape those decisions so as to maximize their contribution to the goals of the enterprise." In this sense, "policies are the instruments by which goals are achieved."[29]

All of this may be summarized briefly—perhaps too briefly—as: *Planning is policy formulation and realization through choices and rationalization.*

Most planners tend to converge upon these elements. For a time there was a tendency to overemphasize a formal, rigid, sequential framework: goal definition, formulation of possibilities, choices of policies, execution, and evaluation. Currently, value analysis, policy choice, programming as derived from policy, the constant checking and correcting of projections, and the constant revision through feedback offer more dynamic and realistic models.

Jan Tinbergen, the Netherlands economic planner, sees social elements as derivative, but he also stresses policy development in finding "the principles and methods of designing social policies as a necessary component of general policies for economic development. The design of a policy is another word for its planning."[30] Similarly, Godfredo Zappa of Yugoslavia (not accepting a hierarchy for the economic and the social) suggests, "Planning may be

---

[28] Melvin Webber, "The Prospects for Policies Planning," in Duhl, *op. cit.*, 320.

Compare the somewhat more mechanistic language of the systems design expert who, nonetheless, includes similar components. He talks of systems design (planning?) as "the process of creating a system to meet a set of requirements" (including values?). One must consider functions ("job the system has to do") or components ("the men and pieces of equipment that make up the system"). Boguslaw, *op. cit.*, 101.

A diversity of planning theories and perspectives on process and structure are reviewed by Richard S. Bolan, "Emerging Views of Planning," *Journal of the American Institute of Planners*, XXXII, No. 4 (July, 1967), 233–245.

[29] LeBreton and Henning, *op. cit.*, 3.

[30] Jan Tinbergen, "Social Aspects of Economic Planning," in *Social Progress through Social Planning—The Role of Social Work*, Proceedings of the XII International Conference of Social Work, Athens (New York: International Conference of Social Work, 1965), 61.

defined as the control and guidance exerted upon the socio-economic system by the politically organized community in order to fulfill objectives considered desirable."[31]

## Domains and levels for social planning

Planning, to repeat, is here conceived of as normative activity. It involves policy choice and programming in the light of facts, projections, and application of values. As a process it includes elements of:

- ☐ research (including fact-finding, projection, and inventory-taking)
- ☐ value analysis and facilitation of expression of value positions, sometimes through political mechanisms
- ☐ policy formulation
- ☐ administrative structuring (programming)
- ☐ measurement and feedback.

Here, obviously, is a team activity dependent on subject-matter expertise, research skills, social science scholarship, competence in administration, and capacity to generate expressions of value choices, and the achievement of consensus where possible.

John Dykman has suggested that there are three levels of action in social planning:[32]

- ☐ societal goals: selecting social goals for the nation or a state and setting targets for their achievement
- ☐ testing consequences: "The application of social values and action criteria to the assessment of programs undertaken in pursuit of economic or political goals. . . . The testing of the consequences—in terms of intergroup or interpersonal relations—of everything from broad economic development programs to specific redevelopment projects."
- ☐ social programming: planning the more traditional welfare activities of public and private agencies and the coordination of programming by many groups.

It is Dykman's thesis, as it is ours, that the third level of activity has developed "without an adequately specified set of objectives at the first and second levels."

This is an early moment in the history of social planning, and any system of classification will soon be outdated. Nonetheless, the listing of circum-

---

[31] Godfredo Zappa, "Social Planning and Economic Planning: Similarities and Differences," in United Nations, *The Problems and Methods of Social Planning,* Report of the Expert Group, Dubrovnik (November, 1963, SOA/ESWP/EG/Rep. 4), 31.

[32] John W. Dykman, "Social Planning, Social Planners and Planned Societies," *Journal of the American Institute of Planners,* XXXII, No. 2 (March, 1966), 67–68.

stances occasioning social planning, reconsidered in the light of the elements of the definition which has been presented, does permit the creation of a working typology. Its function is to provide some points of reference for our more detailed presentation of concepts and illustrative applications.

Social planning at present addresses the following domains, appearing routinely in some and only occasionally in others. We move from smaller to larger societal units:

*Planning within an agency or organization in social welfare.* (This is properly seen as administrative planning.) Planning has always been understood to be a function of administration. For example, a local welfare department needs (and some do have) a planning staff.

*Planning for a concert of services on a community level.* (This is sectorial or categorical planning on the local level.) The focus is coordination and case integration. As an illustration, we might mention *Planning Community Services for Children in Trouble.*[33] The point of departure for such planning might be a social problem (illegitimacy) or a service system (child welfare). The objective is the creation of a coordinated service system in the public or voluntary sectors or in both combined.

*Planning to introduce (or correlate) social components into housing projects, or into local, city-wide, or regional housing and renewal activities.* (This is the *social* in relation to *physical* planning.) This category includes social planning in New Towns, social aspects of public housing planning, community social facilities in renewal areas, relocation, the Model Cities program.

*Planning nationally or regionally for an intervention system.* (This includes sectorial or categorical planning on a regional or national level; planning by functional fields.) Here, too, the concern might be with the public or the voluntary sectors, or with both combined. While the definition of boundaries of intervention systems is in itself subject to difficulty and controversy, one must periodically cope with such questions nationally, as in child welfare planning, next steps for the social security system, and the design of housing legislation.

*Problem-oriented or social-trend oriented planning.* This may also be seen as planning for the interrelationships among or restructuring of intervention systems, usually with reference to a broad national, state, or regional problem. This type of planning may encompass two or several intervention systems, and the outcome may involve their reconceptualization. For example, antipoverty planning could result in new relationships among social security,

---

[33] Kahn, *Planning Community Services for Children in Trouble.*

public assistance, and tax programs. Coping with juvenile crime may involve and restructure several systems. Planning to cope with the consequences of automation or the causes of urban riots has broad ramifications.[34] In these and other illustrations the outcome may be policy and institutional changes as well as the restructuring of direct services.

*Planning the social aspects of fiscal and monetary policy or other public programs not primarily defined as "social."* Included here are social and family policy concerns with reference to tax policy, tariff, road-building, etc.

*Planning the social aspects of balanced development.* This phraseology best suits United Nations usage. Others may prefer to talk of relating social concerns to economic planning or of social aspects of economic planning.[35]

In another sense, one may classify social planning in terms of levels of comprehensiveness. The model is offered by Albert Waterston who describes stages of development planning: the project approach, integrated public investment planning, and comprehensive planning.[36] In social planning as well, the activity very often focuses on individual projects, occasionally relates to comprehensive efforts in a geographic area (neighborhood or city), often affects given sectors, on a national or state level. Comprehensive social planning in Waterston's sense does not exist in the United States. In fact, once it becomes comprehensive, it will inevitably be fully integrated with parallel physical and economic planning. It would ignore reality and deny obvious interrelationships to talk of "planning the social system" in contrast

---

[34] National Commission on Technology, Automation and Economic Progress, *Technology and the American Economy* (Washington, D.C.: Government Printing Office, 1966); *Report of the National Advisory Commission on Civil Disorders* (Washington, D.C.: Government Printing Office, 1968).

[35] Eugene V. Rostow considers planning as "one of the most ambiguous and misleading words in the vocabulary of our times," used, at one end of the spectrum, to identify zoning and city planning and at the other to describe wartime control procedures to allocate resources and to fix prices and production quotas. He adds, "The word 'planning' is even used occasionally to characterize a 'welfare' state which has highly developed systems of social insurance, and other methods for providing citizens with basic social services." Our argument, in effect, is that these are related processes and that the word planning does apply. See Eugene V. Rostow, *Planning for Freedom* (New Haven: Yale University Press, 1962, paperback), 22–28.

[36] Albert Waterston, *Development Planning* (Baltimore, Maryland: The Johns Hopkins Press, 1965). Along similar lines, J. A. Friedman suggests four types of planning: *developmental* (involving much means and ends autonomy), *adaptive* (most decisions depend on those outside the system), *allocative*, and *innovative*. See J. A. Friedman, "A Conceptual Model for the Analysis of Planning Behavior," *Administrative Science Quarterly*, 12, No. 2 (1967), 225–252.

to the economic and the physical. The United States has not decided to go quite so far in its planning, although there has been serious discussion of the need for either a Council of Social Advisors or a broadly-sanctioned, domestic planning agency to shape basic social policy, interrelate the several sectors, launch new sectors, and seek policy coordination and service integration nationally and among the several levels of government.

## Social policy, community organization, social planning, and social administration

This definitional chapter must inevitably seek to find its way among conflicting conceptions of terms such as those here listed, each in some way related to planning and each conceived by some of its adherents as the primary integrating discipline.

Although what is offered is presented as having some general validity, the minimal objective is to assure consistency of usage, and therefore of communication, in this volume.

"Social policy" is a British concept popularized in the United States by Eveline Burns and in the writings of R. M. Titmuss and T. H. Marshall.[37] To these authors "social policy" is synonymous with "social welfare" as used in the United States. To quote Marshall,

"Social Policy" is not a technical term with an exact meaning. . . . it is taken to refer to the policy of governments with regard to action having a direct impact on the welfare of citizens, by providing them with services or income. The central core consists, therefore, of social insurance, public (or national) assistance, the health and welfare services and housing policy. Education obviously belongs . . . [as does] the treatment of crime. . . .[38]

Titmuss agrees, defining social policy as consisting of:

acts of government, undertaken for a variety of political reasons, to provide for a range of needs, material and social, and predominantly dependent needs, what the market does not or cannot satisfy for certain designated sections of the population.[39]

Sometimes, to these authors, social policy is the core of principle or the guiding ideology behind the series of separate social welfare measures. It is,

<hr>

[37] T. H. Marshall, *Social Policy* (London: Hutchinson University Library, 1965); Richard M. Titmuss, *Problems of Social Policy* (London: His Majesty's Stationery Office and Longmans, Green and Co., 1950); also see Titmuss, *op. cit.*; Eveline M. Burns, *Social Security and Public Policy* (New York: McGraw-Hill Book Company, 1956); Pekka Kuusi, *Social Policy for the Sixties* (Helsinki, Finland: Finnish Social Policy Association, 1964).
[38] Marshall, *op. cit.*, 7.
[39] Titmuss, "The Role of Redistribution in Social Policy," 1.

in effect, *the* (currently) standing plan for the social sector or the several plans for interrelated sectors (social policies).

Social policy analysis, as systematized by Burns, may thus be seen as either field-specific social planning or as administrative programming addressed to social welfare programs.[40]

"Administration" is focused on the definition of the objectives of an organization and the attainment of those objectives. It is concerned largely with converting policy into program but it develops policy on its own level and it feeds back experience into planning. In the terms of our definition it is the vehicle for one kind of social planning ("planning within an agency or organization in social welfare") and is responsible for agency or organizational programming and program implementation.

"Community organization" is social welfare in a more difficult concept to cope with, since some professionals conceive of it as a field of activity which includes both organizing for social welfare and social planning, while others define it as a method. Among the second group several varying concepts prevail.

Certainly at the core of community organization as method is the role of the "change agent" and the "enabler" in community work, the first tending to be a goal-oriented advocate and the other responsible more for process than for program outcome. "Community development," a term also used to describe both field and method, refers to community organization in underdeveloped countries or deprived areas in developed countries with a goal of creating "community competence." It involves adaptation to the special circumstances of the poor, the powerless, the unskilled, and the uneducated.

The planner, whether or not he is also called a community organizer, is obviously performing a role quite different from that of either change agent or enabler. His is a technical "symbol manipulation" task, even though—as we shall see—he, too, may be an advocate. Both roles are essential.[41] When serving either as instigator or enabler, the community organizer is in constant interaction with the planning process. Sometimes he helps to articulate the problems, concerns, dissatisfactions, or goals that launch the planning. At other times, his is a major role in the clarification and advancement of preferences and the precipitation of value choices at several points in the process—a subject to which we shall return. He may also organize groups to help them achieve control over a given planning process or its implementation.

---

[40] Burns, *op. cit.*

[41] See David Popenoe, "Community Development and Community Planning," *Journal of the American Institute of Planners*, XXXIII, No. 4 (July, 1967), 259–265.

Planner, community organizer, and administrator are, then, in closely interrelated and interacting roles. The social policy analyst or policy scientist (an American variation) is sometimes a scholar of social policy, often a planner or administrator. All are interested in and draw upon the work of students of social change theory and organization theory. And, because the roles not only interrelate but also have unclear boundaries, each is readily found functioning in the domain of the other and defining it as his own.

As for the social planner himself, our special concern in this volume, he is, as we have seen, concerned both with the social aspects of general development and with specific social "sectors" or "fields." While he cannot and does not plan fundamental social organization, which is the product of a complex system of checks and balances and of long social evolution, he can have major impact upon his environment. Some of his predecessors were expert in urban design skills and others in reflecting or in helping to shape community aspirations; he (in his collectivity) must be generalist, substantive expert, researcher, and community organizer, if the job is to be done—and done well.

## BACKGROUND NOTES ON SOCIAL PLANNING

A systematic history of social planning in the United States has not been written. In a general context of non-planning or denial of planning, the story is essentially one of partial and unintegrated efforts, of diverse conceptions and limited sanction. A few background notes may nonetheless add perspective to the present widespread effort at theory development and structuring.[42]

In a sense, definition of segments of history as relevant is related to the concept of planning. At least three strands seem to belong in the picture: the early history of city planning, the development of state-level coordination in social welfare, and the community chest and council movement, especially from the nineteen-twenties.[43]

The city planning movement was founded by social welfare personnel, muckrakers, and those from the design and construction side. It may be said to have begun with the 1893 Columbian Exposition in Chicago. The

---

[42] More specific reference to structures will be found in Chapter XI. Further comments on city planning appear in Chapter V of the companion volume.

[43] There are no comprehensive sources. Some review, with emphasis on city planning and considerable bibliography, is offered in Robert Perlman, "Social Welfare Planning and Physical Planning: A Case Study of their Relationship in Urban Renewal" (Unpublished doctoral dissertation, Brandeis University, 1961). Also see Harvey Perloff, Editor, *Planning and the Urban Community* (Pittsburgh: University of Pittsburgh Press, 1961); and William Alonso, "Cities and City Planners," in H. Wentworth Eldredge, Editor, *Taming Megalopolis* (Garden City, New York: Doubleday & Co., Anchor paperback, 1967), II, 580–596.

"city beautiful" was meant as a better place to live and grow—and was seen as based on boulevard design, waterfront use, and neoclassical architecture. Quite early, however, the "city practical" took over; city planning focused on technology and zoning. There was a revival of social perspectives during the Great Depression, a second decline—and then the great, current preoccupation, as the interrelationships of delinquency, poverty, discrimination, and housing patterns became obvious and as the America of President Johnson's Great Society sought intervention on a broad front. Because of fragmented social welfare contributions to project planning, zoning, or more extensive city planning efforts over the years, the arrival of urban renewal, and the subsequent Model Cities legislation occurred in a situation in which there were few people qualified to implement comprehensive city planning from a social perspective. Indeed, there was limited theory available.

State governments began in the eighteen-sixties to coordinate their separate correctional, psychiatric, and "poor law" programs, not as the result of deduction from theory about administration, but because growing commitments demanded some order. For a long period, there was debate as to whether state welfare boards should be advisory or administrative.[44] In both patterns, however, it soon became clear that one group could not administer or supervise or inspect all "social" programs. States soon were organized with separate agencies for a variety of functions; education, health, "poor law," corrections, psychiatry. The separate social "sectors" grew, were cultivated, and became independently specialized and bureaucratized. Various administrative combinations of the elements were attempted. The social security legislation of 1935 mandated a single state agency for the assistance categories, but there was no uniformity in other additions to welfare departments.

Planning and coordination on a state level were faced seriously only after World War II, partly because of pressure to comply with or take advantage of a diversity of federal offerings, which increasingly mandated planning and coordination. Again, for lack of an obvious social planning discipline, states have proceeded in many ways and have employed many types of personnel in a reaching out for improved planning.

With the exception of the land-grant college program of the eighteen-sixties and the post-Civil War activities of the Freedmen's Bureau, the federal government avoided large-scale social sector activity until the twentieth century. Indeed, there was widespread belief that such involvement was constitutionally prohibited. Sector after sector was subsequently

---

[44] Frank Bruno, *Trends in Social Work* (New York: Columbia University Press, 1948).

launched and expanded: public health, child welfare, veteran programs, Indian programs—and later a diversity of efforts ranging from worker protection to income maintenance, education, and housing. Response to crisis and to extreme problems was often the motivation. The issue of interrelationships and coordination was not faced on a large scale until after World War II. Except for the public health field, there was little theory and training in planning per se. Experts in specific program areas or administrators undertook what planning and coordination were attempted. The writing of the Social Security Act of 1935 should probably rank as a major exception: it was coalitional planning in a political and interest-group context.

Since World War II the developments in planning—from the perspectives of both sanction and knowledge—have been considerable at the federal level. While some warned that the country was on the "road to serfdom," Congress continued to expand its social commitments, to mandate planning on all levels, and to complain when components were not meshed. By the mid-nineteen-sixties, the search was underway for a device to coordinate planning in Washington and to assess progress periodically.

The third strand, the community chest and council movement, appeared shortly before World War I with roots in the earlier search for "charity organization." Its continuing preoccupations have been: (a) assessment of social problems so as to guide priority choice in allocation of community chest funds and creation of new welfare programs; (b) coordination of social services, especially the voluntary. At some points in its history and in some places, the movement has coped more aggressively with major social problems, included public welfare programs, attempted policy development and/or programming for the total social service system, conducted experiments and demonstrations. It has housed considerable development and refinement of social survey, social breakdown measurement, and priority research methodology—and has been the locus of development of "enabling" skills and theory in community organization.[45] Most observers are agreed that, in most places, most of the time, the chest and council movement has tended to a relatively narrow concept of the social; that it has underplayed education, housing, and health and that it has stressed services for the disadvantaged more than developmental services relevant to all. There is little

---

[45] In addition to Perlman, op. cit., see Pauline Young, Scientific Social Surveys and Research (New York: Prentice-Hall, 1949); Murray Ross, Community Organization: Theory and Principles (New York: Harper & Bros., 1955); Wayne McMillen, Community Organization for Social Welfare (Chicago: University of Chicago Press, 1945); Fred Ferris, "The First Councils of Social Agencies" (Unpublished doctoral dissertation, Columbia University School of Social Work, 1968).

doubt in most quarters that current broad city commitments to the social sectors demand a more comprehensive, official planning body. Some United States and Canadian welfare councils have made a bid for the role of statutory social planning bodies. Others, particularly in Canada, have sought to become the research arm of the official social planning. Still others see their future in planning and coordination within the voluntary sector and relating it to the statutory.

## ECONOMIC AND SOCIAL PLANNING

Although the science is far from exact, since many of the variables are only partially understood or controlled, economic planning has an impressive record of accomplishment.

Particularly since World War II, the major capitalist countries have discovered that they must undertake economic planning and that such planning need not diminish freedom or eliminate the market. Indeed, successful planning promotes economic growth and increases the opportunity for enhancement of individuals.[46] The prevailing institutions and value systems place planning on a continuum from the "indicative" to the "imperative," from the project approach to the comprehensive.[47]

As economic planning becomes more comprehensive it eventually comes to include and to provide for social planning, as it does for physical planning. The philosophies and mechanisms vary. In France, centrally-directed economic *planification* included social planning, first in relation to capital investment in social resources and then in a broader sense. French social welfare experts learned to coordinate their proposals with the economic planning process. In contrast, as a result of initiative on the regional level, the Netherlands developed social planning independently of the economic at first and moved gradually towards an integrated process.

For countries such as the United States, which have not accepted the idea of comprehensive economic planning, there is, nonetheless, no gainsaying that even those economic and physical interventions which are deliberately inaugurated—i.e., even partial economic planning—must be considered in a social perspective. The Council of Economic Advisors in its 1965 Report commented that "the ultimate dedication is the quality of human life." National economic planning is always subordinated to human goals or political objectives. The attainment of economic targets also demands supporting

---

[46] Andrew Shonfield, *Modern Capitalism: The Changing Balance of Public and Private Power* (New York: Oxford University Press, 1965).

[47] See Chapter II.

developments on the social side, whether through education or health services or coping with personal problems affecting mobility and productivity. Social planning provides a "human resource counterpart" to physical city planning[48] or to economic planning. Thus, even where there is no comprehensive economic planning, social planning must go beyond the more limited social welfare programming into some of the broader domains listed earlier in the chapter. Nor is this conclusion negated by the consideration that, because many such human goals as social justice, happiness, and culture cannot be quantified, some of the economic planning techniques are untransferable to the social realm.[49]

Unless he is clear about the operating context of economic and physical development, a social planner cannot perceive major trends and needs or make realistic choices. Unlike the economic planner who—despite obvious and serious difficulties—can point to the "system" in which he intervenes, there is no clearly, or even vaguely, bounded social system which is a field apart for the social planner and in which the results of interventions are observable. When he is at his most comprehensive, the social planner copes with social aspects of economic or physical development or is part of an effort in which the economic, physical, and social are examined together to promote "development"—or other societal goals. More often, he is limited to the planning in specific social fields, centers, programs, or problem areas. Thus American social planners work, and will probably continue to work in the predictable future, in agencies, programs, and contexts focusing on the social. Clearly, however, more of them must be prepared to "cross over" and to contribute to the social aspects of even more comprehensive economic and political inverventions and physical planning endeavors, which have significant social impact and requirements. By the very same token, economic planning techniques require respectful attention, and economic planners must be welcomed into the narrower social planning activities to offer their perspectives and experience.

---

[48] Harvey Perloff, "New Directions in Social Planning," *Journal of the American Institute of Planners*, XXXI, No. 4 (November, 1965), 300.

[49] United Nations Economic and Social Council, "Methods of Determining Social Allocations" (New York: 1965, mimeographed, E/CN.5/387).

# SOCIAL PLANNING AND AMERICAN SOCIETY

DESPITE reluctance and a contrary rhetoric, Americans are much engaged in planning. However, proposals for increased and improved social planning continue to invite a major confrontation with the manifest ethic. John Kenneth Galbraith has said correctly and somewhat bitterly:

> To suggest that we canvass our public wants to see where happiness can be improved by more and better services has a sharply radical tone. Even public services to avoid disorder must be defended. By contrast the man who devises a nostrum for a non-existent need and then successfully promotes both remains one of nature's noblemen.[1]

In this chapter, we shall examine the historical and cultural inhibitions to planning in the United States and the realities which demand and increase planning nonetheless. Although already familiar to those who are students of the society, this review serves to set the stage for the discussion, in the latter part of the chapter and at subsequent points, of the ways in which a planning process may be shaped to conform both to democratic values and political realities.[2]

## PLANNING AND THE AMERICAN ETHIC

A heritage of continental individualism, a pervasive and still potent Puritanism, a discredited but continuing Social Darwinism, and an extremely important frontier tradition—all merged with the truisms of laissez-faire economics and a respected agrarian myth—leave this country with a public ethic that, at first glance, would appear to have little tolerance for anything

---

[1] John Kenneth Galbraith, *The Affluent Society* (Boston: Houghton Mifflin Co., 1958), 269.

[2] Readers concerned only with the planning process per se may wish to turn immediately to page 52.

28

like social planning. However foolish such response may appear to the acad emician, to the man in the street the words "social planning" immediately conjure up images both of socialism and of extreme regimentation.[3] There is some suggestion, too, that individual merit will no longer be rewarded.

Distinctions between and among the ideological strains mentioned are not immediately relevant to our purpose. Nor are all of the necessary qualifications and notation of inconsistencies essential. Some of the "newer" themes (several of them of significance since the last decade of the nineteenth century)[4] are discussed subsequently. What is immediately to the point is that, until the Great Depression of the nineteen-thirties, a free market ethic tended to becloud and disguise the considerable governmental interventions and pro-business or pro-agriculture supportive activities and to attack the idea that other social interests in the country also required some measure of regulation, provision of services, and assistance. Indeed, it was true that because of the ethic the extent of intervention was limited and much that was done was played down or defined as temporary, exigent, and exceptional. Thus, while the ethic hardly reflected economic or political reality or governmental and business practice even in the heyday of Herbert Spencer and William Graham Sumner, the United States did less in some realms than did other major industrial powers, or it faced the need for new commitments more slowly than they did.

The idealized American farmer was the self-sufficient yeoman, able to work the land with the assistance of his family and to meet most of his needs on the land. He required occasional access to the city for a few items not produced on his own acreage or in his geographic area but needed little outside contact—and certainly not intervention.

The admired city man was conscientious, ambitious, and hard working. If he lived by the precepts of "Poor Richard's Almanac" or Horatio Alger,

---

[3] On the components of the ethic, with particular reference to varieties of individualism, see the following as illustrations from a large body of literature: Ralph B. Perry, *Puritanism and Democracy* (New York: Vanguard Press, 1944); Ralph H. Gabriel, *The Course of American Democratic Thought* (New York: The Ronald Press Company, 1956); Richard Hofstadter, *Social Darwinism in American Thought* (Boston: Beacon Press, revised paper edition, 1955); Charles Frankel, *The Democratic Prospect* (New York: Harper & Row, 1962); Henry S. Commager, *The American Mind* (New Haven: Yale University Press, 1950). For an effort to summarize current strains, see Robin M. Williams, Jr., *American Society* (New York: Alfred A. Knopf, 1965), Chap. XI.

[4] For example, Eric Goldman, *Rendezvous with Destiny* (New York: Alfred A. Knopf, 1962); Arthur M. Schlesinger, Jr., *The Crisis of the Old Order* (Boston: Houghton Mifflin Co., 1957); Richard Hofstadter, *The Age of Reform* (New York: Alfred A Knopf, 1955); Richard L. Heilbroner, *The Future as History* (New York: Harper & Bros., 1959).

his future was set. If "clean living" and strong self-guided industry were supplemented by a degree of innovation and aggression, he was "bound to rise." Others might "sink" but he would "swim"; and if, in the process, he cut some corners and seemed to ignore some of the components of the Golden Rule and some of the teachings of the Judeo-Christian ethic, one might see this as part of a process which in itself was "progressive."

Whether on the farm or in the city, the successful man—as perpetuated in ideology, if not necessarily in real life—was deemed to have earned his success through personal endeavor, exertion, and wisdom. One might ignore his favorable position on the "starting line" of life's race (or, later, the fact that he had inherited his wealth and never raced at all!) in support of the general proposition that, in a land of opportunity and mobility, the able and hard-working should get ahead. While it might have been one's father or grandfather who actually got the breaks, at least this showed the quality of the "stock." He who did not waste the inherited fortune obviously shared these virtues. Under any circumstances, the facts of opportunity, mobility, achievement, and growth were very real and provided the foundation of a great national development—even if the ideology did not begin to face, until well into the twentieth century, the possibility that one could not conduct the entire society on the assumption that the lower statuses, being temporary for the hard-working and deserving, could be left in that state of intolerability.

In a deeper sense, deriving from a possible distortion of Calvinism, worldly success was considered only an outward reflection of "inner light" or moral virtue, of "salvation." If one worked hard and ran fast to achieve the success, the psychologist might see this as a way of satisfying oneself that one was indeed chosen for salvation—for would any God assign the condemned to worldly success, family stability, good habits, and religious obedience? The later economic analyst and sociologist might interpret it all as the creation of a rationale that motivated and facilitated modern capital accumulation and industrialization. But, to the great leaders in the building of the American industrial system and the millions of "troops," from the clerks to the assembly-line workers, the truckers to the storekeepers, the miners to the school teachers, it was all natural and proper and the way things should be. One tried to be self-reliant. One improved oneself, adding to one's talent and capacities. One worked hard. One took chances. And one knew that all of this was or could be rewarded both in a worldly and an ultimate sense. If there were failures, injustices, and frequent periods of suffering for many, it was also true that material and social progress was apparent and visible. In general, individualism and laissez faire seemed to produce progress particularly if the latter concept were not probed too deeply.

There were many failures, non-participants, deviants, dropouts, and victims of catastrophe, of course. Of these, large numbers could be defined as objects of "acts of God," which followed some larger, if not readily apparent, religious logic. These victims could be aided through personal charity and benevolence. The need for such help was the basis for a tremendous, admirable voluntary system of charity and far-ranging social services. As an apparent by-product (but in a deeper sociological sense, also a primary purpose), such services supported the Puritan emphasis on voluntary good works, the primary "work out" arena for the vast "moral gymnasium" the world was conceived to be. Voluntary good works, as acts of free will, demonstrated one's moral worth, fulfilled God's will, recognized that "we are all brothers in Christ," and improved one's character. Voluntary good works make sense in a construct of free will, and such a construct was basic to Calvinism. One may legislate against evil (through Sunday "Blue Laws," for example), but it is a contradiction to think that true virtue can be created by statute. Character is developed by "practice."

Given such emphasis on voluntarism and skepticism about good-by-statute, there is fundamental distrust of any state welfare measures or public efforts to affect the quality of daily experience. Separation of church and state furthers true charity, and privately-endowed and conducted welfare is more important than the potential efficiency and sanction of governmental effort. (Besides, the United States experience in the immediate post-Civil War period, the first era of "large government," was inefficiency and corruption on all levels!)

Those whose problems, characteristics, or behavior tended to undermine or negate the motivational system, or even seemed to do so, were not deemed worthy of voluntary charity and humane treatment, for voluntary charity was humane on its own terms, even if demeaning and insensitive in the perspectives of today's welfare-state citizenry. At different times the composition of the unworthy group shifted, although the general trend was to cover an increasing number with the "act of God" umbrella (or act of social and psychological causation) and to offer help and remediation where Elizabethan "poor law" and its long-lived derivatives called for a punitive and deterrent policy.[5] The able-bodied man, actually or apparently employ-

[5] Karl deSchweinitz, *England's Road to Social Security* (Philadelphia: University of Pennsylvania Press, 1943); Karl Polanyi, *The Great Transformation* (Boston: Beacon Press, 1957, paperback).

able, but not able to find or hold a job, became the object of restrictions implemented through demeaning, punitive, and niggardly poor law programs. This continues to be the case in public welfare programs in a society which may increasingly understand impersonal economic and social forces, but ties income rights to labor market participation in either a direct or remote sense and assumes that the competent and virtuous will find their way.

In the perspective of this long tradition, any private and governmental action that might discourage, discount, or interfere with initiative was suspect from the beginning. Any practice that might decrease the appreciation for traditional voluntaristic virtues was subversive. Any approach that narrowed horizons by offering overall plans, governmental regulation, and emphasis on coordination seemed to sacrifice growth and innovation for safety. In short, the ethic could be enlisted to oppose any activity by government that could be assigned to private business, any social welfare endeavor by a public agency that might be assigned to voluntary associations, and—of course— any hint of avoidable governmental regulation and interference. It would certainly be expected to fire resounding broadsides at even the suggestion of systematic planning.

This discussion has been carried on with little attention to systematic economic or social theory per se, even though such theory was very much at the foundation of the ethic. One may trace a line of influence from Adam Smith and Thomas Malthus and David Ricardo to Charles Darwin and, then, the Social Darwinians. All believed that progress demanded non-interference with basic social processes. They provided the ideological base for those legislators and Chamber of Commerce lobbyists who talked laissez faire and opposed all intervention not desired by business interests. In the process, these champions of the "hands off" policy ignored the long line of "exceptions" from early nineteenth-century road-building to assist agricultural marketing, through tariff policy and fiscal and monetary supports, to the distribution of natural resources and the enactment of legislation aiding the interests of the "in" group and restricting the others. Nor did they read the theory clearly, even though told by John Stuart Mill, among others, that, "strictly speaking the economic rule of non-interference applied only to the sphere of production and exchange but not to distribution where, on the contrary, interferences in the interests of justice and welfare were legitimate."[6]

What is significant for present purposes is that the considerable interven-

---

[6] Gunnar Myrdal, *Value in Social Theory*, edited by Paul Streeten (New York: Harper & Bros., 1958), 245.

tions, which were sought or accepted despite the contrary ideology, were initiated by interests or special groups capable of bending government. Neither theory nor practice would have tolerated the idea of positive governmental economic or social policy or an initiative based on a concept of public interest seen as in some sense independent of, or even opposed to the interests of, first, an agricultural and, then, an industrial "power structure."

The reality did not conform to the ethic, but the latter was seldom challenged until the "Progressive Era." From the late nineteenth century through the New Deal, increasingly telling forays were made against some of the country's most fundamental tenets; as sociology developed, social science generally became more empirical, economic orthodoxy found itself questioned, and new perceptions of social reality made themselves felt.[7] The basic pressure came, however, not from new ideas but from economic depression, protest by organized labor, and interest-group conflicts demanding compromise.

As put by Samuel Mencher, a pragmatic-inductive approach was substituted, by which trends and events are examined in their social consequences and "truth" is tested in its application to reality. Man is seen as a force to affect and even determine events, not as a helpless observer or victim of evolution or the iron laws of economics.[8] Between the New Deal and the 'sixties, most law, philosophy, social science, and behavioral theory had rejected the supposed scientific and philosophical premises of the old ethic. A variety of neo-Keynesian economics had taken over both Republican and Democratic policy-making in the executive branches of federal and state government.

Yet—and this is most salient for our present purpose—the outmoded ethic retained tremendous popular appeal. The 1964 Republican candidate for the Presidency based his entire election campaign on the validity of the "old" truths, and, though he was defeated, the vote cast for him was large. Many state and local election campaigns are still waged on the strength of a laissez-faire economic policy, the agrarian myth, and Social Darwinian premises about the needy; and many of those candidates who present themselves in these terms are victors locally. Any reasonable sampling of the *Congressional Record,* federal legislative committee transcripts, or political

---

[7] See, for example: Robert Bremner, *From the Depths* (New York: New York University Press, 1956); Richard Hofstadter, *Social Darwinism in American Thought* (Boston: Beacon Press, revised paper edition, 1955).

[8] Samuel Mencher, *Poor Law to Poverty Program: Economic Security Policy in Britain and the United States* (Pittsburgh: University of Pittsburgh Press, 1967).

speech-making confirms the extent to which the rhetoric, at least, cannot ignore this tradition. Indeed, it is perfectly clear that those who know that our social reality has changed and who seek to act in terms of what *is*, not what is *alleged*, must constantly walk a tightrope, bowing in appropriate directions at the same time, if they would retain the privilege of serving the public and avoid replacement by those adherents of a know-nothing ideology who believe that Adam Smith and Herbert Spencer actually described how the world is today—or should be.

In short, if only for reasons of tradition and the public stance of political leadership, it has been difficult to discuss planning in the United States. The primary question asked is whether planning is truly necessary and whether it is not foreign to the United States system, not how it is to be done. When planning is undertaken, it is vulnerable to an emotional attack. Furthermore, a variety of euphemisms has developed to describe the process in terms deemed more acceptable. Finally, even under circumstances where the mandate might seem to be clear, the process itself has been inhibited by its vulnerability to attack and the uncertainty of full support.

The anti-planning tradition, now outmoded in theory and practice but still potent in the popular ethic, has another associated effect. It is difficult to discuss and to consider the real dangers and complexities in planning and to face the warnings of friendly critics, without seeming to join an antediluvian horde.

Among many who are sophisticated about these matters, there is another kind of reluctance to encourage comprehensive planning, which grows out of concern with the problem of bureaucracy. The fear of government, which was reinforced by post-Civil War corruption on all levels, has been given scientific status in the analysis of the problem of large-scale organization.[9] In effect "there are inherent limits to what can be accomplished by large hierarchical organizations." The many problems endemic to bureaucracy can be lessened only if one can think clearly about the objectives of programs. This is difficult for a society in which government is the focus of competing interests, however.[10] Thus it is assumed that the pathologies of bureaucracy will conquer—and planning is opposed in principle as increasing governmental activities and giving more power to bureaucracies. These opponents come from all parts of the political spectrum including "leftists," who once favored "more government" on principle.

---

[9] For example, James Q. Wilson, "The Bureaucracy Problem," *The Public Interest*, 6 (Winter, 1967), 3–9.

[10] *Ibid.*

The advocate of planning must thus face both the emotionalism of the ethic, perhaps a decreasing force, and the reality of organizational and political problems. These obstacles cannot be ignored. There is need for mature, serious concern with the question of how planning may be carried out so as to enhance respect for the individual—not to mould him to a preconceived plan—how to protect his privacy—not to undermine it—and, in general, how to avoid a value-blind type of social engineering. We shall attempt to face such matters in our discussion of how democratic social planning is most effectively implemented.

## AMERICANS DO PLAN

It is a tribute to some courageous public servants, scholars, and political leaders that, obstacles apart, considerable planning has developed in the United States, particularly since the nineteen-thirties. It is even more, however, a reflection of economic reality, industrial complexity, urban growth, and world-wide political-economic-social interdependence.

Before examining the relevant forces and noting the inevitability of even more planning ahead, we might briefly list some of the types of governmental involvement in programs, which are the outgrowth of planning, which encourage or mandate planning, or which would fail without planning. Illustrations are conveniently at hand in Appendix A, "Major Legislation and Administrative Actions of Economic Significance in 1965," in the January, 1966, Annual Report of the Council of Economic Advisors.[11] It is apparent that the planning involved is not confined to any narrow concept of the "economic." The comments and interpretations are mine.

*Appalachian program.*  After a period of research and planning, the legislation created a commission which would plan, coordinate programs, and both obtain and grant funds in an integrated economic-rebuilding and social program for a depressed area.

*Elementary and Secondary Education Act.*  After a period of analysis and data-collection, this legislation authorized a three-year program of federal grants to school districts with large numbers of children from low-income families. It also authorized a five-year program of grants for library materials and textbooks as well as authorizing programs to establish supplementary community education centers. Apart from inaugurating federal aid to elementary education the legislation mandated certain local planning as a precondition for funding.

*Manpower programs.*  This legislation extended and expanded the exist-

---

[11] *Economic Report of the President and The Annual Report of the Council of Economic Advisors* (Washington, D.C.: Government Printing Office, 1966), 187–194.

ing Manpower Development and Training Act and brought a previously passed Area Redevelopment Training Program under its wing to assure efficiency and coordination.

*Excise tax reduction.*   These reductions were designed to achieve specific ends for the economy (to stimulate growth) as well as to respond to pressure to eliminate annoying taxes.

*Reduction of duty-free tourist exemption.*   The measure was aimed at an unfavorable balance of payments in foreign transactions.

*Social Security Amendments of 1965.*   Several major pieces of legislation were encompassed under these amendments. A health care insurance title was added for persons over sixty-five, after a long period of public debate and much research in and out of government, followed by committee hearings and planning. An elaborate program of medical care payments for the indigent was passed, building on the experience of earlier, less comprehensive programs. Several new programs to strengthen child health services were enacted, which called for evidence of planning and provision for pilot experiments. Other changes in income maintenance were also made.

*Staffing support for community mental health centers.*   Existing legislation to permit states to build community mental health centers was the result of an earlier research and planning period under the official Joint Commission on Mental Illness and Health, which had been created by the Congress. The legislation permits funding only if planning has been done in the state. The new legislation, a seven-year program, authorized payment for the initial costs of staffing the centers.

*Omnibus Housing Act.*   This act established a controversial program of rent supplements for low-income families as well as extending and amending laws relating to public housing, urban renewal, relocation grants, open-space land, metropolitan organization and planning. It was the outgrowth of a long period of study and planning. It established a new grant program for the construction of essential water and sewer facilities.

*Economic development.*   Extending some of the principles of the Tennessee Valley Authority of the nineteen-thirties and the more recent Appalachia legislation, this act authorized up to $3.5 billion in grants and loans for public works, development facilities, and other projects intended to assist economically depressed areas and to aid planning for economic development.

*Department of Housing and Urban Development.*   The legislation created a cabinet-level department to bring together and coordinate functions scattered among several government agencies and to plan and lead a comprehensive strategy to revitalize American cities.

One might continue or update the listing, but this is unnecessary because the point is already made and our purpose is merely illustrative. Here, in a selection from an active Congressional year, the Council of Economic Advisors refers: (a) to measures of fiscal and monetary policy, an outgrowth of economic planning; (b) to items in the health-education-welfare-housing fields, generally defined as in the social "sectors" or in social welfare and very much the subject of policy debate and planning on several levels; (c) to area development projects, specifically designed to bridge economic, physical, and social planning. Were our 1965 listing complete, it would also describe legislation relating to: development of new metropolitan transportation systems; control of water pollution; creation of regional medical complexes for research and service relating to major diseases; control of air pollution; beautification of highways; training of health personnel; aid to farmers; subsidization of needy undergraduates in higher education; authorization for a National Teachers' Corps for work in the slums, and guarantees of loans for college students. Although 1965 was a particularly full year for President Lyndon Johnson's Great Society legislation and although there were some important innovations, *qualitatively* this listing is continuous with the work of reform begun in the eighteen-nineties and accelerated during the New Deal. It shares with legislation of several decades, but particularly legislation since the beginning of the Kennedy Presidency, the tendency to grow out of research and policy debate and the device of calling for national bodies, state or local authorities, or workers in specific functional fields to develop comprehensive plans as a prerequisite for long-range funding. In some instances, initial grants are for planning money. Increasingly, federal funding bodies (often called "councils") are set up to review plans and to select from among those submitted the plans which are most promising. Several of the funding programs offer special incentives for well-coordinated and comprehensive programs. The Model Cities Act, developed by the Department of Housing and Urban Development, passed in 1966 and characterized by its emphasis on comprehensive (physical, economic, social) planning, was designed specifically on this principle. Cities competed for initial funds by submitting planning proposals in 1967.

Thus, a sampling of recent legislation serves to show how far the United States has departed from its traditional assumptions about "minimal" government and the unsuitability of planning as a way of attaining national objectives. In addition, we of course insist on planning by others in connection with various foreign aid programs, and we send experts to many lands to help in sectorial or comprehensive planning efforts.[12] Andrew Shonfield

[12] Bertram M. Gross, "When is a Plan not a Plan?", *Challenge*, December, 1961 (Institute of Economic Affairs, New York University); also Lawrence K. Northwood, *Urban Development in the United States: Implications for Social Welfare* (New York: U.S. Committee of the International Conference of Social Work, 1966).

even suggests that one of our planning techniques is to import a "foreign" policy or procedure for domestic use by way of an international pact, largely of American making.[13]

The same point may be made through brief examination of the work of two federal agencies created by the pioneering post-World War II Employment Act of 1946—the Council of Economic Advisors and the Joint Economic Committee—as well as those influential "institutions," the *Economic Report of the President*, which is submitted each January, and the related *Annual Report of the Council of Economic Advisers*. No one would have dreamed in the eighteen-eighties, or again in the nineteen-twenties, that a long-range perspective on the Depression of the 'thirties and the economic experience during World War II, as well as national determination to avoid undesirable economic fluctuation and to expand opportunity, eventually would result in overwhelming bipartisan support for legislation, the purpose of which was described as follows:

> The Congress hereby declares that it is the continuing policy and responsibility of the Federal Government to use all practicable means consistent with its needs and obligations and other essential considerations of national policy, with the assistance and cooperation of industry, agriculture, labor, and State and local governments, to coordinate and utilize all its plans, functions, and resources for the purpose of creating and maintaining, in a manner calculated to foster and promote free competitive enterprise and the general welfare, conditions under which there will be afforded useful employment opportunities, including self-employment, for those able, willing, and seeking to work, and to promote maximum employment, production, and purchasing power.[14]

While there are both conservative and expansive interpretations of the intent of this legislation and the mechanisms to be used, the work has been carried out under both Democratic and Republican administrations and has included efforts to deal both with aggregate demand and with structural problems in the economy. A range of fiscal and monetary devices has been employed so as to achieve economic growth and "full" employment (two concepts the interpretation of which is also a matter of debate).[15]

Americans now are accustomed to the comprehensive hearings of the Joint Economic Committee and the debates about fiscal and monetary issues as these may affect employment, business growth, balance of payments.

---

[13] Andrew Shonfield, *Modern Capitalism: The Changing Balance of Public and Private Power* (New York: Oxford University Press, 1965), 73.

[14] Section 2, Employment Act of 1946.

[15] For illustration, see Joint Economic Committee, *Twentieth Anniversary Symposium of the Employment Act of 1946: An Economic Symposium* (Washington, D.C.: Government Printing Office, 1966).

Keynesian-type premises no longer seem strange and free market slogans are no longer taken as basic wisdom. Nor is it considered unusual for the President in his annual Economic Report or for the Council of Economic Advisors, in the comprehensive accompanying Annual Report or in its regular *Economic Indicators*, to be concerned with the relationship of "Strengthening Human Resources" (a major chapter heading in 1966) and economic growth, or to note that "the content and purpose of the Great Society programs are not purely economic." Comprehensive analyses are thus presented of program enactments, needs, and recommended new directions in education, manpower, health, equality of opportunity, and efforts to reduce poverty. Indeed, it was the Council's report in 1964 which initially offered a poverty analysis and provided the basis for the debate prior to the passage of the initial Economic Opportunity Act of 1964. The Council, in turn, had built upon hearings by the Joint Economic Committee as to the status of low-income families.

Eugene V. Rostow, a strong guardian of both capitalistic and democratic values, sees the objectives of the Economic Report as goals in a system of economic planning. The "developing American law of fiscal and monetary policy, of market organization, and of labor fit reasonably well as a workable plan for planning. . . ."[16] To which we might add that the Report is also a vehicle for a degree of social planning, or at least for consideration to some degree of the relationship between economic policy and some high-priority social objectives. Our intent is not to argue that this is comprehensive or "imperative" planning (Rostow suggests the term "capitalist planning," "liberal planning," or "planning for freedom"). Nor do we ignore Congressional reluctance to cooperate with the Executive Branch's "cooling off" proposals in periods when the danger of inflation appears, even though it welcomes tax cut recommendations to stimulate the economy. Certainly, many believe that the United States needs to go further in all kinds of planning.[17] The immediate purpose is only to show that we in the United States are, in fact, engaged in planning and have reason to think about the process.

[16] Eugene V. Rostow, *Planning for Freedom* (New Haven: Yale University Press, 1962, paperback), 22. For a popular history of economic planning in the United States, see George Soule, *Planning U.S.A.* (New York: Viking Press, 1967; Bantam paper edition, 1968).

[17] For example, Bertram M. Gross, "From Economic Bookkeeping to Social Accounting," in *Twentieth Anniversary of the Employment Act of 1946* . . . , 77–80; or Leon H. Keyserling, *ibid.*, 19–26; and *Progress or Poverty* (Washington, D.C.: Conference on Economic Progress, 1964). Also see *Report of the Joint Economic Committee on the January Report of the President* (Washington, D.C.: Government Printing Office, 1965), especially invited comment by Walter Reuther.

The same point may be illustrated more directly in the social welfare field with a review and inventory of federal planning activity in health and welfare and the federal support of and sometime leadership to similar efforts on the state and local level. The conclusion is that the efforts are "large scale," that over one hundred separate programs are involved, that there are multiple mechanisms developing on all levels, but that: "actual practice . . . precedes wide-spread recognition of such practice"; and we have now reached a point at which "we must find some new ways of coordinating and planning to encompass these many programs."[18]

Increased planning on a national governmental level has also developed as a result of another type of pressure, one related to the improvement of management and administrative methods. Proliferation of uncoordinated programs, concern with costs, and increasingly sharp questions about goal achievement in all areas of government led, late in 1965, to a Presidential directive for gradual implementation on a government-wide basis of an approach developed and successfully employed in the Department of Defense, the Planning Programming Budgeting System (PPBS):

> Once in operation, the new planning-programming-budgeting-system will enable us to:
>
> (1) Identify our national goals with precision and on a continuing basis;
> (2) Choose among those goals the ones that are most urgent;
> (3) Search for alternative means of reaching those goals most effectively at the least cost;
> (4) Inform ourselves not merely on next year's costs—but on the second, and third, and subsequent year's costs—of our programs;
> (5) Measure the performance of our programs to insure a dollar's worth of service for each dollar spent. . . . And because we will be able to make sounder decisions than ever before, I think the people of this nation will receive greater benefits from every tax dollar that is spent in their behalf.[19]

The PPBS is a program-budgeting approach which maximizes concern with goals, consideration of payoff from alternative approaches, and detailed working out of implications of decisions.[20]

---

[18] Charles Schottland, "Federal Planning for Health and Welfare," in *The Social Welfare Forum*, 1963 (New York: Columbia University Press, 1963), 97, 166.

[19] Remarks of President Lyndon B. Johnson on issuance of directive, August 25, 1965.

[20] See, for example, Committee for Economic Development, *Budgeting for National Objectives* (New York, 1966); David Novick, Editor, *Program Budgeting* (Cambridge, Mass.: Harvard University Press, 1965); William Gorham, "Allocating Federal Resources Among Competing Social Needs," *Health, Education and Welfare Indicators*, August, 1966, 1–13. Includes bibliography. For a general discussion, see Chapter VIII.

In short, it is potentially a planning system rooted in the concerns of the businessman, administrator, and accountant for efficiency and effectiveness. The President's directives were widely hailed by all elements in the society; a planning rationale had been developed reflecting the American ethic. Thus

> . . . we are already planning extensively. We have planned for prosperity and full employment for a long time. We had to institute a great deal of planning in order to wage World War II and the cold war. We are beginning to plan for the augmentation of scientific knowledge and technological innovation. The programs designed to bring into being the Great Society have required a considerable expansion of national planning.[21]

Moreover, we are a welfare state moving into a stage in which even more conscious planning is inevitable, essential, and desirable.

## INDUSTRIAL SOCIETIES AND PLANNING

One of the most unexpected and amazing phenomena of modern times has been the discovery that common technology and related problems of organization can supersede politics and ideology in mandating governmental actions and industry-government relationships. The generalization should not be misunderstood. Politics and ideology mean much in daily life; and the differences in degree of democratic control of a society, the distributional and redistributional thrust of policies, and the balance of investment at a given moment as between capital or consumer goods certainly do make great differences in the daily lives of entire peoples and in the life-chances of generations. It remains the case, nonetheless, that these factors aside, all urban industrialized societies and those which would move rapidly in this direction face common problems of economic policy and distribution of productivity and they share in certain common solutions. There are differences of degree, style, and emphasis, and even greater differences in rhetoric and rationale, yet modern industrialized societies, even those in the non-socialist Western political tradition, have all undertaken serious and significant economic planning. Committed to economic growth and to raising living standards, they have had no choice. To refer again to Rostow, the planning

> is inescapable for a modern government, especially in a democracy, which seeks to use the energies of capitalists in organizing a good deal of the daily economic work of the society it governs. It is inescapable because a capitalist economy doesn't keep itself at high levels of employment, nor can it accomplish unaided certain other economic goals of the community. And there are no institutions, apart from those of government, to carry out the

---

[21] Harvey Wheeler, "The Restoration of Politics," An Occasional Paper of the Free Society (Santa Barbara, California: Center for the Study of Democratic Institutions, 1965), 1.

essential preliminary function of planning—that of seeing to it that the aggregate of all spendings in the economy is high enough to ensure full employment, and not so high as to produce inflation. This kind of planning —to balance demand and production at full employment—can be done well or badly, in ways which further democracy or in ways which weaken it. The issue is not whether to plan, but what to plan and how to plan.[22]

To *Newsweek* magazine, all of this underscores the decreasing importance of ideology in the face of economic pragmatism and consensus.[23]

Although there is considerable difference of opinion as to how one should characterize a modern democratic society which intervenes in this fashion into the economy, with a careful view to social as well as to economic consequences, some support has developed for the term "welfare state." Before examining the components of the intervention in further detail, by way of developing our thesis as to the inevitability of increased social planning, it is necessary to admit that the term "welfare state" has become so involved in political and ideological controversy as almost to preclude objective usage. Semantic conflicts surrounding it can hardly be resolved through logical argument. Yet the term is also associated with a tradition which should not be lost—nor does that tradition show signs of disappearing. One can only seek precision in one's own usage through definition.[24]

It says too little to talk of the welfare state as one "that assumed responsibility for the well-being of its citizens."[25] Several more precise notions need to be conveyed:[26]

☐ the guarantee of a minimum standard of income, health, education, housing, and other social services deemed essential to full participation in the society

☐ the assignment of such rights and benefits by other than market criteria, even though market mechanisms may be employed to organize production and distribution

☐ maintenance of sufficient aggregate demand to ensure high employment, economic growth, and some stability of income.

[22] Rostow, *op. cit.*, 23–24. Or see, Daniel Bell, "Introduction," in Herman Kahn and Anthony J. Wiener, *The Year 2000: A Framework for Speculation on the Next Thirty-Three Years* (New York: The Macmillan Company, 1967), xxv.

[23] October 4, 1965, 48; or, from the social science end, see Robert A. Dahl and Charles E. Lindblom, *Politics, Economics, and Welfare* (New York: Harper & Bros., 1953).

[24] Were it not for the long tradition and general usage, one might prefer Lawrence Frank's term, the "service state." Lawrence K. Frank, "The Need for a New Political Theory," in *Toward the Year 2000: Work in Progress*, constituting *Daedalus*, Summer, 1967, 812.

[25] T. H. Marshall, *Social Policy* (London: Hutchinson University Library, 1965), 20.

[26] Historical perspective and a related, but different listing is provided in Asa Briggs, "The Welfare State in Historical Perspective," reprinted in Mayer N. Zald, *Social Welfare Institutions* (New York: John Wiley & Sons, 1965), 37–70.

Welfare states go beyond these interrelated categories of action as will be noted, but these are apparently the minimum. They are well put in a recent review of Shonfield's work:

> . . . modern capitalism has thrown off much of its earlier intellectual and institutional baggage. Atomized competitive markets have been replaced by large centers of public and private economic power. These have tamed the violence of competitive swings, provided a measure of coherent decision making and generally taken a longer view of the right conduct.
>
> The state has become a guarantor of a level of effective demand high enough to provide full or even over-full employment. A growing measure of welfare services protects those at the bottom.[27]

The economic devices utilized are now reasonably familiar to the readers of the daily American and European press: monetary policy and fiscal policy. These include use of tax power and incentives, intervention regarding wages, prices, and interest rates, rate and type of government expenditure at a given moment, controls on foreign investment and help or discouragement of certain trade patterns, plus efforts to expand or contract the labor supply by the manner in which money transfers and social services are provided and made available. In addition, by the provision or assurance of roads, harbors, water, power, communications, and the like, government creates conditions for industrial expansion.

The economic devices can be developed, launched, modified, halted, and coordinated in a complex modern state only if there is forethought, research, theory, monitoring, and a structure for developing and implementing policy. In short, the economic responsibilities of the welfare state are premised on planning. Nor are there many options. For over thirty years it has been clear to the economists of the West that anything less than effective demand management means ever-deeper depressions and ever-higher unemployment rates.

It was Gunnar Myrdal who pointed out that the problem and crisis-oriented interventions which were attempted initially demanded a degree of coordination. In the search for coordination the welfare state moved into planning.[28]

---

[27] Bernard D. Nossiter summarizing Shonfield, "Review," in *Commentary*, June, 1966, 95. Harry Jones adds increasing government ownership and operation of industrial and business enterprise as a welfare state characteristic, in Harry Jones, "The Rule of Law and the Welfare State," *Columbia Law Review*, 58, No. 2 (February, 1958), 143–144.

[28] Gunnar Myrdal, *Beyond the Welfare State* (New Haven: Yale University Press, 1960). For a recent United States review of how United States economic realities compel planning, see Sar Levitan, *Federal Manpower Policies and Programs to Combat Unemployment* (Kalamazoo, Mich.: W. E. Upjohn Institute for Employment Research, 1964).

While all major economic powers have elaborate and potent instruments for planning and intervention, there are significant differences in degree and kind. In some countries the market is merely influenced, in others it is interfered with, and in still others it is superseded to a considerable extent.[29] The recognizable patterns range from the countries that make formal, mandated economic plans with mutually consistent and quantified goals and appropriate. means; to the "indicative" planning countries that, like France, stress specified goals and place less emphasis on specified, quantified means in some areas; to those countries that adopt broad objectives and loosely-defined policies, which are expected to move them in the general direction sought.[30] Yet even in this later category, into which the United States has fallen, the instruments and mechanisms expand and the degree of planning increases.

David Bazelon has documented the extent to which the United States government has become what he calls "The Big Underwriter." Noting that large corporations cannot survive without comprehensive planning, even though they object to governmental planning, he claims that, in fact, big industry would fall apart without the federal government's taxing, spending, subsidizing, guaranteeing, organizing, assisting, regulating, and assuring the flow of national income. "Regulatory" commissions, ranging from Civil Aeronautics Board, the Federal Power Commission, and the Federal Reserve Board to the Federal Trade Commission, the Interstate Commerce Commission, the Securities Exchange Commission, and more than twenty others, have become the government-industry meeting and planning ground. For, in his view, "Our economy is not unplanned—it is just planned badly. And the purposes served by the planning are for the short-term and short-sighted benefit of minority groups. . . ."[31] Further, since planning is the essence of technology and since large organizations can continue to exist only by virtue of technology, "it is not a question in the modern world, of planning or not planning. It is only a question of who does it, and how well. And for whom. And how soon."[32]

---

[29] T. H. Marshall, Class, Citizenship, and Social Development (New York: Doubleday & Co., Anchor paperback, 1965), 308.

[30] See Shonfield, op. cit., Chaps. XIII–XV. Also see, Albert Waterston, Development Planning (Baltimore: The Johns Hopkins Press, 1965).

[31] David T. Bazelon, The Paper Economy (New York: Vintage paperback, 1965), Chap. X, quotation on page 243. The Wall Street Journal (New York), June 22, 1966, 24, confirms the thesis about regulatory agencies becoming vehicles for government-industry coordination and planning under the heading, "Invoking Antitrust Laws: More Firms are using Federal Legislation in Own Battles to Further Coporate Ends."

[32] Bazelon, op. cit., 370.

Government's potency as intervener and underwriter derives from the complexity of the modern economy and the lack of a substitute mechanism, from government's general power today, from the significance of its own large-scale purchases, contracts, and employment commitments. Free market advocates are convinced that the United States is well on the "road to serfdom"; whether or not their readings are correct, the fact remains that two-thirds of our economy is no longer fully controlled by private enterprise in the sense that decisions are determined only by market mechanisms.[33] Fully one-fourth of our gross national product and up to two-fifths of our employment are directly and indirectly accounted for by the not-for-profit sector of the United States economy. Government and nonprofit groups (health, education, foundations, professional associations, church groups, cooperatives, etc.) employ half of all technical and professional workers, one-third of all service workers, and one-fourth of all clerical workers. The nonprofit sector accounted for half of all the new jobs between 1950 and 1960. Income transfers are approaching 10 percent of the nation's annual output.[34]

As we turn from devices employed to promote stability and economic growth to the interrelated measures to assure a *social* minimum, we approach areas traditionally identified with the welfare state and social planning. Of course economists today appreciate the extent to which manipulation of income transfers and other social welfare measures are basic instruments of general economic policy, even though they are somewhat restricted by social objectives. One does not readily decrease social security benefits or stop a public housing construction program even if the economists see the need for economic contraction.

The basic tie between the two categories of measures is suggested by Robert Dorfman, who notes that there are increasing numbers of enterprises which are deemed socially worthwhile, but which would be considered unprofitable by businessmen. These are sometimes unprofitable, because of the conditions under which a product is distributed or consumed (as with "collective goods," facilities or services available to all comers); with payment being cumbersome or not fair (as in the instance of the patrolman on the street or the view of a lighthouse, or in the case of general benefit from a school dropout program); sometimes because of conditions of production (only government can assemble enough land for highways or urban re-

---

[33] Luther Gulick, *The Metropolitan Problem and American Ideas* (New York: Alfred A. Knopf, 1962), 102.

[34] Eli Ginsberg *et al.*, *The Pluralistic Economy* (New York: McGraw-Hill Book Company, 1965), 209, 138. Also, Joint Economic Committee Report, *Report of the Joint Economic Committee on the January 1967 Economic Report of the President* (Washington, D.C.: Government Printing Office, 1967).

newal, for example); sometimes because the market would undervalue some things society values highly in the long haul (such as preservation of natural resources).[35]

Others argue, and we would consider this as characteristic of the *ideology*, even though Dorfman may be describing the *dynamics*, that a welfare state takes over certain activities because the "economic criterion of profitability has been judged inadequate or *inappropriate* as the basis for the provision of these activities in society." (Emphasis added.) It is not that private schools, medical services, or pension schemes cannot be made profitable, but, rather, that we want all children to enjoy such services whether or not they could command them in the market.[36]

Observers have noted that, in the modern industrialized state, the individual in effect pools his fortune with his fellows, and mutual dependence becomes great. Both regulation and guarantees, which must be planned, implement the responsibility that follows. The essential point is that government in the welfare state thus undertakes and retains a measure of commitment with regard to the status of its citizens, sometimes using the direct operations route and at other times drawing upon the voluntary social service sector or private business.[37]

## THE SOCIAL PLANNING PHASE OF THE WELFARE STATE

The educational sophistication and more widespread distribution of power, which have accompanied technological expansion and industrialization in the West, have led to potent demands for more sharing in opportunities, protections, benefits, and advantages—at the same point that productivity has permitted more investments in and return to the consumer. In fact, both the creation of a competent and adequately-motivated labor force and continuation of economic growth supported the development. At the same time religious and humanitarian objectives became more possible of realization and could actually be updated and broadened. Social welfare programs, using the phrase narrowly, must thus be seen in the context of the general

---

[35] Robert Dorfman, Editor, *Measuring Benefits of Government Investments* (Washington, D.C.: The Brookings Institution, 1965), Introduction, 3–6.

[36] United Nations Economic and Social Council, "Methods of Determining Social Allocations" (1965, mimeographed, E/CN.5/387), 6–7.

[37] Marshall, *op. cit.*, 97. Elsewhere, Marshall suggests that in the welfare state some elements of civilized life are ranked *above* the market economy. In his view, too, a welfare state does not seek to eliminate inequalities but to render them explicable and defensible in terms of legitimate claims. Some pooling of risks and sharing of resources renders consumption in some senses cooperative, as in the pattern of a mutual benefit society. See Marshall, *Class, Citizenship, and Social Development*, 298.

forces shaping the welfare state. Where once they met limited and inescapable necessities and modest consumer claims, they now face more options and demands. All of this is worthy of some elaboration because it clarifies one's conviction as to the necessity of even more social planning.

In one sense, "poor law" was a point along the road to social security, yet the differences between the two approaches are of such significance as to make the latter a radical departure.[38] Public policy and provision for the deviant, the needy, and the poor were dominated historically in both England and the United States by the central concern with controlling, developing, and motivating a labor force during the period of capital accumulation and investment. The entire labor force was poor and "poor law" affected directly or indirectly all those who worked for wages. Little was provided as a "right" to meet contingencies. Exceptions eventually were made for those categories of needy whose more considerate treatment would not undermine the motivational system and could be financed. Private charity increasingly took the "bite" off the system by dealing somewhat more adequately with those defined as "worthy." However, for most of the poor, the consequences were a constant ritual of humiliation, inadequate aid, and loss of full status as soon as help was needed. This was assumed to be appropriate policy. The channeling of private charitable impulses was another matter but it, too, for other reasons was often concerned more with donors than with recipients.

The shift came in the late nineteenth and early twentieth centuries with social security laws and related protective legislation on working conditions, safety, hours, child labor, and so on. These developments reflected the growing political strength of urban labor, religious and secular humanitarian impulses, socialist ideologies, and a stage of industrialization that permitted more attention to people as ends, not merely as means. Safety regulations and workmen's compensation could be afforded and child labor was generally unprofitable. Major shared risks could be predicted and the individual insured against their most severe consequences. Costs could also be shared. Social welfare as an institution and a social work profession could develop and could involve programs and premises that went beyond labor force considerations.

In this country, for example, the New Deal dramatized the urgency of making all economic statuses viable, although once it had been assumed that the competent would always rise to the top and achieve success. Insurance against old age, unemployment, the loss of a breadwinner became morally respectable. A drive for personal security ceased to be a sign of inadequacy.[39]

---

[38] DeSchweinitz, *op. cit.*

[39] Goldman, *op. cit.*, 370–371.

A floor of assistance for those not covered by insurance could also be accepted in principle, "guaranteeing" a minimum of health and decency. The "dignity of the client" became a slogan—if not always a fact.

This phase is often called the beginning of the welfare state. If so, it might be described as the *social security phase of the welfare state*. With few exceptions, in this stage the market continues to govern. Social insurances addressed to specified risks are based on contributions and generally follow the private insurance model or pretend to do so. (The fact that there are increasing inroads on the model is part of the evidence for an emerging new phase, to which we shall turn below.) General assistance (for those not in the categories defined as in need for reasons unrelated to motivational problems) is left to the locality, is generally inadequate, and carries negative consequences for social status and sense of competence. Punitive activity and renamed "work tests" characterize relief. "Solutions" are sought through rehabilitation of *individuals*. Stigma-free helping programs for the old poor law category of "able-bodied unemployed" are confined to subparts of the public sector and to parts of the voluntary sector. In short, poor law is formally gone but far from forgotten. Its institutional and attitudinal residues are everywhere visible.

Yet, while all this continues, economists and political theorists remind us that the United States is fast reaching—or has already arrived at—a point of affluence and technological development that makes the social security stage and its assumptions, as well as the remnants of poor law, completely inappropriate as an approach to problems of the individual and his income.[40] Furthermore, as the economy moves continually in the direction of more production of services because more manpower is available for such functions, some of it in the profit and some of it in the nonprofit sector, the possibilities of social provision increase.

One might elaborate this thesis of the new affluence of a technological society (and its variations) at some length, but the general outlines are now familiar. There are, of course, significant debates as to how much of what is discussed is already with us and how much immediately on the horizon.[41] Yet the central core of the analysis reflects considerable consensus.

---

[40] John Kenneth Galbraith, *The Affluent Society* (Boston: Houghton Mifflin Co., 1958); and Jacques Ellul, *The Technological Society* (New York: Alfred A. Knopf, 1964).

[41] W. W. Rostow, *The Stages of Economic Growth* (London, England: Cambridge University Press, 1960); and Robert Theobald, *Free Men and Free Markets* (Garden City, New York: Doubleday & Co., Anchor paperback, 1965). See also, Alvin L. Schorr, "The New Radicals: The Triple Revolution," *Social Work*, 10, No. 1 (January, 1965), 112–114.

We cannot do "everything," but we can do much. We are in control of tremendous productive capacities and face many options as to how to distribute benefits among people and to a person over his lifetime. An economic growth rate, which is adequate to provide employment to all the able-bodied in their productive years, in turn generates resources on an unprecedented scale.[42] Individual and collective interests need to be interrelated and harmonized. We need to set our priorities and clarify the quality of life which is meaningful to us. We may eventually face what Theobald sees as already upon us—but what most economists consider a task of the future, if a task at all—the need to redefine work and to find a basis for fundamental separation of consumption rights from labor market participation.[43]

The United States anti-poverty effort of the nineteen-sixties provides an illustration of the new scope and scale of social welfare concerns and the rapidity of movement in both philosophic premises and intervention concept. At the start, pronouncements aside, the programs which were offered coped primarily with questions of competence, motivation, and access to opportunity for actual or potential members of the labor force who either were not literate or sufficiently skilled, possessed outmoded skills, were not at employment locations, or were denied their chances because of discrimination. So-called community-action programs emphasized self-help as the path to increased social competence for all citizens and as a device to assure the adaptability of training and rehabilitation programs to local needs.

These were welcome efforts. The preoccupation with knowledge, skill, and role training for the disadvantaged individual was a decided improvement over the considerable tendency a decade previously to define rehabilitation or habilitation needs largely in motivational terms. Yet this was only part of the story, obviously. Under pressure from economically depressed areas, the civil rights movement, economic analysts, and others, strategists of the anti-poverty war added area and regional development and redevelopment programs. Americans could understand that one does not win an anti-poverty "war" without creating jobs and making local economies viable. At the same time, the President and the Council of Economic Advisors were concerned with the general performance of the economy and were developing necessary guidelines. Increasingly, discussion of anti-poverty strategy

---

[42] *Technology and the American Economy*, Vol. I of Report of the National Commission on Technology, Automation and Economic Progress (Washington, D.C.: Government Printing Office, 1966), 73 ff. Also Marshall, *Class, Citizenship, and Social Development*, 258–259.

[43] Theobald, *op. cit.*

was found to be interlaced with the general attention to fiscal and monetary policy, publicly created jobs, business and farm loans, and minimum wages. Anti-poverty policy clearly was also general social policy or—in the vocabulary of this chapter—welfare state policy.[44]

Soon the focus also included the possibilities for an expanded policy of income transfers (pensions, social insurance, public assistance, negative income tax, family allowance, etc.); a much larger public commitment to the reconstruction of cities; construction of housing, schools, and other "public goods"; and considerably increased health services. The listing already presented of 1965 legislation, on pages 35–36, illustrates the type of measures considered appropriate, within the scope of government, and urgent. It emphasizes the sense in which an anti-poverty effort cannot be seen apart from all social policy. It serves to point up the arrival of the welfare state at a new stage in the 'sixties—*the social planning phase of the welfare state*— in which human preferences and values, democratically determined, may guide allocation of consumption rights and other large areas of public policy. These steps may be taken in our present mixed economy without affecting the role of the market at the production end, at least in the view of some economists. Yet in contrast to the earlier phase, there is concern with basic institutional innovation as much as with remedying discrepancies between individual capacities and institutional demands.

These are large generalizations. Listen, however, to W. W. Rostow, an economic theorist who believes that we are already in "the age of high mass-consumption":

> In a quite technical sense, the balance of attention of the society . . . shifted from supply to demand, from problems of production to problems of consumption, and of welfare in the widest sense.
>
> . . . As maturity approached. . . . Men were prepared in a sense to take risks with the level of output—and the incentives in the private sector— in order to cushion the hardships of the trade-cycle; in order to increase social security; in order to redistribute income . . . and, generally, to soften the harshness of a society hitherto geared primarily to maximizing industrial output and the spread of modern technology.
>
> The third possible direction opened up by the achievement of maturity was the expansion of consumption levels . . . which the mature economies of the twentieth century can provide.[45]

---

[44] See Chapter II in the companion volume.

[45] W. W. Rostow, *op. cit.*, 73–74.

It should be perhaps noted that we here discuss "stages" descriptively, not assuming inevitability or cycles. In a work first published in 1941, Alva Myrdal analyzed the history

To Rostow, the realities of the arms race and of American responsibilities in a complex and costly world political environment, plus the growth of the "dependency ratio" after a long decline (the relation to the labor force of the consumers under twenty and over sixty-five), perpetuate the scarcity problem for quite a while.[46]

But, whether all at once or gradually, we face the emergence of the social planning phase: the importance of preferences and value decisions, the need to invent new pathways to consumption rights, the ability of individuals to dispose of larger segments of their lifetimes to other than market-defined production or service, the possibility of implementing human ideals long seen as utopian in a world of scarce resources. For the first time our response to social problems may be made not in an emergency context, but in a perspective that considers fundamental social goals.

From a somewhat different conceptual stance, Bell has described the transition from contractual to *communal* society. Rights and claims against the community become the central phenomena. Thus the issues become: (a) social choices and collective decisions; (b) participation; (c) privacy.[47]

By way of concluding note for this section, it should be emphasized that none of this is meant to exaggerate the case. *The United States is a welfare state and engages in social planning, but the contrary ethic remains strong, the concerns about unresponsive bureaucracies are considerable, and the bias continues in favor of a context of maximum permissiveness, market-dominated decisions, and diversity. The planning is partial and Wilensky's term is apt: Ours is a reluctant welfare state.*[48]

One might cite exceptions and contrary pressures, but the tradition and the strength of opposing forces move the United States toward increased planning only very slowly, perhaps happily so. The preference and value debates, essential to democratic social planning, thus have platform and opportunity. Some programs, such as education, have tended to do more for middle- and higher-income groups than for the poor. Yet to be faced seriously is the extent to which priority is to be given to the goal of extensive

---

as covering a "paternalistic conservative era" (government must cure the worst ills); a "liberal era" (safeguards against inequality are created through the pooling of risks— our "social security" phase); a "social democratic era" (attempts are made to prevent ills, and social planning thus emerges). See Alva Myrdal, *Nation and Family* (Cambridge, Mass.: The M.I.T. Press, 1968, paperback edition).

[46] W. W. Rostow, *op. cit.*

[47] Daniel Bell, "Summary," in *Toward the Year 2000 . . .* , 977.

[48] Harold L. Wilensky, Introduction to the paperback edition, *Industrial Society and Social Welfare* (Glencoe, Ill.: The Free Press, 1955).

redistributional effects for programs. Both in England and the United States there are those who would see redistributive justice as the large contemporary issue.[49] To others the question is contained in the larger one of how the richest society of all time can become a progressively better place in which to live, work, and develop to one's full potential.[50]

## PLANNING AND DEMOCRACY

The United States plans more than the "popular culture" says that it does, but it does so hesitantly. The hesitation is part of the source of incompleteness, gaps, and inadequate coordination. The movement is toward stepped-up and more comprehensive efforts, but there is concern that extensive planning is not compatible with democracy.

The anti-planners are often identified with the general stream of anti-intellectualism which refuses to look beyond so-called fundamental truths to economic and social realities. On the other hand, some of the opposition comes from the well informed and the thoughtful: they are concerned about the possible connections among planning, control, loss of freedom, and decline of democracy. One must acknowledge at once that these are real dangers and represent serious problems. However, unless one would undo modern technology and industrialization, large-scale organization and bureaucratization, specialization and interdependence, the forces requiring planning are irresistible. Thus the issue is not one of whether or not to attempt planning, in view of the inherent risks, but rather *how* to undertake planning so as to protect and enhance democracy.[51]

To advocate planning is not necessarily to advocate a completely planned society. The stance of many planners is that one takes as an issue the question of how much planning, on what levels, in view of the goals which are sought and the values which are most precious. As do the economic planners, social planners may continue to utilize the private market place and to introduce it into new arenas.[52] The sectors to be planned, the degree of coordination, the conceptualization of planning tasks are all issues to be debated and resolved. What is more, greater or lesser degrees of planning may be ap-

---

[49] Richard M. Titmuss, "The Role of Redistribution in Social Policy," *Social Security Bulletin*, 28, No. 6, (June, 1965).

[50] *Report of the Joint Economic Committee to the Congress on the 1965 Economic Report of the President* (Washington, D.C.: Government Printing Office, 1965).

[51] The classic statement appears in Karl Mannhein, *Freedom, Power and Democratic Planning* (London: Routledge & Kegan Paul, Ltd., 1951), 29.

[52] Shonfield, *op. cit.* Also see Chapters VI and VII.

propriate in various realms of activity (or, for that matter in different countries).

There is, however, a more fundamental point. The very values which are most precious to a democratic society may be translated into planning objectives. While resource or service distribution may be instrumental goals of a planning process (to illustrate), the core goals may be set as enhancing capacity and opportunity for participation in community decision-making and activity. Then one must seek both means and specific ends consistent with such goals. In short, to return to the previous theme, our wealth and our social development increase the possibility of translating aspirations and preferences into social reality. If social planning is seen as a vehicle toward this end, it will implement and enhance, rather than subvert, democracy. A perspective of this kind places the issue of identifying and implementing values and preferences at the heart of each phase of the planning endeavor. A value-free social engineering is not involved here, but, rather, a normative activity in which means and ends are constantly monitored and adjusted.[53]

A number of things would seem to follow with reference to the conception of planning, the status of plans, and planning structures. Most will require subsequent elaboration elsewhere in this volume.

First, even in highly-centralized countries plans are quite incomplete. The well-publicized "five-year" plans tend to provide frameworks and to be quasi-plans. Those who would plan and mandate details on many levels find that they know too little to do so and that the complexities of minute coordination often defeat them.[54] During the past several years the Soviet Union and many of the countries in its orbit have been experimenting with increasing the number of "free zones," with further decentralization of responsibility and with employment of market mechanisms as a substitute for extremely comprehensive and centralized programming.

Among the Western countries which plan, there is much respect for the French system of *indicative* planning, loosely translated as "permissive" planning and defined as "a system which relies on pointing out desirable ends rather than giving orders to achieve them."[55] Hackett has shown that, in fact, the French plan is far more detailed and specific in relation to some parts of the economy than in relation to others. The system involves an effort to achieve a considerable measure of consensus as to goals. The concept of "concerted economy" calls for involvement of Frenchmen at all levels in the

[53] See Chapter IV.

[54] Gross, *op. cit.*

[55] Shonfield, *op. cit.*, 84.

elaboration of the plan, selection of options, and translation of general goals into implications for the various sectors and different parts of the country. The main "power" behind the plan is the proportionately large governmental expenditure, which is governed by the plan and affects much of the remainder of the economy.[56] Yugoslavia, too, tends to prefer decisions affecting incentives rather than direct national decision-making and quotas. The scope of essential decisions and the levels on which they must be made preclude highly-centralized, detailed plans and encourage considerable decentralization (which, again, may or may not provide for comprehensive decision-making at the local level or for extensive free zones).

The issues of strategies for decentralization and the balance between central policy formation and accountability, on the one hand, and authentic decentralization, on the other, thus become major ones for the democratic planner.

Mannheim notes that planning requires strong central power, since without it there is no true coordination of policies. But "coordination is essential only in certain basic policy issues," so one must not let centralized institutions "usurp all function."[57] Local options, extensive local participation in policy choice, programming, and resource allocation would appear to be among the important vehicles for combining planning and the protection of democracy. However, one must probe the limits of decentralization as well, the "rights" of the non-local group, and the question of what level is relevant to what type of decision. One must also explore beneath formal structures for decentralization to the possibility that favored cadres or political groups make the real decisions, while local committees go through a ritual of what can only be endorsement. Decentralization is an asset if it is utilized to make the "consumer" also a policy participant, an initiator, an evaluator, and a cooperator in programs—whether the consumer is operating on his own or in voluntary associations and official bodies.

Thus, in the context of a planning discussion, one must probe the question of centralization and decentralization and the balance in the continuum between the French *indicative* and the contrasting *imperative* approaches. Or one may consider something less than what the French have, stressing a large voluntary component in the search for consensus on objectives and

---

[56] *Ibid*. Also, John Hackett, *Economic Planning in France* (London: Asia Publishing House, 1965), 14–15; and Edmund Taylor, "Permissive Planning and the French Economy," The *Reporter* (May 6, 1965), 25–28.

[57] Mannheim, *op. cit.*, 112–115.

seeking merely for more coordination of: (*a*) the components within each social sector, (*b*) the sectors with one another, (*c*) economic, social, and physical planning, and (*d*) activity on different governmental and geographic levels.

Perhaps the two major safeguards of democracy are, first, the encouragement of a pluralism and diversity of planning efforts and, second, the assurance that the planner is not permitted a final decision-making authority. With reference to the former, there is much protection for all if, apart from what is undertaken by official bodies, there are independent research and planning efforts, narrow or broad in scope, undertaken by special-interest groups, political parties, commercial interests, and others. Then, through the political mechanisms on all levels, alternative policies and programs are debated and resolved through the political process. A diversity of planning avoids rigidity and domination by biased technicians. Resolution within the political system protects the principle of "consent of the governed" and makes it possible for planning to increase democracy by bringing vital issues into the arena for public inspection. Similarly, this implicit recognition that, in a democracy, planning must be seen essentially as a political function with technical underpinnings will lead to a pattern of organization and administration which will not assign executive authority or final, independent decision-making to the planner. In the sense suggested, his real function is to improve and facilitate administrative and political processes.[58]

This is fundamental. Furthermore, some of the risks that accompany extensive planning—or any considerable expansion of the social welfare activities of government—also may be countered by the development of necessary doctrines, procedures, and resources.

*Information.* Access to information about services, benefits, entitlements, procedures, rights, and channels for appeal is essential to the citizen in a highly-organized society. The British Citizens' Advice Bureaus and similar types of programs offer one possible model.[59]

*Rights.* Even more basic, as the state's involvement in services and benefits increases, is the need to assure that these are not conceived and defined as a matter of largesse. Much human history illustrates how irrelevant con-

---

[58] See Walter Stohr, "Planning for Depressed Areas: A Methodological Approach," *Journal of the American Institute of Planners,* XXX, No. 2 (May, 1964), 125. Organization for planning is discussed in Chapter XI.

[59] Alfred J. Kahn *et al., Neighborhood Information Centers: A Study and Some Proposals* (New York: Columbia University School of Social Work, 1966). The general subject is discussed in Chapter X.

ditions and the sacrifice of constitutional rights may be attached to the distribution of what is defined as largesse. To counter such tendencies, a number of legal scholars, among whom Charles Reich has been in a leadership role, have urged the development where possible of a concept of legal rights as attaching to social insurance and various other social services, facilities, and welfare programs. These rights to the "product" of the welfare state become "the new property." Such "property," in turn, helps avoid excessive dependence and is the material base for civil liberties. In addition, also by way of offering protection for the citizen in the welfare state, Reich would limit the discretion of regulatory agencies to the purposes for which they were designed and would avoid assigning policy-making tasks to private "research and development" or consultation organizations.[60]

Legal rights need full definition through the process of their employment and enjoyment; the individual citizen cannot go far without access to legal guidance and assistance on occasion. In this connection, the democratization of American social welfare was advanced considerably by the development of pioneering neighborhood legal services for poor people under the antipoverty effort and by the decision to permit such services to function well beyond the boundaries of traditional legal aid for accused defendants. In fact, the early work of such services tended to concentrate on the rights of public welfare recipients and applicants and public housing tenants and highlighted long-standing and never-challenged infringements on constitutional rights, invasion of privacy, and arbitrary exercise of administrative discretion. Although several scholars had reported the existence of a "dual system" of law, operating to the disadvantage of the poor,[61] this needed to be demonstrated and challenged in the courts and through administrative tribunals.

*Administrative reviews and appeals.*  As government service, regulation, and planning increase, there must inevitably be developed a large network of administrative agencies. The welfare state must be concerned with provisions to detect and expose inefficiency, corruption, and abuse by such agencies and to assure appeal from them. There has been world-wide interest in the Scandinavian *Ombudsman* program, even though experience thus far would suggest its suitability to small, relatively homogeneous countries. Walter

---

[60] Charles Reich, "The New Property," *Yale Law Journal*, 73, No. 5 (April, 1964), 733–787. Also see, Jones, *op. cit.*

[61] Jacobus tenBroek, *California's Dual System of Family Law*, reprinted as a monograph from *Stanford Law Review*, 16, Nos. 2, 4 (March, July, 1964) and 17, No. 4 (April, 1965).

Gellhorn has studied these adaptations and considered possible implications for the United States.[62]

At the same time there is general recognition of the need for formal machinery of the kind represented by Britain's Council on Tribunals. Wheeler has suggested that the welfare state, in its social planning phase, will require a substantial revamping of the United States court system to include both an "administrative and statutory appeals court" and a "court of planning."[63]

This section may then be concluded with a simple summary quotation:

> . . . to some, equating planning with democracy seems paradoxical, since they claim that planning subjugates and makes people dependent. Planning in a *closed* society does have this effect. Planning in an *open* society can only facilitate democracy by reducing the inequalities, maximizing the range of choices, educating people to use the choices they make and making the choices more widely available.[64]

## LIMITS, LIMITATIONS, AND DIRECTION

Important to some fields, programs, places and often quite limited, social planning continues to develop and to seek codification. This appears inevitable and desirable. Yet planning is certainly not the only source of social change and seldom qualifies as the predominant element. It probably achieves more when targeted on programs than on institutions. Carefully evolved policies are often swept aside at key turning points in a nation's history as a result of unpredictable occurrences, acts of political leadership, and technological breakthroughs. Certainly, too, at the present state of knowledge in the social sciences, unanticipated consequences of purposive actions are equally as interesting as the anticipated ones and often more so.[65]

Even the most ambitious of social planners (with only occasional exception) do not seek to plan a "social system" in the sense that the economist plans an "economy." There are many high-level abstractions about society,

---

[62] Shonfield, *op. cit.*, 385–427; Donald C. Rowat, Editor, *The Ombudsman* (London: George Allen & Unwin, Ltd., 1965); Walter Gellhorn, *When Americans Complain* and *Ombudsman and Others* (both, New Haven: Yale University Press, 1966). This topic is discussed here in Chapter X.

[63] Wheeler, "The Restoration of Politics," 10, 29–30.

[64] Leonard Duhl, Editor, *The Urban Condition* (New York: Basic Books, 1963), xi.

[65] See *Toward the Year 2000.* . . . Also, H. Kahn and Wiener, *op. cit.*; and Robert K. Merton, *Social Theory and Social Structure* (Glencoe, Ill.: The Free Press, 1957, rev. ed.), Part I.

but social scientists have not successfully conceptualized social system in a fashion which could be operationalized by planners. The key dimension remains in dispute.

Political realities limit planning. There are powers and interests which do not want planning, which contract for pseudo-planning, or which undercut established plans; and these powers are often in the ascendency. The stakes of competing community groups, geographic sections, program sectors, occupational groups, or bureaucracies are often resolved through a bargaining and power process which would appear to allow little play for rationality. To recognize this, however, is not to hold that planning is impossible. Increasingly, even such groups carry out planning so as to clarify, specify, and advance their own interests; or they accept the need for a broader planning process because the society cannot manage otherwise. They shift the political battle to an effort to control such process or the components of task definition, preference, and priority which are so vital to it.

Despite problems of prediction and politics, planning takes place because it is needed. As the ability to assess and to look ahead improves (and there continue to be debates as to what is feasible), there may be anxiety over planning's becoming more potent and more dangerous. However, such new capacities need be assigned only for that planning which societies wish to undertake. Scientific knowledge in all fields lends itself to misuse, but this does not mandate a decision to end potentially enriching research and development. Neither planning nor technology poses an unmanageable hazard to human values so long as the democratic mechanisms which can guide it are protected and the choice components kept in focus. Planning is neither more nor less dangerous than politics or physical science.

The social planning here described may be comprehensive or synoptic on occasion, if such terms are understood as covering many elements, but never everything. It is often incremental and partial, based on the premise that a system is in equilibrium and that one needs to understand and affect only specific elements.[66] It is a process incompletely understood and described, with little experience accumulated. Yet it is an expanding and growing activity, mandated by complexity, competition, resource limitations, and a desire to protect precious values. The limitations debated are real; but they obviously must be regarded as helping to define what planning is and how it may be strengthened, not as reasons to dismiss it.

---

[66] Gulick, *op. cit.*, 87–88.

The present work concentrates on the components of a planning process per se and not on its degrees of freedom from or its intertwining with politics —the preoccupation of many eminent scholars. Once such a process is specified, however, and the critical question of preferences addressed (Chapter IV), it becomes possible to attempt (in Chapter XII) a more systematic statement of the problem and its resolution.

Within our scope are both

- [ ] the planning of social aspects of overall balanced economic and physical development, and
- [ ] the planning of what are specifically recognized as social sectors and the relationships among such sectors.

As will soon be discovered, available practice experience and knowledge lead to a concentration on the second of these spheres, while we are constantly preoccupied with enhancing the first.

# III

# DEFINITION OF THE TASK: FACTS, PROJECTIONS, AND INVENTORIES

PLANNING is a developmental process in which the several levels of intellectual undertaking are in constant interaction. Although a logical sequence may be listed, it is not necessarily a temporal one. Even as we organize for planning, we must provide for the interplay among levels. For our concern with assuring a planning outcome which gives appropriate weight to all relevant elements implies a readiness to refine and revise the outcomes of earlier stages as we move into later ones.

If a straight line depicts planning as a deductive process in which a sequence of specified formal steps is followed, our approach may best be seen as a series of interlocked spirals and circles. Changes in one place affect the entire system.

The total scheme to be developed in Chapters III through IX is represented by Chart B and summarized in Chapter XII. The present chapter is concerned with the *definition of the task,* an intellectual undertaking with much room for creativity. Subsequent chapters introduce the other components of the process.

In the real world, planning tends to begin because there is complaint, tension, disagreement, dissatisfaction, conflict, suffering, need for choice, a bill enacted by a legislative body with too little forethought, some combination of these—or a dream. As these actions and feelings are pursued and their sources and rationales formulated, we emerge with a somewhat more formal statement of substantive issues and circumstances which may generate planning. A series of such statements has been presented in the first chapter.

Since our present focus is not on the community organization, interest-

Chart A    *Simplified Outline of Anchor Points in Planning*

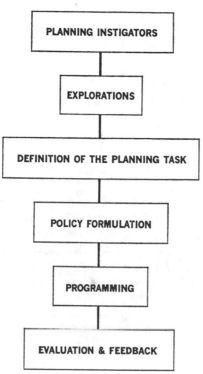

group, or political aspects of the process, we merely assume for the moment that the planner, planners, or planning group are assigned the problem and have adequate sanction to begin. We assume, too, that the assigned or assumed charge takes the form of an expression of problem, need, or concern—or is presented in its broader frame as a case of priority determination, coping with serious social disorganization, need to build social services into physical redevelopment of an area, and so on.

The planner's most serious decision and major contribution is what may be called the *formulation or definition of the planning task*. The "task" is formulated through *a constant playing back between an assessment of the relevant aspects of social reality and the preferences of the relevant community*. Each of these two factors affects and modifies the perception of the other. The task definition appears as an integration of the two. Much else in social planning follows from the outcome of such integration.

Traditionally, planners talked of "goals" or "objectives" as given at the beginning of a planning process. Then, in fact, the assignment might be conceived of in deductive terms: one weighs resources and obstacles and

CHART B    *Interlocking Circles and Spirals: Planning in Action*

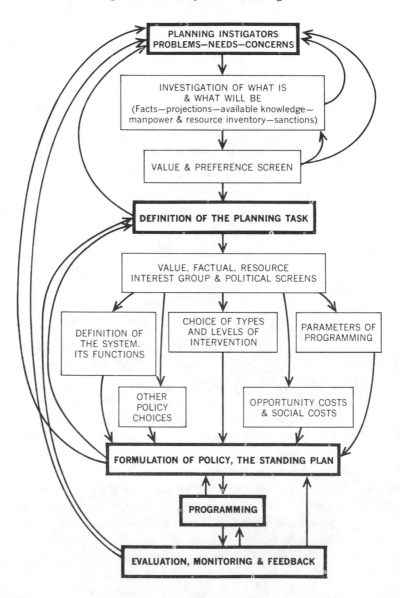

one programs the approach to the goal. Similarly, the assumption that planning seeks to satisfy "needs," as though these were fixed and readily discoverable personal manifestations of social goals, tends to a static view of what is essentially a very complex and unstable reality.

In effect, "needs" are social definitions, representing a view of what an individual or group requires in order to play a role, meet a commitment, participate adequately in a social process, retain an adequate level of energy and productivity—at a given moment of history. "Needs" are biology interpreted through and very much supplemented by culture, to a point where the universal, stable biological core is a small component of the whole. The need is defined with a view of what the social institution or the broader society expects of the individual or the group, and what the resources and possibilities are to make a given level of expectation realistic. Entering into the definition is an assessment as to whether the social or economic price of meeting the need at a given level is justified in the perspective of the expected results. In short, a value judgment enters.

Thus to talk of the goal of "meeting" certain needs is to be involved in a complex human calculus—not starting with a fixed and readily formulated "given." The goal both derives from a concept of need and also helps shape that concept. For this reason we have tended to think of the definition of the planning task as the formulation of the appropriate *needs/task concept* —a concept to guide the planning in which needs and task are shaped together, each affecting and modifying the other. Only the clumsiness of the phrase in its written or oral form leads us to employ the less complete: *definition of the planning task*.

Almost all goal statements made at the beginning of planning enterprises are very complex statements in this sense. Once they have been made, much of the value debate and assessment of social priorities is over, at least temporarily. In fact, much of the evaluation of social reality has already taken place. The definition of the planning task is "the idea sword" in planning, to borrow Constantinos Doxiadis' phrase for the "processing" key through which the planner orders his learning and actions.[1]

An emphasis on the formulation of the planning task as a first phase may, therefore, be seen as an effort to make conscious and deliberate the entire process. We begin by illustrating its significance and then move to its two major elements: *investigation of the relevant realities* (in this chapter) and *assessment of preference* (in Chapter IV).

---

[1] C. A. Doxiadis, "Learning How to Learn," The *Saturday Review*, January 1, 1966, 107.

## SIGNIFICANCE OF THE DEFINITION OF THE PLANNING TASK

Recent American social welfare history provides a series of dramatic illustrations of the significance of this element in planning.

### Delinquency control to youth development

At one time, police, courts, and correctional institutions dealing with young people who committed crimes or were otherwise unmanageable viewed their jobs as one of controlling and punishing the deviants so as to protect the larger community. The offenders were seen as willful and deliberate sinners or exploiters of the larger community who deserved punishment and would be deterred by it. A "planner" in this field in the eighteen-eighties, if he existed, would have surveyed the efficiency of police in detection, the adequacy of court machinery to adjudicate, and the sufficiency of deterrent-oriented places of incarceration. True, some individuals at work in the system were operating on somewhat different concepts, but community decisions were directed by a general consensus.

It was during the second half of the last century that a series of forces, not here recapitulated, converged in the decision to define young offenders somewhat differently from adults who broke the law and to offer them opportunity for re-education and rehabilitation. The problem was lack of education or mis-education, and the deficit could be determined and filled in. The offender was considered capable of taking the help. The juvenile courts invented for him a status which was not to carry a stigma ("juvenile delinquent") and strengthened both community-based probation services and specialized institutional resources. Much emphasis was placed on character reform and vocational training. Again, there were some who went beyond this and many who never quite implemented the theory, but the guidelines were there and governed most policies and programs.

Gradually, from the late nineteen-twenties, but particularly after World War II, this general strategy was given new content by a combination of sociological and psychological findings, especially by psychoanalysis, and by shifts in the social ethic which were concurrent. The locus of the strategy shifted from character reform and retraining to treatment of the delinquent. From the premise of free will—or a large component thereof—the ideology of anti-delinquency programs shifted to emphasize "sickness" and lack of capacity to do otherwise. Because of the nature of their own institutional rationales, most police systems and many juvenile courts still conducted their "rituals" on the free will premise, but the dispositional authorities operating probationary, foster home, guidance clinic, and institutional services were charged with treating adjudicated delinquents on the assumption that environmental and intrapsychic life forces had created behavior patterns of which the antisocial action was a normal outcome. Moreover, with only a token effort to change the environmental part of the equation, they could seek enough personality change to assure future adjustment. For this was the key: to help an unsocialized or disturbed personality to achieve enough control or rationality to adjust and to begin with the assumption that he needed treatment to achieve this.

Again, this is an oversimplification. Each of these views had its opponents and its variations, and the leading students of the subject were far more sophisticated than this summary allows.[2] For most workers in most agencies, and for the commissions, committees, and executives planning and projecting programs, these were the guiding ideas.

The application to delinquency of a sociological approach known as "anomie theory" marked the transition to a new phase. As developed and modified by Richard A. Cloward and Lloyd E. Ohlin, in *Delinquency and Opportunity*, and then used in a planning context in a document called *A Proposal for the Prevention and Control of Delinquency by Expanding Opportunities*,[3] this theory held:

> much delinquent behavior is engendered because opportunities for conformity are limited. Delinquency therefore represents not lack of motivation to conform but quite the opposite: the desire to meet social expectations itself becomes the source of delinquent behavior if the possibility of doing so is limited or non-existent.[4]

Therefore, according to Mobilization's plan, "in order to reduce the incidence of delinquent behavior or to rehabilitate persons who are already enmeshed in delinquent patterns, *we must provide the social and psychological*

---

[2] A more comprehensive presentation of shifts in delinquency theory and a more detailed illustration of consequences for delinquency services of a re-definition of the planning task will be found in Alfred J. Kahn, "Social Work and the Control of Delinquency," *Social Work*, 10, No. 2 (April, 1965), 3–13, and his "Trends and Problems in Community Organization," in National Conference on Social Welfare, *Social Work Practice, 1964* (New York: Columbia University Press, 1964), 3–27, or his "From Delinquency Treatment to Community Development," in P. F. Lazarsfeld, W. H. Sewell, and H. L. Wilensky, Editors, *The Uses of Sociology* (New York: Basic Books, 1967).

[3] Richard A. Cloward and Lloyd E. Ohlin, *Delinquency and Opportunity* (Glencoe, Ill.: The Free Press, 1960) and *A Proposal for the Prevention and Control of Delinquency by Expanding Opportunities* (New York: Mobilization for Youth, 1961).

[4] Cloward and Ohlin, *A Proposal for the Prevention and Control of Delinquency by Expanding Opportunities*. . . .

*resources that make conformity possible."* Now, in place of the traditional delinquency-program emphasis on personal counseling and on psychiatrically guided treatment, programs such as job counseling, placement, job training, and cultural experience which would enhance capacity for participation in the larger society all became central. In fact, treatment programs became secondary to what were seen as these preventive efforts.

Furthermore, when confronted with the problem of disadvantaged and "closed out" youth, the new predilection was to ask what there is about the school, the job placement center, the social agency which closes them out, where once the only question asked was why they did not adjust or how they could be made competent to conform.

To phrase this somewhat differently, in the language of those who do not read sociological tracts, the adolescents congregating on the streetcorners of urban ghettos and constantly at war with the police were redefined from "drop-outs" to "push-outs," and the society had now directed its attention to the rejecting forces, where once it looked at the rejected only as a group to be treated.

Obviously, the shifts were generated not by the theories alone but by social forces which validated and gave them support. Thus, at the beginning of the Kennedy Administration, while traditional child welfare and mental health programs continued with their basic programs, a new organization, called the President's Committee on Delinquency and Youth Crime, was created as the vehicle for the new efforts—efforts based on redefinition of the task.

In 16 cities community groups looked at the facts and trends anew and sought, in the general framework of the "opportunity theory" described above, to develop two, three-, or five-year plans for assisting their youth. Given their social settings and the need to cope with a broader social welfare system, which emphasized treatment and deterrence of delinquency, they did not ignore the old entirely. They sought instead to improve treatment programs by "reaching out" efforts, which took the services to young people who could not enter agencies as they were set up, and which adapted treatment techniques to the social, economic, and ethnic groups served. Furthermore, they sought to implement proposals for service coordination and case integration, as developed by critics of the current patterns of welfare organization. However, the core of the programs was job counseling, training, placement, educational services, and access to new kinds of socializing experiences. For the problem, to repeat, was defined as one of lack of access to relevant resources, knowledge, skills, habits, and attitudes.

Thus, the emphasis had moved from delinquency control to re-education, to treatment, to *youth development*. And once this transition had been made, most of the cities involved decided that the new programs should not be in the hands of judges, probation personnel, clinicians, youth gang workers, or family service agencies. All of these had parts to play, but new community coalitions concerned with youth development were to be created as sponsors and operators of the new efforts. In many cities or sections of cities the traditional community welfare councils were eclipsed entirely or assumed secondary roles as Mobilization for Youth, Action for Boston Community Development, Haryou, Action for Appalachian Youth, and others took the center of the stage.[5]

What had occurred was a new definition of the planning task and what emerged were new social strategies, service approaches, sponsoring organizations, staffing patterns, public definition of access, and much more. Furthermore, variations in the more detailed specifications of the planning task among the cities chosen for experiments by the President's Committee and granted funds for planning led to variations in emphasis significant enough to identify and characterize each.

Several stressed "target population" participation in community planning with obvious socio-therapeutic intent, in a community organization tradition, but Haryou, which saw Negro "powerlessness" as the center of the problem of Harlem youth, gave training and organization for political participation a central position in the plan.

Most of the cities placed emphasis on improvement of educational and employment programs, the better to serve the formerly closed-out youth, but several undertook larger institutional change targets and found themselves fighting not only for improvements in the systems but for a role in controlling educational, housing, employment, or welfare policy. As they did this, they became aware of the artificiality of the pretence that a *youth* program could open opportunities or "change the opportunity structure" (Mobilization for Youth's attractive new slogan). Was this not a program for the total community?

New Haven defined its youth employment project in the context of its comprehensive manpower projections and plans and emerged with something quite distinct from those plans that coped with the needs of disadvantaged and delinquent youth as though the economy of their neighborhood were independent of the city-wide or regional economy. Several planners found it necessary either to attack or to ignore traditional case services

---

[5] See detailed bibliography in Kahn, "From Delinquency Treatment to Community Development," *op. cit.*

(counseling, treatment, group guidance) in order to demonstrate that their efforts were basic and sought institutional change. Other viewed case services, basic educational and vocational programs, and more radical individual change as mutually interrelated aspects of a total approach. New Haven planners saw education and job training as the central "opportunity program" and decided to use counseling and treatment to support access to and use of such services.

By now the point has been illustrated: definition and re-definition of the planning task and variability in such re-definition carry visible consequences for the social plans which emerge. These, in turn, create vastly differing operational programs, professional balance, and staffing patterns.

This observation is further documented by what occurred in 1964 and 1965. Just as many of these community "opportunity" mobilizations were getting under way (and modifying their plans en route), a national shift occurred. For fundamental social reasons, the task definition changed. The central concern was no longer juvenile delinquency but poverty. Moreover, poverty was not merely to be alleviated, it was to be "conquered." Now, freed of the pretence that delinquent youth and specific delinquency prevention were adequate points of departure, local anti-poverty planners could consider more complete community development strategy or even go beyond it, depending on how they conceived of the roots of poverty. The various opportunity mobilizations were soon absorbed by Community Action Programs supported by the Office of Economic Opportunity. Youth employment and educational reform programs were emphasized, but in a far broader context. The President's Committee on Delinquency and Youth Crime now found itself with a far narrower charge, focused once again on individual and group deviance, and developed a more specific "corrections" program, which it, nonetheless, sought to implement with a view to the broader scene.[6]

### "Task," facts, values

While the use of the terms "definition of the planning task" or "needs/task concept" may not be common, recognition of the intellectual process is not rare. Economic planners know the difference between a decision in

---

[6] The discussion of income maintenance programs in Chapter IV of the companion volume illustrates shifting task definitions and their impact. An equally clear illustration is offered by what is now called the field of child welfare after its journey from Poor Law to child-saving to child care. Currently one asks whether child welfare must not be sought through family-based social services and income policy. See Chapter VII in the companion volume, STUDIES IN SOCIAL POLICY AND PLANNING.

Country A to see "the task ahead for economic policy as that of 'sustaining full employment without inflation,' " while Country B announces that "the main economic task of the current Five-Year Plan . . . [is] to insure a further considerable expansion of industry. . . ."

Rein and Miller, for example, illustrate the consequences of various possible task formulations for anti-poverty policy.[7] If the problem is seen as inequality, one stresses redistribution; if it is the lack of a minimum of services, one emphasizes specific amenities. If the issue is defined as the absence of mobility, one "opens opportunities"; but if the concern is social stability, rehabilitative and re-educative measures may be stressed. Similarly, other definitions lead to their own strategies.

A Mobilization for Youth report notes how progressive task redefinition has major impact on an agency's programming, shifting it from individual case approaches to group methods, community organization, and social action.[8]

A United Nations report describes the consequences of task updating, over a period of time, for economic planning in Poland.[9] An economic analyst shows how understanding of the task formulation (growth, full employment without inflation, etc.) adds coherence to British economic planning.[10] Others remark that even the institutional arrangements for planning reflect concepts of the task.

On the other hand, one readily identifies considerable numbers of planning reports doomed to ineffectiveness, because participants could not or would not resolve conflicting concepts and thus emerged from the process without a beacon.

Clearly, the process of task definition and redefinition is critical in planning and offers the occasion for sterility as well as creativity. In the language of systems analysts, it is in the process of task definition that one may introduce new scenarios, exptrapolating beyond a currently-perceived reality.

---

[7] Martin Rein and S. M. Miller, "Poverty, Policy and Purpose: The Dilemmas of Choice," in Leonard H. Goodman, Editor, *Economic Progress and Social Welfare* (New York: Columbia University Press, 1966), 20–64; Martin Rein, "Social Science and the Elimination of Poverty," *Journal of the American Institute of Planners*, XXXIII, No. 3 (May, 1967), 146–163.

[8] Mobilization for Youth, "Action on the Lower East Side" (New York: 1964, mimeographed), 68–69.

[9] United Nations Department of Economic and Social Affairs, *Planning for Balanced Social and Economic Development: Six Country Case Studies* (New York, 1964).

[10] Everett E. Hagen, *Planning Economic Development* (Homewood, Ill.: Richard D. Irwin, 1963), Chap. 10.

Formal task definition deals with the manifest: what is and what is sought. To those who inaugurate, carry out, and seek to implement planning, however, there is always alertness to the latent as well: what can the formulation mean; what does it mean; where may it lead beyond the goals which are stated and outlined?[11]

This volume provides opportunity later to elaborate on these matters. We are now prepared to look at the *elements* involved in any systematic effort to define the task as part of a planning process.

As suggested earlier, the planning task develops out of evaluation of components of the social reality in the context of values and preferences. However, *the fact that the planning undertaking (as represented in Chart B) partakes of a spiral and back-and-forth process creates a complicated problem for presentation. Fact-gathering and research may be presented: (a) as an aspect of task definition, or (b) as part of policy development, (c) in the context of programming, or (d) with reference to evaluation. Preference and value issues are relevant in as many contexts. Each of these elements does of course play a somewhat different role in each of these planning phases.*

*Since one must, therefore, decide either to be quite repetitious or to be arbitrary, we shall here choose the latter option. Fact-gathering and research, as well as the matter of preference, will be discussed in connection with definition of the task. They will be merely mentioned in subsequent sections, although it is recognized that in some planning processes the definition of the planning task takes place with little or no empirical work at all, while these two dimensions are usually explored quite systematically either in connection with policy formulation or programming.*

*Our decision to follow this course may have one virtue. Whereas what many students of the subject define as a goal is taken as a "given," our procedure demonstrates that it derives from calculation and evaluation and offers potential for creativity.*

### FACTS, PROJECTIONS, AND INVENTORIES

Given the availability of many research texts and manuals, the discussion here may be brief. However, what may be described as the exploration of relevant realities is generally the most time-consuming phase of a planning endeavor. The problem, need, concern, promise, or generalized social goal has launched the enterprise. Now one must do some or all of the following:

---

[11] See Bertram M. Gross, prefatory comment, "The 'Drifting Cloud' of Guided Development," in John Friedman, *Venezuela: From Doctrine to Dialogue* (Syracuse: Syracuse University Press, 1965, paperback).

☐ define the problem in detail
☐ "diagnose" the causes
☐ seek relevant theories
☐ get realistic estimates of scope and scale
☐ consider the interrelationship of component parts
☐ project relevant variables into the future
☐ inventory present resources and estimate future resources
☐ compute presently available and potentially available manpower
☐ examine relevant legal rights, sanctions, precedents
☐ translate all this as appropriate into geographic units, time units, or subdivide it by other critical variables
☐ assemble interpretations placed by others on these facts and appraise such interpretations
☐ estimate consequences of various possible interventions.

The above list is long, but it is not complete, since there are many variations in scale, substance, and point of departure in social planning, and this condition obviously affects just what is known and given and what needs to be determined or tested if the process is to move forward.

Planning without adequate investigation of relevant realities, relevant social facts, is utopian thinking or traveling blind. Planning that assembles volumes of data without imposing criteria of relevance and priority in their appraisal is useless ritual. Actually, one does not know what facts to assemble and how to weight such facts without simultaneous attention to preference and value questions. It is for this reason that, while we begin with the discussion of relevant factual investigation, the preference matter is here presented as a co-equal and certainly temporally-overlapping phase in the determination of the planning task. Both fact-finding and preference analysis recur (and sometimes are concentrated) at the policy development or programming phases of a planning enterprise that follow task definition.

In full recognition that: (a) we do little more than offer subject matter headings; (b) all of this section could not be applicable to any one social planning enterprise; and (c) the fact-gathering activity often occurs at a later point, not in relation to task definition—it may be useful to list briefly and to discuss some of the most commonly used approaches to assembling the facts and appraising relevant realities.

We begin with several cautions, however. The planner must himself decide what is relevant.[12] Available series may not tell him what he needs to know. Statistics about post office volume do not cover speed in mail de-

[12] For example, Morton L. Isler, "Selecting Data for Community Renewal Programming," *Journal of the American Institute of Planners,* XXXIII, No. 2, (March, 1967), 66–77.

livery. Totals for children in schools do not clarify the quality of education. Data about the total mileage of highways shed no light on where highways lead.

Similarly, while many types of data are relevant, it is the value system and preference structure, subjects to be discussed in the next chapter, which clarify priorities among data: which aspects of reality must be understood most clearly because of their significance in the choices to be made? How important are the facts in the decision process; how much should one spend to assess the reality, in the light of the probably small (or large) effect on what will emerge from the planning?

Furthermore, the planner needs to remember that even in fields in which many data are available, planning is never a simple matter of summing it all up. Much is unknown in relation to relevant dimensions. Even a country relying on 30 equations for economic planning must resort to much trial and error, according to Tinbergen.[13] The sum of all presently available indicators does not take one very far in understanding social trends, social costs and benefits of measures, and the quality of our national life. Finally, one should underscore that the many institutional threats and blockages to the use of intelligence do not mean that it is not used and do not decrease responsibility to improve it.[14]

### Statistical series

The social planner can seldom move without demographic data—statistical data relating to a population's vital status (birth, death, growth, marriage, divorce, etc.) and characteristics and levels of living (income, education, savings, residence, family size, race, religion, etc.). He often also requires manpower statistics, information about morbidity, facts about resource utilization, program participation, and service delivery.[15]

Fortunately, where once it was necessary to begin from scratch with each undertaking, general improvement of what might be called "social bookkeeping" now regularly produces the kinds of data which are extremely relevant and helpful. At times local supplementation may be needed. Often it is

---

[13] Jan Tinbergen, *Central Planning* (New Haven: Yale University Press, 1964), 38.

[14] Harold L. Wilensky, *Organized Intelligence* (New York: Basic Books, 1967).

[15] Edward S. Rogers, *Human Ecology and Health* (New York: The Macmillan Company, 1960).

For a comprehensive summation of available series in many fields, a substantive review, a critique, and a program to improve indicators, see Eleanor Bernert Sheldon and Wilbert E. Moore, Editors, *Indicators of Social Change: Concepts and Measurements* (New York: Russell Sage Foundation, 1968).

a matter of reassembling available material in accord with the particular geographic boundaries which are of interest or of making critical cross-tabulations.[16] The data derived from two general sources: general census and socio-economic statistics series, and operating statistical series.[17] The latter by their nature, when related to available norms, often are at the same time indicators of need (e.g., average grants for Aid to Families with Dependent Children in various states).

The United States Census of Population in the Bureau of the Census, of the Department of Commerce, may be seen as a continuing survey. The range of questions in the decennial census plus the interim sample censuses and the special local censuses or special subject-matter censuses have converted it from a one-time counting of the population to an excellent cross-sectional view of the composition, characteristics, and exigencies of the population at large and relative statuses of a variety of subgroups, some of it organized for units as small as census tracts, combined for larger areas and available for further analysis in a variety of patterns. Furthermore, trends may now be analyzed readily and "turnover" and "change" appraised in some categories.

To illustrate the possibilities at a national level, we might note how special tabulation and re-analysis of data available in the Census Bureau's Current Population Survey have provided the most important picture of poverty available in the United States and have been of immense value both to the Council of Economic Advisers and to the Office of Economic Opportunity in designing anti-poverty programs and other social welfare strategies.

Mollie Orshansky and her collaborators in the Office of Research and Statistics of the Social Security Administration, relying first on special tabulations of data available in the Current Population Survey and then on some items added to the survey, developed a series of social policy–oriented analyses. Soon, by general consensus, policy and planning personnel on a variety of levels began to utilize these reports. The general discussion generated ideas for further analysis.[18]

---

[16] This is not to ignore the major problem of lack of disaggregated data even where a source has been located, i.e., facts about non-whites by income level, etc. We therefore subsequently discuss both special studies and new proposals for social data.

[17] Despite their usefulness as points of departure for the planner and as base data, available indicators have many limitations, as reported by the several collaborators in Raymond A. Bauer, Editor, *Social Indicators* (Cambridge: The M.I.T. Press, 1966), especially Albert D. Biderman, "Social Indicators and Goals," 68–153.

[18] See articles by Mollie Orshansky, "Counting the Poor: Another Look at the Poverty Profile," *Social Security Bulletin*, 28, No. 1 (January, 1965), 3–29; "Who's Who

Especially helpful in trend-spotting and problem-identification are the periodic analyses of census materials and similar data by scholars associated with universities and research institutes.[19] In general, such studies often inspire and guide the early phases of planning endeavors, but do not provide enough data for the full planning process.

All federal, state, and local public agencies, national voluntary coordinating agencies and many voluntary agencies on a local level produce *operating statistics* which tell one much that is relevant for various kinds of undertakings in social planning. Often one must turn to the original sources for detailed breakdowns and locally relevant comparisons; but several routine, selective national compilations provide enough of a sampling of operating statistics (sometimes in conjunction with basic social statistical trend data) to raise relevant questions, highlight issues, launch explorations, encourage planning, and suggest possible leads.

Careful monitoring of operating statistics may generate a beginning in planning on one of the levels we have described or may contribute in significant ways to the definition of the task:

☐ If most substitute child care is provided in foster homes, what is the significance of the fact that, in a given state, institutional care is extremely important?

☐ Why are so many average state AFDC payments so low? What does this suggest about the programs?

☐ What light does the material about the characteristics of recipients of Old Age, Survivors, and Disability Insurance shed on the issue of the relationship of social services to income security programs?

☐ Why, given an infant mortality rate of 18.3 per 1,000 live births in 10 percent of the counties in the United States, are there 30,000 infant deaths annually in other counties in excess of this rate?

Many planning efforts will require assembling relevant operating statistics from national compilations, as well as from state and local sources, and making comparisons. The operational data raise questions, sometimes offer norms, highlight gaps, and serve to characterize a program or a service. The

---

Among the Poor: A Demographic View of Poverty," *Social Security Bulletin,* 28, No. 7 (July, 1965), 3–32; "Recounting the Poor—A Five-Year Review," *Social Security Bulletin,* 29, No. 4 (April, 1966), 20–37; "More About the Poor in 1964," *Social Security Bulletin,* 29, No. 5 (May, 1966), 3–38; "The Poor in City and Suburb, 1964," *Social Security Bulletin,* 29, No. 12 (December, 1966), 22–37.

[19] For example, Donald J. Bogue, *The Population of the United States* (Glencoe, Ill.: The Free Press, 1959); Joseph S. Davis, "Implications of Prospective United States Population Growth in the 1960's," *Milbank Memorial Fund Quarterly,* XXXIX, No. 2 (April, 1961), 329–349.

obvious cautions need to be observed, of course: data collection may be imprecise, incomplete, or biased; reporting may follow long tradition and not capture important social trends or major program characteristics; reporting may be pointed more toward administration, public relations, or job analysis functions than toward accuracy of program analysis; what appears as a "trend" may actually be accounted for by a technical change in the reporting system. The problem in the labor statistics field was illustrated in 1967 by a United States Department of Labor report of a special survey in ten urban ghettos which found that: "unemployment—or subemployment—in the city slums is so much worse than it is in the country as a whole that the national measures of unemployment are utterly irrelevant." The problem of the slums, where the rate is three times the national average, is masked in the ordinary sense, because of the averaging of high- and low-employment areas and the failure to report limited employment, low-wage employment, and the unemployed too discouraged to remain in the job market.[20]

Demonstrating the need for analytic capacity and caution in looking at statistical reports, Burton Weisbrod points out that, whereas educational measures may solve the problem of employment for a given school dropout, to approach all dropouts in this way is probably to increase unemployment among high school graduates. Focusing on the aggregate demand, rather than the structural, aspects of youth employment, he then makes the case for more careful study of the concentration of the unemployed (age, geography, race, etc.).[21]

Proposals are under discussion to add to the usefulness of available statistical data by combining series relating to individuals through use of computers; but these may not be implemented because of feared invasion of privacy and concentration of power.[22]

Two problems are highlighted in recent reports by experts. First, there is the matter of increasing decentralization of statistical activities in the federal

---

[20] United States Department of Labor, "A Sharper Look at Unemployment in United States Cities and Slums" (Washington, D.C.: The Department of Labor, 1967, pamphlet).

[21] Burton A. Weisbrod, "Preventing High School Dropouts," in Robert Dorfman, Editor, *Measuring Benefits of Government Investments* (Washington, D.C.: The Brookings Institution, 1965), 117–171.

[22] See *Report of the Task Force on the Storage of and Access to Government Statistics* (Washington, D.C.: Bureau of the Budget, 1966). The possibilities are outlined in Carl Kaysen, "Data Banks and Dossiers," *The Public Interest*, No. 7 (Spring, 1967), 52–60.

government. At the present time, 21 agencies have significant statistical programs. The four largest (Census, Bureau of Labor Statistics, Statistical Reporting Service, and Economic Research Bureau—the latter two in the Department of Agriculture) account for 60 percent of a federal statistical budget of $125 million in 1967, a decrease of 10 percent of the share of a smaller budget a decade earlier. The budget will soon be $200 million, and decentralization will accelerate.

Second, and even more important, the technology is obsolete. Publication, the only way to make information available for use, inevitably involves summarization. Details in the underlying data are lost; retabulation of the original data is costly and difficult. Thus,

> information on related aspects of the same unit is collected by different agencies, tabulated and summarized on bases that are different and inconsistent, with resultant loss of information that was originally available, and a serious degradation of the quality of analyses. . . .[23]

The use of a central storage and processing agency would permit both far more efficiency and improved data analyses. Decentralized collection, analysis, and publication to the extent considered desirable need not be given up—so long as integration and storage of all data in a "bank" in accessible form is also provided. Concentrating on "large-scale, systematic bodies of social, economic and demographic data," such a bank could omit police and FBI dossiers, personnel records, and "other dossier information."[24]

Because consolidation of data from various sources would require individual coding—even where samples are used—justifiable fears are raised. Proponents argue that protections are available: what is listed, who has access, on-going review, monitoring of users, etc. Certainly, solution of both policy and technical problems in this realm would facilitate and improve access to data relevant to social planning.

### Special studies and surveys

Both the scope and failings of present statistical series[25] make it inevitable

---

[23] Summarized from Kaysen, *op. cit.* Quotation from page 54.

[24] *Ibid.*, 55–56, referring to *Task Force on the Storage of and Access to Governmental Statistics.*

[25] See Biderman, *op. cit.* The limitations and hazards of using routine statistical series to estimate income distribution is tellingly demonstrated in Richard M. Titmuss, *Income Distribution and Social Change* (London: George Allen & Unwin, Ltd., 1962).

that most planning studies assemble for their own use the data relevant to estimating the prevalence of "need" or to the appraisal of a problem, its severity, and its distribution. They must themselves plan the analysis of service utilization and implementation of policy. They above all must themselves seek indicators of effectiveness, or at least of the relationship between service model and operational reality. Where questions of coordination, case integration, and accountability are at stake, it will undoubtedly require specially designed studies to assemble valid information.

One need not specify all of the possibilities. The full repertoire of social research tools is relevant. To illustrate, sometimes the emphasis is on *how* something works or does not work, so as to generate questions and guides to more systematic study or to document the case for an effort to design new policy. Here a case-study approach is possible.[26]

Service utilization studies on occasion have both instigated planning and guided planners. Special attention has been devoted in health and social work to "high utilizers."[27]

At times one inventories a new service phenomenon and describes it in its variations, as a first step in considering its broader impact.[28]

It is quite common to undertake social surveys to estimate pathology, need, or trends in fields not covered by routinely-compiled statistics or for a population group or areas for which no breakdowns of general data will suffice. Here all the techniques of the social survey are relevant,[29] and one may commission a social survey group to undertake the research.

---

[26] See, for example, Winifred Bell, *Aid to Dependent Children* (New York: Columbia University Press, 1965); or Margaret Purvine, "Into and Out of a Child Welfare Network" (Unpublished doctoral dissertation, Columbia University School of Social Work, 1966).

[27] Paul M. Densen *et al.*, "Concerning High and Low Utilizers of Service in a Medical Care Plan and the Persistence of Utilization Levels Over a Three Year Period," *Milbank Memorial Fund Quarterly*, XXXVII, No. 3, (July, 1959), 217–250.

[28] See, for example, Howard Parad, "Crisis, Casework and Community" (Unpublished doctoral dissertation, Columbia University School of Social Work, 1967).

[29] See, for example, Herbert Hyman, *Survey Design and Analysis* (Glencoe, Ill.: Free Press, 1955).

For general materials on need studies and the distinction between formulative efforts and hypothesis-testing studies, see Norman Polansky, Editor, *Social Work Research* (Chicago: University of Chicago Press, 1960), especially articles by Genevieve Carter and Alfred J. Kahn.

For a specific illustration of conceptual innovation, see David R. Godschalk and William E. Mills, "A Collaborative Approach to Planning Through Urban Activities," *Journal of the American Institute of Planners*, XXXIII, No. 2 (March, 1966), 86–95.

Several large social surveys have made special impact in the past several years, focusing on spotting needs and conceptualizing tasks: *Americans View their Mental Health*,[30] one of the studies by the Joint Commission on Mental Illness and Health; *Income and Welfare in the United States*,[31] a special study from the University of Michigan Survey Center, which also routinely studies consumer expenditure patterns; *Mental Health in the Metropolis*,[32] a picture of many aspects of urban life.

Epidemiology, a valuable tool for planners and scientists, is the study of who develops a disease or problem, where, and under what circumstances. One might cite efforts in the epidemiology of mental health, in estimation of need for day care, in viewing the needs of the aged, in assessment of the adequacy of available information and referral services, or in reviewing the local labor force situation, to illustrate the range of possibilities. Sometimes the focus is on the full picture of a problem. The epidemiological review at other times takes the form of an inventory which brings theories and service strategies into question.[33]

British scholars have produced an impressive group of studies which document the impact and consequences of a policy or program development, sometimes on a case-study basis and sometimes with the tools of a more intensive survey. Quite often the general direction of the possible reform is indicated.[34]

Efforts to look at the total local social welfare system are especially helpful

---

[30] Gerald Gurin *et al.*, *Americans View their Mental Health* (New York: Basic Books, 1960).

[31] James N. Morgan *et al.*, *Income and Welfare in the United States* (New York: McGraw-Hill Book Company, 1962).

[32] Leo Srole *et al.*, *Mental Health in the Metropolis* (New York: McGraw-Hill Book Company, 1962).

[33] August Hollingshead, "Some Issues in the Epidemiology of Schizophrenia," *American Sociological Review*, 26, No. 1 (February, 1961), 5–13; E. Gartly Jaco, *The Social Epidemiology of Mental Disorders* (New York: Russell Sage Foundation, 1960); Bernard Kutner, *Five Hundred over Sixty* (New York: Russell Sage Foundation, 1956); Russell R. Moore, Gerald D. Klee, Eugene B. Brody, Editors, *Psychiatric Epidemiology and Mental Health Planning* (Washington, D.C.: American Psychiatric Association, 1967). See especially, Morton Kramer, "Epidemiology, Biostatistics and Mental Health Planning," 1–68.

[34] In addition to the items cited in Chapters VI and VII, see Peter Townsend, *The Family Life of Old People* and *The Last Refuge* (London: Routledge & Kegan Paul, 1957 and 1963).

for many purposes: problem clarification, policy formulation, etc.[35] At other times one may focus on one functional field or sector, locally or nationally.[36]

The researcher knows from the beginning that there is no such thing as "just getting the facts." Whether in the impressionistic case study or the statistical survey, whether on a large or small scale, the fact-gatherer must know what to look for. He needs some criteria of relevance or, what the researcher might prefer to term, tentative hypotheses. Some of the criteria are derived from the realm of values and preferences, subjects requiring special attention. Some are truly preliminary hypotheses in the research sense.

- One looks at the educational statuses of children in the AFDC because one thinks that receipt of financial aid may contribute to the opportunity for education.
- One asks old people about their patterns of expenditure, because one suspects that they are depriving themselves seriously in some way.
- One asks how individuals would respond to certain types of "cases" in daily life, with specific illustrations, on the assumption that one may identify patterns of exclusion or acceptance which affect the lot of the mentally ill.
- One studies community child welfare patterns comparatively, on the assumption that there are communication variables and value determinants which shape the local network.

As noted earlier, a knowledge organizing scheme is in a sense also a planning framework. Therefore, a systematic review and appraisal of relevant research in an applied field may take one a long way, whether written in response to the interests of researchers alone or directed to issues being debated by practitioners.[37]

Existing social statistics or limited case studies are not adequate conceptually as sources of evaluation of effects and effectiveness of existing programs. To measure effectiveness, one must design special studies. Although

---

[35] Margot Jeffries, *An Anatomy of Social Welfare Services* (London: Michael Joseph, 1965).

[36] Henry S. Maas and Richard E. Engler, Jr., *Children in Need of Parents* (New York: Columbia University Press, 1959); Shirley Jenkins and Mignon Sauber, *Paths to Child Placement* (New York: Community Council of Greater New York, 1966).

[37] For a research review addressed to the researcher but offering much to the planner, see Henry S. Maas, Editor, *Five Felds of Social Service: Review of Research* (New York: National Association of Social Workers, 1966). A research review addressed to the practitioners is Martin L. and Lois Wladis Hoffman, Editors, *Review of Child Development Research*, two volumes (New York: Russell Sage Foundation; I, 1964, II, 1967).

significant attempts have been made and ideas generated, the overall output is not impressive.[38] Several methodological problems continue to plague evaluative research relating to social programs and continue to impose limitations on the output:[39]

*Premature evaluation.*  Innovation often requires a period of exploration and "shakedown" before it is ready for testing. Premature launching of evaluation often fixes the experiment too soon to be useful.

*Specification of the intervention.*  Project and program planners leave the intervention ("input") too vaguely stated to assure consistency over the life of the project. Measurement of effects is then meaningless.

*Inadequate control.*  This covers many issues. Basically, one cannot measure effectiveness or tell whether the experimental component made any difference at all without a control group (a comparable group in the population must be deprived or ignored), opportunity to measure, opportunity to analyze effects of the measurement process.

*Difficulty in specifying or applying outcome criteria.*  Evaluative research is not taken seriously unless those to whom it is addressed agree with the outcome criteria—and unless adequate indicators of outcome are invented and applied.

The dilemma often faced is that one can solve methodologically the evaluation problems related to narrowly-conceived, laboratory-like experiments, and then not know whether the results are applicable to the real world. On the other hand, rigorous evaluation of very comprehensive innovation designed to produce divers outcomes is not manageable. The planner consulting the evaluative research in a given field or contemplating evaluative research as a component of ongoing planning efforts might begin by asking whether the situation has "matured" to the point of evaluation or whether the certainty about the intervention is already so great as to justify "demonstration" (a "planned change" strategy). If evaluation is sought or planned, careful identification of variables *critical to the planning process* may sharpen the focus and facilitate the design: what, in short, would make a difference; what do we need to know for the planning? Such delimitation may justify a narrow, somewhat artificial laboratory experiment or a modest, but rigorous, design in the context of a community development effort which

---

[38] A brief, but sophisticated, summary of problems is presented by Elizabeth Herzog, "Some Guide Lines for Evaluative Research," Children's Bureau Publication No. 375 (Washington, D.C.: Government Printing Office, 1959). Also see, Edward A. Suchman, *Evaluative Research* (New York: Russell Sage Foundation, 1968).

[39] Cost-benefit studies are discussed in Chapter IX.

may be quite diffuse. It may test one technique via the former or develop one precise index about one aspect of output for the latter.

Only rather unusual long-term planning undertakings, such as the early phases of the community development projects of the President's Committee on Delinquency and Youth Crime, the Model Cities Program, or the Community Mental Health Planning process in the United States can contemplate evaluative research or cost-benefit studies as part of initial planning and programming. In most instances, financing, legislation, and program issues have changed before one can mount and carry out sophisticated evaluation. Thus, much of what is here said applies to the planner as evaluative research consumer, rather than producer, in the earliest phases of his work. Yet the responsibility of consulting and appraising such cost-benefit studies and evaluative efforts as are relevant and available cannot be ignored. Nor can the planner fail, as part of a long-term effort, to assure provision for suitable and competent design or to support such research for its knowledge-building contributions.

## Projections

The study of what *is* helps to define or redefine for the planner the problem which is of concern and to offer some assessment of the possible. Planning, however, deals with future situations; policies are being developed with a view to the future state of affairs. Programs are being organized on the basis of a variety of assumptions about events yet to occur. Therefore, when stating that a review of *what is* occurs early in the development of the planning task, one must hasten to add, *and what is expected*.

Just as a combination of objective, knowledge-based decisions and value judgments determines what are the relevant areas of exploration of the current reality, so do both of these elements enter into the areas in which projections are sought. Generalizations are not possible for all social planning; certain types of projections are routine for specific types of studies. And, again, there are certain statistical projections made routinely, as part of ongoing governmental statistical operations, while most other projections relevant for social planning must be prepared in connection with the specific needs of the planning enterprise.

The various census series already cited offer the most routinely-compiled projections. A population projection series from the Census Bureau in fact offers four alternative series based on somewhat different assumptions. While such projections are reducible to the state level, anything for a smaller unit must be based on special work locally.

Similarly, certain labor force projections are made routinely, with reference to projections for the economy, but local work is needed for most planning purposes.

For the most part, local operating departments and planning staffs find it necessary to employ demographers, economists, and researchers with other specializations to apply general national trend data and projections to the geographic unit for which planning is being done, or to conduct special studies so as to develop the detailed projections relevant to specific assignments. Many of the routinely made projections are relatively simple, even though they must be specifically undertaken locally. Thus, if one has national, state, or local *rate* data for such phenomena as juvenile court cases or mental hospital admissions, and if the rate data are either for certain population subgroups (boys between the ages of eleven and seventeen) or for total population groups (all adult males) *and* if one has locally adapted population projections, it is not difficult to combine these and to project future caseloads. Obviously, the errors in projections of each of the two factors entering into the projection (the size of the relevant population group and the current rate) are compounded as they are combined. And one needs to explore the elements in the current rate quite carefully to determine the validity of applying it to a future population.

Should this not prove to be a legitimate decision, there is need to project the rate itself. Again, there is research precedent: the researcher studies the relationship between available demographic data and the rate and determines what each of a series of factors contributes to variations in the rate. Then, given what the demographer can do to project these factors (perhaps a number of socio-economic indicators), one computes possible future rates. Obviously these are complex research enterprises involving specific kinds of statistical expertise not here under review. The planning staff must contain or retain for the purpose appropriately qualified individuals and must probe in some depth the validity of the chain of assumptions on which a set of projections is based. Too often, laymen and non-statistical planners assume that the apparent precision of quantification assures the validity sought.

Projections often have a deceiving and inhibiting type of precision and should always be examined with care. It is often quite inaccurate to extrapolate the "immediate present." The demographers of the nineteen-fifties who expected the United States population to reach 400 million by the year 2000 assumed that preferred family size would remain constant. Because married couples changed their view of the ideal number of children, the actual figure may be closer to 300 million.

Similarly, in the midst of a great despair resulting from projections of the "population explosion," Donald Bogue was able to point out that the crisis might well be expected to end in the twentieth century—precisely because pre-1960 population trends need not be expected to continue. The significant point, in his view, is the phenomenon of *change* affecting relevant variables: "The trend of the world-wide movement toward fertility control has already reached a state where declines in death rates are being surpassed by declines in birth rates."[40]

Some kinds of change based on major technological breakthroughs, key scientific discoveries, or the activities of new charismatic leaders are not predictable by the researcher's projections.[41] This does not negate the value of such projections and their employment as long as "all things are equal." It does serve constantly to remind one that all of a society is never planned and cannot be—and that one is protected ultimately against even the most monolithic and comprehensive of planning endeavors.

Planners must also note the effects of public knowledge of projections on the phenomenon under consideration. Prediction that minority-group members would dominate the central city became a self-fulfilling prophecy, while notice of probable under-utilization of a desired resource like a beach or picnic area may negate the prognostication.

In short, planners must think about projections, not necessarily accepting or being guided by the picture offered of where present forces, policies, or values will lead. The point, after all, is to develop a change strategy.

### The inventory of theory, models, knowledge, and skill

Examination of statistical series, special quantitative estimates, review of evaluative studies all depend, inevitably, on adoption of a working theory about the relevant phenomena, their dynamics and variables. In the process, one may wish to review the literature and tap expert opinion as to the alternative views and the controversies—a complex and exhausting process. Planners cannot go very far in formulating a definition of a planning task or

---

[40] Donald J. Bogue, "The End of the Population Explosion," *The Public Interest*, No. 7, (Spring, 1967), 11–20.

This position is disputed by other experts such as K. Davis and P. Hauser.

Case-finding activity by anti-poverty staffs and agitation from the Welfare Rights movement upset all caseload projections for Aid to Families with Dependent Children in the United States between 1967 and 1968.

[41] See *Toward the Year 2000: Work in Progress*, constituting the Summer, 1967, issue of *Daedalus*. Or see, Herman Kahn and Anthony J. Wiener, *The Year 2000: A Framework for Speculation on the Next Thirty-Three Years* (New York: The Macmillan Company, 1967), on the errors in trend projections. The authors illustrate projection of a "surprise-free" nature as well as "canonical variations from the standard world."

debating policy options without choice of theory in this sense, explicitly or implicitly. Theory provides the knowledge-organizing scheme referred to earlier. Often, as will be seen, a transition in task definition follows innovation in theory.

Sometimes the planner works with what is called a "model"—an abstract representation incorporating a series of theories about the working of a system. Economic planners work with models of an economic system quite routinely.[42] Models of cities and metropolitan areas have been used by city planners in recent years.[43] The entire process of model building and "gaming" is accelerated by the availability of high-speed computers and new possibilities are developing as a result, but applications in social fields are limited at the present writing.

## The resource inventory

To this point, we have not distinguished among

- ☐ efforts to define and specify a problem
- ☐ efforts to clarify relationships and causes
- ☐ efforts to measure scope, scale, and direction
- ☐ efforts to locate just where the need is concentrated
- ☐ efforts to appraise previous intervention.

The fact-finding and research at a given moment may focus on one or several of these. At some point in the process it will also turn to the resource inventory. Again, depending on the nature of the undertaking, one or all of the following may be included, although all are generally of some relevance:

- ☐ the financial and capital goods inventory
- ☐ the manpower inventory
- ☐ the practice-knowledge/skill inventory.

*Financial and capital goods inventory.* The question is one of resources. On what scale may one realistically plan? What monies, buildings, goods are

---

[42] W. Brand, "Planning for Balanced Social and Economic Development in the Netherlands," in United Nations Department of Economic and Social Affairs, *Planning for Balanced Social and Economic Development: Six Country Case Studies* (New York, 1964), 36–81.

[43] See Britton Harris, Guest Editor, *Urban Development Models: New Tools for Planning;* constituting a special issue of the *Journal of the American Institute of Planners*, XXI, No. 2 (May, 1965), 90–171. Also, see Abt Associates, "Survey of the State of the Art: Social, Political, and Economic Models and Simulations," in National Commission on Technology, Automation, and Economic Progress, *Applying Technology to Unmet Needs*, constituting Appendix, Volume V (Washington, D.C.: Government Printing Office, 1966), 203–250, includes bibliography.

already at hand or certain to become available? What is authorized by enabling legislation; what has actually been appropriated; what is dependent on a fund-raising campaign and what is in the bank account? To what extent is there building space, land, or equipment at hand for new program—and to what extent must one wait for these? (The difference between planning a program in a building needing minor renovation or new equipment and one requiring urban renewal, relocation of tenants, and, then, building and furnishing of a facility may be ten years. For some purposes, this is enough to wipe out the idea of a project at the start.)

At times, it is the existence and availability of space or building which is the point of departure for planning, as when the closing down of the Ruppert Breweries on the Upper East Side of Manhattan was the precipitating factor in a community planning effort for education, housing, recreation, and social services.

At times, a planning effort focuses on buildings as the symbol and locus of the enterprise, even though there are service goals, as when the federal legislation for community mental health centers required state-wide comprehensive mental health planning as the prerequisite for the funding of building costs—and then subsequently used the occasion of the construction of centers throughout the country as the basis for support for staff, again insisting on evidence of a specific program thrust.

Resources must be inventoried because there are never enough. In a dramatic analysis based on what he calls "achievement goals" for the American society ("what knowledgeable people regard as desirable achievement and what could be obtained if the specific goal were to have high priority"), L. Lecht, of the National Planning Association, has shown that the total resource requirements, as projected, exceed by far any projection of what might become available.[44] (See Chart C.) There is no way to avoid choice and concern with mix. Similar work is being done by the National Planning Association in the manpower field.

*The manpower inventory.* Often, given the shortages in skilled manpower, the manpower budget is tighter than the money budget. If federal, state, or local revenue is increasing and appropriations are not difficult to come by, or if the local voluntary fund-raising resources support a new program, the issue then is whether the agency or city or region or nation can actually staff what is proposed.

---

[44] Leonard A. Lecht, *Goals, Priorities and Dollars* (New York: The Free Press, 1966). The volume illustrates the fact-gathering and inventorying process in a number of ways and is relevant to the total chapter.

Chart C    *Estimated Deficit in GNP for Aspiration Standards, 1970 and 1975 (in 1962 dollars)*

*An Overall View*

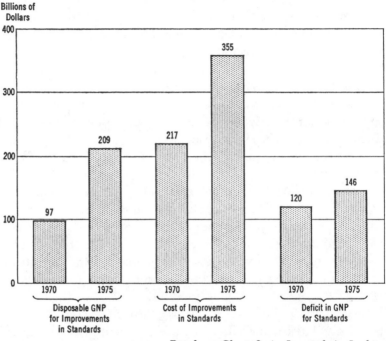

source: Based on Chart 3, in Leonard A. Lecht, "The Dollar Cost of our National Goals" (Washington, D.C.: National Planning Association, 1965), 41.

Here the issue is not one of policy agreement and legislative action alone. It takes a specified number of years to produce a doctor, a social worker, a teacher, or a nurse. What is more, the current output of professional schools may be fully absorbed by existing programs. One must then explore whether existing personnel or current graduates can be attracted to the new programs —and at what price—or whether new training facilities can be created. This of course adds significantly to the time span involved.

These are not rare or far-fetched issues. One country had to postpone utilization of a significant amount of new hospital-bed capacity while medical school building, recruitment, and educational processes caught up. On the other hand, it appropriated funds to create new educational resources for training homemakers at the same time that it helped localities with the financing of expanded services—and took the lead in this field internationally.

Of course the manpower budget may be exaggerated as an obstacle. One can assume that all professional roles are given, all current systems for utilization of personnel fixed, all civil service rules and union contracts unchangeable. Or one can regárd reconsideration of these items, as they are affected by questions of feasibility of alternatives and even the desirability of alternatives, to be the central contribution of the new planning effort.

*The available repertoire of practice-knowledge and skill.* We spoke earlier of the research review as a starting point in planning and as a significant contribution to the formulation of the planning task. In the back-and-forth out of which the task formulation eventually emerges, there is also attention to how much is known by practitioners and what competence is available.

A major element in the task definition is very often the consensus that not only is there significant gap between the service model and the reality, but also that knowledge and available skill are adequate to close the gap.

On the other hand, one retreats quickly from efforts to center the planning task on the achievement of goals which go well beyond the state of the art: "to eliminate all delinquency in X country within five years by reaffirming family responsibility"; "to wipe out all custodial care wards from mental hospitals by offering each patient the treatment he needs so as to accelerate his return to the community."

It is the significance of the knowledge and skill dimension that makes it essential that one or more persons fully aware of the state of the art in the field involved participate in the task formulation. Where there has been a lag, the goal set should assure that practice will catch up; where some pushing out of frontiers is possible, some practice innovation and application of new knowledge should be provided.

One would not want to deal with a child welfare planning problem unless somebody in the group setting the task knew that much of the research on maternal deprivation and institutionalism had been misread by practitioners. One would not want to plan treatment programs for adolescents without exposure to the meaning of research into peer-group culture. To plan income-transfer options without awareness of the consequences of each for the tax system is irresponsible.

In short, we have here evidence that planning in a given field cannot be done by the generalist working alone. In fact, the generalist-planner may go astray quite early unless the knowledge and skill repertoire has adequate representation. At the same time, one must guard against the possibility that what is offered as an assessment of professional resources is in fact a disguised device to protect the status quo. At the very least, where this is a danger, one would wish to initiate a confrontation among two or more experts.

As a protection against premature "closure," it is sometimes useful to begin to develop and explore new possibilities on the basis of only limited "inventorying," and then systematically to review the literature or consult experts once the new doors have at least been opened.

*Should the inventory actually enter into the task definition?* These last comments raise the question of whether one should not define goals, objectives, "tasks" in terms of what it will take to solve problems and implement values, leaving the inventory for the subsequent period of planning for implementation.

The question has several components which may be stated as follows: how can one know what is relevant about funds, building, manpower, or knowledge-skill until one has at least set a general direction? Should not one focus on such matters as these as part of the process of working out a plan? Does this approach not bind the early phases of planning too much to current practice and vested interests?

Here the image of spiral and intersecting circles becomes relevant once again. In connection with the definition of the task, one's desire to solve problems, to achieve goals, and to implement values interacts with some of the reality-touchstones mentioned above, because what is at stake is planning, not the writing of tracts. However, each of the steps requires constant cautions and built-in protections to allow for overcoming vested interests and for departure from traditional grooves of thinking and acting, and the dreaming of "the impossible dream."

One returns again and again to the picture of what is and what will be, first, as policy-level decisions are being made, and then in connection with the working out of programs and administrative plans. Each of these steps moves progressively toward more rigor and completeness in its fact-gathering and more specificity in its projections. In effect, one begins by consulting what is available and using expert judgment, then turns to systematic empirical descriptive work, then to evaluative studies. At times one does all of these in connection with the definition of the planning task, because of the nature of the issues; but, at other times, the more systematic fact-gathering is located in the policy development or in the programming stage.

## MORE COMPREHENSIVE SOCIAL INDICATORS

Advocates of expanded social planning, including those with both modest and ambitious views of what this may entail, have displayed enthusiasm for proposals that an annual Social Report of the President be published in the

United States. The annual Economic Report is seen as the model. In fact, some proponents suggest creation of a Council of Social Advisors and a joint Congressional Committee on the Social Report, thus providing a complete parallel to the Council of Economic Advisors, the Joint Committee on the Economic Report, and the related apparatus which guides monetary and fiscal policy.

These proposals demand careful consideration, but they obviously risk excessive separation of economic and social planning and may entail conceptual confusion about a "social system" seen as something operationally separable from the economic or, for that matter, the political. On the other hand, an annual Social Report, based on a system of *social indicators*, defined as "quantitative data that serve as indexes to socially important conditions of the society,"[45] could be a potent device whether or not a Council of Social Advisors was created. In effect, it would represent systematic trend-spotting, problem identification, and gauging of the "social health" of the nation, much as the Economic Report does in its realm. It would tell us "if things are getting better or worse."[46] While focused on the larger (macro-level) picture, it would also be useful in evaluation of specific agencies, policies, or programs. It could, to some degree, correct the incomplete or inaccurate picture of society derived from economic indicators alone and begin to remedy a tendency to underinvest in social data collection and analysis.

While a Social Report has been urged for several years by a number of advocates, particularly Bertram Gross,[47] Professor of Economics at Syracuse University, formerly executive secretary of the Council of Economic Advisors, the idea did not receive national attention until the summary report of the National Commission on Technology, Automation, and Economic Progress noted the need for "a system of social accounts" in the context of a call for "improving public decision making"—one of many euphemisms for improved planning. The argument offered was that the country has lacked a "continuous charting of social changes" and has been ill prepared in such fields as housing, education, or minority rights "to determine our needs, establish goals, and measure our performance." The lack of base-line

[45] Biderman, *op. cit.*, 69.

[46] Bauer, *op. cit.*, viii. In a trial run, the Department of Health, Education, and Welfare published "Toward a Social Report," in January, 1969.

[47] Bertram M. Gross, "From Social Bookkeeping to Social Accounting," in Joint Economic Committee, *Twentieth Anniversary Symposium of the Employment Act of 1946: An Economic Symposium* (Washington, D.C.: Government Printing Office, 1966), 77–80, or "The State of the Nation: Social Systems Accounting," in Bauer, *op. cit.*, 154–271.

data precludes the testing of policy effectiveness or the weighing of alternative policies which are proposed.[48]

The Commission's objectives are further clarified by its very tentative list of areas for development in this field:[49]

*"Social costs and net return."* National economic accounting is now taken for granted in all industrialized countries. (The United Nations, in fact, is seeking standardization and comparability.)[50] Basic economic forecasting, planning, and intervention has been dependent on such accounting since beginnings in the nineteen-thirties. Several limitations are recognized, however. For one thing, gross national product (GNP), the central instrument, is limited to market transactions, not valuing either household or government service outputs. It in no way reflects qualitative product improvement, or invention with qualitative consequences, or side-effects in the form of social costs and benefits. The costs of a new factory and its payrolls are added to GNP as are the costs of the filtration plant to divert the wastes discharged by that factory and polluting a stream.

> Technological advances create new investment opportunities which are expected to be paid for out of the enhanced earnings they produce. But clearly there are losses as well: e.g., the displacement created by technological change, particularly where the advanced age of the workers or the particular skill displaced make it difficult to find employment at a previous wage. Or, a new plant in an area may create new employment opportunities, yet its byproducts—water pollution and air pollution—may create additional costs for the community. Thus, there is often a divergence between the private cost borne by an entrepreneur and the social cost of production. Such items as maintenance of the unemployed, provisions for the victims of industrial accidents or occupational diseases, and costs of access roads are borne in part by the employer and by the community as "social overhead costs."
>
> National economic accounting does not directly assign the costs generated by one group which are borne by others (e.g., the costs to the community of strip mining which gouges out a countryside). Social accounting would permit us to make such assessments, and, where possible, against the firms responsible. On the other hand, certain costs of technological innovation—e.g., severance pay or maintenance of workers on a firm's payroll—

---

[48] National Commission on Technology, Automation, and Economic Progress, *Technology and the American Economy* (Washington, D.C.: Government Printing Office, 1966), 1, 95–98.

[49] *Ibid.*, 97–98.

[50] Statistical Office of the United Nations, *Statistics of Income Distribution*, E/CN.5/AC.13/R.2, December, 1966.

may be so large as to inhibit the introduction of useful technological devices. Such costs might be borne better by the community than by a firm itself.[51]

*"The measurement of social ills."*   While many statistical series are available, they need to be so compiled and analyzed as to assess the scale, the costs, and perhaps the causes of social ills. Such data might clarify the price of social change and the direction of remediation.

*"Performance budgets."*   How well is the country doing with reference to its general goals? Indexes could describe how adequately health care needs are being met, whether the goal of a decent home for each family is being approached, whether investments are increasing or decreasing equity among regions or groups.

*"Indicators of economic opportunity and social mobility."*   Is it possible to develop a "general index" on the status of the Negro in America? What specific indicators should be combined, and how?[52]

In recent years useful work has been done with a "lifetime-earning-power index." It would be valuable to have a social equivalent of the economists' concept of opportunity costs: social opportunity costs as a measure of what we forgo by not employing human resources in specific ways. Such an index is essential in any calculus of social costs and benefits.

It is no small task to move from the general commitment to the creation of a social indicators series, whether or not within the framework of a Social Report of the President, to the selection of indicators and the creation of indexes. The analogy to the GNP in national economic accounting suggests the critical consequences which follow once the compilation and publication of statistical series become routinized. Some urge a strategy based on gradual improvement and expansion of existing series, while others would make a relatively, but not completely, "fresh" start on a comprehensive system.[53]

As a preliminary to decisions or commitment, preparatory work has been undertaken within the Department of Health, Education, and Welfare

---

[51] *Technology and the American Economy,* 97.

[52] A very elaborate inventory of possible social indicator categories derived from social science and systems theory explorations is offered by Gross, "The State of the Nation: Social Systems Accounting," 154–271.

In their review of the state of the art, Sheldon and Moore, Editors, *op. cit.,* and their collaborators distinguish "the demographic base," "structural features," "distributive features," and "aggregative features" of the society. The state of indicator development is assessed in each realm.

[53] Biderman and Gross represent these two strategies in Bauer, *op. cit.*

(HEW), under the Chairmanship of Daniel Bell, in the Russell Sage Foundation, at the University of Syracuse, and in the American Academy of Arts and Sciences.[54]

The governmental panel in HEW studying possibilities in the categories proposed by the National Commission on Technology, Automation, and Economic Progress has an ambitious series in mind. A tentative list of categories on which work is progressing includes:

☐ health and population vitality
☐ opportunity
☐ standard of living
☐ participation
☐ environment
☐ social costs.

Their preliminary efforts and the general history of the subject disclose very complex problems in an attempt to translate social values or goals into valid indicators,[55] whether of the monetary sort or on other quantitative dimensions. Indeed, even qualitative categorization always involves some sacrifice of conceptual rigor and the danger that indicator may be substituted for concept while important distinctions are lost.

Among the dilemmas to be faced is one that follows from the need to devise a system of indicators comprehensive enough to accommodate likely future public policy issues and even to permit international comparisons, while facing current concerns. Biderman has shown how statistical series, which were very relevant to the goals of 1933, became less salient as the so-

---

[54] Bauer, *op. cit.*; Bertram M. Gross, Editor, "Social Goals and Indicators for American Society," *Annals of the American Academy of Arts and Sciences*, 371 and 373 (May and September, 1967).

A United Nations expert working party, concerned with level of living and the effect of social policies on level of living, urged development of four types of indicators, several of which could be cross-tabulated—in addition to the system of standard national accounts:

"*Natural indicators*" measuring such aspects of well-being as mortality and morbidity rates, life expectancy and other aspects of health, educational attainment, etc.

"*Monetary indicators*" of total disposable income and wealth

*Indicators of goods and services produced and supplied by public authorities, nonprofit organizations*, etc.

*Indicators of such goods and services actually received and utilized* by those for whom they are intended.

See United Nations, *Report of the Group of Experts on Social Policy and the Distribution of Income in the Nation* (New York: United Nations, 1967, mimeographed, E/CN.5/420/Add.1).

[55] One approach is to seek indicators of achievement of allegedly "widely shared social goals." See "Toward a Social Report," *op. cit.*

ciety decreased its concern with production and distribution of basic consumer goods and services and began to address questions of order, integration, and quality.[56] Those at work on social indicators will seek as broad and flexible a social systems model as they can, with full recognition that they cannot plan for all time. Some have urged a period of experimentation before closure of a system of social indicators.

Although the outcome of these several efforts is not fully predictable, since the technical, value, political, and strategic problems are complex, it does seem likely that the United States and other countries will begin to develop and report social indicators to parallel, supplement, or enrich the usual economic accounts. It also seems probable that the value debates and technical problems in this field will exceed those plaguing economic reporting. Nonetheless, however crude the earliest efforts, they will legitimate new variables. As put by Bauer, "There is a strong tendency for the managers of any system to improve the performance of the system on those variables that are regularly measured."[57] This alone would justify the enterprise. Beyond this, of course, one may predict contributions to planning, policy debates, and public education from reports of trends, assessments of specific policies, and assessments of the total impact of a general policy thrust.

## SANCTIONS AND LEVERAGE

One final aspect of the reconnaissance of relevant "realities" that is part of task definition is yet to be reviewed. Its concern is with the right to plan and, then, the power and responsibility to carry through certain measures which may become desirable. These are two different issues, each partaking of components of what may be called sanctions and leverage.

### The right to plan

A democratic society needs a multiplicity of planning centers in its administrative and executive branches and in the voluntary sector, tied both to general political program-making and special-cause concerns in specific fields. In a theoretical sense, then, any citizen or group of citizens has the "right" to plan and to offer policy guidelines and specific programmatic proposals to the politically-established decision-making machinery.

As a practical matter, any group with sound motives will ask itself early in the process how its location in the community structure, the special interests of its members, the expertise it contains within itself or can tap, its re-

---

[56] Biderman, op. cit., 87–89.

[57] Bauer, op. cit., 43.

sources or lack thereof, its very composition, and its experience justify a planning undertaking. Any planning process does imply expenditure of resources; access to relevant materials, observations, clients, interviewees, officials, or others; a bid that the community, in a sense, devote it enough attention to permit planning and some consideration of the outcome.

Most often these questions are solved in a simple and formal way: the proposed planning unit is a public bureau, commission, or department, and the law or administrative code outlines the function. Then, if the executive has issued instructions or the legislative branch voted funds, or both, the right to plan is apparent. Similarly, there is little question about the planning assignments handed directly by legislatures on state and federal levels to certain standing committees, joint committees of two branches of the legislature, or special commissions appointed by the chief executive, the legislative leaders, or a combination of both.

The problem we are discussing then arises for research centers, political parties, social welfare organizations, civic groups, and the like; and it is they who need to ask about the right to plan. Our bias is in favor of a "yea" answer; on the assumption that there is too little policy planning from diverse perspectives, which then tests itself in the market place of public preference and feasibility. Unofficial groups are more likely to concentrate on policy development than on programming, because legal rights and leverage do control access to the details essential for program specification.

*The right and power to implement*

Again, the statutory body has its formal follow-up channels mapped out to a degree by the same legal and administrative authority that assigns it the planning role in the first instance. The reality, however, is that legislative favor, a chief executive's own plans, and the staff "culture" at a given time are also to be reckoned with.

We are here in a subtle area, in which the definition of the task tends to be reflective of the assignment one can accomplish and the consequences for one's agency of what one does. An anti-delinquency agency attuned to operating institutions is handing over a good deal if it calls for expanded youth employment programs, knowing that these will be in the control of the state labor office. On the other hand, an education department is expanding its domain, if it develops adult education proposals in a state in which that territory is not yet claimed.

Ideally, of course, the planning agent, coping with all but administrative planning within a department, should be supra-departmental, so that the assignment issue may be pursued on its real merits.

The general area remains very critical in relation to task definition, however. In effect, it is concerned with the question: "How large a thought may we have while being practical and realistic?" Every planning unit is bound by some limitations, relating to formal sanction and political (in the widest sense) reality. Every unit also faces the danger of being so practical and realistic as never to challenge existing frameworks and definitions of the task. In effect, he who defines the task in any endeavor needs to know what his agency can do and to be willing to operate very close to the fringe, or at a point which may seem to some to be "beyond the fringe," if the problem requires it.

Here we merge into the value and preference issue, a subject to which the next chapter is devoted.

# IV

# DEFINITION OF
# THE TASK:
# VALUES AND
# PREFERENCES

THE PLANNING task (or needs/task concept) often emerges or evolves·quite informally—or it may be a *given* in the social, cultural, or political context. Sometimes circumstances demand or permit fairly systematic exploration of a series of aspects of the relevant realities before the task is set. Such investigation and the related projections may serve to shape, to modify, or to alter the view of the task (Chapter III). Similar generalizations may also be made about the value dimension and community preferences. There can be no rationality without decisions about merit; the planner therefore cannot escape the preference question.[1]

Formal, empirical study of values and preferences occurs more frequently with reference to policy-level decisions (Chapter V) or the specifics of programming than in connection with task formulation, but it does sometimes occur in the latter instance. Or, more often, value and preference issues enter at a point at which the planning activity has moved into later phases of the process, only to serve to bring it back to a reformulation of the task. On the other hand, *informal* attention to values and preferences, sometimes deliberate and at other times indirect, sometimes modest but occasionally quite extensive, may be at the heart of the critical choices made as the task is defined.

Thus, again, as in the instance of Chapter III, we discuss a topic relevant

---

[1] Aaron Wildavsky, *The Politics of the Budgetary Process* (Boston: Little, Brown and Company, 1964), 176.

to several parts of the volume but placed in the discussion of task definition —the point at which it sometimes first occurs as an issue.

## PLANNING AS CHOOSING

It has been argued with considerable force and merit that the characteristic activity in a planning process is choosing. In fact, Paul Davidoff and Thomas Reiner call theirs a "choice" theory of planning.[2] Although one should not downgrade the research, the fact-finding, the programming, the practice innovation, or the evaluation and feedback, a convincing and impressive case can certainly be made for such emphasis. For, does not the planner need constantly to choose his observational categories, his assumptions as to the future, his priority goals, the maximum price he is willing to pay for achievement of objectives, the publics whose wishes he will attend to most conscientiously, the organizational outlets for new programs—as well as the criteria by which goal achievement will be measured? And is this not an incomplete list of planner choices?

Similarly, do not citizens, consumers, administrators, public officials—in fact, all those with whom planners interact—often find themselves involved in these and additional choices? At this level, for example, as we shall argue, competing views of reality and alternative plans and programs are often offered for attention and implementation.

Opinions, beliefs, values, choices are very much in the forefront in planning. At one time some social planners, along with social scientists generally, would have defined the issue as one of achieving a state of disinterestedness and value neutrality with reference to the matters at hand. Experience and reflection on the nature of the planning process would seem to call for another stance. We join Paul Davidoff in the view that:

> The prospect for future planning is that of a practice which openly invites political and social values to be examined and debated. Acceptance of this position means rejection of prescriptions for planning which would have the planner act solely as technician.[3]

Much of the remainder of the chapter is involved in the clarification of the grounds for selection of the above quotation. We begin with some definitions.

---

[2] Paul Davidoff and Thomas A. Reiner, "A Choice Theory of Planning," *Journal of the American Institute of Planners*, XXVIII, No. 2 (May, 1962), 103–115.

[3] Paul Davidoff, "Advocacy and Pluralism in Planning," *Journal of the American Institute of Planners*, XXXI, No. 4 (November, 1965), 331.

At the level of common discourse, the concern is with *opinion*: opinions about what is most important, how problems are to be regarded, what sacrifices are justified for what objectives, whose prerogatives are to be protected, and so on. As Myrdal, Robin M. Williams, Jr., and others have suggested, opinions are in fact made up of beliefs, which are ideas of how reality is or was, and valuations, which are ideas of how reality ought to be or ought to have been.[4] Beliefs in this sense can be objectively judged as true or false. They are coped with by the methods and approaches described in the previous chapter for creating a picture of the relevant reality. But the values (to shift to Williams' more common usage from Myrdal's *valuation*) are "conceptions of the desirable" or "criteria for deciding what we should want." Values are concerned with the ends or goals of action, but they are also heavily invested in the choice of means and they affect the categories in which the reality is "structured" by the viewer.[5]

Williams has noted that, although values have a conceptual component and are often carefully systematized, they represent affect. They are *important* to small or large groups. A measure of group consensus regards them as significant matters of collective welfare. Because they are usually "general orienting principles," on a relatively high level of abstraction which constitute a reference point for "concrete patterns of behavior,"[6] rather than detailed behavioral guides, we might add that values too become the subjects of interpretation and debate.

In referring to values in the sense here described, we shall also employ the term *preferences*. Economists talk of the *preference function* as representing that element in the total equation which takes account of the consumer's actual or potential exercise of choice. A preference in this sense is a value in action.

The analyst of social policy is always involved in affirming, interpreting, and ranking values, and the fact is generally recognized. Gunnar Myrdal argues that even the basic social research process is permeated with value choices as it selects hypotheses, develops indexes and criteria, assembles data. He notes, for example, that in his own work his basic research on the status

---

[4] Gunnar Myrdal, *Value in Social Theory*, edited by Paul Streeten (New York: Harper & Bros., 1958), 71. Policy, according to Alva Myrdal, is based both on "premises of knowledge" and "premises of valuations." Alva Myrdal, *Nation and Family* (Cambridge, Mass.: The M.I.T. Press, 1968, paperback), 101.

[5] Robin M. Williams, Jr., *American Society* (New York: Alfred A. Knopf, 1965), 401, 403, and, "Individual and Group Values," *Annals of the American Academy of Political and Social Science*, 371 (May, 1967), 20–37.

[6] Norman W. Bell and Ezra F. Vogel, *A Modern Introduction to the Family* (Glencoe, Ill.: The Free Press, 1960), 17.

of American Negroes took the "American Creed" as the point of departure. When he studied the Depression, the perspective was that one should seek to develop that kind of insight which would clarify how depressions might be ended. His foci in the analyses of underdeveloped areas were very much shaped by his assumptions about the desirability of "modernization."[7]

Planners are for the most part aware that value choices enter into their work, although there is some tendency to put the process in relatively static terms: the planner deals with facts to predict the future, and then he deals with values, as he seeks to determine what future conditions his present or future clients seek to encourage or achieve.[8] However, there is increasing attention to the idea that, at all stages of planning, facts need constantly to be confronted with values and values need to be confronted with facts. This process is by no means limited to the stage of goal definition or choice.

Thus, New York State supplies the following data with reference to those in the ninth grade four years earlier who actually were graduated from high school.

| Year | Percentage of High School Graduates |
|------|-------------------------------------|
| 1931 | 32 |
| 1941 | 43 |
| 1951 | 63 |
| 1961 | 68 |
| 1962 | 71 |
| 1963 | 74 |

From many points of view, the progress in high school holding power is remarkable. In a given social context and in the perspective of overall values, New York was almost hysterically concerned in 1963 about its 26 percent rate of high school dropouts.

Edward Banfield reminds us that, in governmental decision-making, the satisfaction of the citizen-consumer is, or should be, substituted for "institutional habit" as the ultimate goal of policy. This, in fact, is what he sees as "welfare." How else, he asks, is government to (a) choose between building a zoo or creating a circus; (b) decide the priority to be given to expenditures to control air pollution; (c) approach the problem of estimating demand for expanded education or increased narcotics control?[9]

----

[7] G. Myrdal, op. cit., 260–261. Also, Asian Drama, 3 volumes (New York: Twentieth Century Fund and Pantheon Books [paperback edition], 1968), especially Vol. I, Chaps. 2 and 3.

[8] Davidoff and Reiner, op. cit.

[9] Edward C. Banfield, "Three Concepts for Planners," in Edward C. Banfield, Editor, Urban Government (New York: The Free Press, 1969; rev. ed.), 617.

Or, using a somewhat different vocabulary, a United Nations International Children's Emergency Fund conference on planning for the needs of children faced the fact that it knew how to quantify the *means* of goal achievement but had to fall back on social values when it wished to talk about ends. This remained the case whether the specific arena discussed was family factors, economic programs, political conditions, or social structure generally.[10] Indeed, in many fields in which great precision in quantitative target-setting is actually possible, there are those who stress that productivity, exports, gross national product, construction output, and the like can never be seen except as means. For a human society the goal is a social one, either expressed in value terms or quantitatively stated as an index of a value goal. Donald Michael argues that, as rationalization continues and there is more understanding of and control over logical factors, it is the extra-logical, moral, and ethical consequences of a program (what we are here calling values and preferences) which will become all-important to decision makers.[11]

Robert Dahl and Charles Lindblom note, in *Politics, Economics, and Welfare*, that the major questions of the day are concerned with the choice among complex techniques—but that ideologies enter into the choices.[12] Going even further, Davidoff argues that the basic issues relate to distributive justice; the answers to questions about the share of wealth and commodities to be assigned to different social classes are *not* something to be technically derived at all. Policies and programs which are "based on desired objectives . . . cannot be prescribed from a position of value neutrality."[13] Thus we move from the assertion that a planner must attend to values, something generally accepted even by those who tend to give more emphasis to technological aspects of decisions, to the notion that he should have values, that such values should be made clear, and that he should be an advocate for his values—subjects to which we shall return shortly.

One of the interesting observations to be noted is that of Martin Meyerson and Edward Banfield, who, in a study of urban renewal planning, also comment that there obviously is no purely technical way to choose housing sites. They develop the thesis that many criteria, including the political, enter

---

[10] Herman D. Stein, Editor, *Planning for the Needs of Children in Developing Countries* (New York: United Nations Children's Fund, 1965).

[11] Donald M. Michael, *The Next Generation* (New York: Vintage Books, 1965, paperback), Chap. 12.

[12] Robert A. Dahl and Charles E. Lindblom, *Politics, Economics, and Welfare* (New York: Harper & Bros., 1953, paperback), Chap. I.

[13] Davidoff, *op. cit.*, 331.

into decision-making and note that at the public hearings studied local groups (who, we might note, are generally invited to convey value and preference dimensions) actually were seen to have probed the technical issues more thoroughly than the officials in the Housing Authority.[14]

These and other authors continue to remind us that whether in planning or administration there is no easy way for a housing authority to know that it is working in the public interest. And it is for this reason that the planning literature shows ever-increasing concern with offering full expression to interest groups or with methods of assessing values and preferences. Thus, whether the context is an overview of social planning strategy for a country like Holland[15] or methods of applying cost-benefit analysis techniques to social programs, the value–interest group assessment question becomes important to the planner. In the former instance, the authors pursue the problem of bringing citizens' "criticism on ends and means to bear on the planning procedures," as the only way of accommodating to the realities of regional and group diversity and the limitations of the traditional representation through political groups. In the latter, in the context of discussion of rigorous measurement, an economist quotes John Maynard Keynes to the effect that: "There is no clear evidence from experience that the investment policy which is socially advantageous coincides with what is most profitable." Social projects may be developed precisely because a profit-oriented free market does not allocate sufficient resources to certain areas to meet all public preferences or needs.[16]

Or, in Richard Titmuss' formulation in an unpublished lecture,

> Welfare is concerned with social values and human relations. It may be the embodiment, carrier and expression of a philosophy of everyman's place in society. . . . Those who have studied these problems of welfare have, therefore, to think of themselves not as experts but as social servants able to explain a little more clearly the choices available in terms of alternative policies and courses of action. . . .

There is, then, no real debate as to the belief that valuation is attached to ends, means, procedures, and even to side-effects.[17] The variations, in the

---

[14] Martin Meyerson and Edward C. Banfield, *Politics, Planning, and the Public Interest* (New York: The Free Press, 1964, paperback).

[15] "Holland's Report to the 12th International Conference on Social Work, Athens, 1964" (Amsterdam, 1964, mimeographed).

[16] Juanita M. Kreps, "Discussion," in Gerald G. Somers, Editor, *Proceedings of Seventeenth Annual Meeting of Industrial Relations Research Association* (Madison, Wisconsin: Industrial Relations Research Association, 1965), 205.

[17] G. Myrdal, *Value in Social Theory* and *Asian Drama*.

first instance, are in how the matter is put, in the degree of emphasis, and in the notions as to how the planner personally relates to the value issue. Norton Long stresses that the basic problem of the city is the problem of ethics, the problem of classical political philosophy. Race relations, class conflict, and poverty cannot be reduced to problems of market adjustment; citizenship is not mere consumership. A city planner must attend to issues of ethics.[18] Davidoff and Reiner say simply, "Facts by themselves will not suggest what would be good or what should be preferred."[19] Rein and Miller document that there cannot be an anti-poverty effort which does not make value choices.[20]

Latent values permeate social practice and social policy, with basic implications ranging from the definition of deviance to the conceptualization of treatment programs. Thus Robert Merton notes how the stress on wealth as a success symbol leads to a bias which results in self-criticism rather than a push for structural reform by those with less opportunity.[21] Kingsley Davis documents the extent to which community mental health programs in their very modes of operation "assume[s] the Protestant open-class ethic."[22] Marshall shows how social statuses affecting social security programming and eligibility are not objective facts, but, rather, are created by value-laden political decisions.[23]

The issue is more than one of making the values visible, however, or of noting that at any one moment the culture presents the planner with a list of "givens." Recognition of the presence of the value issue in planning and the determination to cope with it systematically merely serve to underscore the degree of complexity involved and to suggest that almost any of the approaches is in some sense difficult or unsatisfactory. Value analysis and response carry broad implications for planning.

---

[18] Norton E. Long, "Citizenship or Consumership in Metropolitan Areas," *Journal of the American Institute of Planners*, XXXI, No. 1 (February, 1965), 2–6.

[19] Davidoff and Reiner, *op. cit.*, 111.

[20] Martin Rein and S. M. Miller, "Poverty, Policy and Purpose: The Dilemmas of Choice," in Leonard H. Goodman, Editor, *Economic Progress and Social Welfare* (New York: Columbia University Press, 1966), 20–64.

[21] Robert Merton, *Social Theory and Social Structure* (Glencoe, Ill.: The Free Press, 1957, rev. ed.), 139.

[22] Kingsley Davis, "Mental Hygiene and the Class Structure," reprinted in Herman D. Stein and Richard A. Cloward, Editors, *Social Perspectives on Behavior* (Glencoe, Ill.: The Free Press, 1953), 336.

[23] T. H. Marshall, *Social Policy* (London: Hutchinson University Library, 1965), 107.

## VALUE DIMENSIONS

There has been too little systematization of experience to assure identification of all the possible *dimensions of choice* relevant to the exploration of preferences in planning. One nonetheless looks with respect and appreciation both at Talcott Parsons' pattern variables and Clyde Kluckhohn's dichotomies. As summarized by Bertram Gross, these relate to some of the underlying dimensions which may be involved in value conflicts and preference debates. Where the planner seeks preferences empirically, they may serve to guide some of the explorations.

*Parsons' "Pattern Variables"*
1. *Affectivity-Affective Neutrality.* The extent to which people are expected to act in such a way as to achieve immediate gratification or else discipline themselves to renounce immediate gratification.
2. *Self-Orientation–Collectivity Orientation.* The extent to which people are expected to serve private or collective goals.
3. *Universalism–Particularism.* The extent to which people are expected to act in accordance with general standards rather than in the light of particular cases.
4. *Ascription–Achievement.* The extent to which people are expected to judge others on the basis of their attributes or on their actual performance.
5. *Specificity–Diffuseness.* The extent to which people are expected to act toward others on the basis of narrowly-defined spheres or without such confinement.

*Kluckhohn's Variables*

MAN AND NATURE
1. *Determinate–Indeterminate.* The extent to which people believe in orderliness in the universe, as opposed to chance or caprice.
2. *Unitary–Pluralistic.* The extent to which the world is divided into such separate realisms as "mind" versus "body" and "sacred" versus "profane," rather than being seen as a whole.
3. *Evil–Good.* The extent to which nature and human nature are seen as basically good or evil.

MAN AND MAN
4. *Individual–Group.* Much the same as Parsons' self-orientation and collectivity-orientation pattern variable already mentioned.
5. *Self–Other.* The degree of relative emphasis on one's self or on loyalty or devotion to other individuals.
6. *Autonomy–Dependence.* This is similar to David Riesman's "Inner-Directed"–"Other-Directed" polarity.
7. *Active–Acceptant.* This is the contrast between accepting one's fate or trying to help determine it.

8. *Discipline–Fulfillment.* This is the "Apollonian-Dionysian" contrast between safety, control, and adjustment on the one hand and adventure, expansion, and self-realization on the other.
9. *Physical–Mental.* The extent of emphasis on sensual versus intellectual activities.
10. *Tense–Relaxed.* The extent to which tension of any kind is pervasive or is counterbalanced by a sense of humor and calm easy-goingness.
11. *Now–Then.* The extent to which emphasis is placed on the here-and-now, as opposed to either past or future.

BOTH NATURE AND MAN

12. *Quality–Quantity.* The extent of measurement or other standardization beyond purely qualitative considerations.
13. *Unique–General.* The extent to which the world is seen in terms of the concrete, the literal, and the unique, rather than in terms of abstraction and universalism.[24]

These are relatively abstract and noncommital statements of possibilities, especially useful early in research. Many policy experts prefer to state their value stances in the form of general goals. For example, Titmuss, identifying himself with "socialist social policies," urges the goals of "equality, freedom and social integration."[25] A social indicators task force in the United States proposes that the United States seek to do as well as any other country, with reference to living standards, and that we affirm a commitment to "realization of human potential."

In an unpublished paper, A. Kaplan has attempted quite specifically to suggest *some principles for the planner.* While it is doubtful that any list could cover all contingencies, contexts, and stages of development, it is an instructive and inspiring effort, meriting debate and testing.

The following tentative set of principles in planning is far from exhaustive, but may provide a point of departure.

1. *The principle of impartiality.* There is no prior specification of persons or groups who are to benefit or suffer from governmental policy. There is no place for love and hate in policy, i.e., discriminatory treatment of some sectors of the population only because they are the people that they are, without regard to acts or traits that others might conceivably share. Examples of violation of this principle are the Nazi policies against the Jews, or colonial exploitation of a native population on behalf of the master-class.

---

[24] Summarized in Bertram M. Gross, "The State of the Nation: Social Systems Accounting," in Raymond A. Bauer, Editor, *Social Indicators* (Cambridge, Mass.: The M.I.T. Press, 1966), 205, 206.

[25] Richard M. Titmuss, "The Practical Case Against the Means-test State," *The New Statesman,* 74, No. 1905 (September 15, 1967), 308–310.

2. *The principle of individuality.* Values are finally to be assessed as having their locus in the individual. No groups or abstract aggregates, like the State, provide proper substantives for value adjectives, save indirectly, and with ultimate reference to individuals. A "strong State" or "wealthy State" is not a value save insofar as it implies, sooner or later, individuals who enjoy security of a high standard of living. The State is made for man, not man for the State.

3. *The maximin principle.* Improvements in a value distribution consist in cutting off the bottom of the distribution, not extending the top. The achievement of a policy or program is appraised by its minima, not its peaks. We assess a technology, from the standpoint of social planning, by the price of shoes rather than the achievement of a Sputnik. Equivalently, the principle dictates that those with least of a particular value should have the first priority for more of it.

4. *The distributive principle.* The more people that have a good thing, the better. This is the principle that declares against élite formation, part of that aspect of democratic thought that gives weight to sheer number. It implies the use of the method of summation in assessing the values for a set of individuals. However attractive a particular configuration to a philosopher of aristocracy of Plato's stamp, we can never have too many enjoying a particular good.

5. *The principle of continuity.* Changes in patterns and practices are of no value for their own sake, and are subject to established procedures of change. No merit attaches to a break with tradition merely because it is a break. However revolutionary the changes made, their value lies in the substance of the changes, not in the fact of their having been made. It is this principle, in effect, that distinguishes immature rebelliousness from the achievement of mature independence.

6. *The principle of autonomy.* Government is to do for people only what people cannot do for themselves. This is another basic component of democratic theory, repudiating paternalism, dictatorships of whatever benevolence, and the like. It is not necessarily a distrust of government but rather a faith in the governed.

7. *The principle of urgency.* "If not now, when?" The rate of progress toward social goals is to be maximized. The presumption is in favor of dealing with present needs; postponement on behalf of future goods requires explicit justification.[20]

Such listings are extremely helpful to the planner as either a way of sensitizing him to the possible implications of policies and programs being developed or as a guide to him as interpreter and advocate. However, the planner seldom can make—or wants to make—the major choices in a plan-

---

[20] Abraham Kaplan, "On the Strategy of Social Planning" (Unpublished paper, mimeographed, 1958).

ning process only in terms of his own preferences. The question thus arises as to whether there is some systematic and objective way for him to gauge and select the preferences of those for whom planning is undertaken. This question is best looked at in the context of some elaboration of how valuation is introduced into planning, whether or not the planner is able to take responsibility for it in a larger context.

## VALUES, PLANNING, AND COMPLEXITY

The effort of the planner to cope deliberately with the value-preference issue is complex because:[27]

- □ there are conflicting values at stake;
- □ value questions must often be posed in an "as if" form;
- □ it is difficult to clarify just what the prevalent values or preferences are;
- □ values are not always transitive;
- □ there is often dispute as to whose choices are relevant or most relevant to the decisions to be made;
- □ it is difficult to translate technical issues into their value consequences in a completely objective fashion.

### Conflicting stakes

There is a considerable tradition in community organization practice or in urban community development that assumes that competent "enablers," expediters, and technical consultants and a sufficiently long period of time will produce manageable community consensus on any issue involved in policy development or planning and that the community will emerge from the experience better integrated than previously. This may conceivably be the case quite often, if one is judging in the "very long run," and from the perspective of highly generalized social objectives or conceptions of the human community. However, within the time perspective and self-interest conception of the ordinary citizen, it is simply not true that the lack of consensus is a problem reflecting only the lack of time or the failures of community organization. Local home owners are inconvenienced in a major way and have a variety of good and unconfused reasons to oppose certain urban renewal, public housing, or road-building projects when they are proposed. High-income taxpayers do have to give up more if certain social programs are enacted. Some child care programs do implement concepts of child rearing that are unacceptable to some community members or are undertaken

---

[27] For illustrations and somewhat different formulation of the complexity, see David Braybrooke and Charles E. Lindblom, A *Strategy of Decision* (New York: The Free Press of Glencoe, 1963), Chap. II.

to make it easier for women to work—a practice that violates the ethical or religious tenets of some people.

In short, whether one compares cultures[28] or community subgroups, there are divergent conceptions of a good person or of the good life; and there are true interest conflicts always present. A comprehensive child welfare planning study in Houston, Texas, for example, documented significant differences in values held, conceptions of causality, and program-priority choice between board and staff members and among staff members in different types of organization or with differing levels of responsibility.[29] As the amount of planning increases, there are likely to be more rather than fewer value conflicts.

A Rutgers University study described the differences in priorities as defined by planners, on the one hand, and service consumers, on the other.[30]

Behind some of these conflicts is a difference in conception of the public interest, as analyzed by Meyerson and Banfield. These authors identify five differing conceptions of the logical structure of the public interest:

*Organismic.*   The important unit is the plurality which may have ends "different from those entertained by any of the individuals who comprise the public."

*Communalistic.*   The ends entertained by the plurality are "common" in the sense that they are shared universally or almost universally by the individual members. Such shared ends are what is relevant in contrast to the unshared.

*Utilitarian.*   The relevant dimension is the ends of the individual as he selects and orders them; public interest is "the greatest happiness of the greatest number."

*Quasi-utilitarian.*   While the utility of the individual is what is relevant, still all men are not weighted equally.

*Qualified individualistic.*   While the ends of the "whole" are conceived to be the aggregate of those chosen by individuals, only certain classes of ends are defined as relevant or appropriate. Many types of principles may be introduced to guide the selectivity.[31]

---

[28] Orville G. Brim, Jr., *Education for Child Rearing* (New York: Russell Sage Foundation, 1959), 82–83.

[29] Gwynn Nettler, *A Study of Opinions on Child Welfare in Harris County* (Houston, Texas: Community Council of Houston and Harris County, 1958).

[30] Ludwig L. Geismar and Bruce W. Legay, "Planners' and Consumers' Priorities of Social Welfare Needs," in *Social Work Practice, 1965* (New York: Columbia University Press, 1965), 76–93.

[31] Meyerson and Banfield, *op. cit.*, 322–329.

In short, both the procedural and conceptual approaches adopted by the planner to the matter of preference must deliberately or by implication choose a concept of the public interest. The approach must cope with the question of selectivity where there are conflicting stances. It cannot permit the process to be stalled pending complete agreement or consensus.

## The form of the question

The real differences of preference and interest are in themselves quite a difficult matter. The fact that the planner as "preference prober" often must pose his questions in an "as if" form adds to the problem. A reality in itself may be tolerable or even attractive, but many strong fears may be generated for those who must imagine how it might be if a children's treatment center were to be built in their neighborhood or if their high school were consolidated with those in two adjacent counties. Daily interaction may show that a socially-integrated community is tolerable or even interesting, but the response to an "as if" situation is contaminated by the fear of the unknown.

Another problem may also be presented under this general heading. Alan Altshuler has discussed the difficulty in getting a community to sustain a real dialogue about goals and choices in community planning.[32] Scholars and philosophers enjoy discussion on such levels; most citizens would prefer to debate the concrete and delimited. The result tends to be a project orientation toward and decision-making about rather limited programs—not acceptance of statements of long-range goals which might then guide a period of planned activity.

Furthermore, values are not organized in neat hierarchies. If A is preferred to B and B to C, we are not certain that A is preferred to C ("transitivity"). Thus, value decisions in some areas do not necessarily guide one in other areas.

## The complexity of clarifying preferences

What sorts of questions should one ask—and of whom—assuming that we try to cope with the "as if" dimension by conveying all relevant experience which can be drawn upon? A conventional answer is that the average citizen should be expected to respond to goal and priority problems and that one should ask questions in such form rather than specifically translating them into value dimensions. Then the professionals and the technicians take on the decisions relevant to means of achieving the goals.[33] Geismar and Le-

---

[32] Alan Altshuler, "The Goals of Comprehensive Planning," *Journal of the American Institute of Planners*, XXXI, No. 3 (August, 1965), 190.

[33] Samuel Mencher, "Current Priority Planning," *Social Work*, 9, No. 3 (July, 1964), 27–35.

gay argue, however, that few laymen see the value issues on a level of generality permitting such an approach. They would begin by asking experts to measure survival needs objectively. Then, when a floor is guaranteed, they would ask consumers to rank the priorities on the next level of provision, posing quite specific and concrete program choices.[34]

If one returns to the several conceptions of the public interest cited above, it is clear that a basic perspective on the structure of public interest will guide the formulation of the preference issue as it is presented to the citizen-consumer, because each conception is in some way selective as to its view about what is debatable. To some, for example, communal interests in land-use planning are such that "costs" to individuals do not matter. To others, a neighborhood resident's priorities about the character of his dwelling vicinity are so overriding that one should consult him on each bit of public construction or destruction, about which he might conceivably have a viewpoint.

### The limitations of the "social welfare function"

Within social science, the field of welfare economics is devoted to long, complex, and ingenious efforts to cope objectively with the preference dimension as relevant to planning and policy. One may admire both the rigor and ingenuity of some of this work, yet it is not unreasonable to conclude that the social planner will not find solutions to his problem here.

Tinbergen's appraisal is realistic—

The problem of finding the optimum regime is the central problem of *welfare economics*. In this sector of economics we know that among the data of the problem a social welfare function is the first element. This means that we assume knowledge about two things: first, about the preferences of the individuals constituting the economy and, second, about how to weigh the interests of different individuals in determining social well-being or social welfare. In customary economic language this means first, knowledge about the utility functions of individuals, and second about the social utility function. These are far-reaching assumptions, because our knowledge about individual utility functions is very limited and the social welfare function depends on how we compare utilities of different persons. For the time being this is done intuitively only and therefore leaves much room for differences of opinion.[35]

The problem of defining, ascertaining, and deciding how to cope with preferences remains.

---

[34] Geismar and Legay, *op. cit.*

[35] Jan Tinbergen, *Central Planning* (New Haven: Yale University Press, 1964), 82. For a classic statement, see Kenneth J. Arrow, *Social Choices and Industrial Values* (New York: John Wiley & Sons, 1951).

If one accepts Kenneth Arrow's conclusion[36] that a social welfare function is not the solution, because logically it is not possible to achieve social choice which amalgamates discordant individual preferences, one faces the ultimate need to make some decisions politically, using that term in a broad sense. The planning context often supplies enough statutory and administrative "givens" to permit a planner to locate clear parameters for choice and to delineate the options. Under such circumstances, empirical exploration of majority preferences may be appropriate, possible, and acceptable. Quite frequently, however, groups or population elements have their quite independent perspectives on the so-called givens, the boundaries for choosing, the "realities," the locus of the issue. Sometimes one element imposes its will and decides all. More frequently, bargaining and acceptance of trade-offs serve to compromise positions rooted in divergent preferences. The outcome is in no logical sense a balanced amalgam, but it offers a political solution. The planner then has his needed frame of reference.[37]

## The relevant community

These considerations imply and introduce the very difficult question of how one is to select the "relevant" community in exploring preferences. Does one reject urban renewal because the majority of those whose slum dwellings would be destroyed prefer to remain as they are? Herbert Gans argued in *The Urban Villagers* that an attractive village life was destroyed by a Boston urban renewal project—and that those people affected did not want the so-called improvement. To which Peter Rossi responded, "Someone has to mind the metropolitan store."[38] The question is real: are urban renewal decisions to be made by residents of the immediate area, the district, or the borough—or the city as a whole, which is seeking an overall direction for its development? Or, in a characteristic situation, should hospital policy be made by a sophisticated lay board and a related medical leadership group, or must ways be found to introduce other interests, or the "public interest"?

---

[36] Kenneth J. Arrow, "Public and Private Values," in Sidney Hook, Editor, *Human Values and Economic Policy* (New York: New York University Press, 1967).

[37] We here refer to circumstances in which preferences are at issue but there are enough forces to make planning possible. Much in political life involves bargaining and trade-offs not relevant to rational planning, whether modest or synoptic.

[38] Herbert Gans, *The Urban Villagers* (New York: The Free Press of Glencoe, 1962); and review of it by Peter Rossi, *The American Journal of Sociology*, LXX, No. 3 (November, 1964), 382.

Roger Starr complains of the assumption in the housing field that all Americans live in "local communities." See Roger Starr, *The Living End* (Baltimore: Penguin Books, 1967), 45.

On still another level, should the concerns and stake of local mayors impinge on the staff of the Office of Economic Opportunity as anti-poverty programs are planned? Should the United States Department of Agriculture institute a food stamp program where a state government refuses to do so? Finally, should local parents or a local school board settle policy about how racial integration is to be carried out (or with reference to any one of many educational policy or priority issues), or are there potent interests and rights on state or national levels? If so, how are the several layers of interest expected to interact, and how are decisions to be made?

Many planning disputes do not refer to the principle of attending to preferences, but rather reflect disagreement as to which is the relevant community.

## From technical question to value issue

A subtle but important problem is found in the fact that, even under very congenial circumstances, where planners seek to help laymen make the value decisions by translating technical issues into value terms, the task is difficult. The truth is that planners and technicians may find such translation as difficult as would the layman attempting to reverse the process. Does a social security expert arguing for a clarification of the relationship between social services and income supports really know what value issues may be involved for those to whom he turns for opinions? What of the social service expert attempting to guide decision-making by a local community group of "the poor," who are designing a multi-service center in the context of a local anti-poverty program? Does not the problem also exist for the staff of lawyers writing a new state family court act, who want to bring the critical value issues to a citizens' advisory committee?

## Planning controversies seldom offer pure value choices

The difficulty goes beyond the issue of bridging the worlds of technology and of value. In the "real" world of planning or administration, the choices often are made among programs and policies which combine values in various degrees and mixes. One sacrifices a degree of one to enhance a degree of another. Little is accomplished by debate on abstractions, then, because the value problem is in fact always a problem of adjustment at a margin. There is no practicable way for the planner to state marginal objectives or values except in terms of particular policies which are at issue. What is more, men unable to agree at all about abstract values can often arrive at consensus about practical policy issues or can bargain and compromise.[39]

---

[39] See Lindblom, in A *Strategy of Decision, op. cit.,* Chap. 5.

*Community action programs as illustrations*

All of these difficulties and more are illustrated in the efforts, beginning in 1964, to organize local anti-poverty community action programs with "the maximum feasible participation" of residents of the target areas and target populations concerned. Part of the problem has been formulated in an unpublished memorandum by Milton Kotler of the Institute for Policy Studies, Washington, D.C. Dr. Kotler notes the contradiction between the assumption that one can arrange for meaningful "indigenous" representation of the urban poor and the related assumption of the alienation of the urban impoverished. On the other hand, Bertram Beck, of New York City's Mobilization for Youth, cautions: "The technical solutions required for the problems of poverty are not available to people merely because they are poor. A society which looks to the most disadvantaged for the answers to complex economic and social problems is morally and intellectually bankrupt."[40] The anti-poverty program seeks to cope with alienation by offering a stake in programs, and power with reference to policy and program decisions, but it must —as central authorities review proposals or audit programs—introduce criteria relating both to competence and to national goals and policies.

At the same time, when 3 or 5 or even 10 percent of the people in a locality vote to choose so-called representatives of the poor, one asks whether the voting actually serves as a referendum on policy issues or whether so small a rate of participation creates representation. Those who have the authority of political office or of professional training ask whether their views should not be weighed equally or more heavily. In fact, officials chosen through the traditional political system inquire as to whether election by special classes of electors and participation by small numbers of those thus eligible does not subvert the theory and practice of a democratic system. Others respond that, since farmers vote on crop allotment plans, why not the poor on poverty strategy?

Some then interpret "feasible" participation to include consideration of capacity and seek to assure access to the preferences of the poor, as these might guide policy and program, rather than invite the poor to become policy-makers. At which point the complaint from the other side is heard, to the effect that the preferences of the poor have always been ignored because they lacked control over resources and programs; the preferences of the "powerless" are not taken seriously.[41]

---

[40] Mobilization for Youth, Inc., *News Bulletin*, 5, No. 2 (Summer, 1966), 2.

[41] See testimony in *Examination of the War on Poverty Program*, Hearings before the Subcommittee of the War on Poverty Program of the Committee on Education and Labor, House of Representatives, April 12, 13, 14, 15, 29, and 30, 1965 (3 volumes).

There has been a tendency in the United States of late to mandate participation, sometimes of "the poor" (as in the anti-poverty effort), sometimes of the local community (as in urban renewal), sometimes of the affected public and voluntary social agencies and related professions (as in community mental health planning), and sometimes of areas affected (as in area redevelopment legislation). Such legislation seems to assume that skilled "enabling" staff, enough time, open meetings or hearings, and goodwill are enough to produce consensus. We have suggested the obstacles deriving both from real interest-group differences and from complexity inherent in the goal of being guided by or accommodating to preferences. No easy solutions are available —but there is some accumulation of useful proposals and experience.

## SYSTEMATIC ATTENTION TO PREFERENCES AND VALUES

Real value issues, about which there may be legitimate differences, are at the heart of planning. Therefore, whether in the formulation of the planning task, in the derivation of policy, in programming, or in evaluation, one must attend to the value-preference question. Complexity, lack of consensus as to how this is to be achieved, and the recognition of competing stakes in the outcome do not relieve one of this responsibility. When the undertaking is approached in this spirit, helpful precedent and suggestions emerge. This section reviews such leads and possibilities.

In one sense, the assessment of preferences might have been regarded as part of the study of the relevant social realities, as reviewed in the last chapter. However, it is weighed here, since systematic, rigorous empiricism is not always possible and since the issue is not only one of appraising the reality but also of balancing interest-group concerns and creating the possibility of new forms of compromise and consensus.

Davidoff and Reiner provide a list of sources of preference data:

- □ market analyses
- □ public opinion polls
- □ anthropological surveys
- □ public hearings
- □ interviews with informed leaders
- □ press content analysis
- □ studies of laws, administrative behavior, and budgets.[42]

On a higher level of abstraction, Williams notes that one may seek operational definitions of value by beginning with:

- □ overt choices as expression of preference

[42] Davidoff and Reiner, *op. cit.*, 111.

- ☐ attention or emphasis
- ☐ statements or assertions
- ☐ implicit premises
- ☐ referents for social sanctions.[43]

These are useful lists and they include much of what is now done by the most conscientious planning organizations. Because there are many implicit methodological problems (indicator validation, sampling, etc.), there is much experimental work to be undertaken.

It becomes possible to cope with the complexity of the enterprise if we begin with the understanding that a planner is not seeking *the* answer—a worked-out solution to a puzzle.

> We never order all possible total situations according to a system of values, but rather have muddled preferences for aspects and features of a limited number of actual and possible solutions. These preferences change as a result of the discussion and adoption of policies intended to minister to them.[44]

Similarly, the planner must reject the traditional assumptions that values can be discarded or are "to be made explicit in order to be separated from empirical matters." Values are ever present and permeate each phase of empirical analysis and all aspects of a planning discussion. Valuations are affected by what is conceived to be the feasible and are affected by what is projected as the likely. Yet the nature and intensity of valuation activity help determine what occurs. One, therefore, cannot expect in planning to see either ends or means as rigid givens, unaffected by one another and by the interplay of each with valuations.[45]

In this perspective, planners and laymen, professionals, politicians, and citizens at large may all become involved with value issues at all levels and at any point in a planning process. In some contexts, Szeslow Bobrowski's "shuttle" process may have validity: The planning commission works out its first vague sketches and these flow from the minister right down to the factory. This, in turn, stimulates the upward flow of specific projects. The planning commission then optimizes the plan; it goes down and, sometimes, up again. The "shuttle" is a device for popular participation, introducing information not available to central planners. To assure such, one provides for strengthening the capacities of groups to play the role, discovering in turn

---

[43] Williams, *op. cit.*, 408.

[44] Streeten, Introduction to G. Myrdal, *op. cit.*, xxv–xxvi.

[45] *Ibid.*

that real participation in itself is an excellent way to help people "develop."[46]

French social service planning provides an interesting illustration of local level expression of preference, whereas the formal structure for development of the French National Plan illustrates how preference determination may be assigned to a centralized, elective body. For the former purpose, the focus is on the local family association, a group organized for family activities or to support improvements in governmental policy. These associations developed initially as small pressure groups dealing with population policy, but were recognized by and thus encouraged in subsequent legislation. The law now recognizes the union of family associations as representing all French families vis-à-vis the public authorities.

The heart of the policy, which makes the union potent and encourages its development, is the setting aside of a small percentage of family allowance contributions (an important element in the French system of social security) for the work of these associations. A series of possibilities is offered for the expenditure, ranging from general social facilities to treatment resources for specific deviant groups. About one-third of the funds are expended by the national union and the remainder by the associations in the departments.

The sum is small by United States standards, but the services are appreciated, and the opportunity for making decisions about priorities has considerable ramifications. Among other things, the groups do become involved in broader social policy.

One should note, in the light of complaints during 1965 and 1966 of limited participation of "the poor" in choosing their own representatives in United States community action programs, that fewer than 7 percent of the families with children are actually members of French family associations and the general bias is middle class. Efforts have been undertaken to increase worker participation.[47]

On the more central level, when the French economic planners (using reports and proposals from technical subgroups) make their initial projections of growth rate, on the basis of which much else in economic and social planning follows, the options, their bases, and the consequence of the choices are then presented for discussion and action. The National Assembly, with access to expert and interest-group comments, debates the options and elects a growth-rate assumption. Then various technical and expert groups on a national level and regional interest groups join in the process of spelling out

---

[46] Statements by Szeslow Bobrowski, in Stein, *op. cit.*, 94, 75.

[47] The description is based on Alvin L. Schorr, *Social Security and Social Services in France* (Washington, D.C.: Government Printing Office, 1965).

the policies and programs relevant to their respective areas. The planners work with this material, submitting the plan for comment to the Economic and Social Council, and then to the National Assembly for action.[48]

Community organizers react favorably to the French procedure and to similar "group process" approaches to preference. They note that such efforts can be an effective answer to several of the categories of difficulty and complexity outlined above as we examined problems in assessing preferences:

□ A community group process can permit local people more realistically to understand what is at stake and to react more from knowledge and less from fear of the unknown.

□ In the course of such process, the citizens affected can identify the real value issues even if the technicians have not been able to do so.

□ Since there are real decisions to be made, real resources to be allocated, alternative choices to be rejected, the action is considered and responsible.

□ One discovers the "relevant" community by permitting those who care about the issue to be heard and by being sure that all who might care are informed.

□ One does not involve only one population element ("the poor"), but rather the entire community.

The reader will perceive at once that these are excessively optimistic statements. Just as the original listing does not prove that the problem of preference is unmanageable in planning, so this listing does not establish that the complete solution resides in the community organization process. What does seem to be true is that active local involvement by affected people will identify basic value and technical issues which might otherwise be lost and will provide a more realistic basis for response to them. This process is obviously far superior to a traditional public opinion poll, which does not face the question of the minimum level of information essential to a response and does not note that the "real life" outcome of a public issue is changed if a period of community interaction, conflict, and mutual education precedes it, because interests become more visible and intensity of feeling can register.

On the other hand, as we shall suggest below, a community organization process has selective participation and is capable of manipulation. It cannot substitute for the ballot box. It is an asset in the planner's approach to preferences, however. There may also be wisdom in experimentation along the lines of Vernon Miller's proposal for a cross between an opinion poll and

---

[48] On French planning, see "France and Economic Planning" (New York: French Information Service, 1963). Also, Andrew Shonfield, *Modern Capitalism: The Changing Balance of Public and Private Power* (New York: Oxford University Press, 1965).

town meeting, utilizing mass media, sampling, and computerized data processing.[49]

Such a process is, of course, more realistic if the participants have sufficient power to assure attention to their views. This has been the case in much community organization with middle-class participants, but, as noted above, it becomes a problem with the poor and the alienated. They are defined as lacking that sustained interest, competence, and responsible stake in the community which would provide both leverage to advance their views and a perspective for decision-making.

It is here that the anti-poverty program in the United States did offer an interesting answer. By assuring considerable representation of the local poor on the boards of neighborhood and city-wide community action programs which disposed of funds, poor people were placed in the position of making policies and program decisions or participating in such decision-making for programs of wide scope and significance. In many places they could hire, or veto the hiring of, professional workers and nonprofessional personnel. They were dealing with programs and action that could affect them and their neighbors significantly. In short, their "stake" was vital enough to make their preferences real.

The Columbus, Ohio, neighborhood "corporation," created under the consultative guidance of Milton Kotler of the Institute for Policy Studies, carries this process further by incorporating the people in the neighborhood into a legal entity (a "community foundation"), which actually controls property (a settlement house) and receives program grants. Similar logic lies behind the use of neighborhood "corporations" as a community-action device in the anti-poverty effort.

Finally, one might note the increasing practice in the United States from the nineteen-sixties of "consumer" involvement in a policy-advisory capacity in social welfare programs. This does not go so far as the community foundation or corporation, which gives a measure of control over resources, or the French scheme, wherein funds are offered for disposition (all within set parameters). Yet much is accomplished through feedback of program consequences, depiction of social realities, and expression of preferences by organized welfare clients, aged, youth program participants, public housing tenants, school parents, and other "users." Positive experience in such approaches is widespread and the next, obvious step is under way: incorporating such participants as full-fledged members of governing boards and

---

[49] Vernon F. Miller, "The Town Meeting Reborn," *Saturday Review*, 49, No. 30 (July 23, 1966), 34–35.

policy committees of voluntary and public agencies operating all manner of social welfare programs. Such procedure merely utilizes and expresses the fact that, in the modern welfare state, one is simultaneously taxpayer, voter, service user, patient, and potential policy-maker. Boards should be fully representative of all population elements.

No proposal meets all the problems. No method of bringing the value-preference-dimension elements into planning meets the diversity of circumstances. What, then, is a workable perspective?

## AN APPROACH

The components of a total approach may be developed out of what has already been outlined, plus one or two additional ideas. The elements will be presented sequentially. The basic perspective is that "ethics is primary over politics and politics is primary over planning."[50]

More specifically, one might consider, for an overall strategy on preferences, (a) the social welfare function; (b) votes, as reflecting aggregate utility; (c) partisan mutual adjustments; (d) holistic judgments; (e) cost-benefit analysis.[51] Critical is Ruth Mack's distinction between devices like the social welfare function, attempts to measure *objective utility*, and what she calls *holistic judgment*, a person's right to make decisions about the desirable for any reasons. The reasons may range from rationalized self-interest to convictions about how the various alternatives will work out and how such consequences relate to one's own aspirations.

The social welfare function, we have noted, holds no solution. Cost-benefit studies provide data which may affect a value debate but require value decisions to be carried out. Holistic judgment, voting, and mutual adjustment are unavoidable. They can be shaped into a possible total approach.

### Decentralization in policy-making and program control

The subject of decentralization is a large one in social planning and will require considerable subsequent elaboration. For the present we note the desirability of keeping at the lower level all policy and program decisions not addressed to overall policy or resource commitment. In short, people know their circumstances and their priorities and can best visualize realistically the consequences of decisions on a level relevant to their daily experience.

---

[50] Stanley J. Hallett, "Planning, Politics, and Ethics," in William R. Ewald, Jr., Editor, *Environment for Man* (Bloomington: Indiana University Press, 1967), 247.

[51] Ruth Mack, *Planning on Uncertainty* (New York and Washington: Resources for the Future and the Institute of Public Administration, 1969).

An approach to accumulating and gauging the intensity of preferences will be more meaningful if the general pattern is one of decentralization to a level found empirically to be viable—even if, at times, artificially instigated by administrators and planners.

Along these lines let us note the manner in which Yugoslavia had delegated its housing communities, through their representatives, to control decisions about landscaping, child welfare, housekeeping services, appliance repair, and resources for the schools.[52]

## Value decisions with maximum information and understanding

The commitment to attend to preferences is not a rejection of research or the accumulation of relevant experience. One ranks low, among the possible approaches, a simple opinion poll about priorities or values. Where such polling techniques are followed, they should come after a foundation of fact has been laid in the community through the spread of information, educational meetings, public debate about alternatives, and "propagandizing" of various points of view. Miller's computerized, mass media, simulated "Town Hall" is preferable to a simple poll, because information is given and positions are debated before attitudes are tapped.

The technicians and researcher thus have the responsibility to do all that is possible to assist those who would express preferences to choose among options, rank priorities, or enact policies. Their major contribution consists of an unbiased and clear presentation of the facts and projections, an honest identification of the apparent consequences (in both social reality and value terms) of the alternative choices, and a summary of the relevant accumulated experience elsewhere. Cost-benefit analyses may become increasingly helpful in this regard.

None of this is to deny the emotional and irrational, culture-based elements in the choices to be made. It is here assumed, however, that the degree of rationality can be enhanced and that value-choice can be moved from the extremes of emotionalism to that part of the behavioral continuum in which

---

[52] United Nations Department of Economic and Social Affairs, *Planning for Balanced Economic and Social Development: Six Country Case Studies* (New York, 1964); Albert Waterston, *Planning in Yugoslavia* (Baltimore: The Johns Hopkins Press, 1962).

Lisa Peattie notes how the advocate-planner often creates a "relevant community" or may actually talk for an extra-community constituency in the name of community. Lisa R. Peattie, "Reflections on Advocacy Planning," *Journal of the American Institute of Planners*, XXXIV, No. 2 (March, 1968), 80–88.

G. Myrdal cites the Indian insistence on mass involvement in plan development as a device to win support, not as an authentic search for preferences. See *Asian Drama*, II, 852–853.

one articulates values and then considers which course of action is most likely to optimize them. Here, after all, layman and technician must collaborate, whatever the choice, if there is to be successful follow-through on decisions. Myrdal asserts:

> The aim of practical research . . . [we might interpolate, of *some* practical research] is . . . to show precisely what should be the practical and political opinions and plans for action from the point of view of the various valuations if their holders also had the more correct and comprehensive factual knowledge which science provides.[53]

Webber's way of putting it, as already noted in an earlier chapter, is that the planner is concerned with tracing "repercussions and value implications associated with alternative courses of actions [sic], and, in turn . . . explicit evaluation and choice among the alternative matching goal-action sets."[54]

## Value alternatives to be identified and debated in planning

Planners, civic leaders, politicians are in a position to contribute to the quality of a planning process if they encourage researchers and others on the professional staffs to expand available knowledge and understanding as noted above. They themselves must join the planners in seeking identification of value implications of choices—not always the simple matter it is assumed to be.

The goal, too, suggests the case for a community organization process in which people of shared interests are helped to come together to explore a problem or issue and then to develop and express a point of view in relevant forums. Recognizing that a local public is a "pool of values with certain interests surfacing regularly and other concerns causing occasional ripples of response,"[55] one employs the process to fix attention where important actions are pending or need to be proposed.

The debate is most often quite specific in relation to proposed actions and policies: build or do not build the school here; open or do not open a family planning clinic; restrict public assistance programs or do not do so. Civic leadership enriches the entire process to the extent that it helps participants identify key value elements and contributes to a dialogue in which the short-range decision-making becomes part of an overall policy clarification with

---

[53] G. Myrdal, *Value in Social Theory*, 158.

[54] Melvin M. Webber, "The Prospects for Policies Planning," in Leonard J. Duhl, Editor, *The Urban Condition* (New York: Basic Books, 1963), 320.

[55] Peter H. Rossi and Robert A. Dentler, *The Politics of Urban Renewal* (Glencoe, Ill.: The Free Press, 1961), 148.

some consciousness of what is being done. Although this may smack of idealized unreality, if one assumes enough disinterested leadership to keep public discourse on such a level at all times, it is certainly occasionally possible and may be often possible. A continued effort on a national as well as local level has been proposed by a sociologist, John R. Seeley: ". . . I would have public debate . . . of the things we really believe in: what kind of society would you like to bring into being? What kind of person is worthwhile?"[56]

In the real world one might expect some combination of interest-group expression in relation to immediate and concrete issues reflecting value differences; interest-group goal definition which combines values and program elements; and general choice of broader goals formulated in policy or value terms.

## Maximum participation by concerned interest groups

It is often too much to expect members of a community who are concerned with a planning matter or a policy (whether one refers to a local or a national process) to become engaged in value analysis or careful study of the facts and projections. These are left to the planners and other professionals. One expects the latter to become as conscious as possible of value implications and to seek, in disinterested fashion, empirical indicators of community values and preferences by some of the means outlined above, while contributing, where possible, to more profound community debate.

How, then, does one assure a community contribution to value determinations? By avoiding a situation in which planning is defined as a purely technological process and assuring, structurally, that at some point the basic options, policies, or priorities are tested in the political arena or by giving the groups concerned real control over resources, personnel, or policies. This was illustrated above with reference to the Cleveland, Ohio, neighborhood corporation concept or the French and Yugoslavian plans. In the former instance, where the testing is in the political arena, interest groups move into action at appropriate points. *Although all value issues may not be well articulated and clearly formulated, they are enacted by diverse interest groups and thus may enter into the decision process.*

In effect, planning has never been completely objective and value-free even when in the hands of apolitical planning commissions, since these reflect their own biases about the city beautiful, the city efficient, the city equitable, and about solutions to social problems. When seen as instrumen-

---

[56] John R. Seeley, "Central Planning: Prologue to a Critique," in Robert Morris, Editor, *Centrally Planned Change: Prospects and Concepts* (New York: National Association of Social Workers, 1964, paperback), 68.

talities of the executive arm of government or of a department head, planning operations are subject to another type of bias, a term not used here in a derogatory sense.

Departmental planning staffs are extensions of departmental leadership and should reflect, ultimately, the biases of their responsible heads, who would be removed upon consistent public rejection of their work. Thus, the departmental context provides the value-choice guidance necessary to the the work. Because of legislative mandate (urban renewal) or the nature of the task (assessing need for a service which rests on consumer initiative), such staffs will nonetheless do much to seek out public preferences.

In the same sense, planning staffs with a broad assignment, attached to the executive arm of government, expect the value and priority guidance to come from the executive. They make a major contribution if they identify relevant data, "tease out" value implications, and report community preferences accurately. Again, if wise, they will facilitate discovery and expression of the latter.

The department head and executive might go well beyond this, however. Hearings, debates, and educational sessions should be organized in connection with major new program and policy decisions. Major documents would be made available. Interest groups would be informed. Where possible, all of this would occur in response to early drafts of proposals to allow time for study and expression of views. The executive and his staff would make changes in response.

Such process would inevitably move the issues into the political domain, where public-policy choices ultimately belong.[57] An approach of this kind, which makes actions and choices visible, politicizes them. When elements of the public are dissatisfied, they seek to replace the executive and his staffs (and/or legislative arms, as appropriate). For this is the ultimate safeguard in a democracy: no degree of participation supported by, encouraged by, or interpreted by departmental, executive, or legislative planners can avoid some "filtering" and interpretations on the part of those who control the process. There is no way to avoid the tendency to over- or underrate the outcome of a community organization process or interest-group pressure tactics. Those concerned, in turn, must ultimately decide whether they are satisfied or dissatisfied with the response. Their appeal is to the ballot box. They may assure a new team to carry out the process and give it a clear mandate in the course of the change-over.

---

[57] Dilemmas in the relationships among interest groups, and between interest groups and administrative agencies, are illustrated in Charles A. Reich, "Bureaucracy and the Forests" (Santa Barbara, California: Center for the Study of Democratic Institutions, 1962, pamphlet).

In effect, there is no way to know whether polling, research, hearings, and the community process fully reflect community valuations. Planners and their employers must eventually make some judgments about this. In addition they must often act in terms of previous expressions of valuation, not being able at each step to check back. However, in a society organized to select officials who govern "by the consent of the governed," this is not a problem. Interest-group expression often corrects the picture. The several or many "actors" in the situation bargain and seek trade-offs and mutual accommodation. Ultimately there is recourse to the ballot box and a change in the powers who control the process. Our point is simple: anything which improves the functioning of our democracy, whether in the neighborhood, city, state, national government, or voluntary association, facilitates a sound contribution to the formulation of the preference component in planning decisions.

Eugene V. and Edna G. Rostow, who appreciate citizen contributions of value preferences to planning, suggest that democracies need not be limited to that which can be achieved in a town meeting atmosphere. They note that some of the world's most successful cities, in fact, were not democratically planned. Democracy does not condemn us to mediocrity or deny to uncommon men, the élite, an opportunity to wield influence. Democracy permits considerable delegation of authority for considerable periods of time because a veto is always available to protect the public interest: "periodic voting remains the ultimate source of power."[58]

While it is true, as one is often reminded, that elections often do not intervene between the posing of an issue and the choice among alternatives, and while it is also true that the complexity of elements in any one election often results in incomplete or ambiguous guidance as to voter preferences, the fact remains that consent of the governed continues to be the best touchstone of preferences. The democratic *goal* has been defined as follows:

> Control over governmental decisions is shared so that the preferences of no one citizen are weighted more heavily than the preferences of any other one citizen. . . . Governmental decisions should be controlled by the greatest number expressing their preferences in the "last say."[59]

A perspective of this kind also permits some resolution of the question posed earlier: how does one settle on "the relevant community"? The answer is not in the conceptual realm: the relevant community for formulation and choice of the preference dimension in planning must ultimately be

---

[58] Eugene V. Rostow and Edna G. Rostow, "Law, City Planning and Social Action," in Duhl, *op. cit.*, 368–369.

[59] Dahl and Lindblom, *op. cit.*, 41.

that community which has the *right* to make the political decision.[60] Sometimes a sub-unit or neighborhood may be permitted considerable leeway, within wide boundaries, in recognition of the fact that its residents are affected by the decisions and that the results have few implications for others. Community "corporations" are organized on such principles. The unit with power, however, is also ultimately accountable, and groups within it that believe they have a stake in local-level planning decisions (zoning, road plans, school policy, etc.) have a right to be engaged in the community debate and power struggle. Thus it is not the locality which decides whether the higher-level unit and its public enter into the issue. It is the highest level which makes the final decision.

## Feedback machinery to reassess preferences

Feedback machinery per se is discussed later. However, a planner preoccupied with the issue of consumer choice as it affects policy and programming utilizes feedback data constantly to correct generalizations about preferences and to revise task definition, policy, and programming elements. Dahl and Lindblom argue for incrementalism, a planning strategy based on the constant testing of preferences through experience.[61]

## Political outlets for expression of preferences

The possibility of adequate outlets for expression of preferences is maximized if there is encouragement for a diversity of planning efforts. The conclusion follows logically from the earlier material. The rationale has been formulated clearly and persuasively by Paul Davidoff. A major outcome of planning, he notes, is the determination of policy. In a democracy, policy should be the product of political debate: "The right course of action is always a matter of choice, never of fact." Planners should engage in the political process as advocates of the interest of government, on the one hand, or of various groups with which they might work, on the other. The possibility of intelligent choices of public policies would be increased if different political, social, and economic interests produced their own proposed policies or plans. For example, in addition to the city plan developed by a planning commission, several groups in these categories might produce competing city

---

[60] Of course, here, too, there may be need to consider changes—as with reference to regional units, metropolitan areas, etc. See, for example, Jean Gottman, *Megalopolis* (Cambridge, Mass.: The M.I.T. Press, 1961), 744–746. There are serious ideological differences about "relevant community."

[61] Dahl and Lindblom, *op. cit.*, 83.

plans, emphasizing policy—for the most part—but dealing with program, too, as relevant.

The politicization of the planning process in this fashion, offering encouragement to a diversity of planning efforts which may ultimately compete, calls for a structure of governmental planning which places the final decisions either in the executive or legislative arms of government on all levels.[62] At the same time, because the executive branch itself on federal and state levels often serves as a powerful lobby, strong special-interest groups are essential to the process.

Harvey Wheeler, building further on these premises, reminds us that:

> . . . planning requires the participation of scientists and experts, but even more, it requires profoundly popular processes. The legitimacy necessary to a plan cannot exist unless it has both scientific and popular sanctions. The only presently existing institutions capable of combining anything approaching these two characteristics are the political parties. . . .[63]

Wheeler predicts a near future in which a population with much time for leisure, "a guaranteed living standard and enhanced cultural riches," will have much more opportunity for and interest in political activity. As a result of a general "restoration of politics," the parties will have constitutionally-provided staffing and public funding. Social issues will be very much in the forefront and will be dealt with deliberately at all governmental levels as well as in the voluntary sector. Political parties will be staffed for careful research, probing of preference, and the advancing of competing plans on all levels. The President's presentation of a broadly-conceived social plan in his State of the Union Message would follow much study and debate and would lead to new stages in the process:

> The plan affects all levels of government and all strata of society. This means that outside of Congress there is need for deliberate processes comparable to those taking place within it. Each local government agency needs to understand the plan and how its own functions will be affected. This is accomplished by citizens' groups organized under the auspices of local party leaders, conducting hearings and deliberations in conjunction with their immediate government officials. These hearings are, in fact, the culmination of an endeavor that began two years before the national party conventions. At that time a cycle of community deliberations was begun by local party leaders throughout the country, following a prearranged agenda.

---

[62] Davidoff, *op. cit.*, 331–333.

[63] Harvey Wheeler, "The Restoration of Politics" (Santa Barbara, California: Center for the Study of Democratic Institutions, 1965, pamphlet), 23.

These popular discussions are developments from the nation-wide hearings that both parties now conduct prior to preparing their platforms for the party conventions.[64]

In this idealized projection, Wheeler envisages strong party staffing for these activities. He foresees a shift in political conventions from preoccupation with competing candidates to emphasis on platforms which would be at the center of ensuing campaigns.

Whether or not Wheeler's prophecy is accurate, he, in effect, joins Davidoff in encouraging a diversity of planning and politicization of the process wherein value choices are made.

To round out the possibilities, we might add that both of these views are also based on the assumption that many types of voluntary associations (which we might identify as being as varied as real estate boards, committees for the aged or for children, tenant associations, community corporations, or mental health associations) would do well to strengthen their technical staffing and to undertake a range of sectorial, geographic, or social-problem-oriented planning endeavors and to offer their competing proposals in the community market place, where choices will eventually be made.

## FINAL COMMENTS

In short, a pragmatic and not fully satisfactory approach to the introduction of valuations into all phases of social planning involves all of the following:

- ☐ maximum decentralization
- ☐ maximum information for all participants in the process of formulating, assessing, and incorporating valuations
- ☐ efforts to make value issues, alternatives, and consequences highly visible, whether through didactic techniques or facilitating self-expression by interest groups
- ☐ democratization of decision-making, as a way of checking consensus or majority opinions around value questions
- ☐ a diversity of planning devices and centers and the politicization of the ultimate decision process
- ☐ a readiness to take chances, delegate adequate authority to act, and to rely on the "consent of the governed" ultimately to correct errors and misconceptions
- ☐ assigning resources and policy control experimentally to community corporations and neighborhood groups, in which residents or their directly-selected representatives allocate funds, hire staff, and set policy
- ☐ attention to the question of the "relevant community" in decision-

---

[64] *Ibid.*, 25.

making, and a recognition that the right to determine selection of preferences is ultimately associated with responsibility as assigned statutorily.

A few additional, related comments are necessary here. First, it should be noted that widespread participation in social planning–related debates and decisions has two major, valued side-effects. These are the primary goals for some advocates. First, group or individual involvement in social planning, particularly as it is politicized in the sense described above, is an important step in citizen action. It is in fact a major participation outlet. Second, for the alienated and for those lacking communal coping skills, the entire process may also be described as socio-therapeutic. To use other terms, facilitation of interest-group participation in formulation and expression of preferences in relation to any of the phases of social planning, apart from being a desirable thing in its own right, is also a way of increasing community "competence." Brief consideration will suggest that efforts to develop community competence, to increase participation in social action, and to assure effective expression of preference with respect to planning issues may, for disadvantaged communities, be conceived as part of one process. They are all common to community development.

A caution must be sounded. In an era of mass media, controlled information, demagogues, and considerable institutional reliance on advertising, the possibility of induced preferences is a real one.[65] This is particularly the case where the process of introducing preferences into planning results in a degree of emphasis on interest groups, makes visible the conflicting positions of officials or aspiring politicians, and clarifies the large stakes for some people in the decisions to be made. There is incentive to manipulate public opinion or to try in the short run to manipulate the apparent preferences. The available devices are many, from the phrasing of questions in rhetorical form to the exaggeration of costs, from the overemphasis on side-effects to the denial of known benefits, from the appeal to primitive fears to the misrepresentation of tabulations. There is no absolute safeguard against such dangers. Most or many of the devices which may distort the process are not unlawful. Alertness to the problem permits corrective measures and public reporting of what has been done. Here, as in all democratic process, one relies on the power of exposure of the truth and on ultimate recourse to the wisdom of an informed electorate. This holds whether the arena is national policy or the local anti-poverty program.

---

[65] John Kenneth Galbraith, *The Affluent Society* (Boston: Houghton Mifflin Company, 1958), 260–261.

This discussion of preferences has emphasized goal choice and task definition, while merely mentioning the choice and shaping of *means*. Such approach is in order, both because we have thus given attention to the more difficult issues, and because the focus at this point is on the early phases of planning. By way of corrective, then, it is useful to stress the contribution of adequate value and preference data to overall programming. Here the planner has the same interests as does the market analyst in a commercial venture in clarifying how product "image," "packaging," delivery system, and "costs" affect access, continuity of use, intensity of participation, and so on. In social welfare, access and effective delivery are central concerns. Assembling adequate preference data through all the variety of measures described, as adapted to the circumstances of the particular field or program or locale, becomes quite urgent. Special attention should be given to client or user advisory groups and to democratization of boards of directors, so as to assure representation of the range of users.

When legislation for area redevelopment, urban renewal, or community mental health provides that plans submitted for federal funding be shown to represent the broad community consensus of many interest groups, the skeptic may ask, "Why?" To the response that, without such consensus, plans may be narrow and self-serving and unlikely to succeed, he may answer, "Show me." Admittedly, the evidence is flimsy. The case is a rational one, developed by analogy to the marketing problem faced by the businessman. Yet if one had a true market situation, the problem of ascertaining preferences in social planning would not arise. The product which does not reflect preferences gathers dust on shelves, but the user of public services often does not have the option of selectivity. Thus, the core of the case for studying user preferences grows out of democratic ideology. For all their failings, systematic empirical efforts to determine preferences, build interest-group participation and popular control are a wiser approach to valuation than any other to which we have access.

Yet one should not pretend that this is the whole story. To return to a point mentioned earlier, Geoffrey Vickers quite properly reminds us that:

> The men and women in England who abolished slavery, created the educational system or gave women the vote were not acting on hypotheses of what the voters wanted. They were afire with faith in what people ought to want and in the end they persuaded their lethargic compatriots to give them enough support to warrant a change. American presidents from Lincoln to Kennedy do not speak with accents of inquirers seeking guidance about other people's preferences. . . . They *criticize* contemporary values, urge *reevaluation*, and appeal not to what people are thinking now but to

what they ought to be thinking and would be thinking if they exposed themselves with sufficient sensitivity to the subject matter of the debate. A free society is one in which these initiatives spring up freely and in which men are free to espouse or resist them. It depends, like every other society, on the quality and abundance of these initiatives, as well as on the facilities for the debate. . . .[66]

A democracy must at any given moment be organized to protect itself, in the deepest sense. By the same token, and to contribute to continuing democratic renewal, some of the planners some of the time must be prepared to think, to feel, to propose, to leap toward the unknown. Plans need not be seen as always bound by values; they may also be inspired by them. The planner is, by his very assignment, both technician and agent of change.

---

[66] Geoffrey Vickers, "Ecology, Planning and the American Dream," in Duhl, *op. cit.*, 391.

# ☑ FORMULATION OF POLICY, THE STANDING PLAN

THE CHAPTER's theme is most clearly announced in a quotation from the volume on planning in business cited earlier:

> Policies are standing plans. Policies are general guides to future decision-making that are intended to shape those decisions so as to maximize their contribution to the goals of the enterprise. Policies are the instruments by which goals are achieved.[1]

The economist Tinbergen, in discussing the social aspects of economic planning, has similarly defined these as "the principles and methods of designing social policies as a necessary component of general policies for economic development. The design of a policy is another word for its planning."[2] Herbert Simon, a student of administration, agrees: "A large part of planning must be devoted to the determination of a few guiding principles and the dissemination of these principles to key figures. . . ."[3]

This stance immediately introduces both semantic and ideological problems. There are political contexts in which the "goal" or the "policy" is a given; it is something assigned the planner by higher authorities. The planner then becomes a programmer or somebody concerned with administrative

---

[1] Preston P. LeBreton and Dale A. Henning, *Planning Theory* (Englewood Cliffs, N.J.: Prentice-Hall, 1961), 9.

[2] Jan Tinbergen, "Social Aspects of Economic Planning," in *Social Progress through Social Planning*, Proceedings of XIIth International Conference of Social Work, 1964 (New York, 1965), 61.

[3] Herbert Simon, "Decision Making and Planning," in Harvey S. Perloff, Editor, *Planning and the Urban Community* (Pittsburgh: University of Pittsburgh Press, 1961), 191.

structuring. Policy planning does not exist in the sense in which it is here conceptualized when policy formulation is completely a function of the political system.

As will be noted in later chapters, we certainly recognize the validity and creativity of the programming function in planning. There are many important contexts in which the "task" is assigned by legislative mandate or other sanctioning mechanism and does not require groundwork by the planner. Nonetheless, one should acknowledge the centrality of policy development as a planning opportunity. Indeed, it is a major theme of the present volume that the planner makes a most strategic impact at the policy development level. It is for this reason that we have stressed the validity of a diversity of planning centers and of the intertwining of planning with political and interest-group organization. For, that planning which is limited to programming and administrative structuring in the narrowest sense may truly become an entirely technical social engineering within a defined and basically unquestioned framework.

The semantic problem is less serious. There is a tendency in some countries to use the word "programming" where reference is to what we would call "planning" and vice versa. This is usually clear in context. Our own solution is to attempt specific definition and consistency. The *policy* will thus here be seen as the general guide to action, the cluster of overall decisions relevant to the achievement of the goal, the guiding principles, as the "standing plan." It is our view that, while many needed programming skills have been developed in the social realm by those concerned with public and social administration, there has been inadequate attention to "policy planning" or planning that focuses on policy development but goes on to programming as well.

Schematically (*see* Chart A), it is simple to describe policy development as though it were a direct linear descendant of definition of the planning task. Following formulation of the task, the planners, their advisory and policy committees, and the several publics involved consider the overall possibilities in the light of facts, values, resources, interest-group factors, sanctions, and the distribution of power. They formulate and reformulate policy possibilities until there is an outcome which represents a reasonably good "fit" in the light of all these considerations.

Depending on the specific planning situation, this may be an elaborate or relatively simple process. Generally, the major empirical exploration (relevant data, trends, manpower, resources, sanctions) takes place prior to overall task formulation. However, if the task is given when the planning begins, or if its definition is not preceded by empirical work, a considerable empirical phase may intervene between task definition and policy development; and all the phases of Chapter III become relevant. Sometimes the policy choices being debated cannot be resolved without considerable empirical exploration.

Similarly, there are many times when the value and preference issue is not adequately probed before the task formulation and must therefore have major attention in the context of policy development along the lines of the discussion in Chapter IV. In fact, it is consideration of policy options which may highlight preference issues.

While neither of the two stages, task formulation and policy development, can be completely free of both empirical exploration and value analysis, there is some tendency for the study of relevant realities to be clustered in the period before task formulation, while the value explorations quite naturally often are highlighted in the context of policy development when the social significance of choices becomes somewhat more apparent.

The "spiral" or "intersecting circle" nature of the planning process is thus reiterated. In effect, the policy formulation experience frequently results in return to and some modification of the definition of the planning task. Or, more accurately, the two phases are intermingled, even though the planner finds it useful at some point to settle the task definition quite formally as part of the rational foundation on which policy planning may be based.

## DIMENSIONS FOR POLICY FORMULATION

The promise here is that policy formulation is ultimately an intellectual undertaking and can be a creative one. Realities are weighed, sanctions assessed, values considered—and the planner attempts to mould a strategy for achieving what is sought. The planner cannot be a mere calculating machine since he never enters the situation with all options identified or fully defined. Out of the interaction of planner, advisory groups, and policy-makers with the situation's "givens"—and out of the appraisal of knowledge and available experience—new solutions and proposals may occasionally evolve. Planning is not simply programming: it is also a potential vehicle for social invention and social change. However, a planning process does not always lead to a program or to laws embodying new provision. The outcome of the process may also be a policy calling only for restrictive laws and regulations.[4]

While the intellectual process cannot be neatly dissected, the following categories of issues have proven to be of some help in focusing the analysis

---

[4] United Nations, "Report of European Seminar on Problems and Methods of Social Planning, 1964" (Geneva: 1965, mimeographed, SOA/ESWP/1964/3).

in a variety of social planning situations. They are here briefly introduced and then elaborated in this and subsequent chapters:

*Definition of the system to be addressed.*    This decision is tied closely to the task definition. On what level does one mean to intervene: national, state, local; individual, family, peer group, community; income maintenance or social service? At stake is the question of how one identifies and defines the segment of the social system for which planning is to be undertaken and policy developed. If one does not select a viable system, one is unrealistic, at the one extreme—or ineffectual, at the other. The systems perspective alerts the planner to the sociologist's conception of latent and manifest functions and broadens the awareness of forces at work, of points for intervention, and of unanticipated consequences of new programs.

*Conceptualization of functions.*    Here one moves from "function" in the social science sense to the problem of identifying the most relevant components of the system for which planning has been undertaken. The emphasis on functions is the vehicle for rising above agency prerogatives or current legislative mandates and seeking an overall grasp of the process in a fashion strategic for considering basic policy.

*Boundary decisions.*    What should be considered as the major sub-units of social welfare; what is best "packaged" with what else for purposes of social planning and social welfare programming? The boundary question intersects the system concern, but the shift here is toward what one would seek to propose by way of strategic ordering. If, for example, one concentrates on income transfers, social utilities, and case services, the planning soon confronts major boundary decisions.

*The level of the proposed interventions.*    This issue has already been introduced in discussion of task definition; it becomes a major aspect of policy development. Specifically, can or should the problem at hand be addressed through: institutional change; a social planning contribution to economic or physical planning, or to other sectors not generally considered to be "social"; income transfers; social utilities (generally available social facilities); case services? Is this an occasion for a project or for a comprehensive effort? Each of the intervention levels implies a variety of sub-issues of major concern to the social planner at the policy development phase.

*Parameters for programming.*    This is a major, yet a catch-all, category, which includes a series of general policy guidelines relevant to programming specifics. It deals with many issues at the heart of traditional social policy analysis, dimensions immediately translatable into administrative practices. Such questions are relevant as eligibility requirements, the form of benefits, techniques of financing, public-voluntary balance, sectarian or nonsectarian services, distribution of responsibility among levels of government, amount of redistribution sought. As the science of policy analysis develops further, the items in this catch-all may be expected eventually to yield larger general categories or dimensions.

*The price to be paid.* A programmer may calculate opportunity costs in the economic sense or social opportunity costs without being clear as to what price can be paid. Social welfare programs are not validated by market criteria. Therefore, policy makers need to estimate the importance of the new policies and programs in the competition for scarce resources—and the priority to be accorded them. Policy includes some perspectives on the scale of resources and other elements of cost to be assigned to the area in question.

The first three categories of issues are explored in the remainder of the present chapter. Chapter VI is concerned with possible levels of intervention, and Chapter VII with additional dimensions of policy formulation and major policy-relevant programming parameters, as well as with the cost question.

One of the difficulties in proposing a fully satisfactory classification of policy-relevant, analytic dimensions derives from the fact that one may be involved (on national, state, or local levels) in: a social planning contribution in economic, physical, or other realms not in the usual or exclusive domain of the social planner; planning for income-transfer payments in programs generally defined as within social welfare; planning for a large or small direct-service sector within social welfare or for the entire social welfare system. These categories of planning obviously must engender somewhat different issues. The most usual arena for the social planner is the third, planning in or for the social welfare system or some of its components on one of several governmental, geographic, or functional levels—in the public and voluntary sectors alone or in combination. Inevitably what follows is reflective of this experience and of the tentative nature of the social planner's claims in the other fields.

## FOCUS ON THE SYSTEM AND FUNCTIONS

Planning should conceive of its object, whether a local community or a national network of services, as a comprehensive system. About this there is general agreement. However, it is far more difficult to arrive at a degree of clarification, much less consensus, as to the process for identification of the appropriate system to be addressed in a given enterprise or as to the most relevant system elements.

The difficulty begins with somewhat divergent but nonetheless interrelated conceptions of social system and of the meaning of a system approach to planning. Sociologists such as Harry Bredemeier and Richard Stephenson describe social systems as involving "interrelated statuses" and as fulfilling certain "functional requirements" of human society.[5] The notion of system in this sense is useful in emphasizing that group life on various levels has certain requirements and that social organization has a meaningful, rather than random, relationship to such requirements. However, comparative studies also document the existence of "structural alternatives": there may be a variety of ways of fulfilling the function. All solutions are not successful; i.e., they do not all contribute to integration or adaptation of a social system to its task. Some may impede adaptation and are seen as dysfunctional. Furthermore, some of the consequences of a structure for a given system may be apparent or understood by participants or those exposed, but other of the consequences are not recognized. (In either instance, the outcome may or may not be desired.) The unintended and the unrecognized consequences are referred to as latent, in contrast to the intended or recognized, the manifest.[6]

This is a functional approach to social analysis; Robert Spencer defines this approach as follows:

> [to] assay the place of a particular element of culture or social institutions in relation to other elements. The question may then be posed as to whether an institution leads to or assists in the perpetuation of the social entity in which it appears.[7]

Because functions are "system relevant effects of structures," the functionalist becomes preoccupied both with the issue of what is "system relevant" and with the conceptualization of structures[8]—problems which the planner immediately recognizes as meaningful despite differences in vocabulary. Elaborating on functional prerequisites, Talcott Parsons has said that any social system must concern itself with: pattern maintenance and tension management; goal attainment; adaptation and integration.[9] Others

---

[5] As used here, a *status* is a set of cultural specifications for action in given context.

[6] Harry C. Bredemeier and Richard M. Stephenson, *The Analysis of Social Systems* (New York: Holt, Rinehart & Winston, 1962), Chap. II.

[7] A useful overview is presented in Don Martindale, Editor, *Functionalism in the Social Sciences* (Philadelphia: The American Academy of Political and Social Science, Monograph 5, 1965); the quotation is from Robert F. Spencer, "The Nature and Value of Functionalism in Anthropology," *ibid.*, 1.

[8] Robert T. Holt, "A Proposed Structural-Functional Framework for Political Science," *ibid.*, 87.

[9] *Ibid.*, 92.

have developed these in terms which come close to the planner's levels of discourse.

On a somewhat more abstract level of analysis, another sociologist, Charles P. Loomis, puts it this way:

> Society is constituted of reciprocal activity which is structured into a variable number of systems, some of them quite distinct, highly structured and persistent; others are not so directly visible, are more amorphous, and more transient. . . . one sees different systems according to the perspective taken. Whatever system one is viewing, whether it be the "master system" society or any of its component subsystems (community, family, etc.) *the elements that constitute it as a special system and the processes that articulate it remain the same.* . . . certain persistent elements and processes appear at all levels of orderly interaction.

He considers the following as key social system elements: belief-knowledge; sentiment; end, goal, or objective; norm; status-role or position; rank; power; sanction; facility. Elements are meshed, stabilized, and altered in interaction within and among systems. While Loomis' terminology for such processes is idiosyncratic, several terms will be universally recognized. Their relationships to certain of the policy dimensions and programming parameters and to administration will become apparent. First, there are what he calls the comprehensive or master processes, categories which resemble several of Parsons': communication, boundary maintenance, systemic linkage, institutionalization, socialization, and social control. Then there are the so-called elemental processes:

1. Cognitive mapping and validation (knowing)
2. Tension management and communication of sentiment (feeling)
3. Goal attainment activity (achieving)
4. Evaluation (standardizing)
5. Status-role performance (dividing the functions)
6. Evaluation of actors and allocation of status-roles (ranking)
7. Decision-making and initiation of action (controlling)
8. Application of sanctions (sanctioning)
9. Utilization of facilities (facilitating).[10]

We need not for the moment consider the variations on these definitions among sociologists of the same school or the differences between functionalists and non- or near-functionalists. Thus far, sociologists have worked with the systems approach without being able to move from specification of the functions, which a large social system apparently must satisfy, to identifica-

---

[10] Charles P. Loomis, *Social Systems* (Princeton, N.J.: D. Van Nostrand Co., 1960); quotation above is from page 5, and the listing from page 8. See "Essay 1."

tion of system components for a total society, which have known interrelationships. For this reason, one cannot, as indicated in Chapter II, talk of planning the social system in the sense that economists plan an economic system.

However, recognizing both the status of these theories and the conceptual unreality of separating a large social system from the economic and the physical, one does work in fields (income security, medicine, education, housing, etc.) which may be viewed as smaller social systems with discoverable functions and identifiable components. To touch one part is often to set the whole in motion. For the planner it is significant that, whatever the objective and object of the planning, one is entering into a *system* (the way in which processes are developed) and rationally contemplating acts designed to change it. Seen in this less ambitious (but by no means simple) perspective, the work of Parsons, Loomis, and others is quite suggestive. Successful policy development would seem to require:

- ☐ careful delineation of the system in focus
- ☐ attention to the manifest and latent functions of the system as currently constituted[11]
- ☐ attention to functional and dysfunctional aspects of the system as currently constituted
- ☐ alertness to structural alternatives as currently manifested elsewhere or as proposed
- ☐ consideration of those specific characteristics of the system that may facilitate or impede intervention.

In short, one attempts for the smaller system what cannot be conceptualized for a total society. Here the social planner needs the insights of and consultation with sociologist, anthropologist, social psychologist, and political scientist as he considers options for change, the leverage for change, and change strategy.[12] The policy analysis is not merely a matter of considering what *is* and what is *valued*, prior to rational mapping out of steps. One needs to seek as complete understanding as possible of what is, of the direction likely to be followed if there is no intervention, and of how alternative policy choices may affect not only the system component which is the intended

---

[11] Merton comments: "To seek social change without due recognition of the manifest and latent functions performed by the social organization undergoing change, is to indulge in social ritual rather than social engineering." Robert K. Merton, *Social Theory and Social Structure* (Glencoe, Ill.: The Free Press, 1957 revision), 82.

[12] For example: Ward Hunt Goodenough, *Cooperation in Change* (New York: Russell Sage Foundation, 1963); Roland L. Warren, *The Community in America* (Chicago: Rand McNally & Company, 1963).

object, but other elements in this and other systems as well. This is why, for some planning purposes in realms in which there is limited codified understanding, there is little choice but to study a small social system completely as a "case." The basic social researcher thus becomes a member of the planning coalition.[13]

All of this while seemingly abstract and remote is a very real and practical matter, as will become increasingly clear in the illustrative chapters of the companion volume. To suggest what may be at stake, we note the following diverse examples here.

A negative income tax proposal for a guaranteed income to any individual or family unit could actually facilitate or encourage husband-wife separation or adolescent independence from family. These may or may not be desirable consequences or prices worth paying for a general social good; but they may not come into focus in the policy debate, so as to allow such choices to be made deliberately, unless one considers the entire family unit as an income-receiving and disposing system and as having a complexity of motives with which it responds to a new income transfer measure.

A new mental hospital policy of transferring patients as rapidly as possible from in-patient care to community aftercare reflects current thinking about service to the mentally ill. The mental health planner who sees the system as composed only of mental hospitals, clinics, and their patients may do more harm than good as he returns ill patients to homes without provision for protection of or service to their children and other members of their households.

A social service planner who helps develop a proposal to free public assistance caseworkers for more counseling of and social service to public welfare clients may find himself attacked by employee organizations and witness a period of great disorganization and decline in morale in the service. Staff, who filled their days with paperwork and financial investigations (while complaining that they had no time for casework), suddenly find themselves with time, but no preparation, for the long-discussed assignment. A system often depends for its stability on "busy" work, "paperwork," and "static," even though these are formally defined as interferences.

Despite long, formal commitment to "prevention," delinquency and truancy programs are found to achieve very little. Brief investigation discloses that one must redefine the systems for prevention purposes. Service

---

[13] For example, see: Herbert Gans, *The Urban Villagers* (New York: The Free Press, 1962); Harry M. Caudill, *Night Comes to the Cumberlands* (Boston: Little, Brown and Company, 1962).

networks related to delinquency or truancy do not deal with the dimensions of human experience essential to (primary) prevention.

The United States Congress, which voted the first Economic Opportunity Act in 1964, found itself strongly divided by 1966, when the unanticipated (to some people) consequences of the Community Action Programs under that Act created local political activity some members found distasteful. There was a similar reaction in some places to ramifications of the Act's provision for "maximum feasible participation" in program development and operation by residents of so-called target areas. Since this intervention, while devised for the anti-poverty legislation, inevitably affected the entire local service system, it created general pressure for democratization of boards of public and voluntary social agencies and for participation of clients in policy development. The results were widespread, and the power struggles were often more significant on the local level than the anti-poverty program's direct operations.

Jobs for Negro teenagers in Harlem, an outcome of an anti-poverty program, added to the disruption of family life. Fathers had no money, but their sons did. The target system should have been the family, with priority given to getting money to the head of the family.[14]

A state-wide anti-poverty effort found that its multiplicity of goals could be translated into operational programs only if it launched several state-level centers to impinge on administrative machinery, which was state-wide, several regional units, and two somewhat different types of local entities. Anything less would have ignored the locus of systems to be affected and the distribution of prerogatives.

In calling for a systems approach to social planning, David Hunter urged:

In planning and carrying out specific programs agency representatives who wish not to waste their time will examine the problem with which they are dealing in all its aspects, noting all of the systemic elements impinging on it, and then attempt to mobilize and systematize as many of these elements as possible so as to accomplish the objective. . . . It is incumbent upon social welfarists to think more in terms of human development systems in contrast to disparate elements such as casework, settlement house, relief check, homemaker, employment office, legal aid bureau or what have you. . . .

. . . This means for example that when you are trying to meet a need for

---

[14] See Bayard Rustin testimony, Subcommittee on Employment, Manpower and Poverty, United States Senate, *Examination of the War on Poverty* (Washington, D.C.: Government Printing Office, 1967), Part 1, 239.

day care you exploit the situation and make it really *educational* for the children, *educational* for the junior high school girls who could be assigned as day care aides *by* the school as part of *their* education, *educational* for the mothers.

It means that you build the neighborhood school into a real community institution, used the day 'round and at night, too, by adults and children alike, housing such community services as legal aid, employment service, family service, and the like.

It means that school and private employers operate as a team to set up work opportunities for youngsters that really contribute to their education and education that really contributes to their ability to work.

The systems analysis approach lies at the heart of the community action program of the Economic Opportunity Act. . . .

. . . This is a clear call to take the comprehensive view—to start the local planning for the abolition of poverty from an analysis of the condition of man in the total community. *Then* move to the development of a strategy and battle plan. *Then* to the designation of which troops, that is to say, which agencies, or institutions, or segments of the community are to carry out the plans.[15]

These concepts have become increasingly formalized and routinized. The sociologist's systems theory becomes, to some planners, a *systems approach*, a diversely used label to pull together what have been variously called systems analysis, simulation, and operations research. These are "computer-using intellectual techniques" dependent upon a technology which permits simultaneous control of a large number of variables in an analysis and also simulation of developments, given specified assumptions (in a sense, a type of projection). Banfield has contrasted systems analysis with the traditional "requirements" approach so familiar to the urban community welfare and health council planner from World War I well into the nineteen-sixties.

With a requirements approach, one lays out a course of action expected to lead to the attainment of the ends sought and then presents an itemized list of the means (requirements) in the form of a budget request. This would be ideal were resources unlimited, but in actuality it is wasteful because it does not face the problem of deploying a fixed stock of resources to maximize attainment of ends.

Offered as an alternative is what Banfield would call an "economizing" (systems) approach. Its premise is that nothing is free. Gains in terms of some ends are losses in terms of others. The decision-maker, aware of the intertwinings, attempts to search out and measure gains and losses from

---

[15] David Hunter, "Seven Motive Ideas," *Public Welfare*, XXIII, No. 3 (July, 1965), 171–176.

possible actions and to identify the course with the greatest possible net gain. Computer technology makes it possible to seek an optimum "mix."

The Planning Programming Budgeting System (PPBS) will illustrate what is at stake.[16] Cost-benefit analyses are basic tools. The planner is called upon to achieve clear formulation of objectives and to translate them into performance terms as a point of departure. Costs and expected payoffs of different assumptions and approaches are then spelled out. Moreover, the search for the optimum "mix," with alertness to desirable and undesirable side-effects (unanticipated consequences, functional and dysfunctional), forces the analyst into a comprehensive analysis which is alert to interrelations within the system.[17]

Those who contend that systems analysis and operations research simply cannot be applied to public affairs point out that such planning methods assume several things which do not exist in the normal context of public affairs: a degree of goal consensus; a measure of social benefits; reliable prediction; a hierarchy of command; a degree of control over the interrelated system components.[18]

The criteria imposed by operations research and PPBS personnel are often more than sufficient to discourage social planners who would approach their analysis in systems terms. By way of seeking balance, it is useful to quote at some length Gross's realistic assessment:

> The term "system" often gives one the impression of referring necessarily to a tight set of relationships that are fully deterministic, predictable, or controllable. Actually, models in natural science are mainly probabilistic rather than deterministic. The models of the cybernetic engineers not only deal with probabilities, they also include "black boxes" to indicate areas of ignorance and presumption. Any realistic social system model must be still looser.
>
> A social system is rarely a taut system. A change at any one point does not necessarily mean a significant change at some other point. There is usually considerable slack in the system.
>
> A social system is only partially knowable. There are not merely "black boxes" but "black regions" with amorphous boundaries. There are always

---

[16] For details, see Chapter IX.

[17] Edward C. Banfield, "Three Concepts for Planners," in Edward C. Banfield, Editor, *Urban Government* (New York: The Free Press, 1969, rev. ed.), 612–613. Also, *Technology and the American Economy*, Volume 1, Report of the National Commission on Technology, Automation and Economic Progress (Washington, D.C.: Government Printing Office, 1966), 99–101.

[18] Melvin Webber, "The Role of Intelligence Systems in Urban-Systems Planning," *Journal of the American Institute of Planners*, XXXI, No. 4 (November, 1965), 291.

unforeseeable (not merely unforeseen) consequences for good and evil (and usually both together). Although myths of perfect knowledge, wisdom or infallibility may be cultivated by some governors, central omniscience . . . is impossible.

A social system is never fully controllable. The myths of central omnipotence always hide imperfections; internal disunity lurks behind the facade. Perfect coordination can be achieved by neither hierarchy, bargaining, nor any combination of the two. There are always uncontrollable aspects of the biological and physical environments in which social systems are imbedded. Tight control of some elements may usually be achieved only at the cost of diminished control over others.

In sum, social systems are so loose that one may well ask skeptically, "Is this a system?" Perhaps the best answer is, "An unsystematic one."[19]

In this spirit and taken flexibly, the systems orientation serves to widen the vision of the social planner, alert him to relevant dimensions, prepare him for the "unexpected," and force him deliberately to make strategic decisions about the range of what can and will be attempted. Whether he conceptualizes the system in structural or performance terms, new alternatives apparently are opened.[20] He seeks constantly to identify and evaluate all such possible alternatives and their consequences and to select those which are preferable in the light of valued ends. Employing social science insights, he continues to design operational models, which may predict the repercussions of alternative public or private actions in one subsystem or in a network of subsystems. He does not claim ability to control or to plan a total system, but seeks thus a sounder method in pursuit of goals.[21] As progress continues to be made with PPBS and its variations, computer technology will probably strengthen the process, but will never be able to take over in relation to policy matters.

## DEFINITION OF THE SYSTEM TO BE ADDRESSED

Acceptance of the idea of system-alertness or a systems approach in social planning does not solve the problem of defining the system to be considered in a given venture. In fact, the difficulty in such definition is often the prime obstacle to a systems approach. Although social science analysis has an important contribution to make, decisions about how to define the system are in the realm of policy.

The issue varies with the level of social planning.

[19] Bertram M. Gross, "The State of the Nation: Social Systems Accounting," in Raymond A. Bauer, Editor, *Social Indicators* (Cambridge, Mass.: The M.I.T. Press, 1966), 178–179.

[20] *Ibid.*, 179–185.

[21] Webber, *op. cit.*, especially 292 ff.

When one is talking of social aspects of general economic policy, what is, in effect, involved is the effort to achieve a definition of the system which goes beyond the economic. Here the social planner is often seen as an intruder, attempting to stretch the boundaries and to introduce the idea that, in any society, the ultimate criteria must be social—and that growth rates and other economic indexes are only intermediate criteria.

In planning activities of this kind, the intellectually complex challenge resides in selection of the aspect of social organization which should be in focus in considering the social dimensions of a general policy. Thus, one may look at the consequences of tax policy for the family,[22] the effects of tariff enactments on certain elements in the labor force, the consequences of government procurement policy on population mobility in certain areas of the country, etc. And one may consider potential ramifications in these and similar realms as they suggest implications for economic, physical, and political policy. Given the usual modes of thought in fields in which social considerations have not been in the forefront, concerns of this kind call for attention to what in the past have been unanticipated consequences, latent effects, informal organization, and so on.

As one turns to more conventional social planning arenas such as planning for a functional field on one of several levels, or the planning of service networks on a local level, the issue of system definition takes other forms. One knows that school planning is best seen in the larger context, to include community activity and the employment entry system. Medical planning should obviously include community mental health. Child welfare planning is unreal unless it devotes attention to income maintenance and to health services. These illustrations are in themselves narrowly conceived and could be multiplied.

In effect, in any sectorial or geographically-based social planning enterprise, one can eventually trace a chain of interlocking effects among any one concern and all other social sectors or programs. A complete analysis of any program would lead to the social subsystem addressed (family, community, etc.) and its several components. Full attention to the interplay between subsystem and programs would eventually also lead to that "master system," society.

Does this not suggest that any seriously intended systems approach is self-defeating, since no matter where one begins, one is led to the need for a comprehensive effort? Here, then, is one of the inherent tensions in any planning effort: the choice of a proper balance between the specific and the

---

[22] Harold M. Groves, *Federal Tax Treatment of the Family* (Washington, D.C.: The Brookings Institution, 1963).

comprehensive. Experience suggests no formulas. Those who are "too narrow" miss critical dimensions, and their work does not seem relevant. Those who are "completely global" miss critical things in specific sectors or programs and also seem irrelevant. No resolution seems to satisfy all parties. The planner can only seek an informed compromise, a pragmatic resolution, based on alertness to possibilities and to the implications of decisions which he makes. Systems-alertness makes the choice more conscious, visible, and perhaps rational.

Any national functional field will need periodically a comprehensive review which challenges its boundaries and fundamental conceptualizations. Occasionally, at somewhat longer intervals, one will need nationally, on a state level, and on a regional or city level, an even more comprehensive planning effort interrelating all major social policy components and social welfare programs. The former type of review is most useful if it can with confidence refer to the latter. Then, those planning a local service network or planning for a specific social problem may with increased confidence undertake the assignment knowing what system is being addressed.

At the same time, the planner on any level, including the most local and the most restrictive, needs freedom to consider whether what he learns about the problem addressed, the effectiveness of the earlier efforts, or the conceptualization of the intervention does not suggest some broadening of the system addressed and thus more fundamental innovation. In short, one advocates systems-alertness at all levels of planning at all times and a pragmatic resolution of the issues of what systems actually to address during a specific planning process in the light of

☐ whether there have been recent, authoritative comprehensive reviews
☐ sanction available in the planning process (is one in a position to plan more or less comprehensively?)
☐ whether it is the case that only attention to x system will permit successful implementation of the particular planning objective, whether or not this is what is usually done.

Although these guidelines may seem ad hoc and inefficient, they are consistent with the notion that it may be necessary to encourage a diversity of planning efforts and to win politically the right to plan as comprehensively as one is convinced one must in order to be effective. Competing plans may in fact differ in their choices of the system to be addressed.

## CONCEPTUALIZATION OF FUNCTIONS

In the earlier section of this chapter, the term "function" was employed in its social science sense to mean "system-relevant effects of structures."

Boguslaw suggests: "the jobs the system has to do."[23] Illustrations cited included pattern maintenance, goal attainment, tension management, adaptation, integration, control, sanctioning, division of labor, and so on. For the purposes of the remainder of this chapter, as we continue with the subject of policy development, it becomes useful to employ the term in the form most relevant to the planner. *Functions* in this sense are the manifest *groupings or types of activities* within a service system or social institution, as conceptualized with reference to goals of the particular system. "Subfunctions," while clumsy, would be more accurate. The reference is to the *components into which the system's "job" is divided so that it may be accomplished*. In effect, system-alertness does not pay off unless the system, in turn, is successfully conceptualized as consisting of functions, tasks, or types of activity to which the planner is oriented. He becomes preoccupied, first, with system-wide policy issues, then with strategic conceptualization of functions, and finally with policy and programming ("the men and pieces of equipment . . ."[24]) for each of the functions. An alertness to functions in a system often assists those involved in planning to rise above narrow agency perspectives and to introduce concerns going beyond organizational boundaries. Waste and gaps become apparent.[25]

There is very little precedent in this realm in most of the social fields. We shall suggest, subsequently, the usefulness of the notion of channeling for the planning of case services, as an elaboration on the concept of case finding. In general we shall illustrate how a somewhat expanded and sub-specified application of public health concepts may offer anchoring points for planning of case services. The next chapter offers a scheme for social service functions. City and regional planners have made some relevant and helpful beginnings in the specification of functions which assure a comprehensive perspective.[26]

---

[23] Robert Boguslaw, *The New Utopians* (Englewood Cliffs, N.J.: Prentice-Hall, 1965), 10.

[24] Boguslaw, *ibid.*

[25] Alfred J. Kahn, *Planning Community Services for Children in Trouble* (New York: Columbia University Press, 1963) offers an illustration of analysis of an urban service system by functions. Alfred J. Kahn *et al.*, *Neighborhood Information Centers: A Study and Some Proposals* (New York: Columbia University School of Social Work, 1966), is a study of the importance of several functions and options in the manner in which they may be discharged. Child welfare is examined as a network (system) with known functions in William Ryan and Laura Morris, *Child Welfare Problems and Potentials* (Boston: Massachusetts Committee for Children and Youth, 1967).

[26] Harvey Perloff, "Social Planning in Metropolis," in Leonard J. Duhl, Editor, *The Urban Condition* (New York: Basic Books, 1963), 331–347. And "New Directions in Social Planning," *Journal of the American Institute of Planners*, XXXI, No. 4 (November, 1965), 287–304; also Webber, *ibid.*, 289–296.

Yet, all of these must be seen as quite preliminary, reflecting attention only to specific fields. The relatively limited precedent for the specification of functions for the social welfare system or for its subcomponents is a reflection of limited planning experience. As planning increases, we may expect alternative models to be proposed and tested.

## BOUNDARIES: DEFINING THE SUBSYSTEMS

Given the varying conceptions of the range of social welfare and of its components, it follows that there is no generally accepted scheme for delimiting subsystems. Yet, at any given moment, legislation is written, organizations set up, and programs implemented which reinforce, breach, or relocate existing boundaries. Therefore, we examine the significance of the boundaries question and the search for criteria. Then, in the absence of any definitive resolution, a tentative, workable classification is offered.

Although we shall follow common usage and refer to *fields*, it may also be convenient to use the term *intervention system*. As employed in the present context, either term is meant to describe a segment of the social welfare structure. Some of the characteristics of a field or an intervention system will unfold in the course of the discussion.

### Background perspectives on boundaries

There is an interesting, and as yet unwritten, story of how current intervention systems developed. We sometimes forget that there was a time when practically none of them existed: child welfare, public assistance, mental health, family welfare, corrections. Then, voluntary and, finally, public concern took the form of an undifferentiated "charity" and "poor law." Out of this there gradually emerged the recognition that all those in need of help were not the same.

At first the major differentiations were on the moral level—"worthy" or "unworthy." As the efforts persisted to refine these moral definitions, more attention was paid to the circumstances which created the problems people faced. Distinctions were made between "acts of God" and "acts of defective moral will," the latter being a convenient summing-up of a variety of euphemisms. One could at first distinguish as victims of circumstances the widow and the orphan, the physically handicapped, the severely ill. Other categories were eventually recognized: severe mental disturbance, delinquency of a child, handicaps resulting from industrial accidents. Several generations of an increasingly complex industrial system and a series of economic catastrophes finally sufficed also to give recognition to those unemployed who were the victims of that system.

At each stage, moral evaluations persisted in the culture and in programs of aid. The assumption of moral defect or its equivalent often accompanied the attribution to an "act of God"—even though the trend was towards scientific understanding which—intellectually at least—eliminated "blame." The field of mental illness is an extreme example, but even in the realm of unemployment, workmen's compensation, or programs to aid the widowed or the handicapped one finds residues of attitudes involving blame and shame, long after available knowledge has made this irrational. Moreover, the attribution of moral failure became the justification for limited response. The "unhelpable" of one decade became the "unmotivated," the "un-reached," and "multi-problemed" of the next.

For present purposes, what is especially relevant is that out of this process there arose distinctions between and among interventions systems. At one time an all-purpose almshouse might have contained all those who needed public help or supervision except for the few deemed to merit "outdoor" aid and those "contracted out": the poor, the physically ill, the mentally ill, the criminal, the dependent child. As each group was re-evaluated in the light of recognition of socio-environmental realities, it was "differentiated out" of the poor-law mass and new programs or facilities were created. The program unit or facility specialty followed the new perception.

Thus, in the late-eighteenth century there were a few—and in the nine-teenth century, a good many—special orphan asylums for children of par-ticular backgrounds. After the first quarter of the nineteenth century, there were special schools and facilities for a variety of handicapped children and some for delinquents. During the eighteen-forties, the campaign was launched to provide state hospitals for the mentally ill. Indenture had been the desired form of child care under poor law from Elizabethan times and then almshouses were favored; but in the eighteen-fifties the modern foster boarding home concept began to emerge, and most of its components existed by the eighteen-eighties: board payment, social study, supervision, child–foster parent matching. General assistance was the residual poor law cate-gory after some specialized programs for favored groups emerged slowly in the late-nineteenth and twentieth centuries: the blind, the aged, the veteran, the widow, and eventually some of the disabled.

While indenture began as a program for children of parents who could not support them (and whom the public did not wish to support), the foster care of the late-nineteenth century was addressed increasingly to the children without parents. Mothers' aid, later Aid to Dependent Children, became the program for holding families together where the sole problem was an economic one created by the father's absence.

Additional detail about sheltered programs for the handicapped, educational and cultural as contrasted with assistance programs, and so forth, could be added to this sketch, but the point would seem to be made. It was not any modern scientific or professional conception of human needs, personality dynamics, or intervention strategy that created the complex differentiations which now exist between and among systems. The historical processes were embedded in the social philosophies of the times and the emerging evaluations of those who needed help. Inevitably, for the professional workers, these specific intervention systems became distinguishable "fields of practice," with their special emphases, interactions, and applications of professional knowledge.[27] The normal process of bureaucratization and specialization solidified the boundaries, distinctions, and special requirements.

There have been counterprocesses, however, particularly in the past several decades. On the one hand, the discovery of poverty as a product of industrialism—not of moral defect—and the understanding of social disorganization as the price of urbanism and social change have focused some attention on common social forces and possible broad social remedies: employment opportunities and retraining, neighborhood organization, public housing, city planning, public education. Neighborhoods, groups, and families became the unit of attention, not only "dependent" children, mentally ill individuals, or handicapped people. On the other hand, the considerable permeation of the insights of both dynamic psychiatry and behavioral science into education, corrections, social work, psychology, and health services has provided for the many independent intervention systems a common core of understanding of the individual in trouble and recognition of the basic unity of the socialization and helping process, whatever the symptoms, handicaps, and available points of leverage. Especially important has been the emphasis in psychiatry, psychology, and social work on the need to involve a total family in the diagnosis and service, no matter which member presents the original basis for contact. Equally emphatic has been the recent stress on intervention at the institutional level and on coordination of the multiplicity of efforts involved in dealing with the complex ramifications of human problems.

---

[27] Alfred J. Kahn, "Social Work Fields of Practice," *Encyclopedia of Social Work* (New York: National Association of Social Workers, 1965), 750–754; Harriet Bartlett, *Analysing Social Work Practice by Fields* (New York: National Association of Social Workers, 1961); Genevieve Carter, *Fields of Practice: Report of a Workshop* (New York: National Association of Social Workers, 1965).

For these reasons, the social planner may find it useful periodically to pause in his work to look at the ways in which boundaries among intervention systems are currently drawn. Are they basically sound? Are revisions necessary? What of relationships among systems? The data to be presented are fragmentary and the concepts only partially formed.

## Boundaries and discontinuities

Health has been characterized by Dr. Leona Baumgartner as a "many-splintered thing." How well this statement also describes much of social welfare today; a small library could be written about what would appear to be irrational splintering of services, uncovered gaps between intervention units, and the consequences of all this. Indeed, the literature on the subject is already extensive.[28] Several representative illustrations are presented to clarify and specify the problems being addressed. Splintering, discontinuity, and gaps raise questions about what are useful and what become dysfunctional boundaries.

Bradley Buell and his associates have developed comprehensive documentation of the degree to which human problems do not fall neatly into the discrete packages defined by the traditional intervention systems. Dependency is very often associated with health problems, community-disapproved disordered behavior with dependency, indigent disability with other needs.[29] A relatively small segment of a city's or county's population requires a considerable proportion of overall services in these categories.

These facts are neither surprising nor unexpected, but they do serve to dramatize the need either to reconsider boundaries or to provide for some assured relationships among intervention systems. We shall argue that both approaches are needed. Available studies and testimony reveal that the problem as yet is largely unsolved.

---

[28] Kahn, *Planning Community Services for Children in Trouble, op. cit.*; Women's Group on Public Welfare, *The Neglected Child and His Family* (London: Oxford University Press, 1948); Elaine Cumming, *Systems of Social Regulation* (New York: Atherton Press, 1968).

[29] Community Research Associates, *The Prevention and Control of Disordered Behavior in San Mateo County, California* (New York, 1954); Community Research Associates, *The Prevention and Control of Indigent Disability in Washington County, Maryland* (New York, 1954); Community Research Associates, *The Prevention of Dependency in Winona County, Minnesota* (New York, 1953); Bradley Buell, "Preventing and Controlling Disordered Behavior," reprinted from *Mental Hygiene*, XXXIX, No. 3 (July, 1955); Bradley Buell, Paul T. Beisser, and John M. Wedemeyer, "Reorganizing to Prevent and Control Disordered Behavior," reprinted from *Mental Hygiene*, XLII, No. 2 (April, 1958); C. Howe Eller, Gordon H. Hatcher, and Bradley Buell, "Health and

In its most difficult form, the splintering is a matter not only of discontinuities among related agencies dealing with the same person, but of actual
differences of service strategy. Thus it is reported that mental hospital
workers and child welfare workers are often at odds on the wisdom of return of a mental hospital patient to the home, on the use of a day program
as an alternative to hospitalization, and so on. Or—from another field—
there are often differences between probation officers or protective workers
and the staff of child guidance clinics on the approach to allegedly neglectful
or abusive parents.

On another level, child welfare staffs discover many cases which need
psychiatric consultation and perhaps treatment, but—according to an extensive study in one major metropolis—"no agency has greater difficulty in
trying to refer disturbed children to outside psychiatric resources."[30] Several studies by child guidance clinics have also shown that frequently the local
child guidance clinic renders practically no service in the situations involving
the greatest community concern: problem behavior about which schools and
juvenile courts feel that something must be done.[31]

The illustrations to this point have referred to distinct intervention systems, but problems, which may also be relevant to the planning of system
boundaries, arise among units within one overall system. Of major concern
in mental health planning,[32] is the basic discontinuity between the mental
hospital and the community psychiatric clinic. The Joint Commission on
Mental Illness and Health and others have stressed the need for a close
partnership between the two, with special reference to the aftercare role of
the clinic with the released mental patient. Although some states have made
progress in this direction, there are others in which clinics have refused to
accept the responsibility. There are states which, in fact, see their clinics in
an education-consultation-prevention role and give priority to treatment of
psychoneurotics and the relatively milder disturbances, systematically sepa-

Disability," reprinted from American Journal of Public Health, XLVIII, No. 11 (November, 1958).

[30] Wayne MacMillen, Mental Health Survey of Los Angeles County (Sacramento: Cali-
fornia State Department of Mental Hygiene, 1960), 380; M. J. Rockmore and Elias J.
Marsh, "Community Planning as a Support to Treatment," American Journal of
Psychiatry, CXVI (February, 1960), 723–728.

[31] Community Research Associates, A Study of Salisbury Health Center Child Guidance
Clinic (New York, 1962); Community Research Associates, A Study of the Division of
Community Services Clinic (New York, 1962).

[32] Joint Commission on Mental Illness and Health, Action for Mental Health (New
York: Basic Books, Inc., 1961).

rating the clinics by policy from the mental hospital system and differentiating their patients from those who need hospitalization.[33]

An exploration of the consequences for children of the decision to discharge mentally ill parents to the community, or to use day or night hospitals in lieu of full-time hospitalization, disclosed that wise decision-making and effective practice, considering both the interests of the adults and those of the children, are not possible without a finely coordinated system of practice. Such a system does not exist. There are experiments which are seeking to identify workable patterns.[34]

There has been considerable national attention in recent years to the separation between child welfare services and public assistance affecting families and children.[35] For a variety of historical reasons, federally supported child welfare services tended for a long time to have better qualified staff, more stable personnel situations, and higher standards than the assistance programs in most places. A considerable number of counties developed integrated programs. Yet the usual administrative arrangements have created a general separation of child welfare and the assistances, even though the children receiving Aid to Families with Dependent Children (AFDC) and general assistance far outnumber the child welfare cases and derive from backgrounds which create desperate need for qualified social services. These children are born out-of-wedlock or living with divorced, separated, deserted or widowed mothers; their fathers or mothers may be disturbed or handicapped; they tend to experience the most disorganized and deprived environments. Mental health services are available in such cases to only a limited degree.

Other boundary questions are raised by the separation which tends to exist between institutions for children and community services generally—a

---

[33] Herbert Dorkin, "Minnesota's Progressive Community Mental Health Services," *Mental Hygiene*, XLIV, No. 3 (July, 1960), 442–444; Department of Public Welfare, Medical Services Division, *Minnesota's Community Mental Health Services* (1960). For more details, re trends and issues, see Chapter VI in the companion volume.

[34] Citizens' Committee for Children of New York, "Young Children of Mentally Ill Parents" (New York: 1962, mimeographed); Child Welfare League of America, *Child Welfare as a Field of Service* (New York, 1961).

[35] Elizabeth Wickenden and Winifred Bell, *Public Welfare: Time for a Change* (New York: New York School of Social Work, 1961); *Report of the Ad Hoc Committee on Public Welfare to the Secretary of Health, Education, and Welfare* (1961); *Health and Social Security for the American People*, a report to President-elect Kennedy by the Task Force on Health and Social Security (1961, mimeographed); Alfred J. Kahn, "The Social Scene and the Planning of Services for Children," *Social Work*, 7, No. 2, (July, 1962), 3–14. The Congress mandated correction of this situation in 1967.

parallel to the hospital-clinic problem already described. A comprehensive national survey has reported:

> In many communities . . . institutions stand quite apart from the main stream of services. Most institutions are tradition-bound and find it difficult to take first-steps toward participation in broad community planning for children. Yet institutional services must be integrated with preventive, diagnostic, and treatment resources if they are to be of major value for troubled children in the community.[36]

In a large city, within the services of several sectarian welfare federations, one finds a "paper" network without clear rationale, structuring of roles, communication, or planning. By contrast and to suggest the difficulty in generalization, in other places independent sectarian networks show close and impressive integration and no undesirable fragmentation or artificial boundaries. Smallness and informality tend to characterize the latter situation.

To conclude this section, we may turn to an illustration from the field of public health. In a rural area of one western state, before new legislation in 1965, an ill child was not eligible for examination and service at a "well-child conference," and his family had to make a 60-mile trip for care—until a state official became concerned. Equivalent practices exist in much of the social service structure but are not so readily perceived, because of the degree to which even the incongruous, when long familiar, may cease to be outrageous. Traditional boundaries are so well established and accepted that none of us is able for long to depart from them in his thinking.

### Boundaries and peoples' needs

There would seem to be urgent need to rethink definitions of function, conceptualization of services, and the nature of the intervention units thus far created by a combination of history, public attitude, organizational bureaucratic dynamics, patterns of financing, and professional prerogatives. The problem goes beyond fragmentation and splintering, which are somewhat correctible through various modes of coordination and service integration. For one thing, in a bureaucratized world, the "customer" often thinks of his needs in categories suggested by the manner in which professionals structure their services.[37] And, presumably, one type of self-image is more desirable than another, under given circumstances.

---

[36] Reginald Robinson et al., Community Resources in Mental Health, Joint Commission on Mental Illness and Health, Monograph Series No. 5 (New York: Basic Books, 1960), 113–114.

[37] See Peter M. Blau and W. Richard Scott, Formal Organizations (San Francisco: Chandler Publishing Company, 1962).

Nor can one expect self-correction by agencies and fields. Organizations have a tendency towards self-protection, excessive expansion, and "imperialism," whether or not it is desirable in terms of the interests of the larger network or the consumers.

Some of the consequences are suggested by illustrations on a diversity of levels, referring to programs for people in trouble.

A foster child displays disturbed behavior in school or in the community. A child care agency refers the case to a child guidance clinic which rejects it because the clinic pattern of work requires the involvment of the child's mother. As the result, a group of experts recommends that "child welfare agencies provide therapy to children within the agency."[38] Would this, in fact, be sound general practice?

"Since the eligibility requirements [in public assistance] involve at least two problem areas—financial need *and* age, financial need *and* handicap, financial need *and* loss of parental support, they [clients] more often than not require other services along with provision of financial assistance."[39] Should the social services be integrated with the assistance? What of insurance beneficiaries? What interrelations contribute to effectiveness?

A very substantial part of the current juvenile court workload consists of the dependent-neglected child segment of court jurisdiction. It is far from clear what a sound and useful boundary is between child welfare and probation. In fact, child welfare staffs often carry probation responsibilities and vice versa.

Everywhere juvenile courts and family courts face the fact of the considerable portions of their caseloads which require clinical services: emergency help, diagnosis, treatment. Should sharp differentiations be made between probation services and court clinics or should clinical competence–consultation be built into probation? Is it desirable to have a clinical system serving courts, differentiated from that serving the community at large?

A state mental hygiene department provides hospital resources for psychotic children. A county sets up an excellent, sophisticated residential treatment center for the more disturbed, adjudicated delinquent girls. However, the county center must reject certain girls who are extremely disturbed. Because the state system will not take acting-out girls or character disorders who have not had a psychotic break, such girls must be sent home to see

---

[38] Jerome Jungreis *et al.*, "Foster Mothers in Child Guidance," *Child Welfare*, XLI, No. 4 (April, 1962), 147–152.

[39] Elizabeth Long, *Homemaker Service in Public Assistance*, Public Assistance Report No. 31 (Washington, D.C.: Government Printing Office, 1957); also see, Alfred J. Kahn, "Social Services in Relation to Income Security: Introductory Notes," *Social Service Review*, XXXIX, No. 4, (December, 1965) 381–389

what will occur next. This is an illustration of a discontinuity which creates a serious gap in provision. It also raises questions about the ways in which boundaries are best drawn: in the light of diagnostic technicalities (state hospital approach) or program realities (the treatment center).

Some family agencies are known to sustain in the community people who would be seen in psychiatric clinics if there were clinics available in their communities.[40] Which type of service *should* be provided?

There are, too, communities with both of these facilities in which agencies are quite unclear about the boundaries. Some family agencies resemble adult mental hygiene clinics. The confusion results, in part, from the existence of a psychotherapeutic "commons" shared by psychiatry, psychology, and social work and the resultant lack of any clear guide to efficient personnel deployment into programs.

The boundaries between detention and shelter are blurred in a state which developed court services while its family and child welfare programs lagged. Because of the prior development and more extensive professionalization of probation, probation officers are assigned to both programs and transfer children between them, even though shelter is meant only as temporary substitute child care during parental incapacity and detention is a court device to protect an allegedly delinquent child or the community from harm or from the commission of unlawful acts pending court decisions. The boundaries have been more closely guarded elsewhere. Should they be reasserted in this state?

There is some tendency for an agency to be biased toward offering the service for which it is set up. Thus we find a family problem taken into a children's agency which specializes in foster care may be more likely to result in placement than the selfsame case in a family agency. Although the history of family agency–child welfare mergers gives no cause for optimism, it is perhaps necessary to examine the question of boundaries between family and children's agencies.

In one large, eastern seaboard city, publicly and foundation-supported "reaching-out" casework demonstrations, projects, and innovations were carried out independently under the following auspices: family agencies, voluntary child welfare agencies, child guidance clinics, public delinquency services, and the schools. Apart from the questions this raises about deployment of "venture capital," the boundary issue looms large. What is professionally valid and strategic? What achieves results most efficiently?

---

[40] Dr. Milton Rosenbaum, Milbank Memorial Fund, *Programs for Community Mental Health* (New York, 1957), 104.

In a number of states, where public and voluntary agencies share responsibility for foster care and adoption services, there is a tendency for tradition, law, and agreements to converge in a pattern that leaves the "hard to place" to the public facilities, which tend to be least adequately staffed. Is it possible to draw boundaries in any more satisfactory fashion?

Robert F. Bales has noted that social systems tend to swing between two poles. Sometimes there is optimum adaptation to an *outer* situation at the cost of *internal* malintegration. At other times there is optimum internal integration at the cost of maladaptation to the outer system. Michael Olmstead points out that the problems between an agency and a system of services may be analyzed in these terms.[41] The evidence would seem to suggest a distinct tendency in social welfare to value internal integration at the price of relationships with the remainder of the system. However, internal needs of a profession, agency, or intervention system do not adequately take into account problems of boundaries and integration between units or intervention systems. The times would seem to demand some exertion of effort in the direction of the opposite emphasis. Waste, inefficiency, conflict, and the suffering of people dependent on services are everywhere apparent.

## The inevitability of difficulty

People and their problems simply do not divide up as do agency functions and professional specializations. Illness (and, we might add, mental health or effective social functioning):

> is a state of the total organism . . . when a human moves from a state of "health" into a state of "illness," the "illness" is likely to be manifested by a variety of syndromes appearing concurrently or consequently, their nature being dependent upon the various factors acting upon the organism at that time. [In fact,] all illnesses are more likely to occur in periods when the individual is having difficulty in adapting to the total configuration of his life.[42]

Thus, the need for help often means that there are any number of potential entry points into a situation. People can be fitted, consequently, into patterns of service involving variously established boundaries. But the initial fitting is no guarantee that the decision is strategic or that the various relevant components receive needed attention.

---

[41] Michael Olmstead, *The Small Group* (New York: Random House, 1959), quoting Bales, 127.

[42] Lawrence E. Hinkle, Jr., and Harold G. Wolf, "Health and the Social Environment: Experimental Investigations," in Alexander Leighton *et al.*, Editors, *Explorations in Social Psychiatry* (New York: Basic Books, 1957), 117.

A single case frequently requires, for successful intervention, a variety of services; the problem often calls for a successful community effort as much as it does a patient-therapist effort.[43] Where there is evidence that either the setting up of patient-therapist contacts or the marshalling of the community components is complicated constantly by a system of boundaries that, although traditional, does not permit the application of what is most needed, the matter merits concern.

Nor is it possible to devise solutions which remain adequate for all time or all places. A wise decision at one point may have undesirable results in the future. Each agency or service tends, after a while, to attract a characteristic clientele, to routinize its procedures, and then to become preoccupied with technique. Such a "ceiling of routinization" is conquered only by means of a succession of new goals for the agency.[44] The preoccupation with boundaries must apparently be a constant one for those in policy or coordination roles. It is a central issue for the social planner.

For the legislative or civic initiators of programs are usually responding to one specific problem or need and, in their dedication and enthusiasm, can hardly be expected under ordinary circumstances to trace all ramifications of the problem or of the new service. No one perceives the creation of boundaries problems in a program all at once, and they seldom appear in bald terms. There is, instead, the gradual emergence and fixing of a policy, a tradition, an administrative decision, or a professional stance, which is the intervening variable between boundaries and consequences.

For example, a family caseworker becomes preoccupied with relationship skills and consequently is less useful to many of the cases which come to the agency door, or which other agencies refer as needing concrete services or support over situational stress. A foster care agency, in turn, does not perceive of its foster parents as prospective adoptive parents; in fact, the rules may forbid the transition. A public welfare staff does not conceive of the possibility that some of its public assistance recipients are the kind of people who might provide sound foster homes for children.[45] A series of policies in community clinics and family agencies about what they will or will not do may lead to overhospitalization of many psychiatric patients.[46]

---

[43] Robinson et al., Community Resources . . . , 375; and Kahn, Planning Community Services. . . .

[44] Nelson N. Foote and Leonard S. Cottrell, Jr., Identity and Interpersonal Competence (Chicago: University of Chicago Press, 1955), 129–130.

[45] Patricia Garland, "Public Assistance Family: A Resource for Foster Care," Child Welfare, XL, No. 7 (September, 1961), 1–6.

[46] Paul H. Hoch, "The Changing Role of State Mental Hospitals," in Programs for Community Mental Health (New York: Milbank Memorial Fund, 1967), 132.

The countercurrents also exert their influences. Positive and constructive experiences contribute to more complete understanding of the phenomenon and of the road to improved planning. To turn once again to the illustrations of the above paragraph, we note that increased community concern with unmet need or unsolved social problems may provide the leverage needed by professional innovators from within or without. With the concept of "reaching out," family casework begins to add to its service repertoire and its concept of skill. Foster care agencies permit foster parents to become adoptive parents. There is experimentation in placing foster children with public welfare recipients. New forms of screening and emergency service decrease hospitalization of the mentally ill. Experience in integrated services may create agency policy flexibility.

Boards, executives, and practitioners in many places seem to respond to their accumulated experience and to community needs by stretching traditional boundaries. Increasingly there are executives and board members who solve the problem in one place by affirming that "an agency has a responsibility to offer multiple services to its constituents."[47] One such agency then develops appropriate long-term foster care for those for whom there will probably be no adoptive homes; it organizes a family-centered, rather than a child-centered casework service so as to seek for the long-term foster child some of the security of adoption; and it facilitates adoption by foster parents. A multiple-function child care agency offers counseling services in the home itself, following application for placement of a child. It also includes in its program: foster home placement, adoption service, unmarried mother service, group placement, residential treatment for the emotionally disturbed and aftercare. In a number of places, welfare leadership and qualified staff drop the distinction between child welfare and Aid to Families with Dependent Children, except for accounting-reimbursement purposes, and develop a pattern of staff deployment and service which reflects client needs and the potential for change. The blurring of the lines between family agencies and clinics may be seen in this positive sense as well—a refusal to allow traditional boundaries to block service which does not express itself in the form of traditional distinctions: organic complications, environmental pressures, need for reorganization of personality structure.

In other places, boundaries have been shifted to create unified family and child welfare agencies to assure family counseling if it will avoid breakups— just as there are child welfare agencies with their own clinics, recognizing that the circumstances which bring a child to child welfare channels often

---

[47] Jane Edwards, "The Hard-to-Place Child, *Child Welfare*, XL, No. 4, (April, 1961),

produce the need for clinical help, help too often unavailable to child welfare on referral. Some child guidance clinics do give highest priority to those forms of serious child behavior of greatest concern to schools and courts. French social security programs initiate and maintain a wide range of social services, with attention to continuity of care, accountability, and diversity.[48]

These are not comprehensive solutions to the boundaries problem and do not pretend to be. Nor will solutions be found in any yet-to-be-evolved magical programs which serve all purposes for all people at all times. Partial and piecemeal improvements are to be expected—if any. The exploration would seem only to provide several "handles" for examination of possible approaches. Some combinations of an urgent problem, professional ethics, citizen concern, practitioner inventiveness, and planner ingenuity obviously are pre-conditions of change.

### Elements in a boundaries decision

It is doubtful that one should address the boundaries problem unless there is enough service. No plans or agreements can be satisfactory, given excessive deficiencies. As long as clinics are in very short supply, family agencies cannot clarify their tasks. For lack of qualified public welfare services or decent AFDC budgets, an entire community network must continue to improvise. The nonexistence of a parole staff for the training schools may create major problems.

Similarly—or perhaps as part of the same point—across-the-board personnel shortages preclude much planning. Evaluation of personnel strengths and gaps would provide as legitimate a basis for launching an analysis of boundaries as would a theory of need or of how a service should be conducted.

There is concern at overuse of clinical resources in one community because of the poor levels of training of personnel in agencies serving masses of people where the incidence of mental illness is high: courts, public assistance, child welfare. If this problem is not immediately remediable by upgrading of staff in these agencies, it suggests the possibility of easing boundaries by moving clinical consultants into these services, thereby decreasing the flooding of clinics with inappropriate referrals.

It may be said that any intervention approach exists only in the people who implement it. Planning for boundaries must therefore reflect projections and realities in relation to *personnel*. Successful upgrading of personnel may wipe out boundary problems, since the staff members' range of perceptions and competencies may be increased.

---

[48] Schorr, *Social Security and Social Services in France.*

It also remains true that the degree of specialization must continue to be a function of the size of the population served. A middle-sized county would want to define protective services as a function of an integrated child welfare (or, better, family service) program. A large city probably requires several offices to which complaints of neglect or abuse may be brought and out of which emergency services might move.[49] The crucial consideration in determining whether such specialization is validly carried out is the frame in which the problem is seen and the way in which the case finding does or does not affect what ensues. If the existence of this specialized protective service intake leads to the creation of specialized shelter and service methods and cuts the families off from comprehensive evaluation and from the most appropriate of a full range of potential treatment resources, an undesirable boundary has been created. If, on the other hand, the boundary is set up to maximize case finding in the light of public perception of problems and the desirability of making it easy to get to services, it has validity. In general we would argue for conceptual clarity about intervention system boundaries, as well as for patterns of service delivery, which would be free to combine elements from several intervention systems.

Public definitions of why, how, and when people need help are affected by profesional definitions and educational efforts. They are also reflections of some basic social forces. They must be taken into account in thinking of boundaries, as the protective services illustration indicates. Some have argued that public child welfare should not be integrated with public assistance because of the warm public regard and support for the former and the negative image of the latter. It will take careful fact-finding and wise leadership to determine what public definitions actually exist, how rigid they actually are—and when they must be determining. There may prove to be more adequate financial support for separate than for merged family and child welfare agencies, as some have claimed. It would be wise to probe and absorb the lessons inherent in the fact that, while many states could not use all their day-care funds in 1965 and 1966, they rushed to use available Head Start funds for preschoolers.

Despite the theoretical arguments to the effect that most services to delinquents overlap with public welfare and child welfare services, the public concern with delinquency may make it possible to establish and support special programs by retention of these boundaries. On the other hand, this ceases to be an advantage if it requires rigidity of service boundaries and channeling of a sort which closes off to delinquents necessary clinical

---

[49] Alfred J. Kahn, *Protecting New York City's Children* (New York: Citizens' Committee for Children, 1961); Laurin Hyde Associates, *Protective Services for Children of New York City* (New York, 1962).

and institutional treatment resources—or, in general, supports their isolation and self-definition as outcasts.

More basic issues of public definition and perception also enter. Is a person in need of relief like every other citizen—in which case he may share counseling services with everyone while his relief check comes from another office? Or is he perceived as a social failure who cannot be evaluated adequately for eligibility, will not use funds most constructively, or cannot be "reached" for rehabilitation unless the casework service is tied to the check? If this is the case, public assistance needs its own casework service.

Probing of these matters leads one to the community values and goals, which are the foundation of the perceptions and definitions—and which either set boundaries or determine the limits for such setting by those especially concerned. Is the community ready to encourage doctors who are preoccupied with health as much as with treatment? This has consequences for programs. If there is support for focus on family welfare, not on child therapy, one is less likely to permit family treatment to become a number of independent treatments serving members as though they were isolated individuals.[50] Community readiness to rehabilitate offenders has consequences quite different from a policy of isolation and exile. It would not seem possible, in short, to discuss boundary clarification outside a context of values.

The example of the out-patient mental hygiene clinic might serve to introduce several other elements. On the one hand, there are those who would stress its ties to the state hospital and to day or night community-based services, emergency services, and so on. It would carry a major aftercare role and would concentrate on the more serious mental illnesses. On the other hand, there is the clinic as part of the "prevention" network, closely allied to schools and health services, related to mental health education and consultation, early case finding and "preventive" intervention. In its treatment role, such a clinic does more with neurotics and relatively milder cases of mental illness than with the severely ill.

How are we to approach this type of conflict? What should shape the decision about the clinic and "boundary" ramifications? Some leads may be obtained in the implied premises of each of the positions. Part of the debate stems from differences in point of view about public perception of mental illness and what should be done about that perception.[51] There are

[50] Otto Pollak, *Integrating Sociological and Psychoanalytic Concepts*, (New York: Russel Sage Foundation, 1956), 33–34.

[51] Gerald Gurin *et al.*, *Americans View their Mental Health*, Joint Commission on Men-

those who hold that the public refuses to see the continuum between illness and health and perceives a qualitative difference between the mentally disturbed and others. Once a person is defined as mentally ill, this public would cast him out of the community and place him in an isolated state hospital, with little likelihood of return. It may also be, advocates of this position suggest, that the internal family dynamics which lead to the illness of one member may demand such isolation. Given this type of analysis, there is a tendency to define much of the treatment problem as one of rapid reintegration of patient into community and family. The out-patient clinic is an important instrument of such reintegration. If it is also the admission channel, it may obviate the need for hospitalization. Furthermore, if it is the selfsame clinic which deals with neurotics and behavior problems and which conducts educational efforts, the image of the mentally ill may be altered.

Those who question this description of the public image believe that there is public acceptance of the notion of a continuum. Most important in their view is the fact that the problems of working with the severely mentally ill on an aftercare basis or in relation to possible hospitalization are different from other out-patient psychiatric clinic tasks. They would therefore see the need for separate hospital out-patient psychiatric clinics or aftercare programs and community clinics. Sometimes they find support from holders of the first of the above positions on mental illness on the grounds that while hospital-clinic continuity and a stress on community return are the crucial things, the clinic task is complicated by too wide a range of clients-patients or tasks. They call particular attention to the fact that the clinic has quite different sanction (leverage) in relation to the client on the borders of hospitalization or in an aftercare status than it has in certain less severe situations.

A third group projects a concept of community mental health program which is broader than any clinic and which involves the general doctor, the clergy, nurses, teachers, court personnel, and social agencies. These personnel, in the words of the late Dr. Luther Woodward, contribute to the "many-sided job" involved in the "achievement and maintenance of mental health." A clinic oriented to this task looks to the community, not to the hospital, and needs its closest ties to community services. In other words,

---

tal Illness and Health, Monograph Series No. 4 (New York: Basic Books, 1960); also, Elaine Cumming and John Cumming, *Closed Ranks* (Cambridge, Mass.: Harvard University Press, 1957); Joint Commission on Mental Illness and Health, *Action for Mental Health.*

those who turn to clinics for school-court-police–health center consultation and who refer all manner of behavior problems to child guidance clinics see them as community counseling centers with medical ties to be drawn on as necessary. Others see the clinic, as several Community Research Associates' studies state, as the center of medically directed efforts to deal with child adjustment problems that require the skills of the multidisciplinary team. Here it is the conception of the intervention specific which makes the difference. Some would debate the assumption that medical direction makes a qualitative difference in the counseling. Others ask whether the team concept would not make sense in non-clinical settings.

Tinbergen introduces similar concern in arguing that one cannot organize governmental bodies around *targets*, since there is much interdependence in economic and social life. He proposes, instead, that governmental bodies be so organized that each handles a given *instrument of action* (our intervention specific), by which he means taxes, investments, health centers, or schools. Government planning, in his view, should lead to instructions to the various bodies as to the relative weights to be allocated to different targets.[52]

Alvin Schorr and others have looked at the boundary problems between child welfare and Aid to Families with Dependent Children in similar terms. The AFDC worker and the child welfare worker perceive of the family quite differently, and this has real consequences for the service. There is little systematic accumulation of comparative data, which would clarify whether or not there are in fact major similarities or differences with regard to a variety of contiguous systems.

We need not here seek policy conclusions about these specific matters. What is immediately relevant is that each of the positions implies knowledge about community, about clients, and about the consequences of specific forms of organization and service. Such matters can be formulated systematically, discussed, and evaluated in relation to values and goals and can be tested through research. Also inherent in many of the positions are value premises, capable of exploration, debate, and resolution.

Conceptual, rather than "power," resolution of boundary questions, then, would seem to demand that the following elements be brought into the picture:

☐ the public and the professional views of the social problem or disability being addressed (attitudes, values, and theory)

---

[52] Jan Tinbergen, in an unpublished, mimeographed paper, "Targets and Instruments of Economic and Social Policy" (1964).

☐ the self-perception of the person who has the problem or need and the perceptions of those immediately involved (family, peers, and friends)

☐ the decision as to what the service is to accomplish

☐ the way in which the given group of practitioners perceives the client or family (which may or may not coincide with broader public and professional perceptions)

☐ available sanctions or socially-defined leverage into a problem and the potential for changes of self-perceptions and community definitions

☐ the conceptualization of the intervention specific and its differentiation from other intervention specifics. To what degree does it demand specialization?

☐ the quantity of required service. To what extent could it sustain specialization?

In the vocabulary of the more generally used professional shorthand, these listings reduce themselves to a *need-diagnosis* concept (a definition of the phenomenon being treated), a definition of what is known about *how* to serve or treat (*intervention specific*, or instrument of action), and the *public-social context and sanctions* as these affect the decisions. Professional workers can make their direct contribution in relation to the definition of need and the specification of what they know how to do. In this they influence and help shape public-social perceptions and goals. They may also, as indicated, seek to influence the community directly.

To put it in somewhat different terms, the crossing of the boundary from one intervention system into another should involve entering a territory with a unique perspective on some aspect of a client's need or problem, and an identifiable armamentarium of intervention specifics in some way related to the perception of the potential client and to a cluster of available knowledge and skill. What is more, each of these territories should be different enough from the others so that it is possible to establish that desirable uniqueness would be dissipated or undesirable tensions set up by the razing of existing walls.

*Fields for planning within the social sector*

Are there any guidelines at all as to the boundaries of systems for social welfare planning? The assumption is of course that some planning must be carried out nationally, some on a regional or state basis, some in cities and counties, and some in the neighborhood. It is also here assumed that units dealing with larger populations (metropolitan areas) will tend to subdivide their concerns and activities into more subspecializations than will small cities and towns. It is taken for granted, too, that, within social welfare in a diversified society which values local preferences, decision-making will never be taken to a higher level if it is possible to leave it to the lower. Finally, as already stated, service delivery systems on the local level may join together, integrate, or at least offer entry into a number of fields.

The need for system boundaries remains. What we have offered is suggestive of an approach, not a workable method. There is no way to avoid a considerable period of inventorying of what we know, what we know how to do, and what we value—followed by research, as well as experiment, in concrete situations, with constant attention to the issues outlined above. Such process should eventually produce a conceptual model with strong empirical underpinning.

In the interim, we offer a tentative listing for use, based largely on a period of trial and error. The short descriptions call attention in each instance to an element or characteristic particularly relevant to the differentiation, from the writer's point of view. Later chapters will elaborate several.

In brief, one can make a case, in planning within the social sector (or within social welfare, in the United States sense of the term), for specific attention to the following fields or subsystems. Within each, all the issues about social utilities or case services, cash benefits or help in kind, universal or selective services, and so on remain relevant. On an operational level, one is much interested in complementarity among systems:

- □ *a medical system* (and a community psychiatry subsystem), characterized by the need for medical control, but defining medical interventions broadly
- □ *a correctional system*, characterized by the potential for deprivation of liberty
- □ *an income-maintenance system*, characterized by its use of a variety of transfer-payment devices to assure a socially-defined minimum for those variously qualified
- □ *a leisure time and recreation system*, characterized by its concern with pleasure and self-enhancement
- □ *a family and child* (or *"general"*) *social service system*, characterized by "perfective," preventive, and therapeutic efforts to support and enhance individual and familial role enactment and to guide family formation, reproduction, and child rearing
- □ *an educational system*, characterized by its socialization, culture transmission, and professional or job preparation responsibilities
- □ *a housing renewal, and relocation system*, characterized by introduction of nonmarket considerations into the provision of housing and development of community facilities and urban amenity
- □ *an employment system*, concerned with discovering and enhancing talent, offering job counseling, and facilitating placements
- □ *a rural welfare system*, consisting of facilities, instruments of action, and programs designed to revitalize the economic, cultural, social, and communal life in rural areas.

Some systems omitted from this list are found occasionally in the social planner's orbit. They are those systems that relate to the production and distribution of goods, maintenance by a society or community of internal and external order, maintenance of motivation and continuity with spiritual and religious heritage, and assurance through governmental and private effort of a supply of transportation, communication, and governmental services necessary for urban-industrial interdependent living. Also omitted is the general realm of culture and creativity, a field in which it is not yet possible to separate completely what is of the market place from what is of social welfare.

To recapitulate, an effort has been made to develop a very preliminary basis and to elaborate a classification system for the subdivision of social welfare into fields relevant to planning. Such fields are appropriate sub-units for the "packaging" of service. However, even these large and helpful subdivisions do not solve the problem of fragmentation and discontinuity. The individual's needs and problems never subdivide themselves neatly to coincide with institutional provision. If such needs and problems are treated as though they do, new community-created problems occur.

Therefore, no matter how adequate this classification system may be as a starting point for planning and as a guide to bureaucratic structuring, there will still remain the task of so organizing as to assure the person in need of help and services of:

☐ easy access to the relevant subsystem
☐ integration of service components required simultaneously
☐ continuity of components over time.

In short, as we shall suggest, there is need to convert the social welfare system as confronted by the individual into a well-coordinated *network* and to "organize" it—to introduce the terminology of later chapters—for channeling, case integration, continuity, and accountability.

# VI

## POLICY: TYPES
## AND LEVELS
## OF INTERVENTION

AFTER specification of the object of the planning, the subsystem, one approaches the strategic question of the types and level(s) of intervention which may be considered.

The economic planner may seek only short-term control over the business cycle, on the downswing, or he may go beyond it. He may also attempt to preserve or to contain an upswing, without reversing it. He may attempt general demand management—or he may intervene in production. He may focus on strategic development projects, on guiding public investment, on broad fiscal and monetary strategies—or may undertake even more comprehensive planning.[1]

Social planners face similar possibilities as to levels of intervention. Planning may involve modest projects, more ambitious programs, or comprehensive change. It may take as its point of departure "formalistic designs" or ideal models; "heuristics" (generally-accepted principles); or available skills or organizational precedents; or it may avoid commitment to models, principles, or units and "proceed with a view of present reality as the only constant in its equation."[2] Planning may be "patchwork" or "incremental" —the choice of word depending on the evaluation—or it may represent a basic, new fresh start. Scope, depth, level, and type of planning are issues to be explored at the policy development phase in the light of the reality appraisal, the access to sanction, and the value exploration.

---

[1] Andrew Shonfield, *Modern Capitalism: The Changing Balance of Public and Private Power* (New York: Oxford University Press, 1965); Everett E. Hagen, Editor, *Planning Economic Development* (Homewood, Ill.: Richard D. Irwin, 1963).

[2] Robert Boguslow, *The New Utopians* (Englewood Cliffs, N.J.: Prentice-Hall, 1965), 21.

166

For many social sector planning undertakings, but not for all, it is useful to identify the following intervention types:

1. In brief, does the planning assume working *within* an existing system or existing systems or does it contemplate a major modification or breakup of systems? The latter is often referred to as an *institutional change* goal.

2. Does one operate within the traditional social welfare sectors at all, or do circumstances and goals require pioneering in the *introduction of social considerations* into realms generally seen as the province of economic planning, physical planning, or of other social institutions or fields?

3., 4., and 5. If, as is usually the situation, certain system boundaries, laws, or policies are "givens" and the task calls for concentration of the planning in what are generally conceded to be the social "sectors," is the concern to be with *income transfers* and with *nonmonetary social benefits* and services —or is the planning to focus on individual helping, guidance, and treatment (*case*) *services?*

These last three categories are not mutually exclusive. They often merge into one another or even combine with the first two. Social planning activity in relation to a given problem and field may emerge with some proposals in each area, as when mental health planning deals both with treatment and prevention. It is urgent, however, that the planner be deliberate about each of the possible intervention levels and that the "mix" of levels be a conscious one. Many planning pitfalls derive from unexamined perpetuation of given emphasis and mix. Much progress in some fields has derived from a re-examination of the question and a new start. As suggested earlier, this was the nature of the progress in the youth programs under the President's Committee on Delinquency and Youth Crime (*Chapter III*). It was an arena for major debate after the anti-poverty program was launched in 1964 (*Chapter II in the companion volume*).

In effect, our listing together of these five levels of intervention is somewhat misleading since an action under categories (2), (3), (4), and (5) may be seen by some as fundamental in the institutional change sense and may have unanticipated consequences which are far-reaching. Furthermore, whereas the social planner quite frequently discusses and considers possibilities in categories (3), (4), and (5) in quite systematic fashion, (1) and (2) are often unsanctioned or not even considered. There is little precedent for an approach to them. The accumulation of social planning experience is in the latter three categories.

In recognition of this distinction, we shall attempt in this chapter mere identification of the nature of the possibilities in (1) and (2), making the case for their consideration, while (3), (4), and (5) will be presented as somewhat more sharply defined options some of whose dimensions are known. It is obviously in the spirit of the present volume that (2), in particular, undergo growth and development and that, where appropriate, planning seek basic effects in the sense of (1).

## INSTITUTIONAL CHANGE AND INTERVENTIONS BEYOND THE SOCIAL SECTOR

### Change

When the question of institutional change is raised in a planning context, the issue generally is whether what is being attempted is seen in some sense as fundamental. By contrast, much planning deals with projects, a reorganization within a sector, a new effort in a limited area, a new way of coordinating the work. Even where so-called master plans are projected, what often emerges in practice is that much more modest series of consequences which has been called "disjointed incrementalism."

The "institutional change–disjointed incrementalism" dichotomy and all the intervening stages in what is probably a continuum tend to be evaluative categories as much as objectively described possibilities. Few clear guidelines are available for the planner. Unlike utopians, revolutionaries, and charismatic political leaders, planners are not involved in attempts to plan basic social organization except early in the history of planning in some developing countries. It is doubtful that basic social organization can truly be planned. Fundamental institutional changes evolve gradually out of many forces and are only partially understood; or they may be the outcome of dramatic revolutionary shifts, carried out through either the legitimate political and social channels available or in an extralegal fashion. A planner may, of course, conclude that such changes are necessary, but he is not likely to be in a position to effect them formally.

In what sense, then, may planning be concerned deliberately with institutional change? Here we refer to the earlier discussion of alertness to the relevant system. In the planning context, institutional change refers to

- [ ] legislative or administrative enactments of policies, which are qualitatively so different and new as to have widespread ramifications
- [ ] organizational and administrative changes so fundamental as to have widespread repercussions and to represent, in effect, simultaneous policy changes
- [ ] a shift in the balance between the employment of income transfers, social utilities, and case services to cope with a social problem or to achieve an objective (since such shift involves both new policy and the launching of a chain of fundamental organizational and administrative consequences).

The institutional change category is a qualitative one, then. It refers to a planning outcome which shakes things up and does so to a degree recognized as probably starting a chain reaction and carrying many unanticipated consequences. It may manifest itself completely in the categories discussed subsequently: income transfers, social utilities, case services. It often involves policies with major ramifications for the structure of the family.

To illustrate, there had been many studies of the situation of American Negroes in the twentieth century, many proposals and plans and considerable activity in the fields of employment, education, and social services generally. However, the series of laws in the Civil Rights field related to voting rights and banning many types of discrimination and the related and resulting compensatory and preferential employment, as well as educational and housing policies, may be described as institutional change. An even better example is provided by those governmental statutes and policies and actions by the business community to support local economic and social programs controlled by local minority groups in their search for "power." Quite typically, the chain of events then subsequently launched may be better described as a social movement than as social planning.

The United States Model Cities Program offers another illustration. Funding is provided for comprehensive overhaul of cities or significant sections of cities only after submission of convincing plans dealing with renewal, relocation, public housing construction, public facilities, social services, and related issues. The basic objective here is a *qualitative* change in the nature of community life and in the life-chances of residents. It is this that we are describing as planned institutional change.

Planning for the modernization of underdeveloped countries perhaps provides our best illustration. Forces are deliberately set in motion which will change the modes of work, family and kinship structure, capacity for political participation, levels of aspiration, cultural life, and relations among tribal and ethnic groups within a country. The daily modes of living are destined for change: housing, clothing, food, transportation, sanitation. Population is redistributed within the country by providing work opportunities in various localities. Land-tenure changes start a major chain of events. Here, then, is planning which brings about institutional change; the United Nations' "development decade" program has asked that the planning focus on assuring that the development is balanced.

Though considerable planning in this category is manifested in the levels described below, much of it is reflected in proposals for legislation (civil rights, economic incentives to investment, giving women the vote, India's constitutional privileges for the "untouchables," etc.). Much of it is reflected in new administrative policies (salary levels in government enterprise, collective bargaining procedure, or preferential hiring). Some of it involves modest "project" planning with potential to serve as a change force (the creation of a new type of higher education institution in a developing country).

### Social planning outside traditional social sectors

The institutional change level is often "entered" through a second relatively-underdeveloped category of social planning activities.

The relationships of the levels may be illustrated by noting briefly and over-simply that an anti-poverty effort may: *emphasize aggregate demand* (fiscal, monetary, and related efforts to improve the performance of the economy) on the assumption that poor people will benefit in the general prosperity; *undertake redistribution programs* to give poor people additional income in one of a number of ways; *emphasize structural measures* to build up the capacities of the poor to earn additional income.[3] The cumulative result of all these measures would be institutional changes in the sense that dramatic shifts in political participation or in income distribution may result. Structural measures, whether as social utilities or case services (*see below*) are quite "normal" areas of social planning concern. A social planning contribution to fiscal and monetary policy, here urged as desirable, is not at all common.

The social planner, however, should be permitted to consider economic policy as an arena for intervention, just as a number of other fields traditionally outside his scope become legitimate as the society considers how its productivity may be translated into the good life. This entire realm may be introduced with a brief digression on the problems of improving the modern city as an illustration.

The modern city cannot fulfill its economic, political, cultural, or social functions unless it constitutes itself as a viable environment for human existence. Universal experience suggests the need to provide adequately for:

☐ distribution of food, materials, and services
☐ water supply and public utilities
☐ sewage disposal
☐ traffic management

---

[3] James Tobin, "The Case for an Income Guarantee," *The Public Interest*, I, No. 4 (Summer, 1966), 31–41; Margaret Gordon, Editor, *Poverty in America* (San Francisco: Chandler Publishing Company, 1965); Louis Ferman, Joyce L. Kornbluh, and Alan Haber, *Poverty in America* (Ann Arbor: University of Michigan Press, 1965), Chap. 7.

- ☐ public transportation
- ☐ clean air
- ☐ postal service and other types of communication
- ☐ protection of the population and the control of crime and delinquency
- ☐ recreational, cultural, and religious activity
- ☐ housing
- ☐ education and socialization
- ☐ so-called welfare services
- ☐ health services.

Eliminating the last four categories, which are generally recognized as relevant concerns of the social planner, we are saying in essence that there can be no city that does not offer certain protections against those hazards to health and public safety which are concomitants of population concentration. There can be no city that does not organize adequately to provide for water, gas, electricity, telephone service, or to transport people, goods, and mail with reasonable reliability, speed, and comfort. Under the heading of recreational, cultural, and religious activities are grouped a diversity of functions showing great variations from society to society—yet suggesting that urban man does not live by bread alone.

The purpose of this listing is to recall that, though all of these provisions are basic, they can be implemented more or less adequately, their costs distributed more or less equitably, and access to them be made more or less universal. Cities or their parts may be—and already have been—hell-holes or jewels of civilization.

It has become clear only in recent years that the choices among these alternatives are in significant degree political (using the term in its broadest sense) rather than wholly technical. It is only recently that men have fully appreciated that all of these are, in fact, arenas for choice and are not determined by forces beyond communal influence. Among the variables for decision are the specific service designs—involving many dimensions—as well as priorities for resource and manpower allocation. The relation between people's preferences and specific measures becomes important; and the ramifications of proposed solutions on individual, family, and group life come into focus. As this has become more apparent, the concept of social planning has expanded to include the notion of introducing "socio-economic and human behavior considerations in the making of decisions by all governmental and private agencies and groups in the community."[4]

---

[4] Robert Perlman, "Social Welfare Planning and Physical Planning," *Journal of the American Institute of Planners*, XXXII, No. 4 (July, 1966), 238; United Nations,

To put it simply and directly, the decision about how seriously and in what manner to cope with air or water pollution is only in part a scientific and technical matter; it is also a political matter and a value question. Is this not also true of public transportation or police services? And if these are areas of decision in which human priority, preference, response, and participation have significance, should not one consider how to provide a social planning process which addresses such matters?

This choice of illustrations in fields which have seldom been associated with social planning is meant to suggest the validity of departures and the urgency of the need. Such development will take place only if efforts are launched in the next several years to educate social workers, social scientists, or other social welfare personnel who are technically competent to join with engineers, economists, transportation experts, and physical planners so as to add to the planning process a human dimension, a preoccupation with what the choices to be made will mean for individual development, family life, neighborhood, and community. Furthermore, sufficiently high priority will have to be given to the education of personnel qualified to inspire and facilitate the widespread urban community development activity through which citizens will express their preferences in these matters and utilize democratic political machinery to implement their choices.

All of this would seem to follow if there is commitment to significant efforts to humanize the urban environment, making it supportive of man's potentialities, where it so often has appeared reflective only of greed and powerlessness.

One might similarly demonstrate the relevance of social planning to tax and tariff policy—already acknowledged in a significant number of countries. As societies ponder their increased affluence, the expansion of social planning may also convert such fields as urban transportation from the domain of engineering into a coalitional activity of several professions. The process is already visible in the Department of Housing and Urban Development and the Department of Transportation, the two new federal departments developed by the Johnson Administration to help realize the Great Society.

## MORE TRADITIONAL SOCIAL WELFARE OPTIONS

In contrast to the above categories, we now turn to intervention options which are somewhat more familiar to social planners and which are better

"European Seminar on the Problems and Methods of Social Planning" (Geneva: 1965, mimeographed, SOA/ESWP/1964/3); *Social Progress Through Social Planning—The Role of Social Work,* Proceedings of the XIIth International Conference of Social Work (New York: International Conference of Social Work, 1963), 259–265.

conceptualized—although it will be clear that these are by no means completely refined or sufficiently comprehensive intellectual tools. To repeat, at times these may be seen as mutually exclusive categories of intervention. At other times they may be components of a carefully conceived "mix."[5]

## Intervention through income transfers

Money is the key to the market economy, and one possible planning outcome is the development of legislation which will assure certain categories of people enough money to participate fully in the market.

For much of modern history this has been considered a completely inappropriate policy—at least from the end of mercantilism (which did in some ways protect the rights and capacities of different economic statuses) until the beginnings of modern social security. The income transfers available under the assistance provision of "poor law" in its many manifestations were intended to do little more than keep body and soul together, while the recipient was rehabilitated or motivated to return to the employment arena. For the unemployable categories, the intent was to offer a very modest subsistence base, but not enough to discourage all-out effort by all those in the labor market to provide more adequately for their own old age or for any other dependent status which they might suffer in the future or leave their families to face.

In recent decades, income transfers have become a fundamental element of social policy. A planner now is in a position to consider very seriously the possibilities inherent in such transfers as vehicles to achieve social objectives. There is little dispute about the use of transfers except in societies which still live under extended kinship systems and only partially in wage economies, or in which the stage of industrialization supports a deterrent approach to labor-force members in difficulty. A number of scholars have documented the scope of such transfers as well as their contributions and limitations as devices for "redistributive justice."[6]

There are many significant and difficult issues faced by a modern society

---

[5] Health and social work personnel will note that, although we do not consider public health categories helpful in this context, we do employ them in relation to some aspects of programming. For example, see Chapters III and VII in the companion volume.

[6] Robert Lampman, "How Much Does the American System of Transfers Benefit the Poor?" in Leonard H. Goodman, Editor, *Economic Progress and Social Welfare* (New York: Columbia University Press, 1966), 125–157; Richard M. Titmuss, "The Role of Redistribution in Social Policy," *Social Security Bulletin*, 23, No. 6 (June, 1965), 1–7; S. M. Miller and Martin Rein, "Economic Equality," reprinted from *I.U.D. Agenda* (Washington, D.C.: Industrial Union Department, AFL-CIO, 1965). More detailed reference listings for this topic appear in the next chapter, on pages 193, 195, 197, 198.

as it seeks to develop overall policy for social insurance or other income transfers.[7] For the present it may suffice to note that the planner considering a response through income transfers faces a repertoire which includes:

- ☐ minimum wage or a wage tied to family obligations
- ☐ family or children's allowances
- ☐ social insurance in a variety of categories
- ☐ non-contributory pensions
- ☐ public assistance
- ☐ tax allowances and deductions
- ☐ training allowances
- ☐ negative income tax
- ☐ farm and industrial subsidies.

The level of grant may or may not be intended to assure a specific level of living (to meet a "needs" test) and may or may not be conditioned by assets (a "means" test). It may or may not impose conditions on the recipient. It may be available as a justiciable right or through administrative discretion. Future recipients may contribute to their ultimate benefits through any number of devices, or funding may be completely the responsibility of employers, unions, or the general treasury—out of tax funds. Programs may be public, private, or a combination of public and private.

Long experience with the complexities of achieving adequate organization of social services and dissatisfaction with a variety of types of administrative discretion and bureaucratic red tape, which make social services very costly, have created in mid-twentieth century a strong public shift toward income transfers as a major device to achieve socially desired ends. In effect, some of the inhibitions described above have been wiped out by fuller recognition of social realities. The society does not need to keep in the labor force its aged, its handicapped, its young children, its mothers who would like to care for their children. Actually, modern technology and high productivity levels, combined with demands for considerable education, make it socially useful to prolong dependency for education and socialization as well as for periodic retraining—and to permit the young, the old, the ill to stay out of the labor force. Furthermore, economic theory has increasingly highlighted the value of supporting the purchasing power of those not in the labor force as a contribution to aggregate demand.

Ours is a society reared on laissez faire, committed to diversity, and aware of the ties between capacity to make one's own choices as a consumer in a free market and basic democratic protections. Therefore, once increased appreciation of current industrial and economic realities helped modern coun-

---

[7] See the companion volume, Chapter IV.

tries overcome earlier inhibitions about income transfers, such transfers achieved high priority policy status.

The new ease with and enthusiasm about income transfers as policy in the United States developed only gradually during the nineteen-sixties. The Economic Opportunity Act of 1964 did not follow the "obvious" strategy of giving the poor money to make up their income deficits. The anti-poverty effort and Negro rights revolution had reached the point of serious discussion of income guarantees by 1966. The strongest support was for an income guarantee as a back-up element in a total social policy which included guaranteed work for the able-bodied and income for those not available or suitable for the labor market.

The shift toward money was real, but ambivalent. Social security cost-of-living increases in 1965 and 1967 lagged behind the actual rise in cost of living. Much public discussion centered on the negative income tax and similar income guarantees during the same period, but it was clear that the majority of the population was not willing to consider a complete separation of income rights from labor force status, or to ignore one's contributions to one's "insurance." "Guaranteed work" attracted some support as a possible policy. Demogrants, especially children's allowances, were also added to the agenda, as the debate about income strategy entered 1969.

All of this has taken place at a time of general rediscovery of the market both in Western-type economic systems and in the communist economies of Eastern Europe. Even the proponents of strong centralized planning have come to appreciate the allocative efficiency of the market mechanism.[8] It provides a direct pathway to preferences and gives the consumer leverage to deal with suppliers of service.

As this has increasingly been understood and the market recommended to the social planner, not as a case against planning but, rather, as one type of programming mechanism to be chosen within planning patterns, there has been more rational effort to confront proposals (such as those made by Milton Friedman and endorsed by James N. Morgan and people at various points in the political spectrum) that certain traditional social services be returned to the market.[9] Thus, it is variously suggested that one supply people with funds (or vouchers) and permit them to buy education via tuition, rather than continuing expansion of a public education system, that the health

---

[8] Charles E. Lindblom, "The Rediscovery of the Market," *The Public Interest*, I, No. 4 (Summer, 1966), 89–101. Albert Waterston, *Development Planning* (Baltimore, Maryland: The Johns Hopkins Press, 1965), 46–61.

[9] Milton Friedman, *Capitalism and Freedom* (Chicago: University of Chicago Press, 1962).

insurance schemes provide the patient with money (or vouchers) with which to buy services in the free market, that one subsidize the disadvantaged tenant and not build public housing. In all instances, the proponents argue that public services directly rendered are inferior, wasteful, coercive, and otherwise undesirable, in various degrees, or that market mechanisms are needed to coordinate supply and demand, to attract new "producers" of services, and to improve quality through competition.

John Kenneth Galbraith argued in *The Affluent Society* that our major ills derived from the overdominance of a market system which, by artificially manipulating preferences through advertising and related practices, dramatized the inadequacy of complete resort to a market system in which the individual consumer must find his way.[10] When critical social values and communal goals are at stake, he would increase the investment in public goods, or what we call social utilities. Thus the issue is posed of how and when one departs from market instrumentalities and chooses social provision in other forms, whether as facilities available to all or as services to the individual. The next section will suggest possible criteria to assist the planner, but it is most important to note that this is one realm in which preferences are critical: what do people want; how will they behave?

Given the experience to date and the economists' difficulty with a "social welfare function," an American social planner would do well to begin with a bias toward assuring people income adequate to permit them to manage on their own in the market. One would depart from such an approach if the planning process revealed relevant and convincing things about (*a*) the nature of the service ("indivisible" goods such as public safety cannot be sold in a market); (*b*) the character of the communal stake in the availability of the service; (*c*) the capacity of the subsidized consumer actually to do well in an open market.[11]

### Social utilities or case services

Once the decision has been made that the social goal at stake in the planning, or the social task to be implemented through the planning, will not be satisfied by positive or negative legislation, by new administrative policies alone, or through income transfers alone, the planning process turns to consideration of provision of social services. Here there are two major options, social utilities and case services. Each ideally carries a philosophy of rights

[10] John Kenneth Galbraith, *The Affluent Society* (Boston: Houghton Mifflin Co., 1958).

[11] These and related criteria are explored below. See pages 182–184.

and assures the dignity and integrity of the user. Each rejects the deterrent and punitive social service approaches of the past.

Since both the idea of utilities and the philosophy with which they are recommended are by no means generally shared, a fairly detailed elaboration is undertaken here.[12] It may aid clarity to adduce a recent experience.

When New York City was subject to a power failure in 1965, which affected a large section of northeastern United States, people were trapped in elevator shafts and subway tunnels; hospital services were curtailed; traffic signals ceased to operate. One could listen for points of view about the causes of the failure and attributions of blame. Since the crisis was dramatic and the inconvenience and suffering considerable, data accumulated over several weeks. One heard a good deal about overconcentration of utility companies and about the rigidity of bureaucratized organizations. Street-corner philosophers even speculated about the relation between technological sophistication and the vulnerability to sabotage and conquest.

But, for present purposes, what one did not hear is especially relevant. No one blamed the people in an elevator stalled between the twenty-third and twenty-fourth floors of a skyscraper for not carrying pocket generators, or perhaps pocket parachutes, for use in such an emergency. Nor were the people in the subway tunnels told that it served them right for not being accompanied by their own emergency horsepower or for not at least having pocket flashlights!

These reactions occurred to no one. Why? Because in some realms we understand modern industrialization, urbanization, and technology—and the interdependence which these bring. Man is more potent and powerful but also, in some spheres, far less self-reliant. We protect and provide for him institutionally, because there is no way for him to manage this new type of environment on his own. The occasional citizen who continues to make the attempt is defined as an eccentric or even as severely ill. Thus our society develops its water supply, general electricity systems, roads, the post office, and sewage systems, without much concern that it will thereby undermine the moral fiber of citizens, destroy family life, or even decrease free enterprise. Indeed, with reference to the latter, every schoolboy knows that the automobile industry is one of the pillars of the free enterprise economy and that the public road system is an essential public subsidy to Detroit.

---

[12] This material was presented, in somewhat different context, in Alfred J. Kahn, "Social Services as Social Utilities," in *Urban Development: Its Implications for Social Welfare*, Proceedings, XIII International Conference of Social Work, Washington, D.C., September, 1966 (New York: Columbia University Press, 1966).

Public utilities and public services are taken for granted as essential concomitants to industrialization, urbanization, and technological progress. It would appear useful to urge upon champions of modern social welfare a continuing effort to interpret to the public the notion that there are also essential social utilities that are no less necessary and the use of which carries no more stigma than do general public utilities and services.

A *social utility* is a social invention, a resource, or facility, designed to meet a generally experienced need in social living. It is defined as so vital that the broader community suffers from the results of the deprivation faced by an individual. Because of this, the provision is not left to the market economy even though some especially affluent people may continue to resort to the market.

The concept "social utilities" carries the social welfare system beyond the traditional limitations of social services.[13] In many places, social services have been considered as addressed to failures, the maladjusted, and the sick and as consisting only of facilitating and rehabilitative efforts. As the recent professional literature has noted repeatedly, the general post-World War I preoccupation with remedial and therapeutic interventions led to a conceptualization of social welfare programs as services that came into play only when the normal primary institutions and the forces of the market place had broken down. Inevitably, social work was seen as a helping, liaison, therapeutic, and rehabilitative activity. Its clients were perceived as casualties, failures, victims, and deviants in a world of generally self-sufficient and self-sustaining individuals. The assumption was that all social welfare programs and social work services were basically temporary and transitional.

In recent years another perspective has been articulated, the institutional view of the social welfare.[14] In this view, society takes account of technological and social changes which alter the relationships of man both to primary institutions and to the general social environment. New social "inventions" appear in response to the functional prerequisite of life in this changed social environment; and they are as "normal" in their way, in their relationship to these changed circumstances, as were the originally developed primary social institutions of a primitive agricultural economy. Nor are they to be considered temporary or transitional. Social insurance, public housing, services

---

[13] Bell prefers the term "communal goods" for services and resources which cannot be relegated to the market and are not divisible among people (clean air, etc.). See Daniel Bell, in *Toward the Year 2000*, constituting a special issue of *Daedalus*, Summer, 1967, 966.

[14] Harold L. Wilensky and Charles N. Lebeaux, *Industrial Society and Social Welfare* (New York: Russell Sage Foundation, 1958), 130–147.

to the aged, day care services, or counseling programs may be seen as social response to new challenge and circumstance. To stigmatize or penalize the user is no more rational than it would have been to have called a nineteenth-century American farmer excessively dependent because of the many ways in which he counted on the other members of his family and primary group.

*Social services may be interpreted in an institutional context as consisting of programs made available by other than market criteria to assure a basic level of health-education-welfare provision, to enhance communal living and individual functioning, to facilitate access to services and institutions generally, and to assist those in difficulty and need.*

The emphasis on the notion that some social services are social utilities while others are case services represents, first, a conviction that community well-being and the success of the economy depend on the existence of social utilities and, secondly, a belief that we must organize such utilities so as to make them as accessible and non-stigmatic as the water supply and postal service.

Although vocabularies vary, there is now considerable convergence upon these perceptions and goals. In fact, while talking of "provision according to need," Beatrice Webb apparently used the social utilities phrase at the turn of the century.[15] In a discussion of child welfare issues, the British Ingleby Committee said that the state should

> assist the family in carrying out its proper functions. This should be done in the first instance by the provision of facilities such as housing, health services and education. Some families will need greater and more specialized help through the welfare services. . . .[16]

UNICEF's Bellagio Conference on child welfare planning heard from the Secretariat a plea to

> break with the traditional belief that a national policy for children should be confined to dealing with the underprivileged and the handicapped. A national programme should cover all children . . . irrespective of their social class, their place of residence and economic status.[17]

In many countries the description "collective consumption" or "social benefits" is preferred to convey the idea:

---

[15] Beatrice Webb, *Our Partnership* (London: Longmans, Green and Co., 1948), 149.

[16] *Report of the Committee on Children and Young Persons,* "The Ingleby Report" (London: Her Majesty's Stationery Office, 1960, Cmnd. 1191).

[17] Herman D. Stein, Editor, *Planning for the Needs of Children in Developing Countries* (New York: United Nations Children's Fund, 1965), 11–12.

. . . all persons meeting certain qualifications such as attainment of a prescribed age and having a certain period of citizenship or residence receive
benefits without regard to any previous contributions or taxes paid or demonstration of individual need.[18]

The several sources quoted differ somewhat in emphasis. It becomes useful in sorting out issues of access, financing, and service delivery to distinguish *three types of social services.* First, there are two subcategories of the
general *resources and facilities,* which we here call social utilities—something not understood by those who see social services as completely encompassed by case service. Included here are:

1. Services or resources *to be used by the individual as he chooses to do so*
(the park, for example). Symbolically, at least, such facilities have no locked
door.

2. Services or resources *available to users by status* (the kindergarten or
day nursery available to children of a given age who have developed nor-
mally). One's status provides the key for opening the door.

Then there are the more traditional *case services,* needed by a smaller
population, but also available as right and removed from "poor law" stigma
and moral taint. These are:

3. Services or resources, which become *available on the basis of professional judgment or evaluation* (the residential treatment center) or some
assessment of need (special slum schools for compensatory education). An
appropriate diagnostic judgment or social evaluation opens the doorway to
service.

While these are relatively clear-cut categories, there would by no means
be world-wide consensus as to which are social utilities or social resources
and which are case services. In many places in the United States, for example, strong forces define day care as a diagnostically assigned service. Some
status services for senior citizens, taken for granted in the Scandinavian
countries, are unknown or cannot be afforded elsewhere. On the other hand,
diagnostic accessibility is a luxury in many poor and developing areas. (The
very definition of a status that opens the way to service is created by a public
decision: is the aged person to be defined as seventy, sixty-five, or sixty years
old?)[19]

Despite the desirable and necessary variation, the emphasis on social
utilities and on diagnostically-rendered facilitating and remedial case serv-

---

[18] Charles Schottland, *The Social Security System of the United States* (New York: Ap-
pleton-Century-Crofts, 1963), 1.

[19] T. H. Marshall, *Social Policy* (London: Hutchinson University Library, 1965), 107.

ices as a right represents a considerable advance. It is one of the prime characteristics of the welfare or service state under its many euphemisms. In the United States a group of legal scholars has recently developed the doctrine:

> The new expectations progressively brought into existence by the welfare state must be thought of not as privileges to be dispensed universally or by arbitrary fiat of government officials but as substantial rights in the assertion of which the claimant is entitled to an effective remedy, a fair procedure and a reasoned decision.[20]

Charles Reich has suggested that the individual's relationship to these new benefits, entitlements, resources, and facilities be recognized as constituting "the new property," the rights to which can be maintained under law.[21]

Although rigorously-compiled consumer preference data are limited, Ludwig Geismar has found, in fact, that in contrast to planners, consumers place high priority on universally accessible social utilities, to use our term.[22] By the tests of the rate and pattern of use and the response to availability, there would appear to be little doubt about this, despite periodic pronouncements of warning from conservative political quarters. Public preference is ahead of organizational and professional practice in some sectors of social welfare, sectors which derive secondary gains from an accent on a charity-philanthropy concept of all social welfare and a view of clients, problems, and programs that is best described as residual.

As suggested in the previous section, there are those who might regard an emphasis on social utilities as a diversion in the context of world-wide discussion of guaranteed minimum income, improved social insurance, and humanized public assistance. The argument is increasingly heard that one should assure people enough money and permit them to buy needed services. The market mechanism is cited as an ideal way to engender healthy competition and assure accountability.

While the issue is real and complex, the assumption that an income guarantee makes it unnecessary to plan utilities is of course a false one. Most proponents of social utilities, precisely because they appreciate current social realities, favor liberalized income transfer policies as well. Nonetheless, one

---

[20] Harry W. Jones, "The Rule of Law and the Welfare State," *Columbia Law Review*, 58, No. 2 (February, 1958).

[21] Charles Reich, "The New Property," *Yale Law Journal*, 73, No. 5 (April, 1964).

[22] Ludwig Geismar and Bruce W. Lagay, "Planners' and Consumers' Priorities of Social Welfare Needs," in *Social Work Practice 1965* (New York: Columbia University Press, 1965).

must recognize that the issue essentially is: what *mix* of income and utilities is most likely to advance what social objectives? (To round out the picture one would need to ask, what mix of income policy, social utilities, case services, and institutional change, to advance what social objectives?) Schorr has suggested that the mix is affected by: the *significance of the service* (can it be left to individual choice or do we wish to assure a child a nutritious breakfast, for example, whether or not a mother who has been provided an adequate children's allowance actually prepares it for him?); considerations of *economy or organizational effectiveness* (do we achieve better education for most people by investing in a public educational system or giving people funds to compete in the educational market place?); the view of what *people are entitled to have* (do we offer and even mandate some use of health services whether or not people choose to use their funds for such services?); *complexity* (can the family provide the resource, even given access in a market, or is it too much to expect the typical family to distinguish among the types of professional counseling available in the market place and seldom subject to adequate standard-setting and regulation?). We might add also: the issue of whether the service imposes or depends on *public sanction* (one could hardly expect probation services or compulsory day centers to be used if left to the market); the question of whether *diversity* and great variability are to be tolerated or promoted (would the option of purchase of education or health service by users create useful diversity, variability, experimentation?); and *divisibility* (collectively consumed goods, such as park beauty, are not readily sold to individuals).[23]

Brian Abel-Smith has cautioned that leaving certain services to the market may saddle the larger society with unnecessarily high administrative costs. He also warns that, under the guise of assigning some programs to the market, there is often an inadequate policy of transfers or insufficient investment in public services. The result is an increase in the gap between "private affluence and public squalor" in such fields as housing, education, health, and social security.[24]

Other negative consequences may follow in some fields when the profit motive is encouraged in what might be publicly assured services. For, people are not equally sophisticated, they often confront professional monopolies, and the possession of funds does not assure ability to purchase "equal" serv-

---

[23] Alvin Schorr, *Poor Kids* (New York: Basic Books, 1966). (Examples supplied.)

[24] Brian Abel-Smith, "Labour's Social Plans," Fabian Tract 369 (London: The Fabian Society, 1966). Also see, Richard M. Titmuss, "Choice and the Welfare State," Fabian Tract 370 (London: The Fabian Society, 1966).

ices. Abel-Smith suggests the general rule: the community should not allow the profit motive to enter into social services, where dependent people will be unable to protest or to remove their patronage, or where unethical conduct, inspired by a search for profit, may have very serious consequences for the consumer. On the other hand, his position is to favor "more benefits which people can choose how to spend, at the expense of some services now provided in kind—as long as the state ensures that the services are available and limits the adverse effects of the profit motive."

If needs are too varied and complex to be left to cash purchase, and services are too technical, the selfsame objectives may be protected by experimenting with what Anthony Pascal calls "categorical vouchers," or by assuring that services rendered in the public sector leave a maximum number of choices and alternatives to the consumer.[25] The United States social planner has access to a stance between the "cash" and "benefit in kind" schools, as exemplified by the Medicare and Medicaid legislation of 1965. A service program in which rights are sharply defined and protected, and which offers the beneficiary service options for choice may permit some of the advantages of the market to operate (sensitivity to preferences, decentralization), while imposing standards and protecting the unsophisticated consumer.[26]

---

[25] Brian Abel-Smith, "Freedom in the Welfare State," Fabian Tract 353 (London: David Neil & Co., 1964). Also, Anthony Pascal, "Poverty, Dollars and Urban Problems," Paper No. 13, Workshop on Urban Problems (Santa Monica, California: The Rand Corporation, 1968, mimeographed). The case for housing vouchers as a strategy for offering choice is made in Eugene Smolensky, "Public Housing or Income Supplements—The Economics of Housing for the Poor," *Journal of the American Institute of Planners,* XXXV, No. 2 (March, 1968), 94–101.

[26] Alternatives to the market in ultimate choice-making are decisions by leaders or by voters or decisions through political bargaining. Somewhat beyond our scope in this context, but extremely fruitful is the discussion in Robert A. Dahl and Charles E. Lindblom, *Politics, Economics, and Welfare* (New York: Harper Torchbooks paper edition, 1963), Chap. 14, "Price System, Hierarchy, and Polyarchy for Choice and Allocation."

Stated in the vocabulary of the economist, our argument may be summed up in this comment by Wilbur R. Thompson, in "Toward a Framework for Urban Public Management," in Sam B. Warner, Jr., Editor, *Planning for a Nation of Cities* (Cambridge, Mass.: The M.I.T. Press, 1966), 232.

"None of this denies that pricing urban public services would be very difficult and in many cases impossible. Economists have, in fact, erected a very elegant rationalization of the public economy almost wholly on the base of the nonmarketability of public goods and services. The public economy is, for example, assigned the provision of those goods which are so indivisible that they must be collectively consumed (e.g., justice, public safety), and since individual benefits cannot be determined, nor can voluntary payment be relied on when exclusion from consumption is impracticable, compulsory pay-

Certainly one should not offer social utilities as a substitute for essential cash or where the direct services are a vehicle for discrimination and unwarranted control. The considerations listed make a case for social utilities in some instances, for money grants in others. The planners are here called upon for careful analysis, fact-gathering, and promotion of general discussion. These issues ultimately demand democratic decisions.

To conceive of social services as made up of resources and facilities available at user initiative or by status rights—what we call social utilities—and of case services available on a diagnostic basis is to recognize that several patterns of financing are available. It is likely that each country will develop its balance among possible sources in a manner most suited to its other institutions. Included among the possibilities are general tax revenues, a portion of the earnings of communally owned factories or other enterprises, social insurance trust funds, user fees, industry, industry-labor contributions, foundations, and individual contributions. What is crucial is the mode of access to the service, the guarantee of the right, and the definition of the user, not the financial device—except insofar as the device conditions these other factors.

Similarly, while most social utilities will probably be administered as statutory services on a local or central government level, they may also be operated by nonstatutory (voluntary) organizations (voluntarily financed, or financed by public subsidy or purchase of care) or by nonprofit and profit-making corporations, which accept public payment, vouchers, and user-fees. In general, as the right is affirmed for a widely needed service, it seems unlikely that coverage will be possible without either public operation or at least public subsidization and standard-setting.

Richard Titmuss has reminded us that:

> Universalism in social welfare (free, on-demand services) though a needed prerequisite towards reducing and removing formal barriers of social and

---

ment (taxation) becomes mandatory and government responsibility is indicated. Again, because some goods are considered to be especially meritorious, we may elect to subsidize them to increase consumption of them (e.g., education, museums), and subsidies are often handled most easily through direct government provision of the service.

"Where in the case of 'merit goods' the majority induce ('coerce' through price) the minority to change their *personal* spending habits to a more *socially* beneficial (acceptable?) one, we can distinguish a separate rationale for public enterprise in the provision of those public services designed expressly for the poor. *Market prices* are clearly inappropriate for any public service that is designed to redistribute income in kind (e.g., social casework, unemployment counseling). In sum, the private market may not be able to process certain goods and services (pure 'public goods'), or it may give the 'wrong' price ('merit goods'), or we simply do not want the consumer to pay (income-redistributive services)."

economic discrimination, does not by itself solve the problem of how to reach the more difficult to reach. . . .[27]

Martin Rein talks of the "creaming" of services by the better situated and more competent users. In short, the decision to convert social services into social utilities and case services available by right, although a necessary step toward equity and implementation of social goals, does not per se offer any guarantee of access. One must still face questions about organization for service delivery and staffing of programs.

## The types of social services

A review of social services currently encouraged by government in the United States or locally initiated in programs being funded by Community Action Programs under the anti-poverty effort provides the following illustrative list. There is some overlapping; the order is random.

☐ casework and personal counseling
☐ services to encourage participation in developing and extending community resources
☐ day care
☐ homemakers
☐ foster care for children and adults
☐ literacy training
☐ employment counseling
☐ training for self-care
☐ information and referral
☐ legal services
☐ auxiliary services such as baby-sitting and shopping assistance
☐ health education
☐ diagnosis of rehabilitation potential
☐ community care and follow-up for hospital dischargees
☐ family financial counseling
☐ low-cost credit services
☐ home improvement information
☐ housing and home-management instruction and service
☐ consumer information and education
☐ child development programs
☐ neighborhood community centers
☐ pre-college educational counseling
☐ library services.

The recent United States emphasis on neighborhood legal services and multi-service centers would probably impress social workers in other countries

---

[27] Richard M. Titmuss, "The Role of Redistribution in Social Policy," *Social Security Bulletin*, 23, No. 6 (June, 1965), 6.

as innovative and exciting. On the other hand, American practitioners are painfully aware of the almost token nature of their homemaker and home-help services, as contrasted with British or Scandinavian tradition, and are impressed with the programs of cheap family vacations in a number of European countries, which, in turn, may wonder at the extensive counseling programs here.

Yet, although there are exciting developments and programmatic forms which should be assisted in their migration from place to place, one is struck by the relatively static picture in social utilities. The approach has been timid. Not enough is happening—if one takes as criteria the fact of massive social change and the range of need for new patterns of social coping. What is more, although the list is long and impressive, it becomes less so as one adds data about caseload totals and geographic coverage. With some notable exceptions, this is the situation around the world.

A strong case exists for an escalation in social invention so as to produce new social services suitable to the present era. The interventive repertoire needs to be enriched to reflect new philosophies. At the same time support must be achieved for a sufficient quantitative development.

Some of the newer possibilities and challenges may be more clearly perceived through the device of a classification of the several manifest functions of social utilities and case services.[28] Though the categories are preliminary and tentative, they do illustrate the conclusion that earlier conceptions of social services encompass only a portion of the whole.

*Access: information, liaison, and advocacy.* The liaison function has long

---

[28] An alternative classification of functions, which implies a somewhat more expansive conception of social services, is offered by a United Nations publication:
1. the progressive improvement of the conditions of living of people;
2. the development of human resources;
3. the orientation of people to social change and adjustment;
4. the mobilization and creation of community resources for development purposes; and
5. the provision of institutional structures for the functioning of other organized services.

See United Nations, *Economic Bulletin for Latin America*, XI, No. 1 (April, 1966), 79.

Titmuss offers yet another classification by functions:
- □ as compensation for socially caused disservices where no specific causal agent may be held responsible (as in industrial accidents)
- □ as protection for society
- □ as investment in future personnel for collective gain (manpower programs, etc.)
- □ as immediate or deferred increment to personal welfare.

See Richard M. Titmuss, "The Practical Case Against the Means-test State," *New Statesman*, 74, No. 1905 (September 15, 1967), 308–310.

been recognized as a critical one in social work, but it was devalued somewhat in the nineteen-fifties and early nineteen-sixties, a period of emphasis on therapeutic activities. The recognition that many services had become "hard to reach," that some services "disengaged" themselves from the poor, and that, in general, modern, large, specialized, and bureaucratized institutions inevitably confront complex problems when they seek to render individualized services has made these several types of access functions respectable again.

Renamed as a "social brokerage" or "urban brokerage" service, the liaison activity has new status and appears in new forms. Often, in multi-service centers, it is found together with outposts of many other programs. In the Community Action Program, which is part of the United States anti-poverty effort, it includes or is carried on in close partnership with a program of case and policy advocacy and a broadly-conceived community development effort.

There is currently world-wide interest in the British Citizens' Advice Bureaus, a widespread service which elevates the value of information and the organization to deliver it accurately and well, and which finds that such service may also serve as a useful "window on the man in the street." An American study proposed adaptations of the service to accommodate to our social welfare and governmental system, and a development is apparently under way.[29] Equal or greater attention has also been addressed to ombudsmen or similar administrative complaint provisions.

Emphasis on possible new organizational arrangements for some of these functions does not reflect any intent to deprecate more traditional auspices for facilitating and liaison services. However, it does seem clear that modern cities will be experimenting with new and expanded information, liaison, advocacy, and complaint mechanisms to counteract complexity and depersonalization. The possibilities of group approaches are relatively untapped.

*Developmental provision.*   Access and liaison services are an attempt at bureaucratized solution to a problem inevitable in bureaucracies. Other social services may address another task, one which grows out of recognition of what family and other interpersonal relationships become under industrialization and urbanization.

In effect, once it became apparent that the unit family could not do everything related to production, socialization, education and training, cultural enrichment, maintenance of motivation, and facilitation of family forma-

---

[29] Alfred J. Kahn *et al., Neighborhood Information Centers: A Study and Some Proposals* (New York: Columbia University School of Social Work, 1966).

tion, the process was under way. What characterizes the present situation is the quantitative change. If a society wishes to protect some of its core values and to assure intimate primary group experiences and the fruits thereof, it must find other institutional vehicles for some of the functions of the family, the traditional neighborhood, the extended family, the peer group, the religious institution.

The thesis here is simple. Social change creates new prerequisites for adequate socialization and role-training in industrial communities. Since these are recognizable as meeting functional requirements of the broader society, they ought to be socially created in the same spirit in which earlier societies invented public roads and public education. The user is "citizen," not "client." There is no personal defect implied in the need for the service and no penalty involved in the use. Those social utilities designed to meet the normal needs of people arising from their situations and roles in modern social life might be thought of as "developmental provision." Full comprehension of what it means to be mother, adolescent, retired adult, or child without one parent is a starting point in planning such provision.

Thus day care programs are needed for young children, younger children than one would have released from the shelter of the family ten years ago. Or we sustain old people in the community by a diversity of communal provisions (such as meals-on-wheels and home-helps), since the intimate family is no longer available for such service support.

This is only a beginning. Consider some of the major life-transitions and what primary group institutions once offered and still seek to offer in many places so as to assist people through them: entry into elementary school, the beginning of adolescence, the transition to the world of work, the early days of marriage, the period of pregnancy, the first days with a first baby, adjustment to the death of a spouse, retirement, old age. These are normal, everyday, universal experiences, and the institutional efforts to help people meet them represents social wisdom and communal self-interest, not charity or sympathy for victims.

The response ranges from group counseling and education for parents whose children enter school, through organized activities for adolescents— including coffee houses and "hangouts," to work guidance and counseling services, to family-life education and counseling, to group activities for "young marrieds"—down to specialized services for older people.

Day care (or better, child-development centers) and homemakers are very high-priority developmental services too often miscast in case service terms. The former is now experiencing major United States expansion under the impetus of Operation Head Start, an anti-poverty program. A degree of inventiveness might now be applied to form and name for a related program, the short-term or emergency baby-sitter. Is it not time that the city dweller had access to a resource more routinely available and reliable than the teenage baby-sitter or the neighborhood exchange arrangement for a function whose requirements grow out of current living conditions? Is it necessary to spell out the consequences for personal health (parents need rest, change, and diversion), involvement in children's education (parents need to attend parent-teacher meetings and adult classes), and emotional security (children and parents need to be comfortable about the substitute arrangement for brief periods for shopping or clinic visits and longer periods, which may occur several times a week), of some mothers' never having secure arrangements for care of their children no matter how urgent the other demands upon them? Facilities can and should be located in parks, shopping areas, and in conjunction with other major facilities such as a medical center.

Priorities must vary from place to place. Several sections of the United States could profitably devote resources to:

☐ new types of family (or adolescent) vacation resources

☐ new opportunities for peer experiences for adolescents, including group trips, cultural-educational activity, and camping

☐ new supports for induction of young people into marital life and help after birth of a first child (to include information and guidance in furnishing and maintaining an apartment, furniture loans or grants, practical nurse's aid after child's birth, consumer information, more adequate family planning information).

All of this is merely illustrative of the challenge and the opportunity. Many new forms of developmental provision are certain to emerge as the need grows and the stigma is removed.

*Basic educational, health, and housing services.*   This is a mixed category which partakes of social utilities oriented to *developmental provision* (education and some public health services) and *case services* (medical care). It is set apart here to note that a point arrives at which some social services become so *basic* as to merit elaborate institutional underpinnings. At that point one often forgets that they are, analytically at least, part of social welfare.

Education, in particular, was recognized as a basic social utility so early and is given such high priority everywhere that it is often omitted in United States social service listings. This is less often the case in the developing countries where the health, education, and welfare categories are defined as parts comprising the total social welfare system. Health is enjoying much of the same recognition despite complications inherent in the professional ideologies of physicians.

All welfare societies guarantee minima in these fields, but one notes the rapid raising of the level of guarantee as society's demands upon the individual are matched by needed resources for expansion of services.

For reasons not immediately relevant much of the provision of housing and housing-related services for middle- and low-income people has been removed from the market place (or the market has been considerably controlled). The variations here are greater than in health and education, and the extent of current provision is far less comprehensive. It is not yet possible to specify the boundaries of programs, major solutions to the market-nonmarket balance, relation of other services to the provision of dwelling space, and so on. Here, nonetheless, is a field in the midst of development and expansion, for the modern state recognizes that the city family must have an adequate dwelling as the center of its life activities.

*Recreational and cultural opportunities.* Much in these realms remains in the market place; but modern societies continue to expand these programs through direct public operation and partial or complete subsidy. Sometimes the cultural or recreational program has the function of developmental provision, as in the instance of some pioneering recreational activities for senior citizens or those cultural programs which speed up the socialization of "closed out" groups. At other times the goal is directly and plainly pleasure, enhancement, and the fostering of creativity. A society's dreams and desire to enrich the lives of its citizens—with no ulterior ends in view—are also a legitimate basis for *social utilities.*

*Help, therapy, and rehabilitation as case services by right.* Case-oriented social services remain urgent in a world of considerable personal pathology, breakdown, and problems. Psychiatrists, social workers, and psychologists have developed their most refined skills in this arena; some people, in fact, see social work only as a clinical profession even though it trains for broader roles as well. There are places where social workers are not considered competent to administer the facilitating and therapeutic social services which they render.

The general community acceptance of the validity of *case services* is accompanied by a tendency to overemphasize them when utilities are needed. While devoting energies to the development of the more generally needed facilities and resources, planners must continue to cope with manpower problems, inadequate expansion of many kinds of counseling and treatment programs, and large scale failures in service for specified client groups. The entire service repertoire is in constant need of updating in the light of requirements, new knowledge, insights into the effects of patterns of organization, and information about successes and failures.

*Packaging, administration, and priority.* This preliminary effort to classify social utilities and case services by type is meant only to outline possibilities. Programs often serve several functions. Programs in several of the categories may at times belong together. In fact, what is developmental provision in one part of the world may be therapeutic elsewhere.

Administrative logic, local practice, and case-finding strategy may suggest certain combinations operationally. Thus information services may usefully include emergency case services as well, whereas developmentally-oriented services should often include case finding and referral resources.

The issue is how the "mix" affects access and image, while still deploying resources efficiently. We have argued in the United States, for example, that it is now necessary to separate income maintenance from social service programs if the latter are to develop without traditional "poor law" stigma.[30]

Basic issues of service delivery thus remain to be faced once overall policy is accepted and a philosophy of social utilities adopted. Universal answers are not likely for communities at various stages of social welfare development, but there does appear to be some convergence on the concept of planning for decentralized service-delivery systems, while retaining a degree of centralization to implement standards, protect overall policy, and assure sound use of specialists.

## THE TIME PERSPECTIVE

The issues relating to timing and staging in planning are matters relevant to the programming phase. As Shonfield has shown with reference to economic planning, however, the time perspective may also become a policy question.[31] In effect, it is the *project* and limited plan which are short-term (one to three years). As planning becomes more comprehensive, five- and ten-year periods are involved. Thus the time decisions also become decisions relative to type and level of intervention. Value issues, in particular, must then be faced, debated, and resolved—or deliberately avoided through "working consensus."

---

[30] Alfred J. Kahn, "Social Services in Relation to Income Security: Introductory Notes," *Social Service Review*, XXXIX, No. 4 (December, 1965).

[31] Shonfield, *op. cit.*

# VII

## THINKING ABOUT POLICY: ADDITIONAL DIMENSIONS

THE QUESTION in focus is: what issues, questions, possibilities, considerations, and concerns do or should come to mind in the transition between task definition and policy derivation? The answers come from that social policy experience which has been consciously monitored and analyzed. In a given context, the planner requires anchor points in values and facts, so as to select the viable options from among the possibilities that actually may be relevant to his particular planning enterprise.

The schema in the last chapter for considering "levels of intervention" derives in part from the work of several students of social policy. It will be apparent at once that neither the dimensions suggested in that schema nor the several other types of issues elaborated in the present chapter provide adequate intellectual anchoring points to guide *all* social planning processes as these seek to order their data and to evolve policy guidelines. Fortunately the policy literature does offer some additional aid, especially as one considers health and educational programs, income transfers, and the local organization of social services. Since none of the authorities in the field of social policy has produced a widely accepted *generalized* schema to be employed in all fields, the planner who seeks inspiration and specific assistance will want to review the literature relevant to the activity in which he is engaged.[1]

---

[1] An impressive number of students of social policy in England and a smaller number in the United States and elsewhere have begun to identify some of the major dimensions relevant to the policy formulation phase of planning. All in turn owe debts to major predecessors in social science, philosophy, and social welfare policy (or social administration in the British sense). Since this is not the place for a comprehensive survey, we merely mention here such figures as Beatrice and Sidney Webb, R. H. Tawney, L. T. Hobhouse,

What follows is, therefore, essentially illustrative and a source of possible leads. Much of it is relevant to more than one social field, but little of it to all fields. Some of the proposals are more widely accepted than others as ways of formulating issues or possibilities. In a sense, this state of affairs is disappointing, yet the ferment among scholars of social policy has produced stimulating and helpful suggestions, which give promise of further results in the future. We have deliberately avoided the temptation to consolidate the several approaches or to offer a unified outline at a time when it is more important to develop experience along several lines.

Richard M. Titmuss, of the London School of Economics, is widely recognized as a leading current student of social policy in the West. Professor Titmuss, his colleagues, and his students have worked systematically with

---

Karl Mannheim, and William Beveridge. Our presentation is illustrative, and the following bibliography offers only an introduction and a sampling, the criterion being that these authors have provided the illustrations used here, even though the works of only a few are mentioned in this section.

Richard M. Titmuss has contributed the following to the discussion: *Essays on the Welfare State* (New Haven: Yale University Press, 1959); "The Role of Redistribution in Social Policy," *Social Security Bulletin*, 23, No. 6 (June, 1965), 1–7; *Income Distribution and Social Change* (London: George Allen & Unwin, Ltd., 1962); "Social Policy and Economic Progress," *The Social Welfare Forum, 1966* (New York: Columbia University Press, 1966), 25–39; and his, *Commitment to Welfare* (New York: Pantheon Books, 1968). Also, Brian Abel-Smith and Peter Townsend, *The Poor and the Poorest* (London: G. Bell and Sons, Ltd., 1965, paperback); T. H. Marshall, *Social Policy* (London: Hutchinson University Library, 1965); and *Class, Citizenship and Social Development* (Garden City: Doubleday & Co., Anchor paperback edition, 1965); D. V. Donnison and Valerie Chapman, *Social Policy and Administration* (London: George Allen & Unwin, Ltd., 1965); J. A. Ponsioen *et al.*, *Social Welfare Policy* (The Hague: Mouton and Co., I, 1962; II, 1963); Eveline M. Burns, *Social Security and Public Policy* (New York: McGraw-Hill Book Co., 1956); and *The American Social Security System* (Boston: Houghton Mifflin Company, 1949); Robert J. Lampman, "How Much Does the American System of Transfers Benefit the Poor?" in Leonard H. Goodman, Editor, *Economic Progress and Social Welfare* (New York: Columbia University Press, 1966), 125–157; Martin Rein and S. M. Miller, "Poverty, Policy and Purpose: The Dilemma of Choice," in Goodman, *op. cit.*, 20–24; Martin Rein, "Welfare Planning," in David L. Sills, Editor, *International Encyclopedia of the Social Sciences* (New York: The Macmillan Company and the Free Press, 1968), 142–153; and "The Social Service Crisis," *Trans-Action*, I, No. 4 (May, 1964); S. M. Miller and Martin Rein, "Economic Equality," reprinted from *I.U.D. Agenda* (Washington, D.C.: Industrial Union Department, AFL-CIO, 1965); Alvin L. Schorr, *Social Security and Social Service in France*, Research Report No. 7, Social Security Administration (Washington, D.C.: Government Printing Office, 1965); and *Poor Kids* (New York: Basic Books, 1966); Gunnar Myrdal, *Challenge to Affluence* (New York: Random House, 1963); Timothy Raison "A Strategy of Social Provision," *New Society* (London), 7, No. 190 (May 19, 1966), 6–8; Eugen Pusic, "The Political Community and the Future of Welfare," in John S. Morgan, Editor, *Welfare and Wisdom* (Toronto: University of Toronto Press, 1966), 61–94.

an evolving pattern for analysis, criticism, and advocacy, which—while not codified—is recognizable in several of its preoccupations.

## REDISTRIBUTION?

The central question to which Titmuss alerts one is whether a given policy or program is actually redistributive. On the assumption that the welfare state, in a commitment to equalitarian justice, seeks a degree of redistribution of resources, he examines policies in terms of redistribution over time, among groups, and among parts of a country ("territorial justice"). He notes the inadequacy of most available data.[2] The central and occasionally startling finding is that, in general, there has been far less redistribution than commonly assumed and that many of the welfare state programs, especially the most expensive ones, favor the middle and upper classes. The results are compounded by a frequently regressive tax system. The planner who would consciously implement a redistribution policy therefore must adopt specific means to do so. (Robert J. Lampman, Schorr, Rein, Robert Lekachman, among others, have pursued this question in the United States.)

The adoption of redistribution as an objective—in itself controversial in an era when real income grows almost annually—does not resolve all issues. Scale and timing are variables on which countries differ. The choices between leveling down or leveling up has considerable consequences. In effect, does one leave the "haves" where they are, distributing more widely the results of new productivity, or does one redistribute previously allocated shares? Specifically, for example, does one maintain traditional distinctions between "capital gains" and "income" or does one re-examine these categories in relation to concepts of equity? What of inherited land and other wealth? What of maldistribution of so-called fringe benefits?

S. M. Miller joins those who underscore the relativity of the poverty concept by noting that the emerging issue may be, not the specific income levels, but *inequalities*. In modern times, mass communication and physical mobility have created great awareness of gross discrepancies in income, access to resources and facilities, and styles of living. This new visibility highlights redistributional possibilities, but does not settle strategy and tactics.

Ultimately, policy-makers face the question of whether they seek equality or equity. Does equality imply leveling or an equal start ("equality of opportunity")? What are its components? Thus far, the almost universal choice, in socialist and free-market countries alike, has been in favor of a

---

[2] Titmuss, *Income Distribution and Social Change*.

guaranteed minimum standard and a commitment to equality of opportunity, rather than absolute equality. All countries assume, and some report, disincentives deriving from efforts at extreme leveling.

Because some redistributional devices achieve their effect only as a secondary consequence of other major purposes, whereas others are adopted deliberately for their redistributional function, the settling of a policy perspective still leaves much to be decided. A brief listing of potential measures in both categories suggests some of the range of social planning concerns—in both industrialized and underdeveloped countries. The listing also serves to underscore the arbitrary nature of any attempt to separate economic from social policy. Indeed, a recent United Nations Secretariat document states a principle known to legislators everywhere, which constantly guides them as they seek to protect the interests of their constituents:[3] "There is hardly a government policy which does not, in some way, affect the distribution of income or level of living." Every governmental budget affects distribution directly and indirectly, as does each contract, purchase order, or decision to expand the armed forces. As much might be said of large elements in agricultural policy. The headings which follow are therefore arbitrary and incomplete, only highlighting major vehicles for redistribution that may be considered or initiated in the context of a planning undertaking with a conscious social component.

*Vehicles for redistribution*

*Tax policy.* Direct and indirect taxes of many kinds are employed primarily to raise revenues. The selection of the specific measure results in more or less redistribution. The technical problems are less limiting than social or political questions and issues of economic development strategy: is there to be a large inheritance tax, a capital gains tax, a truly progressive income tax, a sales tax on essentials or luxuries, and so on? At what level is income to be considered excessive and to be taxed heavily? Should "negative taxes" be used for income maintenance?

*Distribution of land and wealth.* Though difficult of implementation, land reform is a component of overall redistribution policy in large numbers of developing countries. More controversial, in this realm, are proposals for

---

[3] See United Nations Economic and Social Council, "Social Policy and the Distribution of Income in the Nation," E/CN.5/AC.13/R3/ Add. 1, (1967). Much of the presentation in this next section follows this report. Also, Social Development Division, United Nations, "Report of the Group of Experts on Social Policy and the Distribution of Income in the Nation," E/CN.5/420 Add. 1 (1967). Quote is from page 24.

nationalization of industries (and expenditure of their earnings through governmental programs) and very stringent inheritance taxes. Views about these policies vary with basic philosophies of government and involve major questions relating to the importance of incentives (leaving wealth for heirs) and industry responsiveness (said to be impossible with centralization of government ownership)—among many other factors. Less radical approaches to wealth-redistribution include anti-monopoly legislation, distribution of industry shares as bonuses to workers, and the policies which give special concessions to those who would start new enterprises. Special "ghetto" programs in the late nineteen-sixties in the United States may be viewed as redistributional in this sense (territorial and racial redistribution).

*Labor and wage policy.* Governments differ in their labor legislation, particularly as it permits and supports collective bargaining, and thus they indirectly affect redistribution. Minimum-wage laws illustrate a more direct device which has been much debated in developing countries: the issue is at what point in development it is possible to introduce minimum-wage legislation without undermining economic growth. This issue has its counterpart even in industrialized countries, which find it difficult to estimate precisely the point and degree to which rises in minimum wage lead to investments in technology as a substitute for expensive labor.

*Social assistance, social security, and social services.* Vocabularies to describe these measures vary, but they are the most clearly recognized of social redistributional measures. Although some of the other methods on the list —especially tax policy and wealth distribution—are potentially far more potent, they are not employed in many political contexts or may be used in a modest degree. More important, most of the potentially redistributive activities listed above are concerned primarily with other goals. The redistributional effects may be a by-product and, therefore, not sharply directed exactly as most needed. The social planner is not generally invited to participate in these decisions.

By their very nature, social welfare measures (the generic term most used in the United States) represent public provision by nonmarket criteria (and therefore as part of a redistributional strategy) of goods, services, and funds deemed essential to help assure what society defines as a social minimum and to guarantee what are considered basic amenities.

Other chapters introduce public policy issues relevant to the several domains here listed. We therefore may limit the present discussion to suggesting some of the planning problems within social welfare especially relevant to redistributional effects. For illustrative purposes, we may here focus on developing countries.

## Redistribution in developing countries

*Education.*  Educational services are most effectively redistributive in so far as they refer to the basic, compulsory minimum and are implemented through a universal, uniform, centrally-administered system. While the ideal is not approached, given regional and district differences, variation in home interest and support, and limitations in resources, the overall results have been most impressive in many developing countries. Dropouts, poor performance, and incomplete enrollment are seen as high-priority problems for solution.

At the level beyond the required (and sometimes enforced) minimum, the differentiations often are extreme. The educational process is dependent on motivation and family supports at each stage of the process. Socio-cultural and economic background thus has a way of creating a self-perpetuating cycle unless special measures are taken. Everywhere one finds that the children of the affluent, the educated, the higher-level civil servants and administrators choose the educational "streams" which open the most extensive opportunities. In the poorest societies, a kind of intuitive cost-benefit analysis convinces the most deprived that they cannot forgo the assistance of their children during the time it would take them to complete school. At a somewhat more developed level, farm and working-class youth may be sent to technical and vocational courses, which have visible pay-offs, but not to the less-understood advanced education, which is actually the pathway to professional status.

Another type of problem also develops. A pattern of imitation results in heavy investment by some countries in advanced education or even quite specialized technical education before the structure of industry and professionalization can absorb the graduates. Since the credentials gained in such a system do not offer access to the expected benefits, the process is not redistributive and has negative political repercussions. In addition, people who could and should become qualified for skills which are needed for development are thus misdirected.[4]

*Health.*  Richard Titmuss' generalizations for the United Kingdom seem to reflect much of the situation in less-developed countries as well:

> We have learnt from 15 years' experience with the Health Service that the higher income groups know how to make better use of the Service; they

---

[4] For elaboration and documentation in relation to this entire section, see text and footnotes in: United Nations, "Social Policy and the Distribution of Income in the Nation" and "Report of the Group of Experts on Social Policy and the Distribution of Income in the Nation." Also, Gunnar Myrdal, *Asian Drama,* 3 volumes (New York: Twentieth Century Fund and Pantheon Books [paperback edition], 1968).

tend to receive more specialist attention; occupy more of the beds in better equipped and staffed hospitals; receive more elective surgery; have better maternity care; are more likely to get psychiatric help and psychotherapy than low-income groups—particularly the unskilled.[5]

Some studies show that the very poor delay visits to doctors longer, rely more heavily on out-patient services, and may even be among the last reached by universal public health measures. (Doctors, for example, concentrate in more affluent parts of a country and in the most developed cities.) Major impetus toward the creation of a basic health network and assurance of a service minimum has come from the need to carry out and sustain the results of mass campaigns to eradicate contagious diseases.

*Social security and assistance.* The redistributive role of social security is very much dependent on risks covered, the extent to which the system is contributory, the use of means tests, and a series of other conditions.[6] In developing countries, where only a portion of the most skilled labor force may be covered by social security schemes and where public contributions are not made, such programs have limited impact. Public assistance based on a means test, family or children's allowances whether or not related to need, and various direct subsistence schemes (school lunches, food distribution to families) related to such programs have the larger redistributional impact. While sharply "targeted" at those in greatest need, such programs carry the burden of stigma and potential deprivation of rights—a frequent concomitant of means-test programs in countries in which the individual in need of such help is defined by the motivational system as in some sense inadequate and, perhaps, morally to blame for his plight.

*Social services.* Nonmonetary services such as day care for children, delivery of meals-on-wheels to the elderly, home-helps for the sick or the aged, specialized programs for youth, counseling, home-care training, and the like are relatively modest redistributional measures, if measured in fiscal terms by imputing values to what is utilized by a recipient. From the point of view of the low-income user, however, such services may mean the difference between keeping an aged parent at home or having him institutionalized, releasing a child for foster care or having him at home while his mother works,

---

[5] Titmuss, "The Role of Redistribution in Social Policy," 19.

[6] See "Income Redistribution through Social Security in Western European Countries" (Geneva: International Labor Office, 1966, mimeographed). For a recent United States report, see Robert J. Lampman, "Transfer and Redistribution as Social Process," in Shirley Jenkins, Editor, *Social Security in International Perspective* (New York: Columbia University Press, 1969).

purchasing a nutritious diet or continuing unhealthful food consumption habits. Thus, monetary measurement alone does not convey the significance of such services to level of living.

In the American anti-poverty program, launched in 1964, the concept of "opportunity programs" was introduced to suggest social services, broadly conceived, to facilitate social mobility of the poor. Vocational training, counseling, corrective health programs, and child care arrangements were specifically organized and made available in a fashion calculated to contribute to social mobility. Under such circumstances, of course, social services are a major force towards equality of opportunity and where successful, are significantly redistributional in ultimate consequences.

Because the evidence suggests that, even in relation to such programs, the poorest and most disadvantaged citizens may continue to be deprived, while those a little or considerably above that level may continue to benefit, it should be useful at this point to turn to a final redistributional category, one representing not a "sector" but an organizational perspective.

### Organization for access and service delivery

Available studies document the extent to which investment in the social sectors is not necessarily redistributive.[7] Health services may be set up, only to be used differentially by different social groups—to the special disadvantage of the very poor. Housing investments may contribute most to meeting the needs of the middle class. Educational programs may experience high dropout rates for the very poor, while the more advantaged continue to enjoy the benefits of the increased public investment. Indeed, such investment may serve only to relieve the tuition burden of those already purchasing education, and not to open opportunity to those below the minimum level of resources. Similarly, retraining programs, mental health programs, and family counseling may be structured, located, or conducted so as to close out those with the greatest need.

These generalizations do not necessarily describe the usual pattern, but available data suggest that they describe a not uncommon situation. Hence, we add to the list of redistributional strategies a category along a somewhat different dimension: devices to assure access to service and facilities. In other words, apart from creating new programs and policies, one also achieves redistribution and aids groups in the population to achieve the socially-de-

---

[7] See Chapter X. See also, Alfred J. Kahn, "Perspectives on Access to Social Services" (London: National Citizens' Advice Bureau Council, publication pending, 1969).

fined minima by arrangements to facilitate access to the established rights, benefits, services, entitlements and to assure the actual delivery and use of the intended service:[8]

- ☐ case-finding measures, in the sense used in the public health field
- ☐ advice and information services, usually on a neighborhood basis
- ☐ case advocacy services of the kind pioneered in neighborhood anti-poverty programs
- ☐ neighborhood legal services and legal aid programs
- ☐ provisions for administrative appeals, the ombudsman (in the Swedish sense), and other special tribunals to protect individual rights
- ☐ strategies to develop hierarchies of social services on neighborhood, district, city, and regional levels in such a way as to assure efficient use of resources, adequate program coordination, integration of related services, and delivery to the individual user.

Among the devices frequently discussed are also the adaptation of the intended service to the specific background and characteristics of intended users and the offering of special quotas, admission requirements, or positions to disadvantaged groups as a way to speed up redistribution and the achievement of equality of opportunity.

The redistribution problem is interlaced with another policy issue sometimes put as the question of the balance between public spending and private spending—or assignment of scarce manpower to market-organized services and to public services. Other phrasing refers to private disposable income versus public improvements, an issue introduced in our social utility discussion. Developing countries often focus planning debates, not on the control of resource disposition, but on the direction of commitment: economic growth or "human investment"—a dichotomy that is often challenged.

Behind some of the policy debate arising out of redistribution proposals are two concepts of government and its right to dispose of resources. The "expansionist" position would consider equality and efficiency in deciding what government should do itself and what it should encourage the private sector to do through tax allowances and deductions. The more constricted view considers the government's domain as clearly bound; the rest is a "free zone," not to be indirectly manipulated. Adherents of both views concur in the notion that the mechanisms adopted by government have significant consequences.

It is apparent from all that has been said that redistributional strategy

---

[8] See Chapter X.

requires early confrontation of the universalism-selectivity issue to which we now turn.

## UNIVERSALISM–SELECTIVITY

No social policy issue was more widely debated in Britain in 1967–1968 than what has become known as the universalism-selectivity question. William Beveridge left the British with a tradition of universal provision. The social insurance system would collect flat rates from all and pay flat benefits —a foundation of minimal protection on which to build. The trade unions and the Labour Party opposed the means test as demeaning and as a negation of universalism. Yet, when labor faced a financial problem and wished to increase benefits, the slogan of selectivity and of new, complex, nonstigmatic means tests was raised.

Over the years Titmuss has championed universal services and warned that:

> Separate state systems for the poor, operating in the context of powerful private welfare markets, tend to become poor standard systems. Insofar as they are able to recruit at all for education, medical care and other services, they tend to recruit the worst . . . staff upon whom the quality of service so much depends.[9]

Contributing to the heated public debate in 1967, Titmuss demonstrated the complexity of any effort to establish an equitable means test, consistent with a "socialist" social policy commitment to equality, freedom, and social integration. In theory, one might devise an instrument suitable for some people at the moment of its invention and capable of achieving goals sought. However, it would never be possible constantly to adjust content, scope, characteristics, and frequency of such tests to the type of service, time available, family structural shifts, and the periodic moral-value-policy questions which arise.

For example, does not an equitable approach demand reasoned answers to question such as these:

(1) Should men and women who are cohabiting have a financial advantage over husbands and wives?

---

[9] Richard M. Titmuss, "Choice and 'The Welfare State,' " *Commitment to Welfare* (New York: Pantheon Books, 1968), 143. Nathan Glazer sees the inadequacy of the United States public housing program as related to the fact that it was designed as a program only for "the poorest." See "Housing Problems and Housing Policies," *The Public Interest*, No. 7 (Spring, 1967), 21–51.

(2) Should men who do not work be better off than men who do (the wage-stop problem)?

(3) Should those with unearned incomes have an advantage over those with earned incomes?

(4) Should those who give away their capital assets to kin receive more favourable treatment compared with those who do not or have no such assets?

(5) Should those who save be penalized as compared with those who do not?

(6) Should wives be encouraged or discouraged, penalized or not for going out to work?

(7) Should families be encouraged or discouraged from maintaining at home elderly relations, mentally-retarded children, or other disabled kin?

(8) Should income tests and charges disregard capital assets, house property, discretionary trusts, education covenants, insurance policies, reversionary interests, fringe benefits, tax-free lump sums, share options, occupational benefits in kind and suchlike?

(9) Should those who are on strike, or who refuse employment, or who are in prison be treated differently from those who are not in these situations?[10]

Others argue that perhaps a means test is possible and useful but only if applied to all levels of the social scale. Why not a means test, they ask, for those in the above-average income categories who benefit from British income tax rebates and house mortgage insurance?

Titmuss acknowledges differential need and the problem of costs. There are priorities in resource allocation. On the foundation of an infrastructure of universal services, he would consider selectivity based not on a *means* test (individualized), but on a *needs* test ("more selective services and benefits, provided as social rights, on the basis of certain categories, groups and territorial areas"). Americans will recall area redevelopment programs or special child development programs (Head Start for the deprived) as possible vehicles. The "needs" test in effect becomes an evaluative process which seeks to classify, not to judge, and which opens the doorway to what we have called case services. In stressing its separateness from the demeaning

---

[10] Richard M. Titmuss, "The Practical Case Against the Means-test State," *New Statesman*, 74, No. 1905 (September 15, 1967), 308–310. Also appears in his *Commitment to Welfare*, 113–123.

The distinctions are sharpened and implications in education, income maintenance, health, housing, and related fields are reviewed in the context of a conference report. See *Social Services for All* (London: The Fabian Society, 1968). Mike Reddin lists over 1700 different local means-tested schemes then operative in education, child care, etc. on page 8.

and historically offensive means test, Titmuss shows the universalism-selectivity debate in its full complexity.[11] It has yet to be demonstrated, however, that a needs test to open special services to disadvantaged and perhaps socially unpopular groups will not carry some of the consequences of a means test. Nor, apparently, have even the most egalitarian of societies found it financially or politically possible completely to drop means test selectivity in all fields in favor of universal social benefits available to all, regardless of need.

Faced by financial problems, the British Labour Government reconsidered the selectivity solution early in 1968, while several other European governments decided to add income tests in determining eligibility for free social services, thus departing from their universal social service position under financial pressures. While universalistic premises remain strong, the debate hardly appears to be concluded.

In the United States anti-poverty efforts of the nineteen-sixties, a selectivist strategy brought into focus a similar debate: could programs for "the poor" become stigma-free and effective or was the very concept self-defeating? Should one quickly seek to join special anti-poverty efforts with "normal" manpower and social service programs? Was this unnecessary in face of the special attention to problems and circumstances of the deprived in the anti-poverty war's manpower, education, child care, farm, and related programs? Did these inevitably become "second-class" programs, or could selectivity protect and assure access and participation in policy-making by consumers in the most disadvantaged groups? Would such participation neutralize stigma and protect quality?

The selectivity issue was discussed in these connections in the United States during the anti-poverty debate—but only in part—as it became intertwined with the bureaucratic pressures from operating departments to consolidate manpower, training, education, and general social service programs for all people under such line departments for reasons of efficiency and potential effectiveness. The United States also faces its own version of the financial issue. May it not be, some proponents of selectivity ask, that if one holds out for universalism, one will be able to do little because of costs? The question of higher education is raised. General across-the-board financial aid to higher education may be far too expensive to contemplate, at a time when one can do much for the very poor through scholarships, loans, and part-time work opportunity, even though these require a means test. Stigma

---

[11] Titmuss, "The Practical Case. . . ."

diminishes if most university scholarships require statements of parental resources at any economic level.

As noted subsequently, in Chapter IV of the companion volume, the income security debates of 1968 argued a similar question with reference to children's allowances. A universal program is appealing and expensive. Is it possible to invent devices (a recoupment plan) to recover such automatic grants from the large proportion of families who can manage without help, and still maintain the advantage of a stigma-free right for all? Or does the logic of costs demand a means-test program?

In sum, the debate was not resolved and the policy development process continues to confront it everywhere. Among those who would help poor people, not stigmatize or punish them, it reduces itself to the balance between *solidarity*, a French concept to connote refusal to relegate some people to a poor or disadvantaged category, and *preference*, a desire to target limited resources and assure their delivery where most needed.

## FORMULATIONS OF POLICY-RELEVANT ISSUES

A decision in principle on universalism-selectivity still leaves much to be considered. One seeks "services good enough for every American"—the essence of universalism—while devising non-stigmatic criteria or procedures for the inevitable application of priorities. The authors listed above offer the following possible formulations of issues, which receive more comprehensive attention elsewhere in this volume under such categories as service delivery, staffing, coordination, and integration:[12]

☐ the specific balance between *preferential treatment* and services to the severely handicapped, to help make up deficits and overcome disadvantages, and the non-stigmatic *universal service*;

☐ the balance between use of *market* and *nonmarket* devices to allocate resources, recognizing that the market maximizes choices but allows exploitation, that it leaves some "weak" consumers at the mercy of the unscrupulous;

☐ the balance between considerations of *efficiency* and economy, on the one hand, and *social priorities*, on the other;

☐ the choice between a *guaranteed minimum* at a level which meets basic subsistence needs and a standard which helps protect a *living level*, which one has achieved in the general market during one's full economic participation;

☐ the choice in interpretation of "equality" between permitting "equal opportunity" to become the *"same program* for all" and offering a *di-*

---

[12] See footnote 1 on pages 192–193.

*versity of outlets* in which people may reveal and develop their unequal capacities;

☐ the balance between "means" and "ends" in service organization; or between *system and boundary maintenance*, on the one hand, and a *task orientation*, on the other;

☐ the balance between *specialization*, expertise, and related service fragmentation, on the one hand, and a social and human focus on the *"whole" person or family*, on the other;

☐ the related balance, within the several professions affected, between *general and family-centered practice* and *specialized practice*;

☐ organization of service delivery systems on different levels in a balanced relationship between general and *integrating services*, on the one hand, and *specialized services*, which husband scarce resources, on the other.

Titmuss' delineation of three "types of welfare" may serve to alert the policy planner to additional possibilities and opportunities:

*Social services.* This is the collective provision for certain categories of need, as described earlier but including income maintenance as Titmuss uses the term.

*Fiscal welfare.* This means use of the tax system to achieve social objectives, including dependents' allowances, certain deductions as for education, etc.

*Occupational welfare.* The term designates industrial fringe benefits, broadly defined, including pensions, which are a charge on the whole population ultimately, if the employer gains tax consideration thereby or as they become a substitute for public social provision.

It was actually his analysis of fiscal and occupational welfare that first enabled Titmuss to point out that the welfare state may be doing more for the middle and upper classes than the poor. By referring, in the United States, to a variety of public payments for nonproduction, especially "farm profits arising out of government purchase and destruction of farm products and wages for make work," Lampman has provided a more realistic picture of the scope of current United States income transfers and has dramatized the range of options faced by the social planner.[13]

Martin Rein's discussion, jointly with S. M. Miller, of "the dilemmas of choice" represents a most comprehensive beginning of an attempt to systematize social policy planning.[14] Referring specifically to the poverty problem, the authors describe six possible intervention strategies which will be recognized as largely encompassed by (but as representing a somewhat dif-

---

[13] Lampman, "How Much Does the American System of Transfers. . . ."
[14] Rein and Miller, "Poverty, Policy and Purpose: The Dilemmas of Choice," *op. cit.*

ferent "cut" from) our own categories of levels of intervention. They refer to:

☐ *amenities*—our "social utilities"
☐ *investment in human capital*—our "social utilities"
☐ *transfers*—included in our scheme
☐ *rehabilitation*—our "case services"
☐ *participation*—a method, not a category, in our view
☐ *economic measures*—social planning's contribution to economic policies, in our terms.

Social welfare goals, in the view of these authors, may be implemented in one or several of these ways and the clarification of goals is essential to the choice among options. Again, with reference to the poverty problem, the goals may be seen as: social decency (one should seek not only freedom from want but certain amenities as well); equality (redistribution is essential); mobility (the programs should assure that future status depends on merit, not family position); social stability (programs are not satisfactory, in the eyes of some, unless they make a contribution to social control as well, "encouraging behavior which conforms to widely accepted social values"); social inclusion (economic aid is not enough; there must be simultaneous support for social and political participation); economic stability and growth (the solution to the poverty problem must be such as to contribute to economic growth; the "effective demand of the poor" needs to be expanded).[15]

The analysis of program strategies, when joined with the possible goals, provides Rein and Miller with a formulation of four *policy issues* which face a policy planner. We do no more here than suggest what is involved in each:

*Investment multiplier.* This is a technical-rational issue as well as a political question: in effect, in what intervention category does a possible program belong; what types of effects can be considered? The planner is expected not only to propose a policy but to know what he expects of it and why.

*Effectiveness.* The planner must ask about the evidence for effectiveness of the proposed policies and programs; this forces choices among the levels and types of goals.

*Coherence.* Isolated programs or unrelated policy thrusts cannot be effective. Thus, job training needs to be tied in with job opportunity, rehabilitation services with provision for community reintegration. Where

_____
[15] *Ibid.*, 35–38.

coherence is not attainable, a proposed policy or program becomes a poor investment. This category is roughly equivalent to our emphasis on a *"systems approach."*

*Value conflict.*   Here Rein and Miller introduce a subject which we have discussed in Chapter IV. In considering intervention strategies and their related goals, one must analyze the means and ends in terms of value implications and explore the potency of value positions and the priorities which they are assigned.[16]

As does Titmuss in his definitions of the essential characteristics of the welfare state, these authors, too, call the policy-maker's attention to the need to strike a balance at a given moment between *consumption* and *investment* programs. While, at the extreme, the boundaries are clear (money for food or capital funds for school construction), the classification itself, in most instances, becomes a matter of perspective. Budgets for schools or tuition to an individual may be a consumption expenditure in one sense (his life is enriched), but an investment in another (he contributes more effectively to the economy). Nonetheless, the categorization is useful since the planner is called upon to attend to a sufficient investment-proportion to meet future productivity and manpower demands in many fields. Investment implies "deferred gratification" of immediate consumption pressures; one becomes suspicious if what are called investment decisions are all reflective of short-run, interest-group pressures and do not seem to require delayed or decreased gratification. On the other hand, where present generations are asked to pay a "delayed consumption" price for the general good, one wants to know who has made the decisions and how—and whether the purported investments are real.

These, then, offer further illustrations of possible policy-anchoring points in the planning process. Behind them all are the welfare state's commitments to equalitarianism, maximum freedom of choice, and support of self-enhancement. Accumulated social wisdom, however, does not take one automatically from such goals to fixed choices among some of the options posed above or to the specification of known "mixes" for given planning contexts. The planner must face such issues anew in each context, hoping each time both to solve his immediate problems and to contribute to the accumulation of much-needed experience.

It will be recognized that the discussion in this section has fluctuated between two poles. On the one hand, fundamental policy questions, which

---

[16] *Ibid.*, 39–56. The interpretations are mine.

seem to merge with goal statements, are offered for choices (universalism, equality, redistribution). On the other hand, we are confronted with issues relevant to programs and administration (types of coordination and social service delivery strategy, for example). It would appear that policies are confronted on varying levels of generality and that the choices gradually reach a level that offers guidance sufficiently specific to provide parameters for programming.

## PARAMETERS OF PROGRAMMING

The focus of the present section, which discusses the bridge from policy to programming, is best understood by reference to the work of Eveline M. Burns. Introducing her volume on social security, Burns notes that she has undertaken two objectives:

One, ". . . to identify the major questions about the nature of social security programs which must be answered by every community desiring to assure, through the instrumentalities of government, a measure of economic security to some or all of its members."

And, ". . . to indicate some of the more important considerations which have to be taken into account and evaluated in answering these questions."

Burns's first objective is to develop, for social security programs in particular, a series of policy-relevant dimensions along which choices must be made. Her work thus illustrates, in detail, and in one field, the type of process described in the previous chapter, although the particular model employed is hers.

The second class of objectives both deepens our understanding of the policy-relevant dimensions and clarifies the transition to programming. For, in the sorting out of possible choices and then clarifying the relevance of various elements in the answering, Burns takes one far along the way in understanding how she would organize for the programming and administrative task. An earlier work illustrates programming decisions as tied to policy in greater detail.[17]

The Burns model is here presented in the form of an outline of the four major sections of her general volume, *Social Security and Public Policy*, the related chapter headings, and several selected subheadings, but the added emphases are mine:[18]

---

[17] Eveline M. Burns, *Social Security and Public Policy* (New York: McGraw-Hill Book Company, 1956). The quotations are from page ix. And her earlier volume, *The American Social Security System* (Boston: Houghton Mifflin Company, 1949).

[18] Adapted from, Eveline M. Burns, *Social Security and Public Policy* (New York: McGraw-Hill Book Company, 1956), with the kind permission of the publisher.

### A. Decisions as to the Nature and Amount of Security Benefits and the Conditions Governing Their Receipt

Chapter 1. Benefits Related to *Need*
Chapter 2. Benefits Related to *Contributions*
Chapter 3. Benefits Related to *Previous Earnings*
Chapter 4. Income Guarantees and *Willingness to Work*
　　　　　Controls Embodied in the Benefit Provisions*
　　　　　Controls Through Conditions Attached to the Receipt of Benefits*
Chapter 5. The Bearing of Social Security Programs on the Family System

### B. Decisions as to the Risks for Which Social Responsibility Will Be Accepted

Chapter 6. Threats to Continuity of Income: *Chronological Age or Retirement*
Chapter 7. Threats to Continuity of Income: *Prolonged Unemployment or Disability*
Chapter 8. Threats to Adequacy of Incomes: *The Costs of Medical Care*

### C. Decisions About the Financing of Social Security Programs

Chapter 9. The *Type of Taxes* to be Levied
Chapter 10. The Distribution of *Costs Over Time*
Chapter 11. The Distribution of Financial Responsibility Among *Different Levels of Government*
Chapter 12. Methods of Implementing Intergovernmental Cost Sharing*

### D. Decisions Regarding the Structure and Character of Administration

Chapter 13. Administrative Issues*
　　　　　Organizational Structure*
　　　　　Intergovernmental Cooperation*
　　　　　The Adequacy and Quality of Administrative Personnel.*

Several things immediately become apparent. First, policy issues appear on several levels of generality. Some which may be addressed in one type of planning situation are accepted as givens in another. Thus Burns assumes an income-security and income-transfer policy and begins at that point. We have noted the need at some point to settle the balance among strategies of which income-transfer programs represent one approach. However, having decided to develop a social security program, there remain new policy issues on another level: *risks* to be covered, nature and amount of *benefits*, methods of *financing*. Each of these is in fact a very complex policy arena and requires its own analytic model, as Burns illustrates very well. When these issues are worked out, the planner emerges with that level of policy guidance which facilitates the transition to programming. In the case of the above outline, the asterisks(*), which we have supplied, denote sections devoted entirely to administrative questions, but there are other illustrations.

For example, under the Chapter 3 discussion of "Benefits Related to Previous Earnings," the planner is introduced by Burns to necessary administrative options among which choices will be made if one adopts this general approach. The discussion of "Income Guarantees and Willingness to Work" organizes the experience in using administrative controls to cope with malingering. The "Risks" review outlines the possible technical and administrative approaches to determination of actual retirement—and how different types of programming might be based on different policy thrusts. Thus one level of benefits and one method of policing may actually encourage and enforce full withdrawal from the labor force.

It is also apparent that there are some policy issues which are fundamental and primary in some planning contexts, and derivative in others. A major planning effort might be addressed to public-voluntary relations in health services or to intergovernmental relations in organizing child welfare. On the other hand, a model which begins with some givens and sees these as issues of administrative efficiency in carrying out policies relating to decisions about risks, financing, and benefits, will not devote major energies to the public-voluntary or intergovernmental relations questions. It is in this latter sense, then, that some policy questions deserving of major planning concern at some point become instrumental in others. They are here called programming parameters to suggest that, as a planning process makes overall, basic decisions, it often must deal as well with issues such as those listed below, so as to traverse the bridge towards programming. In other contexts each of these could be the fundamental policy question.

Our listing below is impressionistic and covers several fields. It reflects current concerns within American social welfare. It is not comprehensive, nor would we know how to develop a comprehensive list at the present point. The debt to Burns and to the authors represented in the first section is apparent.

Some major parameters of programming, *largely relevant to planning within and between what are clearly recognizable as "social" sectors*, are noted briefly:

*Eligibility questions.* For whom are the services designed and by what rights?

*Benefit questions.* What range and level of services and benefits is to be provided?

*Financing questions.* Who will pay, when, under what degree of compulsion?

*Public-private balance.*   What is to be the distribution of responsibility and the structure of interrelationships of public and voluntary service sectors? To what extent will one turn to private business to operate programs, a new strategy in the late nineteen-sixties?[19]

*Sectarian-nonsectarian balance.*   If private services are under consideration, what is to be the distribution of responsibility and the structure of interrelationships of sectarian and nonsectarian services?

*Levels of government.*   What are to be the respective roles, responsibilities, and prerogatives of federal, state, local, regional, and other units of government in policy development, standard-setting, financing, and operation of programs?[20]

*Funding.*   Should funding from the higher to the lower governmental level be in the form of *block grants* (general budgetary assistance) or *categorical grants* (matching money for specific programs under defined controls)?

*Manpower strategy.*   What is the program's major manpower strategy: stress on professional staffing, creating expanded opportunities for so-called indigenous nonprofessionals, pioneering in new team relationships, maximizing use of volunteers, etc.?

*Coordination, integration, accountability.*   How central are program and *policy coordination, service integration, and accountability* to the basic policy objectives sought?

*Time and scale dimensions.*   What are the timing possibilities for moving from policy to program, from program launching to full operations, from operation to evaluation and feedback?

With reference to the last item, Whitney Young has argued that all too often the appropriate policy stance has been adopted and legislative instruments created, but goals have been subverted by programming on too small a scale. In this connection he is generally suspicious of "demonstration" programs as diversionary.[21]

---

[19] Alan Pifer, "The Non-Governmental Organization at Bay," *Annual Report Carnegie Corporation of New York 1966* (New York, 1966), 3–15. See also, "Business and the Urban Crisis," constituting *Fortune*, LXXVII, No. 1 (January, 1968).

[20] Roland L. Warren urges systematic research in this area, noting that we know little of the actual consequences of alternatives. *The American Community* (Chicago: Rand McNally & Co., 1963), Chaps. 6 and 7.

[21] Subcommittee on Executive Reorganization, Committee on Government Operations, U.S. Senate, *Federal Role in Urban Affairs* (Washington, D.C.: Government Printing Office, 1967), Part 14, 2944.

## THE PRICE TO BE PAID

Cost-benefit analysis has already been mentioned briefly as a way of making choices among programs or of optimizing the combination of programs or program units. It will be discussed more systematically later in Chapter IX. Program budgeting will also be described, particularly in its PPBS form. It has already been made clear that such systems face difficulties in conceptualizing or quantifying "human benefits"; they do not eliminate value and preference issues from the planning process.

At the point of policy development, the planning phase here in focus, planners face what is essentially a policy issue: how to create the *criteria* for interpretation of the results of cost-benefit or cost-effectiveness analyses, or for reacting to the results of the objective cost estimates of any of the proposed policy thrusts. The question may be simply put: *What are we willing to pay to carry through the task?* What price in money or social consequences are the goals worth?

One has here in clear form a convergence of value-preference questions and the survey of the objective realities. At some point the planners must know, through interaction with executive, legislative, or other policy-making authorities, what price can or will be paid. This, too, is one of the policy dimensions out of which the program is shaped. It is not the product of arithmetic alone. Computations, analyses, and projections tell us what can be known, but system-relevant considerations, political concerns, fiscal and monetary policy, and interest-group pressure answer the cost question. In the Meyerson and Banfield terms introduced earlier, one cannot avoid "end reduction," attaching relative values to various ends and goals and then choosing among the relevant ends. In this process, one decides whether the price one can pay is what can be "afforded," what the analysis shows to be an optimal investment in this sector, what the undertaking requires, or something in between.

We know of no way at present to conceptualize this aspect of policy development fully except to note that fiscal and monetary criteria and interest-group pressures cannot be ignored without ultimate catastrophe and that their balance at a given moment may be an act of political artistry. One justifies mention of this consideration in the context of a rational planning model only to make the case for consideration of a series of hypotheses about the price which can be paid. The planning team, which obviously requires both economics and behavioral science competence, must then proceed to consider the possible consequences of each choice along a series of socially significant dimensions, ranging from aggregate growth rate and the balance of governmental budgets at the one end to social stability at the other.

The economic analyst employs the concept of "opportunity costs" to include in his equation earnings which we forgo, economic gains which we give up, to devote manpower, time, and equipment to a given effort. The question of the price to be paid, posed as a policy issue, must include attention to opportunity costs as well as direct outlays. The opportunity-cost concept, in turn, requires supplementation in terms of a *social-cost* equivalent. The full policy issue, then, may be framed as follows: to achieve the given task, what direct costs, opportunity costs, and social costs will be sustained—and what are the implications of these limits? The rarity of such analysis at present is an indicator of the incomplete development of much social planning.

# VIII

## GENERAL CONSIDERATIONS IN PROGRAMMING

THE STANDING plan, policy, must be translated from general principles into program specifics. In the words of a report on budgeting

> *"Programs"* are time-phased plans for allocating resources and for specifying the successive steps required to achieve stated objectives. They are means to clearly defined ends. . . .
>
> *"Program objectives"* are the specific results to be obtained by the planned commitments of resources. They underlie the subsequent definition of the particular organizational, legislative, financial, and procedural means required. [Emphasis in original.][1]

The history of social welfare legislation contains abundant illustration of legislative enactments or overall plans which were almost flawless in their policies, but which sacrificed the bulk of their achievements through programming defects. Incompetence, carelessness, and administrative sabotage, singly or in combination, may serve to veto the products of careful planning. Poorly coordinated efforts may nulify one another or cause wastage and ineffectiveness. A pattern of appropriations or budgeting which is not staged with reference to operational realities may convert impressive policy commitments into meaningless dreams. On the other hand, creative programming often builds substantial operational achievement upon modest progress in policy. Errors in programming are costly not only in operational terms but also in what they require, organizationally, to undo. As noted by Hitch, it is often easier to change policy—involving only a few people at the top—than programs which may immediately affect thousands of people.[2]

---

[1] Committee for Economic Development, *Budgeting for National Objectives* (New York, 1966), 26.

[2] Charles J. Hitch, *Decision-Making for Defense* (Berkeley: University of California Press, 1965), 70.

The emphasis here is on *means* to implement general principles. As put by David Novick, a program is *"a combination of activities to meet an end objective."* (Emphasis added.) And segments of programs are often called *projects*. Despite contrary uses and inconsistencies in the literature, this is the sense in which the term programming is here preferred.[3] Order, consistency, and balance are central considerations.

Professional practice in all social sector arenas inevitably enacts policy, whether or not there is conscious intent. For example, French and Scandinavian poor law kept paupers at home, the assumption being that relatives would consequently find it more difficult to evade their responsibility and should not be permitted to do so.[4] American programs for the mentally ill, as developed in mid-nineteenth century, permitted a "casting out" of the severely disturbed. By the nineteen-sixties, an effort was under way to reverse the process.[5]

The social planning process represents an attempt deliberately to translate policy into programs and practice. It is no small undertaking. Jawaharlal Nehru, commenting on the Indian Five-Year Plan, spoke for many people when he said, "We are not quite so expert at implementation as at planning."[6] Nor, one might add, at specifying programmatic details which will translate general goal into specific operation.

As indicated in the last chapter, the intermediate stage between policy development and programming involves attention to what we have called parameters of programming. These parameters define the immediate programming-relevant policy issues. In the course of the process, choices are made about the intervention levels and their balance (as relevant) between universal and particularized (selective) services; between and among governmental, general voluntary, and sectarian efforts; between investment and consumption preoccupations; among income transfers, general social benefits (social utilities), and case services—and so on. Basic principles for financing, assigning administrative responsibility to various levels of government, and the use or non-use of the market as a service-distribution device are worked out. Above all, there is clarity as to whether the goals are re-

---

[3] David Novick, "The Department of Defense," in David Novick, Editor, *Program Budgeting* (Cambridge, Mass.: Harvard University Press, 1965), 86–87.

[4] T. H. Marshall, *Social Policy* (London: Hutchinson University Library, 1965), 34.

[5] Joint Commission on Mental Illness and Health, *Action for Mental Health* (New York: Basic Books, 1961).

[6] As quoted by Albert Waterston, *Development Planning* (Baltimore: The Johns Hopkins Press, 1965), 334.

distributional, equalitarian—or, more narrowly, the assurance of a necessary minimum. Specific programming objectives are set.

Where relevant, a working model of the social welfare system is adopted, involving some boundary decisions.

The stage is then prepared for program development. Each of the policy decisions must be translated into operational terms. The details of scale, staging (programming over time), and staffing must be worked out. Budgets then must be specified.

So significant and demanding is this phase that, as indicated, there are those who see it as the *entire* scope of planning. Policy, in this view, comes from political authorities; and the planner then begins his assignment. Without agreeing to dismiss policy planning, we may nonetheless concur about the scope and demands of this phase. The Planning Programming Budgeting System (PPBS) developments and cost-effectiveness analysis alone are major items for consideration. In effect, *the entire field of administration becomes relevant:*[7] executive planning and scheduling; decisions relating to types of organization, line and staff structure, and so on; staffing and staff development; assuring a structure for ongoing directing and decision-making; coordination; reporting; budgeting. Phasing of components is a critical programming task, the objective being maximum consistency, complementarity, and efficiency in relation to manpower and resource utilization. Capital and operational planning require integration.[8]

A study by Melvin Herman and Stanley Sadofsky of "problems of planning and operation" of youth-work programs indicates the complexity of achieving effective phasing in a relatively short-term project involving several levels of government, a number of agencies, and many unknowns. It is clear, nonetheless, that success rides on the solutions of such problems.[9]

It cannot be within the scope of the present volume to discuss all phases of administration. Relevant literature is available. We therefore must choose, in this and the following chapter, to highlight several *selected* programming problems especially significant for the social sector. A number of these reside in the realm of social service organization and delivery and are selected on the basis of experience as to their critical nature at present. In effect, it is the view here taken that, while one cannot ignore any of the

---

[7] Waterston, *op. cit.*, Chap. 8.

[8] Everett E. Hagen, *Planning Economic Development* (Homewood, Ill.: Richard D. Irwin, 1963), 99, 103.

[9] Melvin Herman and Stanley Sadofsky, *Youth-Work Programs* (New York: Graduate School of Social Work, New York University, 1966).

programming categories mentioned, social planning could be enhanced through more careful consideration of these particular issues. In addition, because of the relative newness of the effort and the intensity of the on-going debate, we shall also discuss cost-effectiveness studies and the PPBS approach as programming aids, and the latter as a full planning system as well.

Before turning to the areas selected for attention, it may be useful to note the need at the programming phase, particularly where one is concerned with new programs, to consider whether administrative detail should be enacted into law or left for administrators. Governmental and administrative preference and traditions vary, with reference to these matters, among countries, parts of a country, and disciplines. In general, students of administration prefer the assignment of broad authorization to act. If one is to achieve efficiency and flexibility, it is probably necessary to trust administrators and executives, while still holding them responsible. This policy is often modified so as to capture the specifics of a special program element or policy detail precious to legislators, policy-makers, or interest groups—or to satisfy the needs of lawyers or other strict constructionists who in some voluntary agencies or governmental departments are likely to hamstring administrators when specific procedures, requirements, or authority are not assigned by statute.

Programming in general "should be flexible enough to pose options and to permit alterations to meet unforeseen contingencies."[10] The whole point of reporting, monitoring, evaluation, feedback, and administrative alertness is lost if planners assume that all decisions must be made in the pre-operational phase or that decisions once made are irrevocable. Those countries which experimented with overcentralized and rigidly planned economies after World War II came to regret it. Programming for appropriately decentralized administration-operation is as vital as is a measure of decentralization during the planning process per se.

While other programming items are mentioned in passing or elaborated in the companion volume, which offers illustrations from specific fields, the following have been selected for generalized attention in this and the next two chapters as particularly relevant at the present time:

□ coordination of policy and programs
□ the "mix" among fields
□ capital planning
□ the interventive repertoire

---

[10] Hagen, *op. cit.*, 331.

☐ manpower planning
☐ PPBS and cost-benefit analysis
☐ access and case channeling
☐ service integration
☐ protection against administrative abuse.

## COORDINATION OF POLICY AND PROGRAMS

A subsector in an overall social welfare effort, whether concerned with a single community or an entire country, may involve several operating programs and large numbers of staff members. Consider, for example, the case of a community anti-poverty effort, focused on employment placement, retraining, basic literacy, health, and housing services. Or the plans in a developing country to launch and implement universal elementary education and related health efforts. Sometimes such undertakings involve several fields within social welfare. At other times, many administrative bodies and separate organizations may be concerned with a plan in one field. In either instance, the need for meshing is great—yet the obstacles are considerable. Students of both formal and informal organization[11] have demonstrated the extent to which separate organizations, programs, or sub-units, given supporting boards, staffs, constituencies, and particular ideologies or sense of mission, may begin to compete, work at cross-purposes, and fail to coordinate.

Coordination mechanisms may not solve all these problems, and excessive coordination may in itself become a fetish. However, where a planning process does base itself on a definition of the task by a group with legal sanction, power, and resources, it is legitimate to expect such planning process also to provide for appropriate coordination once operations begin.

The selection of the devices and mechanisms depends on the size, locale, and nature of the program. Consideration may be given to any of these forms:

*Coordination through the structuring of executive and administrative authority.* Here coordination is provided in the way in which one sets up the line organization. Thus, the planning for a multifaceted effort might

---

[11] Robert K. Merton *et al.*, Editors, *Reader in Bureaucracy* (Glencoe, Ill.: The Free Press, 1952); Amitai Etzioni, *Modern Organization* (Englewood Cliffs, N.J.: Prentice-Hall, 1964, paperback), and his *A Comparative Analysis of Complex Organizations* (New York: The Free Press, 1961). Eugene Litwak and Lydia F. Hylton, "Interorganizational Analysis: A Hypothesis on Co-ordinating Agencies," *Administrative Science Quarterly*, 6, No. 4 (March, 1962), 395–420; William Reid, "Interagency Coordination in Delinquency Prevention and Control," *Social Service Review*, XXXVIII, No. 4 (December, 1964), 418–428; Peter M. Blau and W. Richard Scott, *Formal Organizations* (San Francisco: Chandler Publishing Company, 1962).

involve creation of a multifunction agency with one executive who has direct line responsibility for sub-units concerned with job training, placement, education-related activities, and a diversity of social services or self-help activities. (Mobilization for Youth chose this path in 1961 in contrast to the interagency, interdepartmental, or interorganizational committee approach then the most common device.)[12] The entire structure of the executive's office under this pattern is oriented to coordination of policy and program activities among the components.

Similarly one might create a family and children's agency whose executive director would be expected to maintain an organizational structure which might maximize the interplay of family counseling resources, homemakers, day care, foster care, protective, adoption, and unmarried mothers' services. This contrasts with the more common pattern of specialized child welfare services which then must be coordinated with the other services by some other mechanism.

This type of provision for coordination is in many ways very desirable. System boundaries, financing patterns, professional and organizational prerogatives, and the problem of sheer size often preclude it, however. At times, it may not be possible for historical, bureaucratic, professional, and good substantive reasons to combine departments and bureaus in such a way as to achieve desirable coordination, but the results sought may be achieved through budget mechanisms, as when an executive is given control of the operational funds and employs his power to achieve coordination.[13]

*Coordination through formal administrative mechanisms at the level below the executive, often in the executive office.* Often, particularly in complex national or state government, as in the case of the United States, the range of activities and responsibilities is quantitatively too great to assure coordination through the structuring of the line organization. One then turns to the related but somewhat different device of staff-coordinating mechanisms (committees or bureaus) in the executive branch. The President of the United States, for example, has the following in his Executive Office: National Security Council; Bureau of the Budget; Council of Economic Advisors; Central Intelligence Agency; National Aeronautics and Space Council; Office of Emergency Planning; Office of Science and Technology. Several of these agencies have line functions as well and all carry

[12] Mobilization for Youth, Inc., A *Proposal for the Prevention and Control of Delinquency by Expanding Opportunities* (New York: Mobilization for Youth, 1961).

[13] Arthur Smithies, "Conceptual Framework for the Program Budget," in David Novick, Editor, *Program Budgeting* (Cambridge, Mass.: Harvard University Press, 1965), 53–55.

major advisory responsibilities; but each is also a coordinating instrument. Several devote their major energies to coordination. Proposals have been made from time to time that an instrument similar to the National Security Council be invented to coordinate the entire "domestic" sector, but alternative instruments have also been lodged in the Office of Economic Opportunity and the Department of Housing and Urban Development.

Devices of this type are essential for large-scale government. States may employ several (Governors' Committees on Children and Youth, Transportation Councils, etc.), as may large cities. Sanctions are weaker, authority more diffuse, and the possibility of blockage by vested interest greater than in the first type, because here the task is one of bringing together efforts which may have their own constituencies and institutional trappings.

*Coordination through executive-department grouping.* This is a variation on the first form listed, and it is becoming necessary at the federal level, in large states, and in metropolitan areas. The emphasis is on coordination through the line organization, but the executive finds that he cannot possibly manage a span of control which gives him fifteen or twenty commissioners, or more, in charge of line departments. He then attempts a functional grouping of like departments. California pioneered in such reorganization, grouping together Corrections, Adult Authority, and Youth Authority, for example. New York City's Human Resources Administration put the commissioners and directors of the following under one administration: Welfare, Youth Board, manpower programs, and the anti-poverty program. A Health Services Administration joined together Health, Hospitals, and Mental Health programs.

The main issue which has arisen is whether or not certain commissioners are blocked from access to city and state executives on matters for which they have statutory responsibility. There is also some fear that commissionerships are downgraded by a procedure which places administrators between them and the chief executive. These problems will have to be solved, however, for there is no way to achieve executive coordination in very large units without such groupings under persons with authority.

*Coordination through interagency, interdepartmental, or interorganizational committees.* This is a less potent device, although it is quite common. Sanction and pressure may be created through legislative mandate (a state-wide advisory committee on day care), executive action (an interdepartmental task force on multi-service centers), pressure from a united fund (which backs a coordinating committee in a local community council), shared interest (as when a city-wide child welfare coordinating committee is also the joint instrument for requesting increased public subsidy), or good will. In this pattern an assemblage of "equals" seeks to improve communication, interrelate plans, develop devices for cooperation on the operational level, and so on. Unless the convening authority has real power and uses it (with reference to funding, usually) or one or more of the members is especially well located locally for forceful leadership, each significant member of the group retains a veto. Only a superordinate task of considerable moment, usually in response to a community emergency, permits such a body to overcome fundamental vested interests. Otherwise, it accomplishes many things, but leaves enough unsolved so that calls for more coordination persist.

*Coordination through joint or unified service operations.*  Sometimes coordination is achieved by inventing a service-delivery system under which several services are reached through one access point, or a range of responsibilities is carried by one liaison worker. There are many variations on this, as described in our chapters on local-service delivery and the planning of services for children in trouble (*see* Chapters III and VII in the companion volume). The essence of the system is assignment of accountability for case integration to a multipurpose or so-called polyvalent worker—or an inter-agency agreement as to who takes the "lead" when several are involved with one case. If the accountability is clear, pressure grows to "solve" inter-agency roadblocks and red tape. Agreement on several levels, from line practitioners to executive and board, achieves coordination. Even a simple advice and referral service makes a contribution along these lines as it asks questions so as to develop its information files—and as it begins to channel community inquiries (*see* Chapter X).

These are the major coordination patterns as they may be considered at the programming phase. Each has a number of variations. Many opinions about each approach are current, but very little empirical work has been done to validate general principles. Martin Rein has suggested informally that another issue is to consider whether the coordinating device of joint or unified service operations should be lodged in the functional service (school, employment agency, health unit) or placed in a multi-service unit or access service which is not identified with any particular functional service. He suggests that perhaps functional coordination is excellent in "investment" programs (job training), but should not be lodged in stigma-arousing "consumption" programs (public assistance). The concept is stimulating but not fully workable.

*Non-coordination as a change technique.*  It was long the assumption that coordination is essential to avoid wastefulness. If programs are not meshed and policies not interrelated, resources do not have additive effects and potential users are confused or alienated. During the anti-poverty effort in the United States beginning in 1964, and in connection with new programs which resulted from the civil rights effort, questions began to be raised about this view.

Some students of social change, for example, noted that tightly-knit coordinating structures may become a way to create monopoly and protect the status quo. A preoccupation with coordination may become a substitute for service expansion. Most important, a focus on coordination accepts what *is* as a monopoly, assumes that the service pattern is adequate, and aims only at making its output more efficient; this approach does not acknowledge the need for radical change in service content or delivery systems in some instances.[14]

Thus a non-coordination or an anti-coordination "school" in the social welfare field arose, deriving most of its rationale and concepts from "free market" traditions. It urged funding of competing and uncoordinated efforts as a way to make agencies concern themselves with how to win and hold clientele. It suggested giving people funds or vouchers for tuition or medical service, permitting their "market" responses to service to guide agency service patterns.

While this questioning of coordination fetishism has been healthy in calling attention to the self-protective aspects of coordination, the anti-coordination solution is not yet an established one. The anti-coordination school of social services may discover, as did "free market" advocates in other fields, that waste is considerable, that one pays many prices for free competition, and that *a lack of joint planning does not necessarily place the consumer in the position of control.* Indeed the very reason for social services rather than cash benefits may be that one is dealing with a service in which the consumer cannot judge quality and finds it difficult to join with his fellows in exerting pressure on suppliers. Also, the client, given tuition funds, may not necessarily choose optimum education for his children. In a period of service shortages, all agencies may continue to be busy, so that the competition will not affect program.

One does not reject fully the arguments of the anti-coordination school, however. Complete program coordination, if it existed, probably would stifle initiative and block innovation. This is seldom a true danger, however. The degree of coordination that can be achieved among relatively sovereign agencies or bureaus even *within* one department, each of which may have

---

[14] Jean C. and Edgar S. Cahn, "The War on Poverty, A Civilian Perspective," *The Yale Law Journal*, 73, No. 8 (July, 1964), 1317–1352.

the support of professional and lay constituencies, usually leaves considerable free zones and areas for innovation and competition. The freedom is even greater by virtue of the fact that, in many fields, the related services are spread among *several* departments, organizations, or levels of government. In most of social welfare, the problem has been insufficient service and inadequate coordination to an extreme, rather than an excess of monopolistic self-protection. Whether in housing, counseling, job placement, or health, to cite only a few fields, the cry for program and policy coordination emanating from users and staff is not readily dismissed by a planner. What emerges *after* planning for coordination will, and probably should, still seem quite disorderly to the obsessive seeker for neatness and system—but it may come closer to helping the community achieve its objectives with only a tolerable degree of wastage.[15]

## THE SEARCH FOR BALANCE THROUGH RATIONALITY AND PREFERENCES

As suggested in Chapter V, a planning process may be devoted largely to settlement of a boundaries question. This is illustrated further, with reference to mental health, in Chapter VI of the companion volume. However, even after boundaries questions have been solved (or where boundaries are givens), the planner is often preoccupied during the programming phase with the "mix" among fields or subsectors of social welfare.

### The "mix" among fields

Effective program budgeting and feedback from cost-effectiveness studies, subjects to be discussed later, may eventually systematize this phase of programming and objectify the decisions about the size of components. For the present, one is called upon in most circumstances to assemble available experience and judgment. Decisions about mix become a matter of joining rationality to preferences and interest-group pressures.

The issue was noted by the United Nations Children's Fund conference

---

[15] Of some interest is the experience in the anti-poverty effort in the United States. When launched in 1964, it was a center of anti-coordination, arguing that coordination inhibited change strategies. By 1967, there was high priority on strengthening Office of Economic Opportunity instruments on all levels in their coordination roles.

In urging that the programming phase concern itself with coordination, we do not ignore Lindblom's impressive thesis to the effect that most operational coordination is a matter of mutual adjustment. Given the record of programming and operational problems, however, it is clear that we must provide more adequately for central coordination mechanisms as well. See Charles E. Lindblom, *The Intelligence of Democracy* (New York: The Free Press, 1968).

on planning for children in its stress on the complementarity among services in different fields. In the first instance, one considers those relations among sectors which must be planned because of life-cycle factors: children, most of whom are in contact with health services in infancy and early childhood, are then in contact with the educational authorities, for example. Relevant provision must be made. In addition, however,

> . . . there is also the simultaneous relationship in that different services complement each other. For example, it is not economic to push expenditure on schools beyond a certain point if pupils are hungry or ill. The synergistic aspect of the development of various social services has been pointed out in the World Social Survey. . . .
>
> It is clear that inadequate attention to relations among sectors may lead to dispersion of action, bottle-necks, and uneven development among sectors.[16]

One might illustrate the same point in many ways. Case treatment services oriented to interpersonal relationships do not get very far where people are concerned with finding adequate shelter for their families. Or, one cannot expect significant support for a correction program that offers to the antisocial members of the community a level of services not available to the deprived.

Central to our point, however, particularly where the planning is focused on a social problem (neglect, poverty, intergroup tension), on community development, or on delivery of services (city, region, country), is the notion of balance among sectors. Employment strategy must interweave with education, housing with health, and so forth. Here is a central programming task in which general principles are readily assented to—yet where accumulated wisdom is quite limited. Community preference may override planner calculation. One can urge only that each planning process proceed on the basis of the best available research rather than blindly, to permit some testing of hypotheses and assembling of knowledge. Several of the companion volume's chapters related to specific types of social planning illustrate efforts along these lines.

### Capital expenditures

Social welfare planning of a primitive sort has been initiated at times in the past as the result of conflict about capital investment plans. A debate about whether a new juvenile detention facility should be built may lead

---

[16] Herman D. Stein, Editor, *Planning for the Needs of Children in Developing Countries* (New York: United Nations Children's Fund, 1965), 20. On complementarity in programming, also see Hagen, *op. cit.*

to a study of detention needs and criteria and to a review of the anti-delinquency network. A conflict about the location of a community swimming pool may become the occasion for more comprehensive recreation planning.

Quite frequently, the planning of program content has been an after-thought following, or a by-product of, capital investment decisions. Far too often capital planning has ignored the implied commitment to future operational costs.

It is still quite common, for example, to plan schoolhouse space in relation to population trends and to leave programming for a late point in the process; but this occurs a little less frequently in the context of concern with quality education for the disadvantaged and where there is interest in the school's possibilities as a many-purpose community center.

It is quite common for architects to develop plans for institutions or community centers on the basis of limited knowledge of the intended program function—or with access only to traditionalist views. Sometimes, however, the new building is seen as an integral part of a departure in the interventive repertoire, so that service specialists and architects are called upon to plan jointly.

Capital funds are large and require considerable lead time for planning. Not surprisingly, these funds often command first attention and either initiate or monopolize the social planning process. This is true almost everywhere. One notes in France, for example, how social planning concerns at least initially were built into the national planning process by means of a procedure for making decisions about allocations for what is called "social equipment" (hospitals, schools, community centers, and the like).

Whatever the context, the planner will want to seek integrated planning, which encompasses capital investment, service staff, supplies, and operating expenses. Failure to attend simultaneously to all these elements is to court disaster; bricks and mortar which impede service; operational cost commitments which cannot be met; rooms without equipment; classes without rooms. An integrated overall effort is as relevant in cross-sectorial planning, as in attempts to introduce social concerns into a more general planning effort (a New Town, for example), as it is for planning within one field. If the general logic of the planning process, as sketched to this point, prevails, facilities are seen as program vehicles, not as ends in themselves. One would not consider bricks and mortar without providing for the function.

Program budgeting systems which combine capital and expense budgets automatically bring about such integration. They also project future operating costs, burdens assumed when the capital fund decisions are made—a major consideration in social welfare. A number of cities are currently launching such an approach to their total municipal budgeting processes.

## The interventive repertoire

The planner or planning team finds a major opportunity for innovation in the specification and planning of the interventive repertoire or service system (using these terms broadly to include income transfers, social utilities, and case services). There are problems of selection, scale, and mix.

In brief, the question is this: given the specified task and the policy choices made, what are the *possible program forms* and what is the case for each? On what scale should each program be introduced to assure needed complementarity and sound mix? Here the planner draws on the "technology and knowledge" inventory already made or undertakes such inventory if not prepared for an earlier phase. He requires the participation of experts from the relevant profession or technical fields. His task is to master and build on available experience while grasping opportunities for innovation and breakthrough.

Since, in most of social welfare in most places, resources are scarce and qualified personnel in short supply, the planner's office might display the following slogan: "Do not assume that we need *more* service. Maybe more *appropriate* service will do!"

No interventive typology will cover all fields of social welfare programming. The possible choices for consideration must therefore be lined up with reference to the expertise in the fields in which the work is being done. To *illustrate* the undertaking at this point we only can select several fields at random and indicate the types of choices currently facing planners. Further illustration is presented in the case studies of the companion volume.

*Probation and court services.*   To what extent does one wish to build on group methods for community-based treatment and "control" in contrast to the traditional individual "casework" in the community or commitment to an institution? Is the focus to be on the youngster as a family member or as an interacting member of a potent peer group? Should ongoing service be in the hands of the social worker who conducted the predisposition social study or the one who "worked with" the youth while he was in detention? Each of these and related decisions has considerable implications for staffing, organizational structuring, capital investment, and so on.

*Service to multi-problem families.*   Do we wish to develop the program under what is now often called an "opportunity approach," the use of supportive services so as to facilitate social mobility and participation? This would require an emphasis on retraining, basic education, and job placement. Health, counseling, and other supportive services would be built around these, with coordination in the hands of those conducting the "opportunity programs." Staff ratios would reflect this emphasis, as would organizational structure. A quite different interventive repertoire would result from a decision to emphasize cultural, educational, and therapeutic programming to achieve remotivational goals. Under this assumption, once successfully treated, the individuals involved would use the generally available job placement resources. The latter focus would require a much higher ratio of personnel qualified for therapeutic activity and would locate central responsibility in their hands.

A *housing "community."*    One type of planning strategy would assign to the process individuals able to contribute to the physical planning phase all possible social insights as to how physical structure will affect the community as a place to live: where will children of different ages play, given certain decisions about building layouts and relationships; how high may the building be if we want mothers to be comfortable in permitting young children to play outside alone; what kinds of sitting areas are needed for older folks; what are optimal apartment layouts for families at different points in the life-cycle; what type of "community space" must be left in clusters of high-rise buildings to permit future development of resources and programs which residents will initiate or select?

Another pattern involves choices during the programming phase of the beginning pattern of social facilities and resources which will be set up as soon as the buildings are completed: health station, day care, old-age center, youth clubs. Then one also specifies staffing, operational costs, administrative structure and provides for future decisions to be made about governing bodies, tenant participation, and related matters.

The planning staff in either instance is concerned with all possible components of a new housing community and the choices which are open. Economic realities, federal and state requirements, and planning decisions all enter.

*Individual counseling and the family unit.*    How will the projected service provide for aid and counseling, or psychotherapy, to individuals who require case services, taking into account modern knowledge of the family? Recent sociological and anthropological research has documented the extent to which the long-prevailing picture of the urbanized family as an isolated nuclear unit is inaccurate. Psychotherapeutic or counseling activity which ignores the kinship network even among the most sophisticated city-dwellers is likely to founder on unseen rocks. In the case of adolescents and adults, peer groups may also be potent forces, affecting the response to the therapeutic experience and negating the efforts of the helping agency.

As knowledge of this kind has reached psychiatrists, social workers, and psychologists, experiments have been launched in supportive work with family members, designed to facilitate the work with the individual patient; converting the therapeutic effort into a family-involving activity through one of several devices, including conjoint family therapy; making the relevant peer group (adolescent gang, mothers of delinquents, or mothers receiving Aid to Dependent Children) the therapeutic unit. The social service programmer will wish to consider such options rather than assuming that a one-to-one helping effort, *in vacuo*, will be adequate.

*Can "total institutions" help?*    Erving Goffman[17] has noted that certain intervention systems such as the mental hospital and the juvenile training school are often "total institutions," which erect effective barriers to social intercourse with the outside. Since rehabilitation is based on re-integration and re-acceptance, programs which block access become "storage dumps" for inmates—even though they present themselves as rational organizations seeking approved ends. The failure rates are very high if one applies rehabilitative criteria.

Because of this knowledge, social service programmers will want to consider objectives carefully and to determine the balance between community-protection and custody, for the small group of inmates who are not rehabilitable and are never to be released, and effective treatment for the many others. Continuity between institution and community and an easy two-way flow are essential to convert such facilities from total institutions into components of an integrated treatment and service network.

*Internal consistency in interventive components.*    Haphazard program development and fadism tend to create interventive systems which are self-defeating. The planner will want to avoid repetition of these errors. As an illustration, we may take the instance of the juvenile institution organized on an educational model. Its selection of boys, the living routine, and pattern of the discipline and the performance expectations are mutually consistent. Then, in response to development elsewhere, a psychiatric clinic is added to the institution. Rather than supporting the core program as conceptualized,

[17] Erving Goffman, "The Characteristics of Total Institutions," in Amitai Etzioni, Editor, *Complex Organizations* (New York: Holt, Rinehart & Winston, 1961), 312–340. Also, Erving Goffman, *Asylums* (Garden City: Doubleday & Co., Anchor paperback edition, 1961).

the clinic members act on principles more relevant to in-city private psychotherapy: they encourage "acting out," and do not report antisocial activity to authorities or hold high standards for classroom performance. Within a short time, the institution is in complete disarray.

Clearly, the central theme of the intervention, its basic logic and philosophy, must guide all else. The programmer will want to begin with specificity in this realm.

To conclude, the issue is what is the "bag of tricks" available for programming? What of all that is known and desirable is possible (as to costs, staffing, laws, sanction) in this instance? How may the selection optimize goal achievement? What are the implications of the choices for other aspects of the planning? What is "balance," and how is it to be achieved?

Here, as in the case of capital investment or mix from among fields, one assembles available experience, sharpens analysis of consequences of choices, appraises manpower and other resources, and brings preferences into the picture.

The outcome has at times been comprehensive and effective. However, guesswork is considerable, and the ability to balance many variables limited. Program budgeting, to be discussed in the next chapter, represents an attempt eventually to take advantage of the computer and general progress in quantification so as to codify and systematize the process further.

Interventions consist of persons, plus techniques, plus objectives. We turn, therefore, to some aspects of manpower programming.

## MANPOWER

It has been the experience everywhere, during the great social welfare expansion of the nineteen-fifties and -sixties, that the manpower "budget" is as critical as the monetary budget. In fact, the manpower budget is often more difficult to meet. Appropriations may be voted and taxes collected in a relatively short time. Manpower training, on the other hand, may be very complex and may require years of lead time. Inequitable resource distribution may take the form of disproportionate assignment of scarce manpower to programs for the more advantaged segments of the population and a "starving" of programs for the very poor.

One can arouse public opinion and achieve legislation for new educational programs, health services, or services to the mentally retarded (to select fields in which the illustrations are plentiful), only to find either that appropriations are unspent because of personnel shortages or that funds are wasted on inadequate services by an unprepared staff. Everywhere, the gap between a program as conceived and a service operation as experienced by users may be so great as to make any relationship unrecognizable—and the core of the difficulty may be in the domain of manpower.

To illustrate, Richard Titmuss has pointed out that major legislation in Great Britain did not succeed in its goal of abolishing the poor law because:

> The same people—the same administrators and workers—still had to run the hospitals, public assistance offices and welfare services. They poured into the new social service bottles the old wine of discrimination and prejudice. What was needed was a major effort of training, retraining and separation of functions of administrators, social workers and local officials.[18]

Remedies lie in several realms: a decision to create a completely new program rather than to be entrapped in the old organization; overall manpower planning; careful manpower programming for a given field or project; experimentation and innovation in manpower utilization. We here address the manpower questions, briefly, as relevant in the present context.

## Manpower planning

We cannot here examine either the social aspects of manpower planning or overall social welfare manpower planning in any detail. While we have not included it (having chosen other illustrations), one might illustrate the entire social planning process by referring to the need in a given country to undertake long-range planning for the recruitment, education, placement, ongoing training, and effective utilization of professional and technical personnel. The Organisation for Economic Co-Operation and Development offers a straw in the wind in its assertion that

> manpower policy should be dominated more by social and humanitarian considerations than by purely economic ones. . . . productive and freely chosen employment is a vital condition for the proper development of each individual's personality and is consequently the strongest factor for social stability.[19]

----

[18] Unpublished lecture, 1964. Also, see, Richard M. Titmuss, *Commitment to Welfare* (New York: Pantheon Books, 1968), 104–109.

[19] Organisation for Economic Co-Operation and Development, *Final Report, International Trade Union Seminar on Active Manpower Policy* (Paris, 1964), and *Supplement to the Final Report* (Paris, 1964, processed); Garth L. Mangum, Editor, *The Manpower Revolution: Its Policy Consequences* (Garden City, N.Y.: Doubleday & Co., 1965); Sar A. Levitan and Garth L. Mangum, *Making Sense of Federal Manpower Policy* (Michigan: Institute of Labor and Industrial Relations and Washington, D.C.: National Manpower Policy Task Force, 1967, pamphlet); *1965 Report of the Council of Economic Advisors and Economic Report of the President* (Washington, D.C.: Government Printing Office, 1965).

Indeed, so serious are the problems deriving from the lack of such overall manpower planning, as is suggested in the illustrations above, that many of the developed countries have undertaken basic research, projection, and policy planning covering the entire professional and technical manpower field or significant subsectors.[20]

In the United States, apart from the national efforts mentioned, several states have undertaken more or less extensive work, often in connection with the planning of state university and junior college systems, but sometimes to solve specific manpower problems facing the school system or hospitals.

In general, comprehensive manpower planning requires particularly careful estimation and projection as its points of departure. Since such fact-gathering must base itself on some assumptions about service models and staffing ratios, it may become a factor for the status quo or an element in innovation; it may be quite accurate or it may completely mispredict. Thus, the comprehensive manpower planning effort cannot avoid looking at the usual patterns of personnel deployment and seeking to determine the likelihood of change during the period in question. Expert opinion becomes important—as does the most recent and comprehensive experience available in manpower programming on given levels, in various fields, and in special projects. Special attention must be given to experimentation and innovation in manpower training and utilization. In effect, an imaginative manpower planning process may become a major force for change in a total field of service or sector. To some extent, then, unless undertaken in the context of a fairly comprehensive general planning effort, manpower planning almost

---

Shonfield notes in fact that, because in the post-World War II period manpower shortages were the limiting factors in Sweden's economic growth, an active manpower policy has become the heart of Sweden's economic planning. Andrew Shonfield, *Modern Capitalism: The Changing Balance of Public and Private Power* (New York: Oxford University Press, 1965), 201. Broad perspective for the United States is offered in National Manpower Council, *Manpower Policies for a Democratic Society* (New York: Columbia University Press, 1965); and Richard A. Lester, *Manpower Planning in a Free Society* (Princeton: Princeton University Press, 1966).

[20] See note above, as well as National Commission on Technology, Automation, and Economic Progress, *Technology and the American Economy*, Vol. 1 (Washington, D.C.: Government Printing Office, 1966). Also Edward E. Schwartz, Editor, *Manpower in Social Welfare* (New York: National Association of Social Workers, 1966); United States Department of Health, Education, and Welfare, *Closing the Gap in Social Work Manpower* (Washington, D.C.: Government Printing Office, 1965); Great Britain, Ministry of Health, *Report of the Working Party on Social Workers in the Local Health and Welfare Services* (London: Her Majesty's Stationery Office, 1959).

Problems in theory and research are reviewed in "Symposium on Manpower Theory," constituting *The Journal of Human Resources*, II, No. 2 (Spring, 1967).

inevitably faces the basic issues of all planning: the definition of the task and the policies which will support the achievement of the task.

To put it differently, a basic manpower planning undertaking cannot take the "demand" side as a given. Re-examinations of policies, services, modes of staff utilization, and patterns of organization have serious consequences for the projections.

At the "supply" end, the planning effort must relate itself, first, to general population projections as these affect the manpower reservoir. Then there are the projected consequences for the field(s) in question on the assumption of no change in the rate of attraction out of the available pool or of a continuation of existing trends in rate of attraction. Finally, there are the efforts to assemble empirical evidence, from available research generally or from experiments that are directly relevant, of how changes in manpower utilization, changes in salaries and fringe benefits, or other potential variations may be expected to affect recruitment rates.

Careful work is next required in fields such as the following (always projecting from the matching of supply-and-demand estimates, clarifying the assumptions built into each estimate, sometimes pursuing patterns of development based on competing premises—for lack of overwhelming evidence on the side of one):

☐  the creation or expansion of training facilities—including capital investment and training of trainers and teachers,
☐  the recruitment activity necessary to support the projections,
☐  the revisions in civil service and merit system titles, rules for interdepartmental-interagency-interregional mobility and vesting of fringe benefits in private industry, salary scales, and fringe benefits needed to implement and support the projections,
☐  the elaboration and effective introduction of innovations in staffing, interprofessional collaboration, and service modes which constitute the premises of the plans which have been made.

A careful system of reporting and feedback must be provided to monitor the implementation of any manpower plan. Given the complex system of assumptions and projections, and the inability of manpower planners to know everything about the political and overall economic context as it may affect their work several years ahead, there should be constant correction as needed.

## Programming for a field or project

During the programming phase of a given project or work, in a specific area or field, many of the uncertainties listed in the previous section may become "givens":

☐ The interventive repertoire has been defined.
☐ The administrative structure has been specified.
☐ The size of the operation has been generally settled.
☐ Relevant service models have been appraised and some decisions made about the issues posed.
☐ Basic decisions have been made as to a hierarchy of objectives, thus helping clarify some of the qualitative aspects of programming.

And, unless one is talking of a very large, major new national or regional program,[21] one may take as given the structure of education, training, recruitment, salaries and benefits, and so on. Where the program is to be comprehensive, the manpower planning must then be basic and extensive in the sense of the previous section.

Yet even the planner concerned only with a specific project or a limited field, involved in the manpower issue only at the programming phase—not as the heart of his planning effort—cannot completely ignore questions raised by any table of organization or system of job definition. In a sense, any social planning effort must adopt a staffing model appropriate to its policy thrust or must undertake innovation if an appropriate model is not available. In fields changing as rapidly as those which constitute social welfare, innovation looms as a constant requirement for the planner. Each step demands consciousness of what is being built in and of the consequences of decisions made.

An important outcome of the programming phase is a staffing plan based on such considerations as these and the explorations to which they lead. Assumptions should be specified as an aid to the plan's evaluation and processing—and to its ultimate monitoring. The manpower aspects of the plan should be quite detailed (as relevant): job categories, qualifications, salary levels, supervisory hierarchy, work-team organization, schedule for phasing-in (how many of which categories of personnel are to be hired at each stage of the project), staff location among the several program sites, structure of evaluation, and system of promotion.

## Experimentation and innovation in manpower utilization

Of special interest at present to those who undertake comprehensive manpower studies, as well as to the programmers of modest projects, is the accelerated interest during the nineteen-sixties in new patterns of personnel training and deployment in many health, mental health, public welfare, education, and other social service programs. Several factors are involved.

The first factor is the inability to recruit sufficient numbers of highly

---

[21] As in the case of the Joint Commission on Mental Illness and Health, *Action for Mental Health* (New York: Basic Books, 1961).

trained doctors, teachers, social workers, nurses, and so on. Thus, two innovators in use of neighborhood people as social service center staff members
comment that "we have no doubts that the professional service is the superior one." However, the choice is not between nonprofessional and professional service, "but rather between the nonprofessional service and no
service."[22]

Secondly, there is the discovery that nonprofessional paid workers, perhaps even people from the local neighborhood being served, have certain
advantages over highly-trained professionals for some purposes.[23]

As data began to accumulate about the "disengagement" of social services
from the very poor, the failure of school systems to reach certain groups of
pupils, the inability to recruit service-users in certain groups, the apparent
closing-out from programs of certain ethnic, racial, or cultural groups, manpower experiments were launched. Generally, these experiments involved
assigning members of such groups in "helper" roles as a device to make programs more accessible or useful. Schools used local mothers or adolescents
as "homework helpers," hospitals took them on as nurse's aides, public
health centers employed them as health aides, etc.[24]

The entire effort was accelerated by the anti-poverty effort which was
launched nationally in the United States in 1964. The self-help ideology of
the community action program supported the idea that neighbors could best
help neighbors. In some places, in their attack on existing establishments for
ignoring the needs of the poor or for rendering a type and quality of service
which perpetuated poverty, some anti-poverty community action personnel
described traditionally-trained professional workers as "irrelevant" and
argued that only so-called indigenous personnel could serve local needs.[25]

In an interesting variation on this process, there has also been a movement
to employ rehabilitated offenders, delinquents, alcoholics, drug addicts, or
school dropouts in programs of prevention and rehabilitation. People who
have suffered a disability are not readily "conned," yet know what is involved
in real help.[26] Some of the results have been most encouraging. In one

[22] Frank Riessman and Emanuel Hallowitz, unpublished progress report on Neighborhood Service Center project, 1965, Lincoln Hospital, New York.

[23] Arthur Pearl and Frank Riessman, New Careers for the Poor (New York: The Free
Press, 1965); "The New Nonprofessional," special issue of the American Child, 49, No. 1
(Winter, 1967).

[24] See Pearl and Riessman, op. cit., and "The New Nonprofessional."

[25] For an extreme example, see Haryou's Youth in the Ghetto (New York, 1964).

[26] Pearl and Riessman, op. cit.

variation of the process, building on Alcoholics Anonymous and similar self-help experience, *currently* addicted or maladjusted individuals are employed to help others. The very process of serving others provides motivation and support for self-help. (This is a natural outgrowth of therapeutic and rehabilitative techniques which bring groups together for self-help, turn ward management and orientation to ward procedures over to patients, and so on.)

Thirdly, it was discovered that existing systems for utilizing professionally trained staff were not efficient or effective. At a time of service shortages, long waiting lists, and service failures, it was noted that scarce and expensive professional manpower was not being well used. The medical and nursing professions had gone through the process long before, inventing a variety of aide and helper roles so as to conserve and deploy scarce manpower. In education and social work, however, to take illustrations where the process of discovery was slow, teachers were doing clerical work and lunchroom duty while they had insufficient time for educational tasks, and social workers were completing routine fact-sheet data or forms or answering routine questions, while more complex tasks were undone.

The result was a period of serious work throughout social welfare to filter out routine chores for assignment to personnel of other kinds and careful experimentation with differential use of personnel for various professional-semiprofessional-nonprofessional tasks in accord with levels of training.[27] In some places, there was considerable willingness to ignore formal qualifications and to place personnel on levels of job responsibility determined by performance criteria.

In several fields, the notion of team assignment in place of individual practitioner assignment to a case developed as part of the solution to the question of personnel utilization.[28] The doctor and his medical team in the hospital or clinic served as a partial model. Thus, a public assistance caseload or child welfare caseload might be assigned to a team consisting of a highly-qualified social caseworker, several aides, a nurse, and a clerk. A psychiatric clinic load would have a somewhat different team—as would a grade in an elementary school.

---

[27] For example, Edward E. Schwartz and William C. Sample, *First Findings from Midway* (Chicago: University of Chicago School of Social Service Administration, 1966, processed). Also see, Jean K. Szoloci, "Some Conceptual Issues in Social Welfare Manpower Statistics," *Welfare in Review*, 5, No. 3 (March, 1967), 1–12.

[28] Donald Brieland, *Differential Use of Manpower for Foster Care in a Public Child Welfare Program* (Springfield, Ill.: Department of Child and Family Services, June, 1964, mimeographed).

Fourthly, new developments arise from the growing proportion of the labor force available for the service sector, the decreasing need for unskilled workers, and the increased readiness to consider publicly-guaranteed work if the market does not assure a job.

These are three interrelated forces. Industrialization creates the desire for more service and a labor surplus available for service, whether in the market economy or the public and nonprofit sector.[29] At the same time, automation and the general improvement of technology create a labor surplus of the unskilled. Major investment in manpower training, counseling, and redeployment has characterized the 'sixties in the United States and Western Europe.[30] The general pattern involves an effort to upgrade the entire labor force—so that the unskilled move up one notch, so to speak. However, the United States anti-poverty effort has also included an attempt to take the least educated and unskilled and move them into direct service and aide positions of all sorts in the social welfare field.

Supporting this overall push is the call for government guarantee of work and for the government to play the role of employer of last resort.[31] As a practical matter it develops that, whether in business or organized labor, the fewest encounters with vested interests develop if publicly guaranteed work takes the form of jobs for the unskilled, uneducated, the "indigenous" in the social service sector. Health aides, child care aides, community block organizers, and teachers' helpers may be employed in an obvious expansion of service without poaching on anyone's established preserves.

Lastly, there are changes in function of agencies, deriving from new policies or new knowledge. If, within a public welfare program, one separates out the income security from the social service measures, the line job of the practitioner is changed and new jobs are created.[32] Opportunity for manpower innovation is opened up. Similarly, as the function of foster care is

---

[29] Victor R. Fuchs, *The Growing Importance of the Service Industries* (New York: National Bureau of Economic Research, 1965); Eli Ginsberg *et al.*, *The Pluralistic Economy* (New York: McGraw-Hill Book Company, 1965); Garth L. Mangum, Editor, *op. cit.*; National Commission, *Technology and the American Economy*.

[30] See *International Trade Union Seminar on Active Manpower Policy*. Also, Solomon Barkin, "A Current Focus for Industrial Relations Research," in Gerald G. Somers, Editor, *Proceedings of Seventeenth Annual Meeting of Industrial Relations Research Association* (Madison: University of Wisconsin, 1964), 2–19.

[31] A. Phillip Randolph Institute, *A Freedom Budget for All Americans* (New York, 1966).

[32] See Chapters IV and VII in the companion volume.

changed, or as large custodial institutions give way to urban group residences, new roles develop. These several types of motive have created a major ferment in social welfare manpower policy, which opens many new options to the planner at the point of programming. It would appear to be urgent, however, that clarity be sought in any given instance as to what the innovation is primarily interested in achieving. For, although the cumulative impact of the several factors provides considerable sanction for innovation, the motives do not necessarily lead in the same direction, and confusion as to goal hierarchies may prove to be self-defeating.

Thus, personal service and counseling programs, requiring but unable to attract sufficient professionally-qualified manpower, have placed subprofessionals in jobs—only to forget that new functions had to be defined. Unqualified staff attempting the functions actually requiring professional competence naturally lower the quality of service—and may cause damage. If a service is not staffed with over-qualified or inappropriately qualified personnel, a change in staff competence clearly must be accompanied by a realignment of roles.

On the other hand, when subprofessional and aide personnel are employed because they enjoy certain advantages which derive from their identification with the neighborhood and their freedom from certain disabilities which may characterize the professionally trained, the identification and desirable traits should be protected. Those who have worked with indigenous personnel report that apart from the errors made in original selection—since criteria are unclear—the largest problems are those deriving from over-rapid professional identification. Hired as effective communicators with neighborhood people, such personnel may soon be completely identified with the agency and its professional group. Their upward-mobility strivings may be as distorting as are the elements of social distance between middle-class professional workers and lower-lower-class clients. In fact, the job income often permits the newly-employed "indigenous nonprofessional" to move from the neighborhood in which he has been selected as a community link!

None of this is to discourage the process of identifying certain tasks as best filled by local, nonprofessional people. It does suggest the need for clarity at each step on the way—and for organizational supports which will help the new personnel do the job expected and assure that the recognition will come from appropriate job performance, not from identification with agency professionals and separation from peers. This is no small accomplishment, since in some ways it runs contrary to the ethic and to the normal dynamics of social stratification. As successful experience accumulates and is studied, planners will have much needed guidance as to how this vital development may be assured a higher success rate than it achieved in its exploratory phases.

There is a degree of danger that the confusion among the several categories of motives listed above will also result in inadequate development of one of the tendencies which antedated the anti-poverty effort and the employment of indigenous personnel. Specifically, progress was being made in differentiating within social work programs those tasks requiring less preparation. The points of departure were the functions to be filled and ways in which they might be subdivided and "packaged" to coincide with possible support by different levels of education. Comparable work was launched in other fields as well. While some of it has been continued and brought to fruition, part of the effort has been confused and sidetracked by other impulses and motives. Making work for people or enjoying the advantages of indigenous personnel are quite different things and deserve their own full development, but are not a substitute for the continuously-needed job analysis and the matching of function to level of preparation.[33] Nor should this latter process, in turn, be permitted to impede the response to need, knowledge, and social change that should constantly revise programs and thus create new professional and technical roles.

## Additional comments about manpower strategy

Manpower programming opens up a large number of other difficult issues, several of which must be mentioned at least briefly.

First, it should be noted, the planner will be blocked almost completely if he falls victim to the "strategic myth." It is quite "normal" for members of the various professions or technological "guilds" to stress the irreplaceable quality of certain of their skills.[34] The planner, on the other hand, must constantly check claims of professional and technical specialists against experience and research and be open to the lessons available.

Secondly, an alertness to the characteristics of the professions and bureaucracies is essential in programming. One cannot, for example, organize doctors in hierarchies of authority. Yet it is quite acceptable, adhering to

---

[33] Robert L. Barker and Thomas L. Briggs, *Differential Use of Social Work Manpower: Analysis and Demonstration Study* (New York: National Association of Social Workers, 1968).

[34] Robert K. Merton *et al.*, Editors, *Reader in Bureaucracy* (Glencoe, Ill.: The Free Press, 1952), especially Richard C. Myers, "Myth and Status Systems in Industry," 273–281.

professional norms and thus avoiding strain, to define supervision as consultation or advice.[35]

Then there is the issue of the relationship of specialization to efficiency in setting staffing policies. Since different people do different things, some degree of specialization is probably inevitable. The administrative and programming issue is one of finding dimensions for defining specialization which advance the objective rather than impede it. Does one specialize by geographic territory, by task, by institution? One answer will not hold for all professions and all scales of operation.[36] As we shall note in the next chapter, case integration and accountability roles and general information services may be needed to cope with the consequences of some inevitable specialization which complicates the delivery of services.

And service requirements, work rules, and union contracts will also enter into the planners' programming activity. The imposition of a 40-hour week undermines the traditional role of a homemaker coping with a family emergency, for example. Since the 40-hour week—and inevitably an even shorter week—is very much with us, plans must be made to assure coverage and to achieve the program goals in a new way. It may even be necessary to give up some of the older program forms, especially in child welfare, psychiatric care, medical service, and group work, if they depend on self-dedication and sacrifice by staff members to a degree no longer consistent with acceptable labor practices and recruitment of truly qualified personnel.

---

[35] Mary E. W. Goss, "Influence and Authority Among Patients in an Outpatient Clinic," *American Sociological Review*, 26, No. 1 (February, 1961), 38–50.

[36] Herbert A. Simons, "Some Further Requirements of Bureaucratic Theory" in Merton *et al.*, Editors, *op. cit.*, 52; Alfred J. Kahn, "Social Work Fields of Practice," in Harry Lurie, Editor, *Encyclopedia of Social Work* (New York: National Association of Social Workers, 1965), 750–754.

# IX

## PROGRAM BUDGETING AND COST EFFECTIVENESS

As EVIDENCE of the increase of planning at the national level in the United States brief reference has been made in Chapter II to the governmental commitment to a planning, programming, and budgeting system (PPBS). Perhaps symptomatic is the sudden and considerable increase in the literature of the subject,[1] which explores application of the system to the social sector generally and to traditional social welfare programs in particular. Especially relevant to the concerns of the present chapter is the utility of PPBS as a programming and administrative device.

### PPBS AND PLANNING

To many of its proponents the PPBS is a comprehensive and all-inclusive total planning process. The question therefore arises as to why it is here presented in the context of a programming chapter concerned with *administrative realization, including budgeting and staging, of previously arrived-at policies*. To answer, we must clear up confusions arising from the varied uses of the term programming.

---

[1] A comprehensive bibliography is provided by William Gorham, "Allocating Federal Resources Among Competing Social Needs," *Health, Education, and Welfare Indicators*, August, 1966, 1–13. Major sources for what follows here are David Novick, Editor, *Program Budgeting* (Cambridge, Mass.: Harvard University Press, 1965); Committee for Economic Development, *Budgeting for National Objectives* (New York, 1966); Charles J. Hitch, *Decision-Making for Defense* (Berkeley: University of California Press, 1965); Robert Dorfman, *Measuring Benefits of Government Investments* (Washington, D.C.: The Brookings Institution, 1965); Daniel Seligman, "McNamara's Management Revolution," *Fortune*, 72, No. 1 (July, 1965); H. S. Rowan, "Improving Decision-Making in Government" (Washington, D.C.: Bureau of the Budget, mimeographed, 1965).

Although there are inconsistencies, when program budgeters talk of "programming," they usually refer to major delineations of functions as related to core objectives. The illustrations cited in the literature and the efforts at formal conceptualization would seem to confirm our view (Chapter V) that specification of function (or analysis of the mission of a department or agency from the point of view of program) is essentially a policy-planning task whether or not encompassed in a PPBS process.[2] The PPBS advocates see some of this policy determination as an outgrowth of substantive analysis, while other aspects are essentially political. The entire PPBS process as they see it also encompasses the question of decisions relevant to the realization of policy through specific administrative steps and budgeting allocations.

Although one can regard PPBS as a *total* system of planning, our own preference remains for a deliberate, obviously arbitrary, but specific consideration of policy aspects of the conceptualization of functions before proceeding to issues relevant to the staging (or, in our sense, programming) of implementation and assignment of the required resources. Our approach appears especially relevant in fields in which the highlighting of questions of value and preference is important; in short, in the social field. However, as will be clear, this is not to minimize the light shed by the PPBS process on the interplay between policy and programming (in the sense of administrative structuring for implementation). The PPBS experience provides the most dramatic illustrations available of the sense in which the process is a circular one, with administrative and resource allocation considerations feeding back to the policy process and having major effect on policy choice.

As put by Hitch, systems analysis at the national level involves:

> . . . a continuous cycle of defining military objectives, designing alternate systems to achieve these objectives, evaluating these alternatives in terms of their effectiveness and cost, questioning the objectives and other assumptions underlying the analysis, opening new alternatives and establishing new military objectives, and so on indefinitely.[3]

All of this requires further elaboration. Budgets have traditionally served accounting and administrative control purposes, especially in government. They have tended to highlight personnel additions. Expense and capital

---

[2] For example, see Arthur Smithies, "Conceptual Framework for the Program Budget," in Novick, *op. cit.*, especially 34–43.

[3] Hitch, *op. cit.*, 52.

budgets have generally been separated. The units in budgets have been bureaus and departments. The time-span has been the calendar year, or the fiscal year or, in some states, the legislative biennium.

The PPBS reform has focused on the tasks to be accomplished, the functions to be discharged. One no longer assumes that previously-assigned personnel remain and that the budgetary debate is only about additions. A "new start" is not a promise of a growing program. Because capital investment commits one to long-time operating expenditures, the two are part of one budget. Where a function to be discharged covers a series of departments, bureaus, agencies, and levels of government, the analysis encompasses all that is relevant. Since any program may involve ongoing commitments, one computes likely costs for several years ahead, perhaps five. Where required, however, one also sorts out, for a traditional, annual budget, the department and bureau costs for a single year.

The process is many faceted and complex. It becomes possible only as the focus shifts from operating government and agency machinery to accomplishing specified objectives, and because of the development of computer technology. Government, agency, or industry is not relieved by program budgeting of the necessity for choice, but its choices are facilitated by machinery which makes visible as much as can be known about the "implications of alternatives." The skeptic may wonder whether government wishes to be as rational as this. Again our response is that all the tools of rationality should be lined up and available to the decision-maker. Where he deviates for political reasons, because of interest-group pressures or judgment about preferences, he has the right to do so with the facts clearly in mind and as much as possible about the costs known.

For the reality that has shifted the balance in favor of program budgeting is the recognized and articulated scarcity of resources. Even in a prosperous, advanced industrialized country, choices must be made. Funds are not unlimited. Trained and qualified manpower is usually in short supply. The old "requirements" approach which took each project, or field, or "need" on its own merits and translated these into budgets ignored the necessity of reconciling competing demands. Social welfare priority development tools focused only on preferences and interest groups, not on the optimization of resource use. PPBS and other programming systems ask not "A *or* B *or* C," but rather, "Given our objectives and resources, what is the optimum *mix* of A, B, and C?" In short, the crucial question of *mix*, previously presented as an issue for analysis, may be translated into a technical question. The PPBS focuses on optimization: *the particular combination of objectives, resources, and scheduling which comes closest to greatest efficiency and ef-*

*fectiveness.* And it is the careful work required of a PPBS in relation to identification of "output" (objectives) and inputs which makes meaningful both the comparison of alternatives and the search for a "mix."[4]

Banfield illustrates from the field of education:

> ... consider how a school superintendent might act if his budget were raised to permit him to improve the education of his pupils. If he adopted the requirements approach, he would (let us say) hire more teachers because he knows that a higher ratio of teachers to children improves teaching. On the other hand, if he adopted the economizing or systems analysis approach, he would break the end "to improve education" into component ends (e.g., to improve the reading ability of handicapped children, to improve the math of college-bound ones, etc.) and then decide the terms on which he would trade off a marginal unit of benefit in terms of one end for a marginal unit of benefit in terms of another. At the same time he would be examining all the plausible ways of achieving the various ends that he seeks. He would carry on research to find out the marginal rate of return (in terms of his various ends) of investment in (say): 1. additional teachers, 2. raising teachers' salaries, 3. employing television and "teaching machines," and 4. buying additional laboratory equipment. He would take into account as benefits and costs any side-effects that could be anticipated (e.g., the influence this or that action might have on the morale of the parents of the handicapped children). In the end he might well conclude that no course of action was best by all relevant criteria. . . . This in itself would have prevented him from making the most serious errors.[5]

As will be noted shortly, the organizational and conceptual obstacles are considerable and the solutions should not be oversold. At present PPBS is a useful but quite imperfect tool, which is perhaps most valuable for programming in the more restricted sense of this chapter than as intended by expansive enthusiasts. It does, however, hold out the possibility of increasing translation of some of the policy issues already described into empirical questions. Then one becomes less likely to accede to "either-or" solutions, given the possibility of a calculated mix.

The PPBS story is usually told in the connection with its Defense Department applications, sometimes in the context of its use as a device to consolidate a Secretary's power. In the process of popularization the tale has become oversimplified and vulgarized. The development actually involved careful work to specify functions as relevant to all services and as embodying the mission as conceived by the political arm and by the public. Then the

---

[4] See especially, Smithies, in Novick, *op. cit.*, 25–27.

[5] Edward C. Banfield, "Three Concepts for Planners," in Edward C. Banfield, Editor, *Urban Government* (New York: The Free Press, 1969; rev. ed.), 613–614.

groundwork had to be done to identify relevant "impacts" throughout government, develop adequate computer programs, and also facilitate production for Congressional use of the more traditional Annual Budget as well. This is certainly more than the search for answers to "how much bang for a buck?"—or, "what is the least cost for a given defense level?"—even though the cost-effectiveness question, to which we shall return, is part of the analytic process in seeking optimization. The general success of the enterprise, at least in the eyes of its chief consumer, the President of the United States, is attested by the August 25, 1965, order for application of the system to other departments. Subsequently, Defense Department personnel and others involved in developing the system, particularly at the Rand Corporation, moved into strategic locations in the federal government and into many other levels throughout the country to help teach and implement the process. At the present time, all of this remains in an early phase and serious obstacles are encountered in translation into social welfare operations.[6]

One of the by-products of the entire endeavor has been the increased understanding that a well-organized budget is a major tool for both planning and programming, whether or not in the context of a PPBS. One of its enthusiastic proponents puts it this way:

> [Budgeting] is related to the complete administrative range from analysis through planning to management and control. In its end product, the budget, it summarizes (1) the problems to which analysis has been applied, (2) the analytic concepts and techniques brought to bear on these problems, (3) the information relevant to their solution, (4) the proposed (ultimately, the determined) decisions, and (5) the administrative structure through which performance of the approved budget will be executed, controlled, and appraised.[7]

To understand somewhat more completely the bridge which thus has been constructed between policy and programming (in our sense), and between both of these phases and budgeting, it is useful to examine in more detail the components of a PPBS. Special attention will also be given to

---

[6] See, especially, Hitch, *op. cit.*; Novick, *op. cit.*; Gorham, *op. cit.* Also see, Special Section, "PPBS: Its Scope and Limits," *The Public Interest*, No. 8 (Summer, 1967), 4–48, especially William Gorham, "Notes of a Practitioner"; and Joint Economic Committee, *The Planning-Programming-Budgeting System: Progress and Potentials*, "Hearings: September 14, 19, 20 and 21, 1967," and "Report" (Washington, D.C.: Government Printing Office, 1967), in 2 vols. The "Hearings" summarize beginnings in a number of states and cities and include illustrative cost-benefit analyses in several fields.

[7] Melvin Anshen, "The Federal Budget as an Instrument for Management and Analysis," in Novick, *op. cit.*, 1.

cost-benefit or cost-effectiveness studies (terms used here interchangeably), a tool of PPBS but also a procedure which has independent existence and separate importance.

## THE ELEMENTS OF A PPBS

As seen by PPBS adherents, since no country can pursue *all* objectives which citizens consider as desirable, or very many single objectives to their *fullest*, there is a constant process of compromise. Resources, goals, and techniques interact. It is the function of planning, programming, and budgeting in the PPBS sense to seek compromises rationally. Money becomes the common denominator in which various possibilities are expressed. The goal is: "resources (money) used in 'optimal' or preferred ways to achieve policy objectives."[8]

The total PPBS process therefore involves:

1. Appraisals and comparisons of various government activities in terms of their contributions to national objectives.
2. Determination of how given objectives can be attained with minimum expenditure of resources.
3. Projection of government activities over an adequate time horizon.
4. Comparison of relative contributions of public and private activities to national objectives.
5. Revision of objectives, programs and budgets in the light of experience and changing circumstances.[9]

Conceptually, the critical step is the delineation of what the PPBS expert sees as "programs": in our terminology, it is the specification of functions relevant to the accomplishment of the task. Programs are usually, but not always, oriented to the end products of the organization. The pioneering Defense Department system, for example, adopted the following "program structure":

☐ *strategic retaliatory forces*—interchangeable and complementary components, cutting across different services, focused on a defined mission
☐ *continental defense*—while protecting the strategic forces, the continental system also has its own role
☐ *general purpose forces*—ready forces to be transferred to meet non-strategic attacks anywhere
☐ *airlift and sealift*—contributes to the mobility and capability of general purpose force but large enough for special focus
☐ *reserve and national guard force*—another "cut"

---

[8] Smithies, in Novick, *op. cit.*, 25.
[9] *Ibid.*, 26–27.

☐ *research and development*—concentrates on items "beyond the horizon" but constantly transferring to other programs
☐ *general support*—general overhead and items not clearly assignable
☐ *military assistance*
☐ *civil defense.*[10]

A natural resources program budgeting system might be arranged either by functions or resources:

BY FUNCTIONS
☐ natural resources research
☐ natural resources development
☐ natural resources management and conservation
☐ natural resources regulation to resolve conflict

BY RESOURCES
☐ land resources
☐ water resources
☐ forest resources
☐ recreational resources
☐ nonoceanic fish and wildlife resources
☐ oceanic resources
☐ mineral resources
☐ air resources.

The choice of the first of the principles of classification would result in the use of the second for subclassification. Werner Z. Hirsch has illustrated a program budgeting system in which categories of resources provide the major classification and functions offer the subclassification.[11]

A preliminary attempt at program budgeting in health employs the following major categories: control and prevention; treatment and restoration; long-term care and domiciliary maintenance; training; research; other.[12]

In the space field, because "it is possible to associate most space expenditures and most of the effort expended on space activities with specific physical systems," categorization for budgeting appears quite natural and logical. Nor are there problems arising from intergovernmental relations, as is true in most fields. The "projects" involved in a program are identifiable as:

☐ manned space flight
☐ space applications

[10] Adapted from Smithies, in Novick, *op. cit.*, 37–38, or Novick, *op. cit.*, 92–94. Or see Hitch, *op. cit.*

[11] Werner Z. Hirsch, "Program Budget for Natural Resource Activities," in Novick, *op. cit.*, Chap. 9.

[12] Marvin Frankel, "Federal Health Expenditures in a Program Budget," in Novick, *op. cit.*, Chap. 8.

☐ unmanned investigations in space
☐ space research and technology
☐ aircraft technology
☐ supporting operations.

However, the obvious interdependence of elements is a serious complicating factor in subsequent cost-utility and trade-off analysis. Multiple use of facilities and spin-off of results are not readily predictable.[13]

A program budget in education might employ such major categories as: primary education, secondary education, higher education, adult education, library services, research and development, international education. For some purposes, these are better regarded as subcategories under the general headings: grants, loans.[14]

Clearly, the choice of programs is both strategic and difficult. In public welfare, for example, one might create a separate program for eligibility investigations or one might integrate eligibility and social service. The latter reflects administrative reality; the former is a policy advocated by some. Yet inability to separate the two in a budget or organizationally ties the planner's hands. Similarly, if one wishes to classify by categories of recipients, are mothers of young children to be placed with those for whom employment and other self-support investments are to be made?

Smithies, on whom we have relied most heavily on the subject of criteria for programs, suggests that one important criterion for structuring a program is its utility in permitting:

> comparison of alternative methods of pursuing an imperfectly determined policy objective. Thus, the need for public assistance can be clarified and analyzed by breaking down the problem into the needs arising from old age, economic dependency, physical disability and unemployment.[15]

Decision-makers may be presented with very detailed computations of "alternative structures" and their costs, even though the responsible staffs indicate preferences.[16] (Where either quantitative or qualitative data about absolute or relative effectiveness of different approaches are available or can be obtained, these are included.)

One sometimes creates a program as a way of putting a requirement which might be met in several ways—so that alternatives may be compared (reloca-

---

[13] Milton A. Margolis and Stephen M. Barro, "The Space Program," in Novick, *op. cit.*, especially 125–133.

[14] Werner Z. Hirsch, "Education in Program Budget," *ibid.*, Chap. 7.

[15] Smithies, in Novick, *op. cit.*, 42.

[16] Novick, in Novick, *op. cit.*, 95–96.

tion in urban development?). Where one part of an organization supplies relatively expensive services to one or more others (computers, training?), a separate program may be justified. Sometimes a particular time pattern justifies a separate program, as in the already-cited instance of research and development. Clearly, the result involves a degree of overlapping and logical inconsistency. Identification of programs is a process of delineating major categories so as to capture major objectives and goals, doing so in a fashion which makes sense to policy-makers and administrators; utilizing units which lend themselves to consideration of alternatives; while still seeking categories across traditional bureau or unit or departmental lines to sharpen the choices available.

Where two major principles of organization suggest themselves, as in the natural resources or educational illustrations, one set of program categories may provide subcategories while the other offers the major headings. Choice in this instance may be a matter of trial and error. The experiences suggest the utility of classification by two or three principles in a PPBS undertaking to maximize results.

In general, one is suspicious in any large organization, such as a federal or state department or a very large voluntary social welfare agency, of any system of program categories that coincides exactly with existing department or bureau lines. Normal organizational growth creates overlapping, competition, and duplication, and one wants a program budgeting system to be a device towards coordination and restoration of efficiency.

Once classification by program has taken place, there is an assembling of the known and the conduct of empirical investigation to clarify the potential costs and relative effectiveness of alternative program *elements* over different periods of time. With reference to the relocation illustration, relevant elements might be retraining, counseling, day care, refurnishing the apartment, moving the family, etc. Cost-benefit analyses are examined or carried out (*see below*). Interplay among elements, a complicating factor in a PPBS, is explored. Capital investment, lead time, ultimate costs, and ultimate benefits of each, to the extent known or knowable, are looked at. As already suggested, the process is aimed not only at choices among some true alternatives, but also at optimizing the mix of other elements. We shall not here enter into the computer-program aspects of the process.

One of its creative aspects is an ability to relate the impact of new knowledge and technology to the projection of budgets for several years ahead. What is involved specifically is changing the proportion of the whole provided by a specific program. In social services, for example, one might increase the proportion of the total service rendered by home-care facilities, in contrast to custodial institutions. One might also apply changing rates for need of service, after launching prevention programs of known reliability (economic aid, homemakers, and day care), which affect the number of children actually coming into care. The illustration is hypothetical; we do not know of any such comprehensive calculation.

Because some of the assumptions are tenuous, what emerges should be a "rolling plan" or a "rotating plan": it may look ahead for five years, but it is revised annually as the predictions, projections, and chain of expectation are checked with what has actually occurred. A formalized system for corrections is built into the process.

The acceptance of a program budget is followed by the adoption of an annual budget for each of the departments or sub-units which must carry out the subprograms, the implementation of manpower and administrative implications, and the launching of the specified activities and construction. Since, by the very nature of the process, administrative lines at any moment cannot coincide with program lines and are not generally regrouped so as to coincide, executive power, allocational procedures, and internal coordinating devices are needed to assure that a program concept on paper actually becomes an operational guide. At any given moment, program budgeters need to concern themselves with the organizational and administrative steps relevant to achievement of the programs.

## COST-BENEFIT OR COST-UTILITY ANALYSIS

All program budgeters emphasize that the system has no meaning unless it includes cost-utility studies en route. However, such studies have their independent worth and are valuable to planners even where a PPBS has not been undertaken.

What is at stake is an analytical process:

> The heart of the process is emphasis on a systematic examination of alternative courses of action and their implications. This process has a variety of names, such as cost-benefit analysis, cost-effectiveness analysis, systems analysis, operations research, and others. . . . The phrase cost-utility analysis was suggested. Being new, this phrase is probably less confusing than the others.[17]

The growing literature on the methods to be employed in such analyses is quite clear about procedures, even though there are important technical debates as well as serious controversies as to whether, in view of the diffi-

---

[17] George A. Steiner, "Problems in Implementing Program Budgeting," in Novick, *op. cit.*, 310–311.

culty of quantifying "human benefits," the enterprise is useful to the social planner.[18]

Hitch, crediting his predecessor as Defense Comptroller, W. J. McNeil, quotes Benjamin Franklin on the significance of cost-benefit analysis:

> How to make a STRIKING SUNDIAL, by which not only a Man's own Family, but all his Neighbors for ten Miles round, may know what a Clock it is, when the Sun shines, without seeing the Dial.
>
> Chuse an open Place in your Yard or Garden, on which the Sun may shine all Day without any Impediment from Trees or Buildings. On the Ground mark out your Hour Lines, as for a horizontal Dial, according to Art, taking Room enough for the Guns. On the Line for One o'clock, place one Gun; on the Two o'clock Line two Guns, and so of the rest. The Guns must all be charged with Powder, but Ball is unnecessary. Your Gnomon or Style must have twelve burning Glasses annex't to it, and be so placed that the Sun shining through the Glasses, one after the other, shall cause the Focus or burning Spot to fall on the Hour Line of One, for Example, at One a Clock, and there kindle a Train of Gunpowder that shall fire one Gun. At Two a Clock, a Focus shall fall on the Hour Line of Two, and kindle another Train that shall discharge two Guns successively: and so of the rest.
>
> Note, There must be 78 Guns in all. Thirty-two Pounders will be best for this Use; but 18 Pounders may do, and will cost less, as well as use less Powder, for nine pounds of powder will do for one Charge of each eighteen Pounder, whereas the Thirty-two Pounders would require for each Gun 16 Pounds.

---

[18] In addition to the citations already given from the Novick volume, it includes Gene H. Fisher, "The Role of Cost-Utility Analysis in Program Budgeting," 61–80.

Other major sources drawn upon are: Robert Dorfman, Editor, *Measuring Benefits of Government Investments* (Washington, D.C.: The Brookings Institution, 1965); Abraham S. Levine, "Cost Benefit Analysis and Social Welfare," *Welfare in Review*, 4, No. 2 (February, 1966), 1–11 (includes comprehensive bibliography); Abraham S. Levine, "Cost Benefit Analysis of the Work Experience Program," *Welfare in Review*, 4, No. 7 (August–September, 1966), 1–9; Bent Anderson, *Work or Support* (Paris: Organisation for Economic Co-Operation and Development, 1966); United Nations Research Institute for Social Development, *Cost Benefit Analysis of Social Projects*, Report of a Meeting of Experts Held in Rennes, France (Geneva: United Nations Research Institute for Social Development, 1966); Gary S. Becker, *Human Capital* (New York: National Bureau of Economic Research, 1964); Morris H. Hansen and Genevieve W. Carter, "Assessing Effectiveness of Methods for Meeting Social and Economic Problems," in Leonard H. Goodman, Editor, *Economic Progress and Social Welfare* (New York: Columbia University Press, 1966), 92–124; Gerald G. Somers and Ernest W. Stromsdorfer, "A Benefit-Cost Analysis of Manpower Training," *Proceedings, Industrial Relations Research Association, 1964* (Madison, Wisconsin: Industrial Relations Research Association, 1965), 172–185.

Note also, That the chief Expense will be the Powder, for the Cannon once bought, will with Care, last 100 Years.

Note moreover, that there will be a great Saving of Powder in Cloudy Days.

Kind Reader, Methinks I hear thee say, That is indeed a good Thing to know how the Time passes, but this Kind of Dial, notwithstanding the mentioned Savings, would be very Expensive; and the Cost greater than the Advantage. Thou art wise, my Friend, to be so considerate before-hand; some Fools would not have found out so much, till they had made the Dial and try'd it. . . . Let all such learn that many a private and many a publick Project, are like this Striking Dial, great Cost for little Profit.[19]

As noted by Dorfman, a cost-benefit analysis "is closely analogous to the methods of investment project appraisal used by businessmen. The only difference is that estimates of social value are used in place of estimates of sales value when appropriate." While several approaches to accomplishing the analysis are followed, they generally begin with projecting the relevant program output for some relevant unit of time: children to be educated in high school in a given year or over a period of years; dropouts to be prevented; families to be housed; illnesses of a given kind to be cured; delinquents to be apprehended, etc. Then one puts a social value on the product —again in a time perspective: increased lifetime earnings of the high school graduates; productivity and decreased community care costs of dropouts restored to school; improved health and better school attendance of a better-housed family; money saved in care of cured or arrested patients; potential property damage by apprehended delinquents, etc.

Gross benefits are sometimes calculated for a typical year (later to be compared with costs for a typical year). Costs, in turn, consist of current operating costs plus a charge levied on that year's operations of the cost of amortizing the capital costs (construction and installation). Under this approach, the ratio calculated is the relationship of "gross annual benefits to total annual costs." (This is similar to the businessman's calculation of the ratio of sales income to the cost of goods sold.)

Under one of several alternatives, current costs in a given year or a typical year, or over several relevant years, are subtracted from gross benefits—as calculated in the above fashion—to estimate current net benefits. The

current net benefits for each year are discounted back to the date of inception of the project and added up to obtain an estimate of the present value

---

[19] Hitch, *op. cit.*, 74.

of discounted net benefits. The ratio of this figure to the estimated capital cost of the project is then the benefit-cost ratio.

In effect, this is the equivalent of a businessman's estimate of the rate of return on a given investment. One can work with the past alone or project into the future—in the light of given assumptions.[20]

Each of the steps and alternatives involves careful work, defense of assumptions, and—for the social field—substantial difficulties. Since it is our purpose here to introduce the notion of such analytic efforts as essential to any PPBS and as themselves independently valuable in many contexts, rather than to offer a procedural manual, we shall merely inventory some of the complex steps and then illustrate briefly:

*Categorization of groups or units which may be affected by the programs or policies.* At times this is specific and simple; at other times it may be complex or amorphous. Choice of physical boundaries may become quite complicated.

*Listing of various impacts.* One usually evaluates the obvious effects, such as the increased productivity and earning potential of a better educated person. In this instance, however, education may also (among many other things) be said to enrich people's lives culturally, to improve socialization and social control, to serve as a vehicle for redistribution, to add to the demand side of the economy. Different types of indicators are needed for macro-decision-making in social policy (health *versus* educational investments) than for technical choices within a given field. Then there are the direct and indirect effects, as well as the complementaries among efforts which may come together.[21]

*Placing a price on each type of impact.* Even where so-called market-type values seem reasonable (housing units provided by a public program, for example), the price is not readily set. After all, one is undertaking cost-benefit analysis precisely in those fields in which the market does not govern. There are many philosophical and technical questions relative to actual and imputed prices (shadow prices), items which can be counted but not

---

[20] The above follows Dorfman's summary. The quotations are from pages 6–8.

[21] Putting aside the many circumstances in which it is not possible to arrive at conceptual agreement as to what measurement of impact is relevant to assessing benefits, Gorham notes that often the analyst knows what to measure but cannot obtain the data. We do not pursue this problem here, because it obviously can be solved if there is commitment to such analyses. See Gorham, "Notes of a Practitioner," 6.

Burton Weisbrod urges that public programs be examined both for efficiency and for redistributive effects. Burton A. Weisbrod, "Income Redistributive Effects and Benefit-Cost Analysis," in Samuel B. Chase, Editor, *Problems in Public Expenditure Analysis* (Washington, D.C.: The Brookings Institution, 1968).

readily priced, and items for which quantification hardly seems possible or reasonable. (Many social policy analysts argue that it is of the very nature of the social sector that efforts to value all outputs in monetary terms are invalid.)

*Clarifying just which alternatives should be simultaneously investigated, for the possibility of a higher benefit-cost ratio.* Sometimes the issue is: which method will give the needed results at the lowest cost? At other times one needs to know which method gives the largest return for a given fixed investment. Cost-benefit studies in PPBS may be either of these types. In still other cases, one simply wants some assessment of output for a given investment, not in a context where one is making choices or seeking a mix— but rather to know whether a program is worthwhile, by some specified yardstick.

*Choosing the relevant time-stream for the analysis.* Over what period does one allocate costs or measure benefits? A wrong decision may distort the results.

*Choosing discount rates.* The issue of whether an investment is considered a relatively profitable one will depend on the rate selected. Many value and political issues enter. Current analysts tend to find the rate of return on equivalent capital in the commercial market an unsatisfactory criterion.

*Computing opportunity costs.* Determining what other uses might have been made of the personnel or resources over time and, thus, allowing for the earnings which one must forgo in order to embark on the project.

*Determining social opportunity costs.* The issue is not only lost earnings, but also other social costs for the adoption of a particular project rather than some other, or none at all.

With reference to the problem of measuring social or human benefits, one might reproduce an elaborate debate from the literature or just summarize briefly as follows: there are many interesting ideas but no generally perceived solutions as yet. Governmental and voluntary social sector programs are by their nature certainly not meant to validate themselves by the price criteria of the market. Some obviously have positive outcomes that cannot be reported in nonmonetary quantitative terms. One must follow one of two strategies or adopt both in combination:

Limit the quantitative benefit analysis to those things which can be converted into money equivalents or some other quantitative measures, recognizing that this is only part of the picture. One then uses these findings in combination with qualitative criteria and preference material to arrive at final appraisals.

Or, invent ways of assigning money equivalents or other quantitative weights so as to reflect social valuation of the outputs. Though there is a degree of arbitrariness in this procedure, it is not unlike what is done in all types of cost-benefit analyses. When decisions are made about discount rates, shadow prices, time-streams, one emerges with quantification on the foundation of qualitative judgments—even in so-called rigorous cost-benefit work.

Norman Scott has summed up some of the major components of costs and benefits of any single project in an outline, which places the above dimensions in general perspective. When more than one project in a given field, or projects in different fields, are being analyzed, it is also necessary to cope with issues of physical and economic interdependence.

*Costs and Benefits*

*Direct*                                                                 *Indirect*

*Type*
(a) Monetary
    (i) Capital
    (ii) Current
(b) Non-monetary
*Origin or destination*
(c) Individual (problem of averages)
(d) Local (micro-economic)
(e) National (macro-economic)
*Time-horizon*
(f) Immediate future
(g) Near future
(h) Distant future.[22]

Scott, a friendly critic of cost-benefit studies in the social field, sums up his exploration of attempts to cope with all the complexities as follows:

> . . . it is an infant discipline with a very slim dossier of case studies to its credit. Its aims are undoubtedly laudable . . . it is a welcome response to a genuine need . . . its practitioners employ scientific methods. . . .

> But . . . the methods so far developed fail to provide unequivocal criteria of choice in the real world of physical and technical interdependences and budgetary constraints . . . cost-benefit analysis has so far been more suited to justifying decisions already taken . . . than to pointing to *which* project should be understaken. This is so because knowledge of the extent and character of . . . physical interdependence is still lacking, and because sufficiently refined techniques for assimilating nonquantifiable costs and benefits to rigorous comparison have not yet been devised.[23]

---

[22] Norman Scott, "Some Problems of Cost Benefit Analysis of Social Projects," in *Cost Benefit Analysis of Social Projects*, 34.

[23] *Ibid.*, 63.

Some of the work done is useful, interesting, suggestive, and promising. The PPBS upsurge will serve to increase motivation to solve some of the methodological problems and improve procedures.

Under the inspiration and leadership of T. W. Schultz, the major figure in the economics of education, a variety of students have looked at education from a cost-benefit point of view as an investment in human capital.[24] The premise is that resources made available to people in such forms as schooling, on-the-job training, medical care, and migration might be conceived of as investments in human capital. The resultant improvements in knowledge, skills, and health may be expected to increase subsequent monetary and "psychic" income. Interest in understanding the differential return from investments of various kinds in human capital has followed from the widespread discovery that "the growth of physical capital, at least as conventionally measured, explains a relatively small part of the growth of income in most countries."[25] Nor does a readiness to study economic effects of such investment imply denial of the importance of other effects. The premise is that economic effects per se are worthy of understanding.

Within this context, valuable work has been done, and planners may in the future be in possession of valid comparative data, which could be used for programming decisions. For example, there are tentative solutions to the problem of how to differentiate in the analysis such variables as the rate of return, the amount invested, and the investment period.[26] There are suggestions for coping with the problem of the correlation between "ability" and the amount of education. Several different approaches confirm that "college education itself explains most of the unadjusted earning differential between college and high school graduates.[27] While the rate of return for investment in college education is highest for white males who go on to graduate, even when adjusted for differential ability, "rates to cohorts of college dropouts, non-whites, women and rural persons . . . are also far from negligible."[28]

Gary S. Becker has also shown in a retrospective analysis that it is possible to compute changing rates of return for investment over time as well as to look at the pattern for a given cohort. Finally, he has looked at the effects of investment in college education on national productivity, comparing the

[24] Gary S. Becker, *Human Capital* (New York: National Bureau of Economic Research, 1964). Also see, Burton A. Weisbrod, "Investing in Human Capital," *The Journal of Human Resources*, I, No. 1 (Summer, 1966), 5–21.

[25] Gary S. Becker, *op. cit.*, 1.

[26] *Ibid.*, Chap. III.

[27] *Ibid.*, 88.

[28] *Ibid.*, 104.

returns with similar investment in business capital. Because much that is relevant is not known (side-effects, spill-offs, unknown costs), results are incomplete.

Becker and others in this field know that their work is preliminary and many questions have gone unanswered. One would, of course, want to confirm the stability of the data in changing social contexts, but it would seem that the PPBS planner could obtain useful facts about investments in education. He would want to add to such findings other relevant considerations as he assesses alternative investments—but he would find in such analyses useful points of departure.

In another field, manpower training, the efforts of Gerald G. Somers and Ernst Stromsdorfer illustrate the complexities involved in seeking to develop a satisfactory system. The research shows constant employment advantages of Manpower Development and Training Act (MDTA) trainees over relatively similarly situated control group members. In fact (by a regression analysis), training is second only to prior labor-force experience in explaining employment success, and trainees also have significant advantages in earnings. The researchers then attempt to feed "training cost" into the analysis, even though it is difficult to be precise, since one must consider both direct costs and allowances. Even more complex is the problem of income forgone—opportunity costs—during training; there are costs for the individual and for society.

The authors have computed the "pay back" period, the time it takes to "repay" these costs: it is relatively brief for males, longer for females. Finally, an effect is also made to see the training investment in terms of its contribution to the increase of the worker's capital value. A complex formula is necessary wherein gains in monthly earnings and post-training total income are related to costs of the training period by means of a chosen rate of discount.[29]

Here one sees the complexity, ingenuity, difficult assumptions, and general usefulness of current cost-benefit efforts in the social welfare field. One also notes that basically the method does not cope with many "human gains" which may be very important: changes in self-image, status, family response, satisfaction, and so on, which may also be direct results of such training.[30]

Nor do cost-benefit studies have any way to take latent functions of pro-

---

[29] Gerald G. Somers and Ernst W. Stromsdorfer, "A Benefit-Cost Analysis of Manpower Training," in Gerald G. Somers, Editor, *Proceedings of the Seventeenth Annual Meeting of the Industrial Relations Research Association* (Madison, Wisconsin: Industrial Relations Research Association, 1965), 172–185.

[30] Efforts to solve this defect are under way, but there are those who consider the pricing or even quantification of all human gains as conceptually contradictory.

grams or unexpressed goals into account. For example, cost-benefit analyses of the anti-poverty Neighborhood Youth Corps would not ordinarily have assessed the efforts in terms of anti-summer-riot "insurance."

With reference to conscious social goals and manifest human benefits, there are those who do believe that cost-benefit methods can contribute to planning. Such a position would not allow confinement of cost-benefit analyses to economic gains measured in prices through study only of economic efforts, side-effects, and sacrifices of alternative measures. In an ingenious analysis, noting how precarious it would be to rely on dollar measures imputed from market prices to make interprogram or intraprogram decisions in public recreation, Ruth P. Mack and Sumner Meyers experiment with a unit which they call a "merit weighted user day." In brief, relevant criteria (interest in conservation, distributive justice, government yardstick role, desire to encourage private recreation, desire to charge for some types of recreation, "modest" but adequate standard for those unable to pay, etc.) are introduced to assess alternatives and provide the weighting. These weightings are applied to expected use to get the "score" for each alternative. Only those criteria are employed in a given analysis which deal with variables not shared by all the options.[31]

Bent Andersen, in an assignment for Organisation for Economic Co-operation and Development, has developed a model for cost-benefit studies of sheltered workshops and has completed a pilot study in five European countries and the United States. Andersen was able to show net economic gains, whose differential rates may be related to class of handicapped person and to the system of organization for the sheltered workshop. "Human gains" were subjected to separate analyses and not assigned monetary values at all. Andersen comments:

> This is the reason . . . the present investigation cannot tell us whether a certain arrangement should be established or not. It needs to be supplemented by political decision. On the other hand it is in the very nature of politics to make such decisions, to compare incommensurable objects.[32]

Thus, in the rigor and incompleteness of the Somers-Stromsdorfer work, the effort to quantify human gains in non-price terms by Mack and Meyers, and in Andersen's deliberate partialing-out of the human gains issue one has the range of strategies currently being defended. Each continues to have methodological problems and imprecisions on its own terms.

---

[31] Ruth P. Mack and Sumner Meyers, "Outdoor Recreation," in Dorfman, Editor, *op. cit.*, 71–101.

[32] Bent Andersen, *Work or Support* (Paris: Organisation for Economic Co-Operation and Development, 1966). Quotation is from page 21.

As suggested earlier, two choices emerge. One school argues that there is no reason to see the goal as cost-benefit analyses in price terms, because "they are in fact social projects precisely because the free market does not allocate enough resources to their use to meet public needs." To quote Keynes: "There is no clear evidence from experience that the investment policy which is socially advantageous coincides with that which is most profitable."[33]

With relation to social programs, therefore, one does rigorous cost-benefit studies of economic costs, so that all possibly relevant facts are available, and then turns, as proposed by Andersen, to issues of politics and preference. Of course the work to perfect the economic side of the analysis must continue.

Novick, an advocate of PPBS, reminds us that "it is a perversion of human values to push it [economic measurement] into areas where it does not belong."[34] And Rothenberg formulates it clearly:

> Whenever possible, therefore, money magnitudes should be supplemented by the vector of nonmonetary consequences, e.g., serious illness days, murders, incidence of psychosis. While the investigator may not be able to discover unique consensual trade-offs in the community among these different kinds of consequences, society has the option of discovering them by a form of simulation—the governmental decision-making process.[35]

The second school would continue to pursue the task of quantification of preferences and other relevant criteria in such fashion that they may serve as weights to be applied to program outputs. One would then have a human-gains measure. All available case illustrations suggest that this is a distant accomplishment, given the varied programs and services, the complexity of the diverse criteria, and frequently *fundamental* disagreements about values and objectives. Indeed, the plurality of objectives in many programs may make the search for a generally acceptable objective measure truly hopeless in some arenas.

At the present, the stronger case certainly resides with those who would offer the most rigorous cost-effectiveness reports possible on the alternatives, in price terms, noting that ultimate choices do not always move in the direction of economic cost alone, and confronting the planner with the need to determine and find relevant ways to consider preferences, latent functions, and unexpressed goals. The "main role of analysis should be to try to

---

[33] Juanita Kreps, comment, in Somers, Editor, *op. cit.*, 205.

[34] Novick, *op. cit.*, 50–51.

[35] Jerome Rothenberg, "Urban Renewal," in Dorfman, Editor, *op. cit.*, 292–333. Quote is from pages 332–333.

*sharpen* . . . intuition and judgment. In practically no case should it be assumed that the results of the analysis will *make* the decision."[36] Even such limited cost-benefit work must move slowly, not entering upon measurement without careful conceptual analysis of all elements and conscious choices as to what is actually measured and by what indicators.[37] We have here hinted at only a few of the technical difficulties. We must remind those who are impatient that even relatively primitive computation of comparative costs is a step forward in a field in which requirements, on the one hand, and positive motives or response or backing, on the other, were long the only elements in the community equation. It is progress to have introduced economic analyses, awareness of resource scarcity, efficiency criteria, and a willingness to consider alternatives and substitutions.

It should be noted, finally, that any concern for a total system, any serious exploration of "balance" or "mix," also imposes limits on the role of cost-benefit analysis. There are times when a project's cost-benefit ratio is of itself poor, but concern with complementarities and the overall program may make this relatively unimportant.[38]

## PERSPECTIVES

The state-of-the-art is summarized by the Assistant Secretary responsible for the launching of PPBS in the Department of Health, Education, and Welfare, William Gorham:

> Let me hasten to point out that we have not attempted any grandiose cost-benefit analyses designed to reveal whether the total benefits from an additional million dollars spent on health programs would be higher or lower than that from an additional million spent on education or welfare. If I was ever naive enough to think this sort of analysis possible, I no longer am. The benefits of health, education, and welfare programs are diverse and often intangible. They affect different age groups and different regions of the population over different periods of time. No amount of analysis is going to tell us whether the Nation benefits more from sending a slum child to preschool, providing medical care for an old man or enabling a disabled housewife to resume her normal activities. The "grand decisions" —how much health, how much education, how much welfare, and which groups in the population shall benefit—are questions of value judgment and politics. The analyst cannot make much contribution to their resolution.

---

[36] Gene H. Fisher, "The Role of Cost-Utility Analysis in Program Budgeting," in Novick, Editor, *op. cit.*, 67.

[37] *Ibid.*; and Andersen, *op. cit.*

[38] See, for example, *Cost-Benefit Analysis of Social Projects*, 24.

*. . . The less grand decisions, those among alternative programs with the same or similar objectives within health—can be substantially illuminated by good analysis.*[39]

Gorham has put it even more briefly:

While the big choices may not be illuminated by cost-benefit analyses, the narrower ones may be. It is possible to group programs and potential programs that have the same objective and to examine the effectiveness (relative to cost) of each in reaching that objective.[40]

For most public purposes, and certainly in the social field, there is a vast gap between the aspirations of PPBS advocates and cost-benefit analysts and what they are able at this moment to accomplish. Those who assumed that pure technology would replace preferences and politics have begun to appreciate the limitations of these new tools. These generalizations are documented by most students of the subject and are admirably and honestly summarized in the Novick volume.[41]

The entire process is dependent upon clarity about goals and on an ability to distinguish ends and means. It is, therefore, not a substitute for the effort to develop policy planning of the kind described throughout this volume. As a pre-condition to the new methods here described, even in their more modest conception, the public must be willing to have its governmental agencies and large semi-public social welfare enterprises approach programming as seriously as does big business—and with as significant a component of rationality. *Once a context of policy planning is created,* the program budgeting system can do much to strengthen the rational component in the administrative structuring and organizational implementation necessary to the realization of any broad objectives.

This, too, has some pre-conditions.

On most governmental levels, it will be necessary to unify the now-separated and often competitive budgeting and planning processes. It will be essential to overcome some of the legislative tradition of allocation and appropriation that tends to re-inforce small incrementalism and logrolling and to attend little or not at all to rationality and cost-benefit considerations.[42]

[39] "Hearings," *The Planning-Programming-Budgeting . . .* , 5. (Emphasis supplied.)

[40] Gorham, "Notes of a Practitioner," 7.

[41] See Steiner, *op. cit.*, and also Ronald N. McKean and Melvin Anshen, "Limitations, Risks and Problems," 285–307, both in Novick, *op. cit.*

[42] For a political science case study of federal budgeting in the United States, see Aaron Wildavsky, *The Politics of the Budgetary Process* (Boston: Little, Brown and Company, 1964, paperback). Wildavsky sees some contribution by new rational tools in *The Public Interest*, special section cited.

On the operational level, ways will need to be found either to realign administratively at intervals so that organizational lines may coincide with programs in the PPBS sense—or to develop far more efficient coordination devices which will make truly additive the components of a program scattered among several agencies or bureaus.

In effect, program budgeting, as does any governmental effort, faces the problem of all planning: it represents an attempt to introduce rationality into a world of interest groups, bureaucratic rigidities, informal organization, politics, and many uncertainties. If the planner is at all times clear that his mission and capability are not to eliminate all of these, but rather to optimize the rational component in the process, he can work comfortably and usefully. He is willing to be part of a planning process, even though his are not the final plans. He is prepared to introduce and to work with an imperfect PPBS, because it is far more satisfactory than the annual, segmented, "requirements" budgeting and—when seen as a vehicle for programming—strengthens the total planning effort.

In this spirit, too, he is prepared to employ cost-utility analysis as well, under one of its many names. Knowing that crucial, human benefits are not quantifiable, and are as legitimate *on their own terms* as are "pork barrel" and political decisions on theirs, he counts what can be counted, but is not confused about what he has. At times he is satisfied with a "more" or "less," "improved" or "unimproved" generalization, knowing that an exact measure is not possible. Yet, this, too, is worth knowing in the total context of the enterprise, leaving the planner with data not much less precise than the preference data which often enter into the arena of public decision-making. And the commitment to a cost-utility approach alerts one from the beginning to the critical distinction between carrying out activities and accomplishing socially sought results. At the same time, such perspective tends to broaden the choice "menu" at any given moment of policy-making and programming, since it invokes a wider range of relevant concerns and commitments.

In short, we have found no nostrums or panaceas, but rather helpful tools and constructive perspectives for the social planner. The analyses projected do not *make* the decisions and never will; they may serve to sharpen intuition and enhance judgment.

# PROGRAMMING PROBLEMS IN SOCIAL SERVICE DELIVERY

THE DISCUSSION of programming has focused initially on the general problem of coordination and on the development of an overall programming strategy. Given the considerable role of social services in social planning, we now turn to several programming issues which are currently of major concern. The intent is both *to illustrate the process of thinking about programming* and to deal substantively with urgent issues. We begin with provision for access and channeling, then turn to case integration and accountability, as tasks for programming. Following a section on the protection of citizens through *ombudsmen* and related devices, there is a brief summation of decentralization as a programming device.[1]

## ACCESS AND CHANNELING

A central problem in social service delivery derives from inadequate access and inefficient or inadequate case channeling. At the programming stage, the planner is therefore much preoccupied with these matters.[2] The issues are urgent, and consideration of the nature of the difficulties and the possibilities is necessary.[3]

---

[1] The reader will note continuity from the more generalized discussion in the present chapter to the discussion of family and child welfare (Chapter VII in the companion volume) and the urban network coping with children in trouble (Chapter III in the companion volume).

[2] As indicated previously, in Chapter VIII, he must, of course, have considered the appropriateness and quality of the agency or organization's basic service, its "interventive repertoire."

[3] The discussion of boundaries has already suggested that improved channeling might contribute to solution of the problem of gaps and artificial divisions among fields. The

## The price of inadequate provision

There is, on the one hand, considerable case finding. People are constantly asking teachers, doctors, ministers, storekeepers, newspaper columnists, and politicians for information, advice, intercession with government agencies or courts—or for other help. Teachers identify one in ten children as needing specialized help in schools. Child guidance clinics almost everywhere have long waiting lists, as do family agencies. Staff members in public assistance, child welfare, or probation stagger under heavy caseloads. State training schools and voluntary treatment institutions exceed their bed capacities in daily census. Endless referrals are made to many places. Everybody is busy; almost everybody works hard. With only limited exceptions, clients-patients-inmates are in such plentiful supply as to overwhelm all kinds of services and to exhaust staff.

On the other hand, agencies or facilities are often unable to help and to achieve useful results. Sometimes the reason for this is that the people who need service most are not offered help at all or are offered the wrong services despite the activity and pressure. For an example in one field, studies show that child guidance clinics are sometimes not at all involved with the children whose severe behavior problems are of maximum concern to schools, courts, and the community in general. In the meantime, large proportions of the cases on the waiting lists of family agencies and child guidance clinics do not keep first appointments, do not return after first interviews, or drop out after very few contacts, while social workers, psychologists, or psychiatrists consider them very much in need of more help.

A national survey found that one American in four has felt sufficiently troubled to need personal counseling or similar help at some time, while one in seven has actually sought it.[4] What of the other three? Is this self-selectivity wise? Various studies disclose an interrelationship among clients' social status or background, the types of problems brought to agencies-clinics, and the nature of the help actually proffered.[5] To what extent is such selectivity

---

notion has been introduced that general program coordination, as well as service integration at the entry point, could overcome some of the consequences of necessary field segmentation and organizational divisions. We, however, have not yet fully defined the scope of the access-channeling problem or outlined possible administrative devices for its solution. See Chapter V.

[4] Gerald Gurin et al., *Americans View their Mental Health*, Joint Commission on Mental Illness and Health, Monograph Series No. 4 (New York: Basic Books, 1960).

[5] August B. Hollingshead and Frederick C. Redlich, *Social Class and Mental Illness* (New York: John Wiley & Sons, 1958); Jerome K. Meyers and Bertram K. Roberts, *Family and Class Dynamics in Mental Illness* (New York: John Wiley & Sons, Inc.,

functional: does it to any degree impair the effectiveness of community-sponsored efforts?

Questions such as these must be approached from a variety of vantage points. To the planner considering organization for service delivery, they suggest (among the several possibilities) the problem of ineffective or inadequate *channeling* of people into what we have called intervention systems. In a broad sense, they are problems of information and access. We shall attempt to delineate the difficulties and to clarify some of the options available. Much of the focus is on the function which the social scientist would call "system linkage."

The term "channeling" as used here encompasses information, case finding, and referral as closely interrelated processes. The consequence which follows from the structure of case finding, subsequent evaluations, and what is done with them may be rational and purposive or completely haphazard and emotional. Channeling outcomes may reflect deliberate, large decisions or many small, hidden choices.

An empirical investigation in New York City, confirmed by a variety of types of data and testimony, showed that size, "specialization, dispersion of authority, and legislative inconsistency make service bureaucracies very complex; the individual in need of service can find his way through the maze only with the help of generally unavailable expert guidance." Also, "there is much information-advice-referral activity . . . but it does not seem to be enough—either in kind or quality—to meet the needs."[6] Herbert Gans documents in his report, *The Urban Villagers*, how inadequate the information system was at all stages of a Boston West End renewal project.[7]

Let us turn briefly to the family service agencies. Twenty-five percent of all cases are closed at the end of the first interview by decision of the social worker, and another 30 percent, though not deliberately closed after the first interview, involve client failure to return for a second. An official analysis comments:

> Many of these early losses represent inappropriate applications due to lack of community understanding or adequate public assistance or other spe-

---

1959). William Ryan and Laura Morris, *Child Welfare Problems and Potentials* (Boston, Mass.: Committee for Children and Youth, 1967).

[6] Alfred J. Kahn et al., *Neighborhood Information Centers: A Study and Some Proposals* (New York: Columbia University School of Social Work, 1966), 11, 50.

[7] Herbert Gans, *The Urban Villagers* (New York: The Free Press of Glencoe, 1962), 324 ff. For an analysis which relates knowledge of resources to social variables, see Oliver Moles, Robert F. Hess, Donald Fascione, "Who Knows Where To Get Public Assistance?" *Welfare in Review*, 6, No. 5 (September–October, 1968), 8–13.

cialized resources in the area. Others involve clients who come with insufficient motivation or under stress of temporary crisis or other outside pressure. Still others are undoubtedly due to the worker's handling of the first interview.[8]

The problem of case loss is a major social agency problem; it is misperceived if conceptualized solely or largely as a problem in client motivation.

What is to an agency an "intake" department, which is geared to an assigned mission, competence, resources, training obligations, or research interests, may appear to an applicant as "outkeep." Survey after survey points up that many potential "cases" do not ever get to agencies for evaluation at all.[9]

These trends are repeated by many child guidance centers, adult mental health clinics, and all sorts of counseling agencies as well as in a variety of social service programs of other kinds. They reflect a phenomenon of concern to both developed and developing countries.

People who are asked where they turn for help with personal problems mention the clergy and general doctors overwhelmingly. Mental health professionals or social agencies are far less in evidence. Where there is feeling of impending "nervous breakdown," there is less turning to the clergyman and more to the general practitioner: in fact, the psychiatrist is mentioned less in relation to impending breakdown than in relation to personal problems in general. Psychiatrists, psychologists, and social agencies appear more prominently in the listing as sources of help where the respondent *defines* the problem in psychological or interpersonal terms or where there are situational crises.[10] However, even a broader definition than "personal problem" does not suggest to significantly large segments of the population the relevance to their situations of social agency services which may be organized with them in mind.[11]

There thus emerges a confused and sometimes discouraging picture of impossibly long waiting lists,[12] cases rejected at intake, and inadequate serv-

[8] Dorothy Fahs Beck, *Patterns in Use of Family Agency Service* (New York: Family Service Association of America, 1962), 20. Later tabulations show that only 63 percent of contacts lead to in-person interviews; 40 percent of interviewees are seen only once.

[9] Gurin *et al.*, *Americans View . . .* , 38.

[10] *Ibid.*, 302–315.

[11] Margaret Bailey, "Community Orientations Toward Social Casework and Other Professional Resources" (Unpublished doctoral dissertation, Columbia University School of Social Work, 1958).

[12] Stanley P. Davies, *Toward Community Health* (New York: State Association for Mental Health, 1960), 32; Reginald Robinson *et al.*, *Community Resources in Mental*

ice in many communities—while at the same time we know of a large reservoir of the unserved, indeed of non-applicants, who may not recognize the potentials of agencies or services or may not be able to reach them. There is, too, some incomplete evidence that the agency one happens to reach may be more salient in determining the treatment one receives than one's diagnosis or problem.[13]

There are those who would "let well enough alone," preferring not to increase applicants or cases served in a period of manpower shortage and rising costs. There are others who point to limited knowledge and skill in many services and argue that random channeling may not hurt anyone. A third group holds that the client who emerges from the irrational intake maze and receives service is well motivated and makes good use of it.

Were these adequate responses, a discussion of channeling into and among intervention systems would be a useless drawing board exercise. Brief examination only makes the preoccupation more urgent.

The motivation for dealing with these matters might be stated in terms of the need for efficiency: to achieve economical use of funds and personnel. The stakes are, however, even greater. There is urgent need to deploy strategically what is available so as to lessen or shorten the impact of social problems so severe and disruptive as to affect the quality and character of community life: crime and delinquency, mental illness, family neglect and breakdown, dependency. There is a large element of injustice and community foolishness in permitting inadequate channeling to reserve resources for those sufficiently informed, motivated, or culturally pre-conditioned to make use of them. Furthermore, a large price is paid in social pathology, disorganization, and loss for that collective ignorance of the scope of real need that permits a channeling maze to decrease effective demand.

The argument that knowledge and skill are limited, so that channeling does not matter, can hardly be meant to justify selectivity as between those who do and those who do not get to agencies at all. Obviously, professional workers in the fields under discussion believe that they can and do render valuable service—and the supporting community does as well. The reference to professional limitations has another, more narrow kind of validity, if any. The argument is made, for example, that it may not be too serious if Case A reaches a foster home agency rather than a residential treatment institution, because we do not have data which establish that the former or latter plan

---

*Health,* Joint Commission on Mental Illness and Health, Monograph Series No. 5 (New York: Basic Books, 1960).

[13] Hollingshead and Redlich, *Social Class . . . ,* 260 ff.

may be more effective for this type of case. This might be an argument for deliberate experimental channeling so that each program might eventually become an "intervention specific" for certain cases—it is not an argument for ignoring the problem of channeling.

The argument about client motivation would seem to be the most flimsy of all. It is only a modern form of Social Darwinism which would pretend that an irrational confluence of chance, cultural bias, and professional predilection could in some way reflect a basically benign process. True, some types of people "survive" in greater numbers than others given the present characteristics of services and the ways in which they are reached. There is, however, no basis for the social judgment that these are the people most in need of help, the people the community has decided to help first or—most important—that others would not make good use of help cast in somewhat different form or differently introduced. The search for a simply-administered oral polio vaccine was not given up because many people did get to doctors for the more complicated inoculation procedure.

Another aspect of channeling and its consequences also deserves mention: the phenomena of self-definition and community definition of the meaning of deviance. As intrafamilial problem involving a teenage child, when taken to a private psychiatrist, may affect self-perception in the sense that one's emotional qualities or interpersonal competence are characterized in specific ways. It is not likely to affect the way one is seen by the larger community, since the professional contact is a relatively anonymous one. A similar problem taken to the local police station or court may have quite different consequences: the relatively public experience affects the way in which school, neighbors, and peers see one and thus changes one's environment in a significant way. Indeed, it may change one's self-definition. There is some evidence that, if one comes to think of oneself as outcast, deviant, rejected, or attacked, one is changed by the process. The immediate social environment defines and creates one's social roles in significant degree. Ernest Gruenberg has asked whether some mental disorders may not have different outcomes depending on the type of facility which provides treatment and the related self-definition engendered.[14]

John Clausen goes so far as to suggest that to withhold the label "mental illness" may help restoration.[15] Richard Cloward sees the nature of the

---

[14] Ernest Gruenberg, "Socially Shared Psychopathology," in Alexander H. Leighton *et al.*, Editors, *Explorations in Social Psychiatry* (New York: Basic Books, 1957), 349.

[15] John Clausen, "The Sociology of Mental Illness," in Robert K. Merton *et al.*, Editors, *Sociology Today* (New York: Basic Books, 1959), 502–503.

institutional "defining system" as a critical aspect of deviance. (This type of analysis affects our approach to delinquency in Chapter III of the companion volume.)

This same point may be made if we conjure up briefly the community definition and related self-definition of: the social insurance recipient as contrasted with the relief recipient; the child guidance clinic case as contrasted with the juvenile court case; the family in a counseling service as contrasted with a child protective agency or a child placement agency; the family applying for homemaker as contrasted with the family bringing a child to a temporary shelter. Channeling does have consequences. Machinery to facilitate and assure access is a major concern of the social service planner.

### Factors in access and channeling

Socio-cultural definitions, group norms, and broad community factors thus interact with agency-organizational factors and personal variables in determining who asks for help, where, and with what persistence. While it is possible to document these notions in quite extensive detail,[16] it may suffice for present purposes to summarize the several generalizations which the planner of improved access may wish to regard as central. These are offered as strongly documented hypotheses:

To some extent, members of different classes and groups *experience* different types of problems—or the same problems in quite different frequencies. To some extent, even if problem frequencies should be similar, life circumstances are such that members of different social classes acknowledge or are compelled to acknowledge and cope with different problems.

The real differences and social differentiations generally work to the disadvantage of the very poor, the uneducated, the minority-group members. Their problems are defined most negatively; they receive the most punitive, stigmatizing, confusing—and the least hopeful—services. They are evaluated as helped or improved least often.

For any given type of non-stigmatizing amenity or service, those who are poor-uneducated-deprived minority members are least likely to reach the service in proportion to their numbers, or (if they reach it) to get beyond the application point, or (if accepted) to get the optimum, or most intensive or advanced, service.

---

[16] As illustration, see Elaine Cumming, "Allocation of Care to the Mentally Ill, American Style," in Meyer Zald, Editor, *Organizing for Community Welfare* (Chicago: Quadrangle Books, 1967), 109–159.

Cultural attitudes towards given groups and in given places create significant exceptions to each of the above generalizations. For almost all groups there are some problems and needs which are suppressed or deferred or not taken to the most competent resources, despite negative effects on members.

The components of stratification, cultural orientations, and intrafamilial dynamics which block and distort assertion of rights, use of resources, and the search for help also have their organizational and agency counterparts. Agencies often prefer (and thus facilitate service to) clients who are able to conform to their routines and play the client "roles" that support smooth operations. Professional workers often prefer clients who permit them to exercise and refine their skills and who will show progress.

Many agencies offer a service repertoire which, at least in its quantitative aspects, does not coincide with the perceptions by substantial numbers (and sometimes the majority) of applicants as to what they want and need. At times, therefore, the community service output is so completely out of balance that no improvement in channeling will help. At other times, elimination of random movement and wastage through improved channeling would take care of a significant portion of the service deficit.

Thus, in summary, from the point of view of the individual seeking help, the channeling process may usefully be considered as involving

- [ ] the definition of the problem
- [ ] whether a decision is made to use help outside of family or informal sources
- [ ] where one decides to go
- [ ] what is accessible and available.[17]

But in the larger context, channeling is deeply embedded in community definitional and social control factors, which explain and acknowledge needs and shape formal and "lay referral" systems.[18] It involves the stakes of organizations and professional workers in constituencies, recognition, resources, and other goals which are normal for them—and reflects their security in certain modes of operation.

Humanitarian traditions, concern for social justice, legal guarantees of equal opportunity, or newly developed political pressures have all, in various degrees, motivated a strong desire in many places to emphasize improved access to services by the most underprivileged. As we have already suggested, it is no small undertaking to do this while avoiding negative definitions and

---

[17] Gurin et al., Americans View . . . , 293–294.

[18] David Landy, "Problems in Seeking Help in our Culture," The Social Welfare Forum, 1960 (New York: Columbia University Press, 1960), 127–145.

continued stigma—and thus less satisfactory service. Nor can planners ignore the evidence that even for people who have had contact with *some* agencies, there is a high degree of public ignorance of complex social agency networks and governmental programs, how they work, and what one's rights are. This ignorance penetrates deeply into the middle class as well as the lower.[19] A mere glance at a schematic presentation of agency functions and intake policies in a community survey in any middle-sized or large urban area will indicate that anyone except a specialist is more than justified in such ignorance and confusion. Channeling structure will have to take this into account. The problem is not only status factors, emotional problems, and biases but sheer complexity as well.

### Overall implications of the channeling and access problem

The planner who is concerned with these matters will want to do more than provide for adequate access, information, and channeling mechanisms in connection with social service systems, although such mechanisms (which are outlined below) are here considered of great importance.

An overall strategy might, as relevant, also include consideration of the following issues as well.

It is urgent that there be more widespread discussion in social welfare generally of the sort which has begun in the mental health field as a consequence of the work of Shirley Star, Paul V. Lemkau, Elaine Cumming and John Cumming, Gerald Gurin, and the Joint Commission on Mental Illness.[20] When is it useful to identify, isolate, separate, or label certain deviant individuals—and families—and when are broader community objectives achieved through emphasis on integration and reintegration, commonalities and universalities? The mental health field is now moving the services from state to locality and, where possible, from hospital to home. Would similar process be desirable in relation to delinquency? Is there a child welfare parallel?

Explorations on this level have implications for public education, policy, and operation.

The point needs to be made again and again that where resources are in extremely short supply or public welfare budgets too small, little can be done to add rationality to the channeling process. If a community has a child guidance clinic, but no professionally-qualified child welfare staff, these

---

[19] Morris Janowitz *et al.*, "Public Administration and the Public," in Amitai Etzioni, Editor, *Complex Organizations: A Sociological Reader* (New York: Rinehart & Winston, 1961), 279–280.

[20] *Action for Mental Health*; Gurin *et al.*, *Americans View* . . . ; Elaine Cumming and John Cumming, *Closed Ranks* (Cambridge, Mass.: Harvard University Press, 1957).

facts will be reflected in case channeling. If public assistance budgets are too low to feed children at home, there will continue to be unnecessary institutional and foster home placement. *The channeling problem is not the foundation of community health and welfare planning.* It can legitimately have attention, in fact, only after certain other fundamental matters have been attended to. It is most urgent as an issue in urban centers of specialization and proliferation of agencies and services.

Any channeling network should assure early and easy separation of chronic from acute situations. If bureaucratic complications block emergency services, the community will create additional social problems and defeat itself in its efforts to use resources efficiently. (Emergency services are discussed in Chapter VII of the companion volume.)

Since the ultimate foundation of rational channeling is firm knowledge as to the consequences of different intervention strategies as related to specific configurations of problem-diagnosis-family situations, this is a high-priority problem for research and experimentation. Service boundaries need careful examination as already noted.

The channeling problem is obviously tied up with class-ethnic-generational-economic-religious-cultural factors and their impact on development, definition of, and disposition of personal-familial-community problems. Agency response to problems, needs, and applications is just one segment of this whole. Solutions must therefore be sought through many types of exploration, experimentation, and innovation. Decentralization and local flexibility deserve serious attention and will be discussed later in this chapter and also in Chapters VI and VII of the companion volume.

## Organizing for improved channeling

In the planning of specific social services or of a total community-wide network, the following might be considered as possible elements in a pattern designed to overcome some of the channeling problems which do not require the more fundamental policy and program changes alluded to above:

☐ adequate information and referral services as part of most specialized programs (the "open door");
☐ availability of diagnostic and case-evaluation resources at key points in the community service network;
☐ "a door on which to knock," or a person to whom to turn when one needs information or is not sure where to go for service.

Many observers have noted that a potential client would have to be quite well informed about the social welfare structure and in a state of mind which permitted careful evaluation of alternatives before him if he were to make a wise choice among helping sources. Of course, given such a level of sophistication and maturity, the need for outside help often fades away. It, therefore, is desirable that any request to a department, agency, or clinic be seen as an opportunity to render a useful service after careful consideration of whether the service should take the form of steering-advice-referral[21] or of access to the agency's own specialized resources.

Since it is unlikely that every public or voluntary resource could station properly-prepared personnel at its doorway, it is imperative that those points to which troubled people are most likely to turn do have "open doors," and are receptive to those people in trouble who need either the agency's special help or a friendly ear and steering to a more appropriate service. Personnel should be qualified to recognize the need for and to render or obtain emergency help.

Because of their locations in the community and the stance they assume as to their functions, such "open doors" (for American cities, at least) would seem to belong in: police precinct stations, social security offices, employment offices, welfare departments, schools, housing projects, family service agencies, health centers, settlement houses, churches, anti-poverty centers, and hospital out-patient departments. Illustrations may be cited of "open doors" associated in *some* places with each of these agencies, and existing ideologies support the idea. By and large, however, the assignment is not fulfilled, as the previously cited data suggest. The function needs visibility and status.

In addition to what can and should be done by any social welfare program which meets many people daily, and beyond what is routinely done on a large scale by clerics, doctors, storekeepers, and neighbors generally, each neighborhood also needs provision for "a door on which to knock." David Donnison, Peggy Jay, and Mary Stewart, in a British comment on proposed Family Bureaus, capture the intent and spirit of the needed provision in calling for a well-known place "within pram-pushing distance of people's homes." They continue as follows:

> This "door on which to knock" must then be a known door and an acceptable door. In other words, any of a multitude of family problems should result in one call at the Family Bureau—whose whereabouts are as well known as the local post office, and at which a call need cause no more neighbourly comment than a visit to the doctor.[22]

Of course an adequate channeling system must be concerned with more than family problems. Its task includes a large measure of information about

---

[21] For more specific delineation of these and related functions, see Chapter VII in the companion volume.

[22] David Donnison, Peggy Jay, and Mary Stewart, "The Ingleby Report: Three Critical Essays" (London: The Fabian Society, pamphlet, 1962), 14.

services, rights, benefits—as well as help with areas as broad as education, employment, retirement planning, illness, family finances, and community improvement.

We have proposed a system of neighborhood information centers as a variation on the British Citizens' Advice Bureau pattern. Others urge an American equivalent of the French polyvalent worker whose services include information and advice.[23]

## Neighborhood information centers and channeling

The local British Citizens' Advice Bureau is a neighborhood center whose stated purpose accurately describes its operation:

> To make available to the individual accurate information and skilled advice on the many problems that arise in everyday life; to explain legislation; to help the citizen to benefit from and use wisely the services provided to him by the state.

The widely displayed and recognized symbol of the CAB is an owl—who is wise but does not talk.

The Bureaus were created at the outbreak of World War II to help Britons through the confusion and hardship war would bring. Whether in the immediate aftermath of a bombing or to handle continuing problems of rationing, separation, and housing, persons of all social classes found the service invaluable. Today a network of close to five hundred CAB's throughout Great Britain answers more than one and a quarter million inquiries a year. The offices are nonsectarian and accessible; their personnel generally friendly. They are staffed by trained volunteers and paid personnel in a 70:30 ratio, which varies with the locality, working with the help of a central, professional staff at the National CAB office. They are looked to for aid by a wide cross-section of the public.

CAB workers are prepared to answer requests for any type of information, listen to problems, make home visits, fill out forms or write letters for an inquirer, or make informal referrals to public or to voluntary agencies and to specialists such as lawyers. They are supplied with a comprehensive directory of social legislation, rules, regulations, and instructions on how to use these laws. They have guides to resources, public and voluntary, available to those in need of help. The information is provided and continually updated by the National CAB office.

No appointment is needed at a CAB; callers are welcome to walk in off the street. All discussions are confidential. The inquiries are categorized and

---

[23] Alfred J. Kahn et al., Neighborhood Information Centers . . . ; Alvin Schorr, Social Security and Social Services in France (Washington, D.C.: Government Printing Office, 1965).

tallied each month, and CAB records become a source of impartial "evidence" for those studying the needs and problems of the British citizen and the adequacy of the services designed to help him.

Although the Bureaus encourage inquirers to help themselves, the workers also will take action on their behalf: write letters, fill out forms, do accounts, make appointments, telephone other agencies to explain the problem.

CAB workers on occasion will mediate a dispute: between a store manager and a dissatisfied customer, or a landlord and his tenants.

To the question of how far a worker should go with an inquirer, or when does CAB work become casework, the answer depends on the availability of casework services and on the professional-volunteer balance of the particular Bureau's staff. CAB workers are urged to use public and voluntary casework services to the greatest possible extent. When there is no local family casework organization, the CAB worker must become the intermediary between the inquirer and whatever resources are available.

For the most part, CAB's lack a follow-up process. The only ways the worker can evaluate the quality of service the inquirer gets is if he returns to the worker with his problem unsolved, or if the inquirer, his family, or friends make subsequent use of the CAB.

A person might come to the CAB merely for an opportunity to pour out his troubles in confidence to an uninvolved and sympathetic listener. He might come to be given reassurance about an action on which he has already decided. He might come to get leads as to possible alternative actions, based on the specialized information available in several guides which are supplied and the general knowledge of the worker. He might arrive knowing that he needs referral to a specialist, such as a lawyer or another agency. Or he might need the help of the CAB to identify his basic problems and to accept advice and referral.

CAB's receive telephone inquiries and may offer information and advice over the telephone, but the preference is for an office visit, and an inquirer will often be invited to drop in. On occasion, a report from a third party that a person in need cannot get to the office will lead to a home visit, as will other special circumstances.

Some offices receive a significant volume of mail inquiries which are answered by mail. Others do little of this. Systematic data are not available.

An American observer is struck by the CAB range, which contrasts with the usual scope of a social agency in the United States. CAB's are concerned with landlord-tenant problems and with housing, with consumer problems and social security rights, with educational and training services and medical services. They are truly intermediaries between the individual and the statutes and bureaucracies of a social welfare–oriented state. They give information and advice, listen, help in concrete ways, or refer inquirers to specialized services. They are part of the social welfare network, but far broader than social work as understood by most Americans.

The exact balance between giving information and relating such information to the situation of the inquiring individual is hard to measure. One unverified estimate is that 60 percent of the inquiries are handled by giving information and 40 percent go beyond this. The CAB central staff sees expertise in information as the foundation of its work and the entry to other services.

Although partially financed through government grants, CAB's are sponsored and run by local committees of citizens and representatives of public and voluntary agencies in their areas. They work closely with the agencies, and have succeeded in becoming an integral part of Britain's social service system.

The National CAB Council emphasizes:

> . . . the unique contribution CAB can make to prevention because, being nonspecialist and informal, the inquirer is more likely to "drop in for a chat" at an early stage of his problem when he may not even recognize his need for social work help; and knows too that his use of the CAB will not label him as a person with a problem.

Wartime CAB's were on the spot in trailers and makeshift offices as soon as bombings ended, to help victims locate next of kin and to make emergency arrangements. The growth of CAB during the bombings and its use by all persons is unique and the base for an image which cannot be reproduced. As put by one observer, the CAB is "now traditional enough on the voluntary scene to become part of the 'good and the true.'" As such, it continues to have local and national governmental support.

A special history and the mode of operation endow the CAB's with characteristics especially attractive to Americans: they are nonsectarian, nonpolitical, nondiscriminatory, and stigma-free. The user is not a patient or a recipient. He is a person who is assumed to be competent and his requests are taken at face value until experience shows otherwise. He has a right to confidentiality and privacy. The Bureaus are accessible to members of all social classes, although the more prosperous and better educated, who are less often without needed information and advice or have access to other resources such as private attorneys, tend to use the services less. Most users apparently are lower-middle class and working class.[24]

Though we shall leave for the chapter on local service delivery systems

---

[24] For more details, see Kahn *et al.*, *Neighborhood Information Centers* . . . , which also includes a critique.

(Chapter VII in the companion volume) some details about choices among the range of functions to be assigned in the light of overall goals, it is likely that an appropriate American version of a Citizens' Advice Bureau, perhaps better called a neighborhood information and advice center, would do much to improve information-giving and channeling. Detailed exploration of relevant beginnings in the United States provides a convincing case for new approaches to information, advice, and referral services. Many direct service agencies, specialized information and education programs, unions, community councils, civic groups, churches, and others are hard at work and are reaching many people. However, the average citizen in the typical place does not know about or have easy access to an expert, nonstigmatic service not committed to narrow remedies, which will, when necessary to help, meet him half-way. Thus there is true purpose to the search for new social provision.

Our proposals assume that all information, advice, and referral services now offered (by direct service agencies, specialized information services, civic, union, church, professional, and civil rights groups) would continue. People of different backgrounds and social classes will persist in seeking help in different ways, and nothing should be done to close off service to any group.

Nor would one discourage the apparently decreasing but nonetheless important help rendered constituents by locally-elected public officials or political clubs.

Finally, it must also be assumed that even if the neighborhood information office has some capacity for case evaluation, it will not be a fully-staffed diagnostic resource or be capable of certain other types of specialized evaluation. Nor will it be equipped with the kinds of sanctions necessary to a court process or a protective service. Thus, a neighborhood information office will continue to use specialized case-evaluation facilities as a major referral resource—just as people will continue to go directly to such facilities if they think or know that they need them.

What is proposed is something more comprehensive, more expert, better known, more accessible—a doorway to the specialized system, a "neighborhood concierge," a force for integration of components which serve an individual in need and a resource to be drawn upon by more specialized services. It is intended to increase and expand provision, not to compete with or decrease it.

We see need for a neighborhood information center that might undertake a variety of responsibilities if they do not impair the core functions of information-giving, advice, referral, and a component of case-oriented advocacy. Given the many transitions now in process on the American social welfare scene, as well as regional diversities, the function might be identified with a separate entity known as a neighborhood information center in some places—or be part of a more comprehensive service in other places. At the time of the study cited, likely auspices were the public welfare system, local anti-poverty centers, the social security system, and new voluntary efforts. Emphasis was placed both on professional control to assure competence and on a large nonprofessional and volunteer component to provide local relevance. Desirable provision was being made for "reaching out" to those who could not themselves seek services and for a degree of representation and help in attaining services, i.e., case advocacy, for those unable to follow up on their needs and claims.

Educational, feedback, direct-service, and policy-advocacy functions of such centers, the possibilities they hold and the problems they pose, are not here relevant.[25] We, however, would stress the following qualities as basic either to a local information center or to the polyvalent worker alternative to be described below.

An "open door" atmosphere. The service is visible, accessible, and welcoming, in an attractive setting, with evening hours and provision for baby-tending and so on.

Expertise. Accurate answers are available on a wide range of matters, and sound referrals are made because of staff selection, training, and information back-up, plus professional guidance.

Range. The scope is all of social welfare and public service as it affects the citizen in his daily life.

Flexibility. Conscious efforts are made to meet people's real needs and not fit formulas to them, to perceive new combinations of issues, and to approach each as a fresh problem.

Ability to attract and serve all social classes. The "open door," range, flexibility, and expertise make the service a resource valued by all and stigmatizing to none.

Confidentiality. There is opportunity for privacy and confidence that information given is used as intended; "sharing" with others is by permission only, except under defined conditions of clear and present danger.

Nonpartisan and nonsectarian. Auspices, staffing, clientele, and referral patterns open the service to all and avoid exploitation for extraneous purposes.

Unbiased in case channeling. The needs of the inquirer and not the habits or predilections of any particular agency or profession are dominant.

Comprehensiveness. An effort is made to see the total range of an

---

[25] See Kahn et al., Neighborhood Information Centers . . . .

inquirer's needs and to cope with them as a "whole" (if he wishes), in contrast to the usual fragmentary approaches.

*Accountability.* The service is accountable to the inquirer for service and to the public for reporting and feedback. Its own internal procedures assure such accountability.

Each of these qualities affects auspices, staffing, locale, and operational policies. Thus, some staff members require adequate training to assure range and confidentiality, yet one would not want dominance by any one professional interest. Use of nonprofessional neighborhood people on a large scale as volunteers or as paid workers might help achieve an open door. If the welfare department is "poor law" in outlook, it cannot create a non-stigmatizing service for all social classes. Programs should be begun in all types of neighborhoods at once—even if the bulk of the investment is in deprived areas—to demonstrate the validity of the service for members of all social groups and the need to offer service of a quality and range to be used by all.

These are not complete criteria but they do suggest the type of review which would seem to be called for as a locality makes its plans. As anti-poverty, welfare, urban renewal, mental health, library, public health, settlement, and other programs evolve, the specific implications of these objectives and the qualities associated with them may be expected to shift.

Among the possibilities to be considered, in localities where people are accustomed to self-service supermarkets and to the use of public libraries, is a "self-service" information and advice service. After passing a receptionist, the user would be directed to an area containing display cases, tables, reference books, forms, and materials. Then, if he wished further information or specific help, he would go to a desk to consult an aide. Such approach is as essential in an area accustomed to self-service as are "reaching out" and "advocacy" where people need more than the normal degree of assistance.

Public housing projects have experimented with a "neighborhood concierge," a full-time resident who advises, facilitates, refers, and helps other residents. The limited experience thus far in the United States is quite positive.

## Variations

*A one-man CAB in Holland.* A function quite similar to that of the local CAB has developed in several cities in the Netherlands on a municipal level. The situation in The Hague may serve as illustration.

The program, set up late in 1963, is staffed by twelve counselors (*sociaal raadsman*), housed in eleven offices scattered throughout the city. Their core roles are information, advice, referral, interpretation, help with complex forms, and reassurance. Feedback to authorities about program lacks is expected, but the personal service is confidential, nor (as in the CAB situation) does the counselor report individual offenders who come to his attention.

An earlier program in Amsterdam, begun in 1949, employs 24 counselors, employed and paid by the municipality and based in neighborhood centers, which are voluntary associations receiving some public help. The *sociaal raadsman's* function, influenced by the CAB, is to inform, advise, refer, and "lend a sympathetic ear." He also calls meetings and carries on educational activity designed to increase program coordination.

Thus, one has here a one-man, paid CAB operation, without the extensive community involvement or backup of the CAB. One assumes that variations of this kind are essential as an information, advice, and general access system is accommodated to its social environment and the cultural backgrounds of the potential clientele.

*The polyvalent worker as an alternative.* Alvin Schorr has introduced the possibility of an American version of the French system of polyvalent workers as an alternative to the neighborhood information center.[26] In effect, such workers constitute a network of decentralized information centers, combining the information, advice, referral, case advocacy function with first-line social service and counseling to families.

The core of the French system is the *assistante sociale,* the line social worker with the equivalent of visiting-nurse and casework-aide training. At the time of Schorr's report, 4,000 *assistantes sociales* based in social security offices represented a ratio of one per 800 insured workers or one to 1,100 to 2,000 entitled to family allowances. These workers are expected to provide an information and referral service for people with special problems or those who find the usual administrative channels insufficient to meet their needs. The institutional arrangement is known as a *permanence,* an "established time and place in each community where the assistante sociale may be consulted for any reason."[27]

The social security *assistante sociale* is the nucleus of a system that provides similar service to everybody in France. France's 1959 "law of coordination" assures each family of social work "coverage" in the sense of the family general medical practitioner. Public and voluntary social services cooperate and the user may choose whether or not he wishes to avail himself of the voluntary sectarian service as an alternative. The workers are called "polyvalent," or "multipurpose," in that they are general practitioners, offering

---

[26] Schorr, *op. cit.*

[27] *Ibid.,* 32.

first-level counseling as well as information and referral to specialists. They offer entry to many concrete services. Each family is on a worker's "list" and thus has access to emergency help as needed—or to the information service.

The development of such a pattern in an American city would require establishment of the general-practitioner social worker concept. Currently all are assigned to special fields: family, medical, psychiatric, child welfare, and so forth. It would not be conceptually or operationally difficult, however, since family social workers often function in this fashion, public welfare social workers have been expected to, and anti-poverty community development workers have stressed these roles under such titles as "social broker," "urban agent," or "urban broker."

The unique feature of the approach is the establishment of a *permanence*, a time and place, rather than an office. With the exception of an occasional social work outpost worker in a school, public housing office, or similar setting, this has not occurred as an American pattern. If it were to be attempted, these "detached workers" would probably need a base from which to work—so as to have secretarial service and expert consultation and, most important, to draw on adequate information files and manuals.

*Information supports.* Our neighborhood information center study disclosed that the British Citizens' Advice Bureau depends on a unique series of publications and aids.

*Citizens Advice Notes* (CANS) is a comprehensive digest, in looseleaf form, clearly indexed, of social legislation, governmental and voluntary services and their regulations, the rights of citizens, all types of resources, and résumés of reports of committees studying pertinent subjects. It is kept up to date by periodic supplements, and is obviously the definitive work in the field of aid and service to individuals. More than 3,500 subscribers outside the CAB's, including many government officials on all levels, use it in their work. CANS is a publication of the parent body, the National Council of Social Services, but is basic to the CAB operation.

A monthly *Information Circular* is published, with digests of new legislation and useful general information, such as new educational or voluntary services, dates of elections, etc. The circular's information appears in permanent form in the subsequent CANS supplement.

Periodic *Supplementary Circulars* are issued, each dealing in detail with a subject of importance, e.g., legal aid and advice. A circular describes a new law, the requirements for individuals wishing to benefit from it, and detailed instructions for making use of it, with descriptions of necessary forms, their numbers, etc.

The Information Department of the National CAB Council is an office of professionals available to local CAB's to locate obscure information, help solve a tough problem, or to serve as a channel of referral to a government agency or office.

A quarterly *Bulletin of Information* is published for non-CAB workers, such as clergymen and school teachers, in rural areas who come in contact with the general public. It provides them with a summary of recent information from the National CAB Council, or reports made by CAB's on specific subjects (such as consumer problems or property laws), so that these informal advisors can be aware of what CAB's are doing and can refer people to them.

A last, significant source of information and help to CAB workers is a thorough knowledge of neighborhood resources. This is obtained during the training period, when the prospective CAB worker meets local government and agency officials, hears them speak of their work, visits their offices, and is encouraged to form a close relationship of mutual assistance and understanding.

As United States services have evolved they, too, have found such supports necessary. The Office of Economic Opportunity (OEO) has developed excellent manuals of governmental programs (*Catalogue of Federal Programs for Individual and Community Improvement*). There is a useful, privately-published *Encyclopedia of United States Government Benefits*. Many local health and welfare councils publish directories, and many cities issue departmental and service directories, especially in the health field. Specialized information groups (arthritis, retardation, diabetes, etc.) also issue directories. The developing neighborhood information services are finding ways to convert all of this to rollex files, computer systems, or index-card systems, specific and relevant to the neighborhood inquirer—and basic to an access and channeling system.

Each local information unit also requires expert "back-up" by a panel of specialists who may be telephoned for guidance on matters not covered by the index files. This is especially urgent during the developmental period. Experts on the local level also may require telephone back-up on the state and federal levels.

As information services develop adequate localized information files, the foundation of the daily service, they may find ways to share this expertise with functional agencies. One may envision the spread of an information-advice-referral *function* based both in direct service agencies and in specialized neighborhood information centers, "fed" by such files and cooperating in reporting and feedback about inquiries and unmet needs. Computers may in the near future facilitate such developments.

These structural proposals will not make much impact on the problem, however, unless there are central training resources which study the evolving professional, aide, and volunteer roles in this service, develop materials, conduct training programs, and certify personnel as qualified. Special workshops are needed as new and complex legislation is enacted or as administrative procedures change and new facilities for service are opened.

The above-listed qualities are not readily achieved, but they are basic if the access system is to have the expected impact. The keynotes are: expertise, range, "open door," no bias towards any particular service, and accountability. As for accountability, the specialized information center or worker must live by the rule that no question or request is unanswerable. He must pursue the issue until he knows how the inquirer might proceed. Nor does he drop the request after referral until certain that a contact has been made. Telephone inquiries and "self-mailers" are used for follow-up.

Much of what is sought could be achieved if the complete array of resources for an information-advice-referral service assured coverage to all population elements and thus dramatized that the need for or request for service is universal and stigma-free. This is, indeed, the case in the modern state, if we survey all educational, health, retirement, social security, recreational, cultural, housing, social service, and related provisions. The elements of stigma alluded to are historical residues, sticking to small segments of the system, and strong enough in the past to mar the whole.[28]

## CASE INTEGRATION AND ACCOUNTABILITY

David Donnison has commented, "Human needs do not come in self-contained, specialised packets; they are entangled, involving whole families —and sometimes whole neighborhoods."[29]

### The problem

In those social services involving intensive intervention into interpersonal relationships, intrapsychic problems, or traditional behavioral patterns, there is a premium on continuity of service over time and on the meshing of

---

[28] We have here focused on the functions. Details of administrative options available to the planner, with special reference to the issue of information-advice-referral in the context of the local social service system, are reserved for Chapter VII in the companion volume.

In the present context, we have not fully stressed the advocacy potential of the local service in aiding deprived citizens. A broader perspective is offered in Alfred J. Kahn, "Perspectives on Social Service Access" (London: National CAB Council, 1969).

[29] Donnison et al., op. cit., 2–3.

simultaneously-rendered service components. These two types of meshing, sequential and simultaneous, are here referred to as *case integration*. The goal is continuity of service, consistency of stance, and concert of components. The rationale is simple: if one would undo what has resulted from a complex process of learning or socialization or development, only an internally-consistent and mutually-supportive series of actions of equal potency can be expected to make an impact.

The urgency of planning for an effective system of case integration in connection with both case services and those social utilities on which people tend to draw during emergency, crisis, or stress derives not merely from deduction from behavioral theory, however. The literature of social service evaluation and the reports of surveys, investigating agencies, and client responses have long been dominated by persistent findings which show the need for these several types of continuity. An earlier work documented the disturbing frequency, with detailed reference to work with children in trouble, with which case finding leads to lost opportunities because steering and referral of those who need help does not assure that they reach or stay with the helping service.[30] Where "system linkages" are weak, people are often left to fall into the gaps or chasms between programs.

Sometimes the problem is the lack of policy and program coordination, a subject already discussed. Thus, agencies may have standing between them unresolved value conflicts on the handling of cases in which they must cooperate; or the referring agency may have a different perception of the case from the agency to which the referral is made. Or, the total of the functions of the cooperating agencies may not add up to what the client needs.

At other times, however, the problems are in the realm of case integration; simultaneous and sequential meshing is not assured in the operational system. One service does not have any way to know: why the other service has referred the client; how the other service perceives the situation; what the supposedly cooperating service is actually doing; what the referred person has been told, promised, or actually offered. As a consequence, ongoing treatment or services is not additive.

These problems persist beyond the referral stage. Where the situation requires that different agencies reinforce one another in their work with the same or different members of a peer group, this often fails to occur. The

---

[30] The remainder of this section relies heavily on and assumes the documentation contained in Alfred J. Kahn, *Planning Community Services for Children in Trouble* (New York: Columbia University Press, 1963), especially Chaps. I, XII, and XIII.

research literature in public welfare, public health, mental health, housing—to mention only a few fields—documents that most people with complex personal problems are visited regularly by large numbers of representatives of agencies; and that, if anything, the many visitors undermine one another's work—they seldom reinforce one another. To illustrate, without meaning to place blame for a problem which resides in institutional relationships, not in individuals or single programs:

☐ During a long period of institutionalization, a "former" delinquent is told that the community is prepared for his reintegration, since *he* now sees the community differently. On the third day back, his new "homeroom" teacher warns him that the "kids in the class are good" and that she would blame him for any trouble which developed. At the same time, his best friend, still on probation, announces that the probation officer had told him to stay away from his buddy who is a source of trouble.

☐ Several members of a "multi-problem" family (perhaps "multi-agency" is as useful a term!) are being "helped." The teenage son has a probation officer. The welfare department sends an investigator. The mother has been visited·by an attendance officer about her nine-year-old and has also seen the school social worker. She and the enuretic six-year-old go to a child guidance clinic. The husband attends a veterans' mental health center. Family members use several medical clinics and are in constant contact with the housing department's social service center, because a combination of poor housekeeping and the son's court record has placed their tenancy in jeopardy.

The case integration problems here go beyond the need for communication and sharing. For example, the clinic doubts that the husband can work in the free job market, but the investigator is constantly "helping" or pressuring him to find work. The child guidance clinic caseworker has taken a stance with the mother which reinforces precisely the pattern which the psychiatrist at the veterans' center thinks makes life more difficult for the father. The probation officer is trying to get the son to accommodate to a family pattern whose pathology the probation officer does not understand. And this is only a sampling of the difficulties!

The dramatic fact here is not this case but its representativeness of a large universe.

☐ A juvenile court judge, hearing his first case of the morning, disposes of a previously-adjudicated neglect case by telling the mother that he will place the child in a foster home temporarily while a caseworker helps the family get on its feet economically and emotionally. In so doing, the judge ignores the statistical likelihood in the particular city that the child will actually remain in a crowded shelter for a long period of time before he reaches a foster home—if indeed he ever will; that the so-called economic help is far from definite given the circumstances; that, furthermore, once the child is out of the house, this family will get little or no priority attention from those able to offer "emotional" help. In fact, the family pathology will be forgotten. Thus, the foundation of the judge's rationale, the need to break up the family temporarily so as to permit its reconstruction, is built on quicksand.

☐ In his second disposition case of the morning, the same judge instructs the probation officer to seek placement of an adolescent boy in one of three treatment centers, and he specifies the priority. In each instance the appropriateness of the choice rests upon a unique shaping of the components of the center to meet the youth's special needs. However, in referring the case, the probation office mails out a standard case summary form prepared before the session with the judge. The institution, if it accepts the boy, will repeat its own diagnostic study. Those who program for him after eventual admission are very unlikely to talk to the judge or probation office to learn exactly what they had in mind.

Also evident in the foregoing illustrations is the problem of case accountability. The issue is one of the *location of responsibility for continuity of community concern* in the case. Agencies often follow practices which seem foolhardy, cruel, wasteful, and dangerous to any outside observer, yet none is actually failing to discharge its formal responsibility:

☐ A psychiatric hospital finds a child disturbed but not technically committable, so he is returned home, with no further action and the community awaits his next outburst.

☐ Peculiar neurological symptoms in a child are noted in a routine vision screening. The teacher suggests in a note that the mother take him to a neurological clinic. The mother thinks the note silly. There is no follow-up.

☐ A court refers a case to a volunteer big-sister organization; a shortage of personnel leaves the situation unattended, but the court is never informed.

☐ A complex psychiatric situation involving parents and three young children reaches a clinic on referral from a family agency. After a month of attempts, the clinic closes the case for "noncooperation" and does not report back to the referring source or to anyone else.

☐ The agencies in contact with the "multi-problem" family mentioned above continue to find themselves working at cross-purposes. No one agency is responsible for taking the lead in getting things sorted out. There is no device whereby any agency can be assigned this role, and independent initiative may either be welcomed or sabotaged as aggrandizement.

Case accountability, then, involves the designation of a person or an agency as responsible for remaining with a case unless and until there is a decision to discontinue community concern. It locates the obligation of assuring integration of ongoing case service efforts. By its very nature, case accountability in the social service field is closely related to case integration, and the administrative structures available for solution usually attend to both issues.

## Some possibilities

Patients and their relatives often effectively undertake case integration and enforce agency accountability. A research team reports:

> . . . vital to the continued deliverance and receipt of these and of other health and social services, was the assumption of the "coordinator" role by the patient or someone around him. The aggressive prodding and probing of after-care resources and personnel was instrumental in overcoming frequent time-lags, communication failures and other administrative and procedural barriers which patients and their families or caretakers encountered in obtaining needed services.[31]

However, many patients lack the capacities to serve themselves in this way, and they do not have relatives able to take on the role. More formal provision becomes necessary.

Where an agency provides substitute care for a dependent or neglected child and the parents are not or cannot be in the picture, it is urgent that the agency itself provide an internal mechanism to protect the overall interests of the child. Too often goals and purpose are lost to the pressures of organization.

Some agencies in several parts of the world solve this problem by designating a lay or professional person as paid or volunteer child's guardian.[32] It has been proposed in the United States that a guardian in this sense be provided routinely.[33] An Iowa agency concerned with this need has found it desirable for the agency as such to become a "parental force" for every child accepted for care either by delegation (release) by the natural parents or court action. The philosophy is clear:

> The responsibility, once assumed . . . cannot be shed except through the development of some other permanent plan of custody for the child—

---

[31] H. R. Kelman, M. Lowenthal, J. N. Muller, "Community Status of Discharged Rehabilitation Patients: Results of a Longitudinal Study," *Archives of Physical Medicine and Rehabilitation*, 47 (October, 1966), 673–674.

[32] See the pattern in several Scandinavian countries, for example.

[33] A. Delafield Smith, *The Right to Life* (Chapel Hill: University of North Carolina Press, 1955).

back to the natural parent, into adoption, or into self-maintenance. Referral may be made to another agency only for physical care, health services, or therapy, but parental responsibility remains . . . [with the agency].[34]

These are child welfare innovations, but all professional practice requires relevant provision.[35] In general, if any one agency provides all the service or most of it, the agency itself is responsible for case integration, accountability, and continuity. Where the problems are many faceted and several agencies are involved, formal community arrangements are needed. What possibilities might be before the planner of social services as he considers provision for continuity, case integration, and case accountability? One must answer with a listing. The situation is different for the large city with its highly specialized services and for the sparsely-settled county. The problems to be solved and the options open are affected by the type of service involved and the nature of the usual staffing pattern. Legal definitions and responsibilities open opportunities in some situations and restrict them in others.

Many variables affect what is possible, and few of the proposed devices have been tried in many settings with attention to such variables. One thus reports on "possibilities" and leaves for planner consideration patterns which have worked under some circumstances and are hence "promising." The planner must consider both local adaptation and provision for evaluation from the very beginning.

*The case conference—for the many-agency case.*   Where agencies are decentralized and have relatively similar area boundaries, a modern version of the multi-agency case conference[36] may serve in some places to improve case integration and to locate accountability. It is relevant to the complex case whose ramifications require careful meshing. A multi-agency committee must be in existence or there must be a device, such as the service center unit described below, to identify cases for a conference agenda and to convene the staff members of the several agencies involved.

Under one pattern, in which the objective is to use the particular case so as to establish operational principles for the agencies involved, conference participants are generally administrative or supervisory personnel. Then, to cope with the case at hand, line practitioners meet with their opposite num-

---

[34] Edith Zober and Merlin Taber, "The Child Welfare Agency as Parent," *Child Welfare*, XLIV, No. 7 (July, 1965), 389.

[35] We recognize, of course, the great need to protect any child against unnecessary takeover by a "parenting" agency. No case accountability plan is without risks of this kind and legal protections are therefore a fixed requirement.

[36] For background, Kahn, *Planning Community Services* . . . , 450–476.

bers. Before the conference, agency representatives prepare, for advance circulation or for presentation at the meeting, summaries of their contacts with the family and their appraisals. Where administrative machinery exists, an integrated summary may be prepared and circulated.

The conference session itself is usually devoted to a sharing of information and evaluations, culminating in a new, group diagnosis, evaluation, and service plan. Central to such case planning is agreement as to which agency or person is to "take the lead" with the family and how the others are to contribute to or support the effort. A reporting-back date may be set for review of progress and the making of further plans. Once the case is thus placed formally in the center of community attention, it is not quite so readily "lost," especially if a system of recording exists which automatically calls it up for review at a specified time (see below). Accountability may be strengthened by formal agreement that the lead agency will not drop the case and the others will not end the promised services without bringing the case back to the group.

Case conference machinery exists on a large scale and the device is useful for coping with the problems posed. At any given moment, in any specific place, the planner considering the use of the conference to achieve case integration and accountability must face a number of serious limitations. First, generally the pressure for social services and shortages of qualified personnel are such that case conferences can cope only with a small proportion of the load, yet they are conducted as though the caseload is covered. Case conferencing with a small sample is only useful for program and policy coordination, to establish principles for continuity and accountability. Thus far the conference as a device for operation across the board has been most successful in the smaller jurisdictions or where caseloads are limited.

Second, one should not undertake a case conference pattern unless it is possible to invest adequately in administrative machinery that identifies the cases, assembles or prepares the summaries, and assures the reporting back on the dates set. There has been some experience with setting up special units for this assignment in, at one point, the referral units of the New York City Youth Board, some of the projects in several cities inaugurated by Community Research Associates, and special multi-problem family experiments in a number of cities. Experience would seem to suggest that such units can become successful vehicles for case conference machinery if they can resist the temptation themselves to become treatment centers (a valuable device but inconsistent with the role of neutral conference convener) and have sufficient sanctions (an official charge or a relationship to funding sources) to win cooperation.

Nor do case conference committees work successfully unless the urgency is sufficient to overcome the reluctance of some highly-trained professional workers to share materials fully and to work as peers with members of the same or other disciplines who may have far less formal education but who are essential links in the service chain. Social workers with Masters of Science degrees must work with medical social work aides trained at the Bachelor of Science level, psychiatrists must "share" with housing managers, teachers with club leaders, psychologists with institutional cottage parents, and so forth.

Because many of these conditions cannot be met or because the case conference machinery cannot cope with the big-city case volume, other devices will often have the attention of programmers.

*The intensive service unit or worker—for the complex case with many ramifications.* This second device may coexist with a case conferencing scheme. In fact, case conferences are likely to be more productive if several of the major participating agencies work in this fashion as well.

British and American experience[37] and a series of special projects and studies have suggested the possibility of a degree of specialization with some families and individuals found to require particular and concerted attention. Agencies, therefore, may choose to assign to this intensive rehabilitative work staff members who are especially suited on the basis of their understanding, experience, and skill. They carry out treatment procedures while assuming case accountability and integration responsibilities.

Three administrative schemes have been developed for this purpose.

The first employs the intensive worker as a line staff member in an "ordinary" agency whose caseload has been reduced, prerogatives increased, and assignment altered to stress case integration and accountability. In many ways this may be an ideal scheme. The premise is that many users of service do their own "case integration" and need no special follow-up by accountability workers, i.e., the clients coordinate the agencies. However, the very disorganized, despondent, and vulnerable need the added ingredient of care and protection. If each service agency had several intensive workers for such cases as they fall within its purview, and as a case conference or some other procedure clarifies that the problem locus is such as to make it appropriate for the particular agency to "take the lead" with the particular case, the total system of services would not be defeated so routinely by discontinuities and gaps in responsibility.

British proposals in 1954 for definition of this role are validated by subse-

---

[37] *Ibid.*, especially 460–463.

quent experience in the United States. The premise is that it is not a multiplicity of visits or visitors which is the problem so much as the lack of program coordination, case integration, and clarity as to who "takes the lead" for a given case. The requirements are:

☐ Caseloads should be small, consisting of not more than 25 families for each worker. With a larger number than this, the families that are passing through a crisis of some kind cannot be given sufficiently close attention unless other cases are neglected.

☐ One worker should have responsibility for the whole family and for helping it in all its difficulties. Specialist workers will often have to be called in to deal with particular problems, such as poor physical or mental health. But one worker, from whatever service, must have full responsibility for the family, and the others should visit only when necessary and only after consulting with the worker in charge.

☐ Help of this comprehensive kind must be available to a family as soon as its problems grow too complex to be dealt with by the functional services.

☐ Those offering this help must have worked in the same district long enough to have become known and trusted by the families they visit.

☐ There must be close coordination of all services, based on fairly frequent discussions both among those directing the services and, more important, among those actually visiting the same families. It matters little whether this is achieved through formal committees, over a cup of tea in the town hall canteen, or in other ways.

☐ When the immediate crisis is over and families once more begin to lead a fairly normal life, it must be possible for someone to keep in touch with them long enough to prevent a relapse.

☐ People of the right character and experience should be chosen to undertake this personal service, and they should be encouraged to work in an independent and experimental manner and to develop new methods. This is the most important condition of all.[38]

The second administrative scheme uses the intensive case unit, set up within a service or agency, to discharge the function described above on referral or on behalf of specially selected or screened cases. Much of the pioneering work was done in St. Paul, Minnesota, following the research work of Bradley Buell and his associates with multi-problem families. The pattern was copied and then elaborated in many other places. Under the usual arrangement, a special agency is set up as a joint venture of a number of

---

[38] D. V. Donnison, *The Neglected Child and the Social Services* (Manchester, England: Manchester University Press, 1954), 117–118.

agencies or as an experimental unit which is specially funded outside of the ongoing agency system. Cooperating case finding or treatment agencies are supplied with criteria for cases to be accepted.[39]

While reports and analyses of work with individual cases have been positive, the community-wide results of these programs have been a dissappointment in most instances. Extremely difficult cases gradually constitute an increasingly large component of agency time, and the special unit can do little to help solve the community's ongoing need to feed new cases into the agency for special attention. Also, in general, a preoccupation with individual or group treatment techniques rather than with case integration and acountability procedures or with needed changes in service systems tends to characterize the work.

In a variation on this pattern developed out of its public assistance studies, Comunity Research Associates helped several communities develop intensive case service units *within* public welfare offices. An elaborate case-classification system was followed by classification of the entire caseload in accord with intensity of service required. For those in need of intensive help, a special unit was set up, the most qualified staff members assigned, and caseloads made as small as deemed necessary. Here, too, the experience was not very encouraging. Apart from the basic conceptual and policy questions raised by the details of this "caseload management" plan for public welfare, questions not immediately relevant to our purpose,[40] this experience confirms the generalizations already made about intensive units: they tend to accumulate static caseloads and they sacrifice case integration and accountability to concentration on refining individual treatment techniques. This may be worth doing, but it does not solve the problems we are here addressing.

The intensive unit remains on our list of possibilities, however, because its failings might very well be overcome given a clarity as to mission and a pattern of administration and staffing that recognizes the priority of continuity and accountability.

The third administrative scheme relies on the general service unit and polyvalent worker. It partakes of some of the qualities of the first two. It builds on the very successful European experience of the French polyvalent

---

[39] For example, Bradley Buell et al., "Reorganizing to Prevent and Control Disordered Behavior," *Mental Hygiene*, XLII, No. 2 (April, 1958).

[40] See Irving Lukoff and Samuel Mencher, "A Critique of the Conceptual Foundation of Community Research Associates," *Social Service Review*, 36, No. 4 (December, 1962), 444–450.

worker already described and the line social worker in several other western European countries. It also reflects experience in multi-service centers or neighborhood service centers in connection with the American anti-poverty program and the earlier efforts of the President's Committee on Delinquency and Youth Crime.[41] *It has the advantage of implementing the notion that social services should be concerned initially at least with accountability in all case situations, not merely in work with very disorganized families.*

Much of what can and should be said about the place of a general or personal social service unit or of a general (polyvalent) social worker is reserved for the chapter on local social service delivery (Chapter VII in the companion volume). The information and referral role of the polyvalent worker in France has already been described. The relevant notion here, in contrast to the intensive worker or intensive unit, is that the general worker or general unit is assigned responsibility for screening, evaluation, referral, emergency help, accountability, and integration. The role is made comparable to that of the general practitioner in the medical field. The general unit retains the primary relationship with the family, drawing upon specialists as appropriate, but never giving up the case and still being held responsible for the meshing of the components. Status comes from successful discharge of these responsibilities with many cases, not from intensive work with a few.

This pattern of work may be achieved either through the locally-stationed detached polyvalent worker, as in the French system, or by creating what might be described as a neighborhood general personal or family counseling service. The latter would combine the orientations of family and child welfare, adolescent, and senior citizen counseling units, and some of the case advocacy and flexibility characteristic of the anti-poverty local social service programs. As mentioned earlier, local anti-poverty community action programs, seeking to correct the defects of the social service system as it is experienced by deprived people in the most poverty-stricken neighborhoods, have placed high priority on neighborhood service centers, which combine a number of functions, ranging from education and job training to recruitment for social action. Quite often the core function, or an important function among others, is a linkage service known as "social brokerage." Professional

---

[41] See Robert Perlman and David Jones, *Neighborhood Service Centers* (Washington, D.C.: Government Printing Office, 1967); also, Schorr *op. cit.* Even more ambitious recommendations for Great Britain have been made in *Report of The Committee on Local Authority and Allied Personal Social Services,* Frederic Seebohm, Esq., Chairman (London: Her Majesty's Stationery Office, 1968, Cmnd. 3703).

practitioners or locally-recruited, indigenous, nonprofessional staff develop a pattern of working which combines traditional social work liaison services with a strong mixture of case advocacy.

Clearly, one sees here an administrative structure capable of supporting the case integration and accountability assignments under discussion. Successful operations would require some raising of the level of competence and preparation (although one might find it possible to continue with nonprofessionals in the line positions) and further clarity about function. Policy advocacy and recruitment for social action have obvious merit in antipoverty programs. If these are considered the priority tasks of the line staff in neighborhood centers, however, other provision will have to be made for case accountability and integration.

The other major obstacle to this approach in the United States is the absence of a "general practitioner" role in professional social work. Child welfare or psychiatric clinics employ line practitioners on all levels of competence, not functioning as do specialists in other fields who usually build upon a general practice. Given European experience, this could be changed if patterns of operation require it.

The general practice unit and general practice worker constitute very powerful responses to the problems here under scrutiny. The planner should obviously give them high-priority consideration if the obstacles which they face, as described above, can be solved and if they fit into the general model developed for local social service delivery. Other elements of such models and the concept of hierarchical levels for different functions and types of specialization, related to density of service need, are presented in our discussion of local social service delivery (Chapter VII in the companion volume).

*Area teams.* The third device which could be used to achieve integration and accountability may be seen as a variation on the first, a "case conference" operating in the field and covering a defined population or geographic area. A group, consisting of members of several disciplines, or members of one discipline with different specializations or educational levels, is assigned formally—or constitutes itself informally—to render the service. In the former instance, the team has the caseload and the team leader assigns roles and develops integrating and accountability devices. Several welfare, mental health, child welfare, and educational efforts operate on this basis. In the less formal pattern (rural child welfare, public health, work in city neighborhoods facing considerable pathology), agency representatives constitute themselves as a team, meet regularly to share information and to allocate responsibility, and accept accountability as a group.

The device has been effective in specific areas when circumstances demanded strong mobilization but has not been fully implemented on a city-wide basis or evaluated in such terms. Emergency creates unity of purpose and submerges professional and agency prerogatives. These become a problem in the long run. A formal team within an agency improves integration in a welfare or health service, but does not move across enough boundaries.

*Accountability rosters.* Whatever the administrative arrangements for service, each of the three patterns would be enhanced by the addition of a well-functioning, preferably computerized, accountability roster. Little relevant experience exists. There are few technological obstacles in the way, but the planner must cope with serious issues relating to privacy, confidentiality, and the possibility of misuse.

The concept is simple. In any interagency system, whether based on a case conference plan or on general policy coordination, there are some cases which all would concede must not be dropped from the community spotlight until a problem has been solved or until there is community consensus, by responsible authority, to the effect that it cannot be solved but poses no continuing danger. Cases on an accountability roster might thus consist of protective cases in child welfare (neglect and abuse), individuals on probation and parole, mental illness and retardation facility patients on home-care status, about whom there is some concern, victims of some of the addictions, and others. Community legal and social procedures would define when a name could be and is added (at neglect adjudication, for example), by whom, to whom a roster goes periodically for the rendering of a status report (this would vary with the case type), and which agency or interagency group could drop which names—through what procedures. Rights of certain clients to refuse listing or to be dropped demand advance clarification and clear publicization.

Specifics depend on the development of services and legal traditions. Rigorous rules about access and confidentiality are essential. Nonetheless, it is now technically possible to arrange—and a planning process could provide for—such accountability rosters. Case conference committees would use them as points of departure and follow-up. They could help the planners of public service and the purchasers of care from the voluntary sector to locate and follow up on priority cases. Most important, for the serious cases, responsibility for the case integration role and follow-up accountability could be defined and implemented.

## THE PROTECTION OF CITIZENS

The Swedish institution of the "Ombudsman" (*Justitieombudsman*) was created in 1809 to provide a "procurator for civil affairs" whose role would parallel that of a "procurator for military affairs." Originally intended to provide parliamentary scrutiny of governmental activity, the office evolved into a citizen outlet for grievances. Developments in many countries, some quite independent and others under clear influence of the Swedish system— and most of them quite recent—have made the office of the ombudsman the most generally considered protection for the citizen in a world of complex and impersonal governmental bureaucracy. Japan's Administrative Inspection Bureau and the Soviet Union's "procurators" are clearly identifiable and independent variations worthy of special attention in large countries. The United States system of Neighborhood Legal Services, should it continue and expand, would suggest a valuable supplement.[42]

## The problems addressed

Walter Gellhorn, who has done most to analyze the strengths and weaknesses of "governmental grievance procedures" in many countries, reminds us that "organized power makes the wheels of life go round, makes modernity feasible." But public authority may be "oppressive, mistaken, or careless . . ."—even though in any given country these maladies are not necessarily "more widespread among civil servants than among human beings generally." A general spread of democratic impulses and increased understanding of the problem of protecting individual, group, and civil servant rights in an increasingly complex and bureaucratized world of government have led to considerable interest in "protective mechanisms against official mistake, malice, or stupidity."[43]

Social planners addressing urban problems in particular will therefore find themselves called upon to consider governmental grievance procedures as well as, perhaps in conjunction with, and occasionally in place of, the mechanisms for access and channeling already discussed. Since the "movement" for formal provision along these lines is relatively new and experience with actual operations quite limited, it is possible here only to review issues and possibilities, with particular attention to relevant criteria.

---

[42] Major sources for this section are: Walter Gellhorn, *Ombudsmen and Others* (Cambridge, Mass.: Harvard University Press, 1966). [Gellhorn's documentation and citations for programs in nine countries is so complete as to make it unnecessary here to mention any except the several major sources]; Walter Gellhorn, *When Americans Complain* (Cambridge, Mass.: Harvard University Press, 1966); Donald C. Rowat, Editor, *The Ombudsman* (London: George Allen & Unwin, Ltd., 1965); Geoffrey Sawyer, "Ombudsmen" (Victoria, Australia: Melbourne University Press, 1964, pamphlet); H. S. Reuss and S. V. Anderson, "The Ombudsman: Tribune of the People," *The Annals of the American Academy of Political and Social Science*, 363 (January, 1966), 44–51.

See Chapter II in the companion volume re Neighborhood Legal Services.

[43] Gellhorn, *When Americans Complain*, 3, 4, 6.

## Why new provision?

The obvious question, in confronting the problems to be solved, is whether existing structures could not meet the need or could not be augmented to do so. In a sympathetic and detailed analysis, Gellhorn acknowledges the roles and contributions in this field of legislatures ("legislatures control administrators") and courts ("judges are wonderfully capable watchmen"), but he finds a need for additional provision as well. His main concerns are relevant to the ultimate definition of the characteristics of the needed instrument.[44]

Legislatures that would prevent abuse by narrow definition of administrators' power find that they have eliminated needed flexibility and must, themselves, frequently enact the petty details. Procedural mandates in laws may be a real contribution to citizens' protection if substance is not thereby lost. "Question Hour" in parliamentary bodies has symbolic value but covers few cases. The activities of the legislator in his personal "casework" role—as Gellhorn calls case handling on complaint from constituents—serve to speed up action on some cases, satisfying some complaints to legislators; leave the basic problems untouched; burden legislators and take their time from other responsibilities; often result in decisions which are not fair or wise; and in general tend to get handling on varied levels of competence.

The congressional and state legislative roles could be strengthened, particularly through additional resources for "casework" by legislators, but the need for further provision also exists.

Because willingness to pursue alleged abuse through the courts and financial ability to do so, do not often coincide, relatively few cases reach federal court review. Many technicalities, varying with field and statute, block the path to the courts for redress (justiciability). Yet, "matters that do not fit into the pattern of cases and controversies for whose resolution courts were designed may be gravely significant for society as a whole as well as for individual members."[45] In many fields, which are of prime concern in the present volume, and of which public assistance in the United States or educational programs serve as relevant examples, there is considerable legal question as to the nature of rights which have been created. Nonetheless, administrative abuse may exist and may be correctible by nonjudicial machinery.

Acknowledging the relevant and significant educational role of the courts with reference to rights and the boundaries of power, and valuing the judicial

---

[44] *Ibid.*, Chap. I.

[45] *Ibid.*, 27.

review which does take place, one must conclude that the "random" nature of court supervision provides a strong case for other "grievance bureaus" as well.[46] Moreover, their general flexibility makes it possible for such bureaus to enter some situations more readily than courts and to pursue them more basically—or in a needed spirit of compromise. The search may be for a desirable solution, not punishment or assessment of blame.

The attention given new arrangements does not necessarily preclude admiration for efforts to strengthen other institutional protection. There is world-wide respect for the French *Conseil d'État* in its role in administrative appeals, yet the volume of its work demands a system of subordinate tribunals and results in procedures which are difficult of access for the common man. In the United States, the recently-established Administrative Conference on the federal level could become a most potent and sophisticated "special legislature" devoted to administrative matters.[47] Budget bureaus, auditors, inspectors-general and other self-policing in individual departments, citizen "watch-dog" committees, and others have their roles at federal and state levels. Nor are local city complaint bureaus, information offices, radio complaint programs and newspaper columns, direct services by councilmen and legislators without their effects. Nonetheless, a careful review of experience and the continuing, indeed increasing, search everywhere for additional provision confirms the need. Modern society has not yet solved the problem of protecting Everyman against what must be called "mass production" government.

### "Ombudsmen and Others"

Gellhorn notes that there are, of course, major variations among ombudsman systems in different countries, growing out of the political and legal milieu, the particular circumstances which created the institution in each country, and also, perhaps, the characteristics of incumbents.[48] Nonetheless the commonalities are many.

Ombudsmen in Sweden, Denmark, Norway, and Finland are men of professional distinction who "function as general complaint bureaus to which everyone can turn, at little or no cost, to complain about an administrator's naughty acts or failures to act."[49] They themselves may initiate

---

[46] *Ibid.* In fact, where judicial review is not part of the total redress system, Gellhorn has serious question about it. See his comments about the Soviet Union, in *Ombudsmen and Others*, on page 369.

[47] Gellhorn, *When Americans Complain*, 98–100.

[48] Gellhorn, *Ombudsmen and Others*.

[49] Gellhorn, *When Americans Complain*, 9.

inquiries on the basis of general information or routine inspections. They investigate and recommend, for the most part, seldom overruling or prosecuting, although they may have some powers to do so.

Limitations on the role vary by country: some may not investigate courts and tribunals. Others must stay out of the military. At least one sits in on a cabinet and is a critic of proposed actions, in addition to filling a more general role. Several countries divide the role among two or more functionaries, leaving the boundaries vague.

In general, ombudsmen deal with the relatively small administrative actions, each of which is of some significance in the lives of one or more individuals and which, cumulatively, spell out the human relations tone and impact of a total governmental system. For the most part, but not always, this institution provides machinery for redress which may be called into play if other available remedies are exhausted. At times it is not the final remedy, but one of several options.

Ombudsmen's common attributes have been listed as follows:

1. All are instruments of the legislature but function independently of it, with no links to the executive branch and with only the most general answerability to the legislature itself.
2. All have practically unlimited access to official papers bearing upon matters under investigation, so that they can themselves review what prompted administrative judgment.
3. All can express an official expert's opinion about almost anything that governors do and that the governed do not like.
4. All take great pains to explain their conclusions, so that both administrators and complaining citizens will understand the results reached.[50]

Ombudsmen in some countries are limited to the national level; in others they may also investigate local authorities. Some must publicize all their findings, but in most places they have a good deal of discretion.[51]

In a few places they may prosecute, but seldom do so. Most cases are not accepted or not settled in favor of complainants—but the complainant gets a full explanation. Where a complaint is upheld, persuasion is more often used to achieve justice than legal action. Recommendations of a specific or general sort to administrators and legislators are the usual disposition vehicle, where a positive finding is made; and there is variation in the degree of generality of the findings. Gellhorn sees "general proposals" as tending to be ineffectual while recommendations on concrete specific cases are usually

---

[50] *Ibid.*, 9–10.

[51] See Rowat, *op. cit.*; and Gellhorn, *Ombudsmen and Others.*

quickly adopted almost everywhere. While ombudsmen tend to find for the complainant only in about 10 percent of all cases, great satisfaction is also said to accrue to those whose complaints are not accepted but who appreciate the consideration shown them and are convinced by the ombudsmen's reasoning. Initially skeptical or fearful public servants have been won over upon discovering that a system for objective investigation, which sifts out unsubstantiated complaints, actually serves as protection for personnel in "exposed" positions. Therefore, when ombudsmen do find fault, administrators tend to listen. Ombudsmen are often careful to keep out of areas where they can accomplish little, or may find compromises which satisfy the interests of all parties. Although, in contrast to courts or legislators responding to single cases, they are technically free to arrive at generalizations and to propose generally needed remedies, some ombudsmen tend to seize such opportunities more than others do.

Ombudsmen have developed in small countries, but if Sweden's population of 7½ million is an outer limit, only seven states in this country exceed this figure, as Gellhorn notes. Only three United States cities exceed in number New Zealand's 2½ million people who are served by one person. However, as Gellhorn also notes, one may derive, from the Japanese experience or the Soviet approach, evidence that the system may be organized more formally and on a larger scale. Indeed, several of the ombudsmen share their roles in part with other officials. Japan has developed an Administrative Inspection Bureau which, through 50 offices and the support of 3,500 volunteer "local administrative counselors," copes with 5,000 cases per month. (Volunteers also provide an apparently effective citizen information system.) This system is less effective in deriving general lessons from specific cases than are some of the others, but it does seem to be effective from the complainants' perspective. The U.S.S.R. relies on local "procurators"—prosecuting attorneys—but defines them as "guardians of legality,"[52] who are charged with assuring that officials as well as citizens meet their obligations. The system itself would not fit other ideological contexts, but it does support the notion that "multitudinous" ombudsmen are possible.

### Principles for planning

The experience supports those who would pioneer in this realm in the United States—with priority to be given to provision relative to state and local services, since these most often confront the citizen in his daily life. Federal programs often have administrative appeals machinery and may

---

[52] Gellhorn, *When Americans Complain*, 10.

benefit, as Gellhorn notes, from the developing work of the Administrative Conference. In addition, strengthened "inspector-general" functions to improve the processing of complaints within some federal departments would be useful.

General state and local public grievance systems deserve considerable attention on the part of those who would cope with current social concerns and problems. Such systems would not attempt to substitute for the relevant work of legislators on all levels, courts, or internal policing by departments. They would appear to have advantages over complaint boards which single out one department or service and which undercut a department's responsibility for self-policing.

Thus the planners of American ombudsman-type experiments in cities and states, drawing on the available analysis of experience (and with special attention to Gellhorn's work), might consider cases of harm to the public at large (from non-administration or maladministration), harm to a class or group of individuals (traffic violators or relief applicants, for example), and individual grievances (petty or major errors by officials).

To meet the need, accommodate to the American governmental system, and protect existing prerogatives of other grievance mechanisms they should probably:

Be available when remedies built into the department or agency involved have been used and exhausted. And they should ". . . be commentators upon departures from approved norms, advisors about how to achieve widely desired ends. Unconstrained by the grooves of old habits, they would nevertheless be guided by successful administrative experience when criticizing stagnant practices." The ombudsman role is not one of basic policy or administrative innovation.[53]

Be completely impartial, not part of any system of administrative hierarchy and not in a position to implement any actions. This may not require a very large apparatus but need not be limited to the single "National Father Figure" whose image is usually conjured up by the Scandinavian experience.

Be completely nonpolitical. This is the sense in which an ombudsman has advantages over an inspector-general. Nonetheless, there may be terms of office and a basis for removal for cause by the legislative branch. Salaries should be high enough to attract leading professional people, confer status, and remove the office-holder from a search for promotion. Supporting staffs

---

[53] *Ibid.*, 225. Specific proposals and a model statute appear in Stanley V. Anderson, Editor, *Ombudsmen for American Government?* (Englewood Cliffs, N.J.: Prentice-Hall, 1963).

should be sufficient for the investigative load and adequate feedback and reporting.

Be as quick to defend and interpret agencies as to call for correction. The ultimate purpose is a stronger system of administration.

Be free to report publicly, recommend to administrators—as the case may require—while protecting confidentiality and always rendering an account to complainants.

## Information and grievance systems

A Citizens' Advice Bureau kind of information service has been described as having a semi-ombudsman function, yet planners seeking to program in accord with the primary task will want to be clear about distinctions. An information service in a modern American city will wish to include what we have called a case advocacy function and will seek persistently to obtain help and service for its clients. Its policy advocacy will probably be limited in most instances (a conclusion disputed by some observers) as tending to cut off needed direct service and creating an image of community-action militancy rather than service to individuals.[54] Its unofficial standing, lack of access to records and witnesses, and its mediating role in the search for help and service do not make the information service a basic grievance instrument. It will of course hear about grievances and help people plan to cope with them, with referrals to lawyers, neighborhood legal services,[55] various administrative tribunals, and (should the service develop) to the local ombudsman. Identified with the individual in need of help, the neighborhood information service representative may in some instances appear with him and interpret his problem before a tribunal, an ombudsman, or in any agency—should his circumstances and capacities be such as to require aid.

## DECENTRALIZATION AS A PROGRAMMING STRATEGY

In concluding this general discussion of programming for social service delivery, it may be useful to note the repetition of the decentralization theme[56] as it has affected the approach to access, channeling, case integration, accountability, and manpower. The limitations of decentralization must also be recalled.

---

[54] Kahn et al., *Neighborhood Information Centers.*

[55] See Chapter III in the companion volume.

[56] Decentralization in planning is separately, if somewhat artificially, discussed in Chapters II, IV, and XI.

It is not decentralization to create a strong central office and to give it local outlets. Decentralization implies some assignment of the power to exercise discretion, adapt programs, and relate to other programs in accord with local conditions and preferences.

A fully centralized operation could create neighborhood information and case channeling outlets and even devise a system for case integration and accountability. However, the social commitment of a social service system is to *deliver and facilitate use* of certain basic services offered through public and voluntary programs. The human needs which are encountered, to use a phrase suggested by Eugene Litwak and Henry Meyer, represent "non-uniform events." Primary groups and their requirements must be coordinated with bureaucracies.[57] The advantage of decentralization is its potential for innovation, flexibility, and person-oriented integration of components.

Decentralization is no guarantee but offers the possibility of organization (bureaucratization) of these goals. We have mentioned: variations in forms of a neighborhood information center, to reflect the overall service pattern; use of local people as staff and volunteers, to facilitate communication and what sociologists call "system linkage"; employment of intensive workers, able to undertake personally several of the needed helping roles and to integrate service components. We might also have noted that the neighbor-user's identification with a local community and its service is a component of social control and stability. Staffs in decentralized offices may have maximum job autonomy, an important component of worker satisfaction in this era of technology.[58] True decentralization leaves in the hands of staff or local board sufficient power to select from among service options and to devise locally-relevant administrative arrangements. Decentralization also offers the possibility for effective local activity to protect service users against bureaucratic arbitrariness. A major innovation of the United States antipoverty effort from 1965 on was the creation of local boards involving "poor" people, the users of service. Within a short time, the impact on policies and services of all local agencies was noticeable.

Long experience has disclosed that the various program and policy coordination devices become meaningless ritual if the local administrators must return to a central office for each decision. Nor does one obtain a locally relevant balance and service "mix" among fields on the basis of com-

---

[57] Eugene Litwak and Henry Meyer, "Social Welfare and Social Work," in Paul F. Lazarsfeld *et al.*, Editors, *The Uses of Sociology* (New York: Basic Books, 1967).

[58] Charles Frankel, *The Democratic Prospect* (New York: Harper & Row, 1962), Chap. VI.

plete central control. In short, the case for a degree of decentralization in *planning* is also applicable to the *programming* of services whether for state in relation to federal government, city in relation to state, or neighborhood in relation to city. The nature and size of the unit for decentralization must vary with the content of the program, the degree of specialization and separateness which may be desirable, and the intensity of usage.[59]

Banfield suggests the following hypothesis to guide decentralization: one should approach organization (or, in our sense, programming) as a problem of "arranging the situation so that individuals, in seeking to maximize the attainment of their own ends, do not impose so many costs upon each other."[60]

Services which can in some way become unique to the locality, without thereby negatively affecting services in other localities, are permitted their own shape. The board or executive of such units are then permitted to do what they can within the limits imposed by resources assigned and some general policy parameters.

Where local units must interact and substantially affect one another in routine operations, limits are imposed. Where central policy is critical and not routinely implemented, decentralization is controlled. (Complete decentralization would have blocked all racial integration in much of the South, for example.) Where coordination is urgent, central directions may be given. For the ultimate limitation on decentralization is the need in programming to translate policy into reality, to assure coordination, and to use scarce resources efficiently. In the social welfare world absolute decentralization is seldom possible.[61] However, a considerable increase in decentralization in service programming would, in many places, bring programs closer to their targets and actually increase access and effectiveness.

The planning issue became enormously complicated in many American cities, but particularly New York, in late 1968 and early 1969, when the "community control" slogan was raised in conjunction with educational and public welfare decentralization. Broader political goals relating to minority group "power" tended to dominate the debate, and it became difficult to

---

[59] Chapter VII in the companion volume discusses hierarchies of social services for different geographic levels as illustration.

[60] Edward C. Banfield, "Three Concepts for Planners," in Edward C. Banfield, Editor, *Urban Government* (New York: The Free Press, 1969; rev. ed.), 616.

[61] For a thoughtful analysis of New Zealand's experience, see J. H. Robb, "Family Structure and Agency Coordination: Decentralization and the Citizen," in Mayer N. Zald, Editor, *Social Welfare Institutions* (New York: John Wiley & Sons, 1965), 383–399.

locate the balance point between central policy responsibility and decentralization.

## TASK AND POLICY AS GUIDES

We have reviewed here only selected programming problems, with an eye to current priorities. To a considerable extent, the emphasis has been on assuring efficient, humane, responsive, equitable, effective services, despite problems imposed by inevitable specialization and bigness.

In conclusion, one must agree with James Q. Wilson that, "there are inherent limits to what can be accomplished by large hierarchical organizations," and that some of the consequences of bureaucratization are not fully conquerable. Moreover, emphasis on some objectives (accountability, for example) may hamper others (flexibility). Many of the solutions are, however, potent and worthy of attention. Their success depends on the recognition that the task at hand and its resultant policy must be clearly in mind as choices are made. For we can be somewhat more deliberate about trade-offs and gain significant leverage on a problem only "when we decide what we are trying to accomplish."[62]

---

[62] James Q. Wilson, "The Bureaucracy Problem," *The Public Interest*, No. 6 (Winter, 1967), 3–9.

# XI

# ORGANIZATION FOR PLANNING, EVALUATION, AND FEEDBACK

A POINT of view about the logic of a planning enterprise inevitably carries implications with reference to the organizational structuring of such planning and its staffing. A relatively brief and general exploration of such implications is in order here, including provision for reporting, measurement, feedback, and evaluation. This discussion must be limited and general, since full coverage would demand attention to much of the entire substance of research methodology. We begin with the question of staffing.

## STAFFING

A total planning process, when in any sense broad and comprehensive, requires the consistent or occasional support of several types of people on the professional staff:

- □ policy analysts
- □ program developers
- □ administration specialists
- □ measurement people
- □ budgeters
- □ enablers, negotiators, or bargainers.

While the terms used to convey these roles may vary, the competencies are generally understood and sought. Policy analysts contribute to assessment of current realities, to formulation of the planning task, and the evolution of the proposed policy. Program people must specify the details of the steps in moving from policy to operations, while underscoring possible unrecognized implications of policy. They focus on the interventive repertoire and its structural requirements. Administration specialists concern themselves

305

with organizational structures relevant to programming, with coordination, integration, accountability, reporting, and feedback systems; they follow through or cooperate with specialists who undertake staffing.

The measurement experts have roles at all stages: assessing the present reality and projecting it, pursuing implications of alternative proposals, specifying feedback and evaluation designs, carrying out and assessing results of evaluation-feedback-reporting systems. Where cost-benefit studies are to be carried out, theirs is the central competence apart from the policy expertise in development of criteria. Indeed, PPBS and cost-benefit analyses require "measurement" and budgeting people with specialized competences. Budgeters work with programmers, administrators, and measurement staff in specifying implications of alternative proposals, analyzing feasibility in the light of resources, and developing actual budgets once planning decisions are taken. In addition, they undertake annually to translate a general program into next-phase detail, with a view to ongoing fiscal experience.

The "enablers" or community organization personnel are involved at one or all phases:

□ helping to create a planning coalition;
□ developing public and organizational interest, understanding, determination to act in the preplanning phase;
□ exploring, assembling, helping to create statutory or de facto sanction for planning in a given agency or organization;
□ helping to create and finance, where necessary, new organizational structures for planning;
□ facilitating exploration, and expression of community preference through a variety of community organization patterns, both before plans are evolved and in response to publicly promulgated proposals;
□ facilitating or organizing efforts to achieve, block, monitor, or revise the proposals which have been promulgated.

The diversity of planning substance and context is such that one does not envisage all of these roles as appropriate at all times. The single or several organizations, departments, or communities involved in specific planning enterprises do need to give consideration to the critical skills and how they are to be assured. Volunteers sometimes carry some of the roles. Several of the types of activity may be within the scope of a given professional person (perhaps measurement and budgeting, or policy analysis and programming). As one moves from small to large planning enterprises, from interest-group planning to comprehensive efforts by statutory bodies, from project planning to broader focus, from neighborhood to central government, the need for more specialists is likely to increase. Local planning efforts tend to emphasize community organization activity more than do state, regional, or national undertakings.

Mention has not yet been made of substantive expertise: urban problems, social security, delinquency, community psychiatry, and so on. Obviously, policy analysts and programmers either require knowledge of or must be allowed consultation and other opportunity to become acquainted with the particular substantive area involved. In general, the core of a planning staff should have background in the substantive fields which are the ongoing concern of the enterprise.

To some extent, the implementation of this principle must depend on earlier decisions: does one unite or separate economic, physical, and social planning organizationally? Within the general arena of social planning, will one join or separate income security, social services, educational planning? While we shall return to this issue, we might note here that planning tends towards greater unity in those places with planning on a national governmental level. The United States, as an extreme case, and many other countries, with only partial national planning or decentralized national planning, tend to separate the planning sectors. Even the more centralized planning endeavors usually have a degree of sectorial separation on some governmental levels.

Where there is unity, one would expect a staff balanced with expertise from all three realms: economic, physical, social. In practice the emphasis is in favor of economists, whose discipline and method tend to set the conceptual framework for national planning. On an urban planning level, with only limited economic planning considered relevant, the architects and urban design specialists tend to dominate, since the framework is often theirs—but the social welfare experts (using that phrase in its most general sense) should play a larger role than they now do.[1] One would expect competence from among the several social sectors in the comprehensive, more specifically social, planning enterprises: education, income security, social services, health, and so on. This is sometimes, but not always, achieved.

In all of these instances, however, the lesson of all available experience argues against monopoly by one discipline: there should be no economic planning with only economists on the staff, no physical planning completely in the hands of architects, no social welfare planning reserved completely to social workers and sociologists. While this view will be documented more

---

[1] The substantive case for this view is argued in Chapter V in the companion volume.

specifically in the illustrative chapters of the companion volume, enough has been already said to demonstrate that:

- ☐ There is no economic planning without serious social consequences to be taken into account, social programming to support economic measures, and socially relevant options to be assessed.
- ☐ Bricks, mortar, and zoning maps do not make real communities.
- ☐ Social welfare programs that list requirements without assessing costs, resources, manpower, and benefits are truncated, at the very least.
- ☐ Economic plans require capital construction planning.
- ☐ Social welfare efforts need to be staged with reference to the phases of economic development.

These requirements and demands pose a number of different possibilities for the training of planners. The field is in transition and no clearly validated pattern has as yet emerged. Economics departments and various types of economic-development institutes, many of them university-based, provide the bulk of the training in economic planning and some experience, as well as occasional training, in social planning. Schools of architecture have provided basic city planning training from the physical side, have gradually turned to social concerns and often included urban land economics. Many such schools have added special institutes, programs, or courses relating to comprehensive city planning, urban problems, and social planning. Several give special attention to the concerns of developing countries.

Several graduate schools of social work in the past have trained small numbers of planners and researchers for community health and welfare councils and specialized planning and coordinating agencies in health and welfare. At the same time, "enabling"-oriented community organizers have been prepared in such schools. During the past decade, such training has expanded severalfold in scale and considerably in scope. Broad social planning courses are now offered in several graduate social work schools, and the expansion continues. Training for grassroots community organization, social action, and related activity is now carried out on an impressive scale.

Schools of public health have long produced a stream of specialized, highly competent public health planners, and several centers now give specialist training on an advanced level for community mental health. Several graduate schools of education play a similar role in educational planning. Some graduate social science programs also specialize in medical economics and the economics of education.

In addition one should note that, varying by country, university, and discipline, there has been relevant training in applied sociology, applied anthropology, applied behavioral science, agriculture, law, and political science. In some places and on some levels, individuals from each of these backgrounds, as well as those from the disciplines listed above, play the role of planning directors, staff members, or consultants in economic, physical, or social planning and in rural or urban community development.

This would hardly appear to be the moment for closure on the question of training for planners. One would encourage continuation of all these thrusts and more adequate communication and sharing among them, until the further maturity of planning itself and its more complete institutionalization permit more precise definition of staffing requirements. Some generalizations already appear valid:

Planning will remain a *coalitional* activity, requiring a variety of roles and the perspectives of several disciplines.

It will need practitioners from the professions (such as architecture, social work, medicine, nursing) as well as from behavioral and social science (economics, political science, sociology, etc.).

Within each of the several planning patterns, one would wish to train generalists, but every planner should also have specialty competence in one or more of the fields covered.

The supporting organizational framework should avoid imagery, conditions, or requirements which would preclude the above principles.[2]

## CURRENT STRUCTURES

Waterston and Tinbergen in particular, but also Hagen, Shonfield, and others, have charted, compiled, described, and analyzed organization for economic and development planning. There are no comparable summaries or systematic analyses of social planning.[3] Nonetheless, the lessons of economic

---

[2] The following are helpful: Arnold Gurin *et al.*, *Organizing and Planning for Social Welfare* (publication pending); Henry Fagin, "The Problem of Training Planners," in Henry Cohen and Harvey Perloff, Editors, *Urban Research and Education in the New York Region* (New York: Regional Plan Association, 1965, Vol. 2); Paul Davidoff, "Advocacy and Pluralism in Planning," *Journal of the American Institute of Planners*, XXXI, No. 4 (November, 1965), 336–337; Dimitrius Iatridcs, "Social Planners: Strategy and Targets" (Athens: Institute of Ekistics, 1965, mimeographed); Corwin R. Mocine, "Urban Physical Planning and the 'New Planning'," *Journal of the American Institute of Planners*, XXXII, No. 4 (July, 1966), 234–237; Harvey Perloff, Editor, *Planning and the Urban Community* (Pittsburgh: University of Pittsburgh Press, 1961), Part Three; Yehezkel Dror, "Policy Analysts: A New Professional Role in Government," *Public Administration Review*, XXVII, No. 3 (September, 1967), 197–203.

[3] Albert Waterston, *Development Planning* (Baltimore: The Johns Hopkins Press, 1965); Everett E. Hagen, Editor, *Planning Economic Development* (Homewood, Ill.: Richard D. Irwin, 1963); Andrew Shonfield, *Modern Capitalism: The Changing Balance of Public and Private Power* (New York: Oxford University Press, 1965); United Nations Economic and Social Council, "Administrative Aspects of Social Planning" (New York, 1965, E/CN.5/393; ST/TAO/M/26); William A. Robson, "The Governmental and Administrative Framework to Achieve the Aims of Urbanization Policy in Different Fields," in United Nations, *Seminar on Urban Development Policy and Planning*, Warsaw, Poland, 1962 (Geneva: 1962, mimeographed, SOA/ESWP/1962), 168–179; Jan Tinbergen, *Central Planning* (New Haven: Yale University Press, 1964, paperback).

planning do shed light on some of the issues and options to be faced in providing for social planning. First, however, a few generalized statements about present arrangements may be attempted.

Countries with centrally-planned economies, both of the socialist or "market" varieties, and at various points in the continuum between the "indicative" and the "imperative," tend either to include social planning within the general concern of the economic planning machinery at the executive level of government (sometimes with specialized staff and usually in a secondary capacity), or they create parallel social planning machinery to feed its output into the overall product.

In these countries to some degree, and *in most other countries at various stages of development,* many other devices are in use—usually several in one country:

1. Departmental planning staffs in some or all of the social "fields" (the Research and Development Division of the United States Office of Economic Opportunity or the Office for Program Coordination of the Department of Health, Education, and Welfare).[4]

2. Planning undertakings by royal or presidential commissions, legislative committees, task forces, or coordinating agencies directly responsible to the executive or the legislature (Sweden's Royal Commission on Family Policy, Britain's Plowden Committee [education], the United States Joint Committee on the Economic Report or the President's Commission on Law Enforcement and Administration of Justice).

3. Nonstatutory planning by specialized, national, voluntary professional or coordinating agencies, or by foundations, permanent or ad hoc (James Conant's various studies of education, foster care and adoption planning by the Child Welfare League of America).

4. Planning by semi-independent commissions created by legislative action for limited time periods and charged with developing reports in specific areas (in the United States, the Joint Commission on Mental Illness and Health).

5. Planning by political parties (pre-election platform materials in a number of countries).

6. Comprehensive planning or policy development by university-based or other semi-independent, generally nonprofit, research centers and institutes (Denmark's *Socialforskningsinstituttet,* and in the United States, The Brookings Institution, etc.).

---

[4] Gellhorn notes another pattern: Swedish ministries devote themselves to planning since they do not administer. Walter Gellhorn, *Ombudsmen and Others* (Cambridge: Harvard University Press, 1966), 195–196.

To some extent, most of these devices may be and are duplicated at a state level in the United States or on a provincial-department level in other countries. In addition, specialized regional agencies within a country, and those involving more than one country, may undertake either comprehensive planning (Tennessee Valley Authority) or specialized planning with reference to defined spheres of action (river basin development, educational planning, disease eradication, making social security systems compatible, creating a wide labor market). The European Economic Community offers a broad illustration, the Southern Educational Conference Board a more narrow one. Such enterprises encompass considerable social planning.

Cities almost always have provision for physical planning since zoning is unavoidable, and recent legislation has all but required some related social programming. However, it remains the case that when one reaches the municipal level, physical planning departments and commissions are quite common while comprehensive planning bodies with a statutory base are rare. Departmental planning in some of the social fields, and occasionally covering several social sectors, has become less rare under the impetus of the federal anti-poverty effort, the Model Cities program, and various aspects of educational, health, mental health, and manpower legislation. The latter may be illustrated by the planning activities within New York City's Human Resources Administration.

Public planning on a municipal level, particularly public physical planning, was long dominated by the concept of the impartial, nonadministrative planning board or commission, which studied needs and developments, created plans and master plans, and published recommendations—which were or were not enacted by other governmental components. Disinterested expert help was sought in this way. As will be noted subsequently, "task force" and executive branch planning instruments are becoming ever more prevalent at the municipal level and a rationale as to their superiority has developed.[5]

Much of the early history of United States social planning was focused in the health and welfare or community councils, as they were variously called. Long preoccupied with coordination, development of criteria for allocation, and assuring community support and consensus in relation to these endeavors and programmatic thrusts, the councils were the center of development of the earliest social surveys, of priority measurement systems, of work on social breakdown indexes. Their community organization staffs pioneered

---

[5] See, for example, Peter H. Nash and Dennis Durden, "A Task Force Approach to Replace the Planning Board," *Journal of the American Institute of Planners*, XXX, No. 1 (February, 1964), 10–26.

in methods to achieve consensus and support and to assure local expression of preference.[6] While always presumably concerned with both the public and voluntary sectors, councils in fact had sanction only in relation to the latter, because of their formal or informal ties to community funds. With only occasional exceptions, they did not achieve major participation from public agencies. Their planning tended—again with some exceptions—to be indicative in a rather passive sense; their reports generally had little status beyond offering programmatic or policy proposals, which might or might not achieve strong backing from those related to sources of local money and power.

Because they were the meeting ground of the existing agencies, their planning seldom had the leverage for considerable innovation; it usually sought consensus within the "Establishment," making new thrusts with new resources but not often redeploying resources considerably.[7]

During the nineteen-fifties there was a tendency to convert councils of social agencies into community councils controlled by—and thus supported by—elements of the industrial and political power structure. The process was interrupted by the social legislation of the Kennedy and Johnson administrations, which in effect mandated more systematic social planning both in city government and in new, broad neighborhood organizations. The councils were eclipsed in the planning role in most places, although a few sought and even achieved acceptance as social planning instruments for both public and voluntary sectors. Councils continue to carry out extensive community need surveys, priority research, grass-roots community organization. They offer central services (especially information), speak on social policy issues, and continue as coordinators.[8] Few expect them to become planning arms for all of municipal social welfare. In addition to reasons already given, most councils have displayed relatively narrow concepts of the relevant—tending to ignore sectors like education and employment because these are not voluntarily funded.

---

[6] Murray Ross, *Community Organization: Theory and Principles* (New York: Harper & Bros., 1955); Violet M. Sieder, "The Tasks of the Community Organization Worker," in National Conference on Social Welfare, *Planning Social Services for Urban Needs* (New York: Columbia University Press, 1957), 3–16.

[7] Robert Morris and Robert H. Binstock document the process in *Feasible Planning for Social Change* (New York: Columbia University Press, 1966).

The creation of new planning instruments to meet the more comprehensive requirements of the nineteen-sixties is described in Peter Marris and Martin Rein, *Dilemmas of Social Reform* (New York: Atherton Press, 1967).

[8] Some data relevant to staffing and coverage are available in Reginald Robinson, David F. DeMarche, and Mildred K. Wagle, *Community Resources in Mental Health* (New York: Basic Books, 1960), Chap. XIII.

Experienced observers predict that councils in the future will face the inevitability that a city develop "a social planning department with a statutory base, an adequate staff operating within a clearly defined social policy," while the voluntary councils will continue to plan for the voluntary sector, perhaps do research for the public and voluntary sectors, engage in social policy development and promotion, and continue their ongoing efforts to improve individual agencies and service systems.[9]

The purpose of this listing of trends has been basically descriptive, rather than evaluative, yet it would be reasonable to note general dissatisfactions of several kinds. First and foremost, has been the concern arising from the separation of economic, physical, and social planning, with the negative consequences already suggested and further elaborated in the companion volume. Then, there is the frequency with which the several types of instruments are so "located" organizationally that proposed policies, programs, and projects are not implemented; planners produce reports under constant hazard of being confined to dusty shelves. Third, in the United States in particular, departmental, committee, commission, and voluntary-sector planning in the several social fields is not adequately coordinated, especially at the federal level. In a country with a general hesitancy to create monolithic, centralized planning, there is search for some compatible overall coordinating or domestic policy-development device. Fourth, there is a searching for clarification of relationships in planning and coordination from central to state and local (or their equivalent) levels—as there is, fifth, also a search for effective ways to interrelate statutory (public) and nonstatutory (voluntary) sectors. In addition, there is debate as to whether planning groups should have operational responsibilities. Finally, there is concern that the balance between central, specialized, sectoral planning (education, or health, for example) and locally integrated planning (multiple-service neighborhood center, for example) be redressed. All of this is taking place in a context in which planning models and techniques and the training of planners continue to require major attention and upgrading.[10]

## EMERGING PRINCIPLES

There is too little accumulated experience and far too little comparative analysis to sustain many firm generalizations about planning organization and structure. The evolution of planning as a process and the shaping of

---

[9] Robert H. MacRae, "Overall Community Planning: How and By Whom?" in *Social Service Review*, XXXIX, No. 3 (September, 1965), 255–260.

[10] Jane Jacobs, *The Death and Life of Great American Cities* (New York: Vintage Books paperback edition, 1963), 416 ff., for illustration.

such process to diverse political philosophies and cultural biases will undoubtedly hold significant implications for the future organization of planning. Planners will learn, too, what is relevant on all levels, for central governmental effort only, for the local level, for the statutory—and so on.

In the interim, planning expands and new administrative vehicles are created. This would seem to justify an effort at *very tentative* summarization of emerging principles.[11]

*Planning should be so organized as to support a process and not the mere production of a plan.*

Those who, on various levels, must implement a plan, support it, finance it, and take advantage of its output should be included in the process of thinking, choosing, and evolving in various relationships. Waterston illustrates the principle for several countries, particularly France, while D. V. Donnison and Valerie Chapman offer British illustrations, and Robert Morris and Robert Binstock are among many American authors documenting the relevant experience.[12] Though the logic of the principle is readily accepted as consistent with behavioral knowledge, implementation demands overcoming some normal tendencies of specialists and bureaucracies. The frequency with which plans are ignored attests to the difficulty of structuring and sustaining *processes*.

*Whatever the governmental level, statutory planning should be a staff function in the office of the executive—with only occasional exceptions.*

The convergence on this view in recent years for municipal, state, and national planning organizations reflects the analysis and absorption of the lessons of experience. If "impartial" boards and committees produce plans, these may or may not be unrealistic, but they will certainly lack adequate support. If specialized ministries, coordinate with other ministries, are expected to plan, the process lacks adequate sanction and support. Where

---

[11] Waterston, *op. cit.*, offers the most systematic guidance in relation to national planning efforts. Other sources cited below are especially helpful on other levels. Relevant sources in specialized fields are cited throughout. Some municipal and state experience is also reviewed in Alfred J. Kahn, *Planning Community Services for Children in Trouble* (New York: Columbia University Press, 1963), Chap. XIII. Shonfield offers detailed studies of France, Britain, West Germany, and the United States in Andrew Shonfield, *Modern Capitalism: The Changing Balance of Public and Private Power* (New York: Oxford University Press, 1965), while the University of Syracuse paperback "National Planning Series," under the General Editorship of Bertram M. Gross, thus far includes detailed studies of Venezuela, Morocco, Tunisia, Tanganyika, Mexico, Israel, West Germany, Yugoslavia, Great Britain, and Italy.

[12] Waterston, *op. cit.*, 445–450; D. V. Donnison, Valerie Chapman, *et al.*, *Social Policy and Administration* (London: George Allen & Unwin, Ltd., 1965); Morris and Binstock, *op. cit.*

finance ministries take on planning roles, the output is unduly "censored" in terms of budgetary considerations. Budget officers seldom "dream the impossible dream." Where governmental planning responsibilities are assigned to nongovernmental or semi-independent bodies, an additional phase of winning adequate political support within the government must be added on to the planning process.

Obviously, the principle applies only to official governmental planning. Plans may be made more realistic, be given some reasonable possibility of support, and be rapidly translatable into operational terms if the executive helps define the planning task, constantly interacts with those formulating the policy, contributes to the assessment of preferences, sets policy and programming parameters in the light of other commitments, instructs his budgeters to include provision for implementation, mandates the participation of department heads in all phases—especially implementation. Significant planning relates at all times to the core of governmental policy on many levels. An executive's annual program and his annual budgetary proposals should build upon and update a plan. Clearly, the planning office is best situated if it is seen as his arm—unless there are major contra-indications.

In some instances, the executive is weak and the legislature carries some administrative prerogatives—or the real control over resources. This would be a good reason to depart from the principle. Legislative committees and their staffs or special commissions appointed by legislatures should then be assigned major roles. Sometimes an unusual finance minister or budget director combines the vision and power to justify placement of the planning in his department. Occasionally a semi-independent research and development institute may serve as the equivalent of the executive's staff arm. Otherwise, given present experience, the case is strong for the principle as stated above.[13]

Those who hold high hopes for the PPBS approach see budget bureaus in major planning roles,[14] but the evidence is not yet convincing that one

---

[13] For relevant support, Waterston, *op. cit.*, 476 ff.: Hagen, *op. cit.*, 332–347; Joseph M. Heikoff, "Comments," in Harvey Perloff, Editor, *op. cit.*, 121–129; *European Seminar on the Problems and Methods of Social Planning*, Kallvik, Finland (Geneva: United Nations, 1965, mimeographed, SOA/ESWP/1964/3); Nash and Durden, *op. cit.*; John Friedman, *Venezuela: From Doctrine to Dialogue* (Syracuse: Syracuse University Press, 1965, paperback), 36.

[14] For example, George A. Steiner, "Problems in Implementing Program Budgeting," and Melvin Anshen, "The Program Budget in Operation," in David Novick, Editor, *Program Budgeting* (Cambridge: Harvard University Press, 1965), 308–370. Also, Committee for Economic Development, *Budgeting for National Objectives* (New York: 1966, paperback), 38–39.

should depart from the general principle that both "traditional" budgeters and PPBS staffs (whether with maximum or modest charges) should be seen as staff arms of the executive. Should PPBS become the operating planning or programming instrument, the annual budget process would eventually be incorporated as a function of a sub-unit. Under any circumstances, as PPBS methods develop, the executive will wish to assure close ties among PPBS, annual budget, and planning activities, reintegrating and combining them as emerging practice dictates—but as direct instruments of his office.

Already implied, but in need of repetition, is the general view that planning offices should not operate projects or programs. A few experts differ, urging that planners "keep their hands" in operational realities by accepting responsibility for a few projects; the majority hold that operation confuses the role and undermines the status of a planning office.

Also, while there are organizational and governmental circumstances under which policy development and technical (programming) activities may be separated, one would generally seek unification or close interconnections between these aspects.

*Less-developed countries, cities and states with very limited resources, and voluntary agencies with rudimentary organizational structures should not attempt to develop a complete structure for planning all at once.*

Planning activity eventually must become part of the normal, natural activity of governmental or other organizations. Developing legislative and executive systems, particularly on a central level, cannot cope with overcomplex agendas all at once. Waterston, who knows the risk of relying on a *person*, rather than a carefully chosen *institution*, nonetheless notes that on a transitional basis, before one locates central planning in the office of the executive, one may at times profitably begin by using scarce personnel to create programming units in several ministries rather than attempting to create a central planning organization.[15] As a next step, quite often, a strategic

> approach in less developed countries . . . is to locate a central planning agency wherever there is some one especially qualified and interested and powerful enough to give this new and weak arm of government the best chance of surviving and progressing.[16]

Interim structures are often necessary and useful, but the goal of locating central planning as a staff function of the executive branch remains.

---

[15] Waterston, *op. cit.*, 375–378.

[16] *Ibid.*, 470.

*There should be organizational provision for a diversity of planning, official and unofficial, central and local.*

Democratic societies may seek rationality and coherence, while protecting preferences, by avoiding monolithic planning. As indicated elsewhere in the present volume and argued strongly by a number of advocates,[17] this may be sought by a variety of devices:

- ☐ by creating a planning process which includes participation of citizens, specialists, politicians, governmental departments, interest groups—on all levels—in the shaping of *official* plans;
- ☐ by encouraging independent policy formulation and comprehensive planning efforts by special-interest groups, political groups, professional associations, and special task forces in accord with their capacities—and facilitating incorporation of the output of such efforts into public programs through normal political process or, where more appropriate, the adoption of the results by nonstatutory programs;
- ☐ by decentralizing both official and unofficial planning as much as possible wherever appropriate.

We need not repeat the reasons for these specific proposals, since they have already been argued in the present volume. The United States, of course, has resisted central planning. Some planning advocates have been so preoccupied with the poor coordination of domestic policy and the need somehow to create a comprehensive federal planning instrument—or a social sector parallel to the Council of Economic Advisors—that they have forgotten the need also to protect some of the values of present diversity. One would hope for both increased executive leadership in coordination of the total planning endeavor nationally, in the state capitals, and in our city halls, while the diverse, unofficial competing proposals from specialists and special-interest groups continue to appear and to have strong support. At the same time the "official" central planning machinery should be interrelated with efforts on "lower" levels to contribute to choice of preferences and to development of program content. As noted in appropriate chapters of the companion volume (on poverty, community mental health, housing), these goals are not readily achieved even where there is agreement in principle.

Of special interest, because of these thrusts, is the experience in Yugoslavia, which has gone further than most countries in conceptualizing a theory and creating an economic and political base for the decentralization of planning. (One may review the concept without having access to data

---

[17] See Chapters II and IV. Also, Paul Davidoff, *op. cit.*

for appraisal of the charge that a political party system, superimposed on this structure, decreases the freedom which is formally assigned to the commune and to local enterprise.)

Observers are agreed that Yugoslavia experienced spectacular economic growth when it gave up a catastrophic post-World War II effort at centralized, authoritarian control of enterprise and substituted decentralized decision-making through worker-management. All subsequent changes were in the direction of further decentralization. This and similar experience in turn helped launch major reforms in the entire East European bloc of nations under Soviet influence—and in the Soviet Union as well. Reforms of the pricing system and restoration of the market for many purposes have been aspects of this phenomenon, although Yugoslavian decentralization has followed an institutional direction not yet completely copied elsewhere.[18]

The basic feature of the Yugoslavia scene is an effort to create "self-government in every sphere of social and political life."[19] This is more than decentralization; some have called it "de-étatization." Society is a federation of self-governing and interconnected associations. Property is socially owned but does not belong to "the state." Workers in industry elect management councils—as do those in wholesale and retail business, agriculture, foreign trade, and public utilities. Similar self-management devices exist in housing cooperatives, universities, other schools, hospitals, social welfare programs generally, and professional groups.

At each level, the elected management group may make production decisions and dispose of resources. Worker councils operating businesses have many of the prerogatives and responsibilities of management in a market economy; after the council meets tax and normal business commitments, it may allocate additional profits to wages and salaries, a reserve, a reinvestment fund, or added social welfare benefits. Much of the activity of the economy is governed by "the market" and its price system. Tenant groups, professional associations, and local communes also exercise options for expenditure, capital improvement, or investment, as they allocate rent surpluses, their assigned tax funds, and grants from industry among the various

---

[18] Albert Waterston, *Planning in Yugoslavia* (Baltimore: The Johns Hopkins Press, 1962, paperback); Eugen Pusic, "The Interdependence Between Social and Economic Planning, with Special Reference to Yugoslavia," in J. A. Ponsioen, Editor, *Social Welfare Policy* (The Hague: Mouton and Company, 1962), 239–287.

[19] Quoted by Waterston, *op. cit.*, 23, from Branko Horvet and Vlado Rascovic, "Workers' Management in Yugoslavia: A Comment," *Journal of Political Economy* (Chicago), 67, No. 2 (April, 1959), 198.

possible amenities, personal benefits, elements of collective consumption, or general maintenance.

An elaborate network of councils, commisions, secretariats, and advisory specialist groups on the national and state (there are six republics) levels is intended as a device to build the experience, expertise, and concerns of diverse groups into planning and policy development. Similar devices exist in local government; representation is in terms of social role, and diverse perspectives on policy are thus introduced. Details are outlined by the authors cited.

The structure would appear to risk extreme fragmentation and stalemating, especially in a country with a long tradition of ethnic divisiveness. The reality is, of course, that the state provides an overall framework and protects the core elements of policy.

> The state makes the important decisions and enunciates the basic objectives and targets in the federal plans as well as the instruments of economic policy by which they are implemented. . . .
>
> . . . In addition, it relies on a comprehensive network of trade unions, trade associations and economic chambers, as well as on the communes, to guide and coordinate local economic activities with national objectives and on a variety of political organizations to inform and persuade the people to cooperate with the aims of the plans. . . .
>
> Within the framework of a single economic, social and political philosophy, which has the effect of orienting all entities towards the Federation's point of view, the objectives of each entity manage to be reconciled to conform generally with the federal planning goals without unduly undermining the essential autonomy of economic organizations. . . .[20]

What is of interest in present context is the fashion in which the Yugoslav planning system provides for the "feeding" of special-interest group thinking into federal and state planning through the creation of a diversity of councils and commissions, while at the same time federal planning both reflects and sets parameters for parallel planning at lower levels in the hierarchy. Since prerogatives of each level are well defined, each level is permitted to plan what will be executed on its level. Also of considerable interest is the intent to maximize the planning and operational options available to the lower levels. Factory councils can decide to increase fringe benefits or to add to the social welfare resources of an enterprise's employees. Resident groups in a commune may shape the social service pattern to local needs and may so plan as to assure integration of components. At the same

---

[20] Waterston, *op. cit.*, 88–89, 90.

time—and here the debate resides as to how much is controlled and super-imposed—a framework of national purpose and policy is preserved. This is the difficult issue, as the interest in decentralization of planning intensifies everywhere.

On a somewhat less comprehensive basis, French planning, although originally quite centralized, increasingly builds preferences and experiences of specialist groups into national planning and creates options to be exercised by local groups. Grant-in-aid patterns of federal funding to the states have a similar potential effect in some fields in the United States, as in the anti-poverty, education, mental health, and anti-delinquency programs launched in the mid-nineteen-sixties, at which time the states were called upon to plan and were offered federal matching or complete funding if certain general conditions were met. Here, as in all such patterns, the problem is one of allowing enough true options to the local level so that the conceptual stances and program orientations of the federal bureaucracies do not impose one mould on the supposedly independent plans.

In general, the American value system would appear to support the notion of maximizing local planning, particularly in social welfare programs, yet the problem remains of maintaining a framework of goal and policy that is clear enough to protect national (or state) objectives and flexible enough to sustain valued diversity. Testifying before a Senate subcommittee, Paul Ylvisaker drew upon his foundation, state, and national experience to conclude: "You must establish ground rules and parameters consistent with some concept of where society should be going and still maintain freedom and decentralization."[21]

Daniel Moynihan feels that the situation is already out of balance: in a national society more policies must be national, while programming remains local.[22] The dilemma is well known: "plans are manageable only if we delegate; plans are coordinated in relation to organizational goals only if we centralize." Centralization is easiest for the single-purpose organization.[23] Clearly, one needs local, intermediate, and national policy development and programming instruments, and the view of division of roles reflects cultural

[21] Paul Ylvisaker, in *Examination of the War on Poverty*, Hearings before the Subcommittee on Employment, Manpower and Poverty of the Committee on Labor and Public Welfare, United States Senate, Part 2 (Washington, D.C.: Government Printing Office, 1967), 683.

[22] Daniel Moynihan, "The Relationship of Federal to Local Authorities," in *Toward the Year 2000*, constituting *Daedalus*, 96, No. 3 (Summer, 1967), 801–802.

[23] Harold L. Wilensky, *Organizational Intelligence* (New York: Basic Books, 1967), 58 ff.

context and social philosophy. One may expect in the United States a period of experimentation and debate about these matters. Research would be fruitful.

Diverse philosophers in the United States currently express themselves in congressional debates about: federal grants to states for various social programs as opposed to direct grants to cities, which thus circumvent the states; detailed proposal and plan evaluation in Washington as opposed to grants, either to cities or states, based on submission of general plans for given sectors or programs; federal aid to lower levels for specific programs or in the form of formula grants offering general budgetary support. Yet none of the positions would seem to preclude the need for planning and programming capacities at the several levels—and for adequate coordination among them.

*Task force, commission, and other short-term ad hoc and interim planning mechanisms continue to have their place, supplementing departmental, legislative, and overall governmental planning machinery.*

Concern about a major social problem, resolve to introduce new initiative with reference to a specific program area, and a desire to dramatize community commitment all justify devices which supplement or temporarily substitute for ongoing machinery. Though they are no substitute on a permanent basis, since task forces, commissions, and the like have relatively limited longevity in public interest and tend rapidly to exhaust their potential for effectiveness, one should not forgo their capacities to capitalize on crises, rally new resources, and bring new initiative and thinking into areas where the existing networks seem to lack needed creativity. In fact, departmental planning staffs and overall planning organizations do well when they themselves encourage and initiate such supplementary devices.[24]

Special committees of the United States Senate and House of Representatives, and a number of joint congressional committees, have developed a level of member and staff expertise over the years which makes them excellent planning agencies. While these bodies cannot substitute for departmental planning based in ongoing operations or for executive planning which seeks balance and complementarities, they are potentially excellent supplementary instruments for problem-oriented planning and periodic innovation in stagnant program areas. Relatively modest staff expansion and reform in rules, which might decrease political encroachment somewhat at the research and planning stages, would have major payoff value.

---

[24] For proposals on a municipal level for time-limited task forces, appointed by the chief executive with the approval of the legislature, see Nash and Durdén, *op. cit.*

*The decision as to whether to create separate official machinery for social planning or to assume that one planning staff will undertake economic, social, and physical planning, must depend on the total context of government and the view of planning in the culture.*

On the level of abstract theory, few argue for separateness. The interplay among the elements is obvious and the ultimate validity of socially-oriented criteria for all aspects of public policy is recognized. However, there are different degrees of readiness to plan in different sectors, and governmental prerogatives among departments and on different levels complicate the picture. Legislative mandates also limit the executive. In the United States at present, for example, it would be a major step forward if, in addition to departmental planning in the various "social" fields, the executive branch also created some machinery to coordinate the total domestic social program. President Richard M. Nixon's new Council for Urban Affairs apparently represents a serious attempt in this direction.

None of this eliminates the issue of defining appropriate boundaries within the social field to guide both departmental planning and more comprehensive overall efforts. Nor does it preclude "watchdog" or pressure-group activity in behalf of segments of a field concerned with particular population groups (child welfare, for example).

*Whatever the organizational structure, staffing by interdisciplinary teams or coalitions is essential.*

The rationale has been developed earlier in this chapter.

*Devices to coordinate statutory and voluntary planning are needed at all governmental levels.*

Again, structure and prerogatives will vary with the importance accorded voluntarism. In the United States, with its great emphasis on the nonstatutory, coordination of public and voluntary planning becomes vital for city, state, and federal government. Experience to date defines the following as the urgent and sensitive issues:

☐ The need to assure that, where there is public statutory responsibility for "coverage," this is not forfeited to the voluntary sector. (Public authorities may wish to purchase care in some fields where there is advantage in doing so, but this should be within a framework of public planning, policy, and accountability.)

☐ The need to limit use of the voluntary where constitutional principles of "separation of church and state" so decree, while assuring noninterference with people's rights to practice their religion and to employ sectarian programs.

☐ The need to avoid assigning public planning responsibilities to voluntary social welfare agencies or groups, while valuing such groups as legitimate pressure bodies seeking to influence public policy. (This does not preclude research and planning contracts for defined purposes.)

☐ The need to encourage careful joint planning in specific fields of service so as to assure adequate program coordination and case integration.

## REPORTING, FEEDBACK, AND EVALUATION

The inclusion of this final, brief section in the present chapter announces, in effect, that the subject is too vast for coverage in the present volume.

A complete, rational planning model provides for:

☐ task definition
☐ policy development
☐ programming
☐ reporting, feedback, and evaluation.

Task definition and policy development have been discussed at length as the more novel and less frequently analyzed phases. Programming material has required considerable space, yet the selection has been limited and arbitrary: in effect, the entire field of management and administration is relevant. Similarly, full presentation of reporting, feedback, and evaluation would require coverage too vast and detailed to be encompassed without putting the entire volume out of focus. The contents of materials in social science theory, research design, statistics, financial auditing, and management reporting systems are relevant. The status of computer programming and technology is also part of the picture. We have therefore adopted the solution of brief reference to requirements and principles.[25]

Feedback, as Norbert Wiener taught, is part of a system's or organization's adaption to environmental signals.[26] It is of the very essence of the present work's stance vis-à-vis planning that feedback via formal reporting, informal communication, auditing, evaluation, and research be built into each phase of the work. Task definition, it will be recalled, emerges in the interaction among problem posed, reality assessment, and the value screens. Reality assessment and value analysis are guided by, but also affect these phases, in turn guiding and being reshaped by programming activities. The experience in designing programs raises new questions about all that has gone before, and the actual program outputs are appraised for the light

---

[25] The flow chart in Novick, *op. cit.*, 341, suggests the relation of controls and feedback to all phases of planning. The variety of structures is suggested in *European Seminar on the Problems and Methods of Social Planning*.

[26] Raymond A. Bauer, "Detection and Anticipation of Impact: The Nature of the Task," in Raymond A. Bauer, Editor, *Social Indicators* (Cambridge, Mass.: The M.I.T. Press, 1966), 56.

they shed on all phases of the enterprise. They guide continuous readjustment of task, policy, and program.[27]

These are easy generalizations. Their realization depends upon: formal and informal interaction of the people involved in the several phases; the designing of formal administrative control, monitoring, and reporting systems, which will provide ongoing program and population-trend data relevant to the effort and implement appropriate principles of accountability; periodic evaluation of the product—of both the program quality and the program effectiveness, two separate matters. From all that has gone before we need hardly add that planners are concerned both with intended and sought results and with the side-effects of their actions. They are interested in impact on the "target population" and on the public at large. What some systems designers call second-order (unanticipated) consequences, when unmonitored, may throw an entire planning operation out of balance. Soviet planning failures under Stalin have been described in these terms. Whatever the view of particular cases, there is a convergence on the view that since the planner or administrator cannot control or even monitor all details, both must rely on feedback for significant signals—particularly about the unanticipated.[28]

The first of these subjects, assuring the interaction of those with complementary responsibilities, is in the province of administration and community organization. It was mentioned briefly above. Organizational structure, committee process, communication devices (bulletins, reports, sharing minutes, joint meetings) are all needed.

Formal reporting systems are designed to permit administrators to monitor, audit, and control operations. Such systems offer an arena for creativity too seldom appreciated. Computer technology permits great improvement in these systems, but also introduces the hazard of drowning in an excess of data. Planning without task-oriented reporting of all phases is traveling blind. The skills of the designers of reporting systems reside in their ability to select or to develop indicators of variables relevant to the enterprise and

---

[27] A comprehensive approach which holds (unlike some of the literature) that feedback *is* relevant to constant goal readjustment is offered by Robert N. Anthony, *Planning and Control Systems* (Boston: Division of Research, Harvard University Graduate School of Business Administration, 1965), especially 28–29. Also see Raymond A. Bauer, "Societal Feedback," in Bertram M. Gross, Editor, *Social Goals and Indicators for American Society*, Vol. II, constituting *The Annals of the American Academy of Political and Social Science*, 373 (September, 1967), 180–192.

[28] For discussion of second-order consequences, see Bauer, "Detection and Anticipation of Impact: The Nature of the Task," 2–10.

most likely to alert consumers, policy-makers, and programmers to aspects in need of elimination or improvement.[29] At the same time reporting-system design must avoid the kinds of demands on staff and program users which actually have the effect of interfering with or changing operations.

Where one deals with poor or underdeveloped countries, poor or underdeveloped communities in more prosperous countries, and with programs which by intent have large numbers of so-called indigenous staff with limited education, it is necessary to compromise on routine reporting procedures so as to avoid making unreasonable demands. Administrative control through other than reporting devices is highlighted. Here, too, however, the feedback data are essential.[30] Sampling procedures and periodic special studies by technically qualified research staff may have to substitute.

In the area between these two categories of feedback, the interaction of people involved in the work and the formal reporting systems, one may identify the category of consumer or user response. Staff alertness to informal reactions is increasingly supplemented by the self-organization of service "users" to affect policies and programs. In the American anti-poverty effort, "users" also become "policy-makers" in local community action agencies.

The final category of feedback covers the more formal research activities which are the responsibility of any planning agency. Sometimes the research is carried out by an arm of the planning organization; quite often, outside research institutes and researchers are granted evaluation contracts. The studies are basically of two types: evaluation of *process* and evaluation of *outcome*. One wishes to know, first, whether the planned program has been produced at the quality sought, has been delivered, and has been used. However clear-cut and reasonable, these are often unanswered questions. Only after answers are known can we face the even more difficult issue: have the intended results been achieved?

Unrealistic fadism about evaluation often results in legislative and bureaucratic mandating of research designs in connection with all program innovation. While the intent may be admirable, the fact remains that measurement of effectiveness requires extreme clarity about the *input* (the program being tested), *control* of extraneous factors (in the research sense),

---

[29] The "social indicators" discussion of Chapter III is relevant here. Also, see Bauer, *op. cit.* Indicators may monitor countries, groups, or programs.

For a comprehensive review of the state of the art and a possible program of work, see Eleanor Bernert Sheldon and Wilbert E. Moore, *Indicators of Social Change: Concepts and Measurements* (New York: Russell Sage Foundation, 1968).

[30] For a comprehensive review of possibilities, see Robert A. Rosenthal and Robert S. Weiss, "Problems of Organizational Feedback Processes," in Bauer, *op. cit.*, 302–340.

and clarity about *criteria* for effectiveness. These conditions seldom prevail in relation to new enterprises. It is particularly unrealistic and sometimes disastrous to mandate formal evaluation where the real need is for an initial period of program development characterized by considerable trial and error. To "fix" the input is to sacrifice much of the potential of innovating legislation.[31]

Where new programs are couched in relatively general terms and are intended to shape the "possible" in the context of political realities and organizational prerogatives, the goal is obviously a change process and the criteria are unspecifiable. Rigorous research demands may be dysfunctional, as Marris and Rein demonstrated with reference to the Ford Foundation "gray area" projects and the anti-poverty community action programs.[32]

This much said, one must stress the urgency of research provision—albeit realistic provision—in all planning enterprises. Apart from the operational feedback and the informal reports, there is need for identification of strategic program elements so as to provide for systematic study of process. This alone may be of great value, because quantitative and qualitative data about output, delivery, and access have major implications. In addition, evaluative designs, shaped to specific projects, focused on areas where there is enough research control to produce valid results and asking hard questions about effectiveness, may produce major needed review of policy and program.[33]

For the most part, one cannot expect rigorous evaluation of large-scale interventions and comprehensive new policy thrusts: a new policy to end school segregation, the community mental health movement, a major departure in income security, or a community development program in some sections of a large city. Where latent functions are as potent as the manifest, where there are many hidden agendas, where the new policy is part of a larger development and not readily isolated from it, where the arena is so

---

[31] For example, see Melvin Herman and Stanley Sadofsky, *Youth Work Programs* (New York: Graduate School of Social Work, New York University, 1966), Chap. XI.

[32] Marris and Rein, *op. cit.*, Chap. VIII.

[33] A balanced view is offered by Peter Rossi, "The Study of Man: Evaluating Social Action Programs," *Trans-Action*, 4, No. 7 (June, 1967), 51–53.

The evaluative study is often ignored because of other elements, as in the case of the failure of research on the relation of class size to educational impact to affect demand for smaller classes. See Daniel Moynihan in *Federal Role In Urban Affairs*, Hearings before the Subcommittee on Executive Reorganization of the Committee on Government Operations, U.S. Senate (Washington, D.C.: Government Printing Office, 1967), Part 13, 2645. Also see articles by C. Weiss and S. Sadofsky in June L. Shmelzer, Editor, *Learning in Action*, Office of Juvenile Delinquency and Youth Development (Washington, D.C.: Government Printing Office, 1966).

complex that research controls are not possible—we do better to leave evaluation to users or to the electorate. Here the emphases might be on reporting and feedback, rather than laboratory-type measurement.

A final point about access to reports, research results, and feedback materials. Obviously, administrators have the right to their own internal and confidential quality controls, materials relevant to personnel evaluation and to a variety of mechanisms for ongoing program monitoring. Furthermore, it is certainly true that the likelihood of publication will color and often invalidate some reports. Nonetheless, in the general field of public services and policy, there is also the accountability to the electorate and the taxpayers. Thus, in each field, and with the understandable but carefully specified limitations suggested, feedback, reporting, and research systems must have provision for routine publication of specified reports and data and for public access upon request. Moreover, the bias should be in favor of access, withholding being justified only for reasons specified in advance and minimized as a matter of policy.

Access to information is a hallmark of the open society. And an open society is most likely to capitalize on feedback in making its planning efficient, responsive, and effective.

# XII

## THE FRAMEWORK
## IN PERSPECTIVE

THE EARLY chapters have documented that we in the United States have undertaken modest social planning, despite hesitancy in the ethic and fears that planning could undermine democracy. Such planning is carried on, and its scale seems destined to increase in coming years, because there are urgent problems to be solved, social choices to be made, resources to be carefully allocated. Further, exploration suggests that effective planning might protect and even enhance democratic values. The critical questions in this latter regard are: who plans and how is it done?

Among those who have no ideological or political opposition to social planning, there are, however, many who hold either that rationality is not possible in the public arena, since reality is too complex and dynamic, or that political bargaining, not planning, is the significant process. Attempts at planning are regarded as ritual. We have dealt with these matters at various points, but not fully and with specific reference to the terms of the argument. The delineation of the specifics of the planning process permits one to frame a more complete answer. Our response therefore takes the form of a summary of the planning framework which has been offered and comment on several of the most widely-discussed analyses of planning.

### THE FRAMEWORK

Planning is not always appropriate, and some of the most telling attacks on planning actually deal with circumstances in which planning should not have been proposed. Societies must respond rapidly to emergencies, must give scope to impulse and to intuition. At times they need to protect privacy, even if it means waste of resources. In fact, extravagance must also be allowed its place in the total configuration. Furthermore, the protection of core values may at times preclude any type of social bookkeeping.

328

Nor is planning always possible even when appropriate. Major social problems may cry out for solution, and fragmented programs may appear in desperate need of coordination; but little can be expected unless a sanction for planning exists or can be created. The need, crisis, problem, dissatisfaction, or tension must somehow be wedded to enough right, resources, competence, consensus, and power so that an official planning body or the planning instrument of a special-interest group can get to work. In a preplanning phase, whether brief or long, explicit or implicit, political power plays and bargaining, administrative jockeying, or community organization process—singly or in interaction—often settle the question of capability, scope, and sanction before the undertaking begins. And these questions must be adjudicated periodically in the course of any planning process as well.

In addition to settling the outer limits for comprehensiveness, the possible scope of the questions to be asked, the preplanning interaction phase may also define quite specific substantive parameters for the planning—a subject to which we shall return shortly.

Feasibility is also limited at times by the realities of resources, knowledge, technique, and ability to project. For rational planning is concerned with the efficiency of means once ends are known or formulated. This implies a measure of intellectual control over a given domain, adequate technique, as well as sufficient funds and other resources to complete the planning and to implement the policies and programs which emerge.

Yet, at times, resources, knowledge, and technical capability seem to be joined with other essential elements and planning is launched. Its major phases are identifiable—as we have seen.

The first target of the planning process is the *definition of the planning task,* a formulation of the problem to be solved in the light of all the above elements and others. This concept is roughly parallel to what others choose to describe as general planning *goals,* from which they derive specific planning *objectives.* Task, a less-frequently used term, does not yet perhaps carry the ambiguities now associated with "goal" and "objectives" as a result of their long and contradictory usage. "Task" seeks to convey a sense of analytic work and choice of targets, in a conceptual sense, based on careful consideration of realities and priorities. For the task is often not a given in a planning undertaking. Even where offered at the start in tentative form, it is subject to the planner's reformulation. As we have sought to illustrate, the reconceptualization of the issue in the form of a new task formulation is often the most creative phase of planning, "the idea sword." It is seldom less than a very significant opportunity.

The steps or stages of planning should not be conceived of as a linear or deductive process. The imagery of a series of intersecting circles or spirals is proposed, although it is not readily depicted on a readable chart. For the planning task formulation should both grow out of and then be followed by *exploration of relevant realities and consideration of values and preferences.* Depending upon substantive area, planning sanction, governmental or organizational level, and the amount of planning which has gone on previously, the bulk of the activity may be concentrated in the period prior to or the period following formulation of the task.

What is more, the explorations of facts and values interact with one another. Values may dictate that some aspects of reality remain unexplored. Preferences themselves, on the other hand, may be studied empirically. Judgment must be exercised as to the amount of value analysis and factual compilation merited in a given undertaking—and as to what the process can afford in time and money costs. The very assessment of the reports of the several relevant realities, as well as the decisions as to what to explore, are much affected by elements of attitude and value, while social theory and scientific knowledge influence the formulation as to where and how preferences are relevant. Our statements here are inevitably general: few concepts exist as to how they apply to specific circumstances.

The factual explorations emphasize projections and prediction. Like all planning, they are future oriented. The objective is to clarify what is to be done next. One seeks a policy for the *present* in the light of the broadest possible picture, including some understanding of where the present will take us, if nothing is changed. But because the capacity for prediction is limited, especially with regard to major breakthroughs in technology or shifts in leadership, planning remains incomplete and does not profess to be the only source of change.

At times, the planning task leads at once to the formulation of *policy*, which is defined as the *standing plan*, the generalized guide to action. At other times, considerable empirical exploration and value analysis intervene. Such exploration and analysis often result in further refinement of the planning task, as a precursor to sound policy development. Interposed between task and policy is also a large analytic phase which may too have its empirical requirements: the definition of the *system* to be addressed in planning, the conceptualization of *functions*, the delineation of subsections of the system (or *boundaries*), the decisions about *levels* of intervention to be proposed, and an attempt to determine the fiscal and social *price* which could be paid to achieve the new policy.

Each of these considerations, and the empirical or value explorations they may generate in turn, may result in a rephrasing of the proposed policy. The emerging policy formulation is a major guide to the undertaking.

*Programming* follows, taking many forms, in accord with the nature, scope, and policy of the enterprise. We need not here review the general (coordination, budgeting) or social service–specific (case integration, accountability) considerations which were introduced as illustration. Again, programming grows out of, but also leads to, reconsideration of policy. So-called *planning-programming-budgeting systems*, offered by some as comprehensive planning models, may be viewed as extremely interesting—if over-ambitious—efforts at systematic programming.

In effect, the entire planning framework proposed is based on constant feedback, yet one also attempts *measurement and evaluation* of the output and effects of the enterprise as well. The results obtained may have implica tions for any of the earlier phases.

This approach to planning emphasizes process more than final reports; it produces medium-range programs, more often than it does master plans. Amendment, correction, and change are constant, in the light of feedback. However, at times the outcome is and should be comprehensive blueprints, broad legislation, basic policy enactments, or major resource commitments. Even under such circumstances, there are periodic—perhaps annual—corrections and revisions. The concept of the "rolling plan" is helpful: the long-range or medium-range plan which is corrected regularly in its policy or its program aspects in the light of experience and feedback.

## BARGAINING, LIMITING CONDITIONS, DISJOINTED INCREMENTALISM

Efforts to formulate the logical structure of economic, physical, or social planning processes are under constant attack from those who say

- ☐ Reality is too complex to be encompassed by a comprehensive planning effort.
- ☐ Planning is irrelevant in a world of political power struggles and decisions by bargaining.
- ☐ Modest, pragmatic strategics which involve seizing opportunities are more relevant than rational frameworks.
- ☐ Planning decreases freedom, and social planning is thus self-defeating.

We have already addressed the last of these allegations, noting that planning may be an instrument for more, rather than less, freedom. It may promote either more or less government enterprise, more or less reliance on the market, and each of the strategies may maximize individual options. The first three positions require more specific attention.[1]

---

[1] In what follows, the presentation cites, responds to, or relies upon these books and articles: David Braybrooke and Charles E. Lindblom, *A Strategy of Decision* (New York: The Free Press of Glencoe, 1963); Robert A. Dahl and Charles E. Lindblom, *Politics, Economics and Welfare* (New York: Harper & Bros., 1953; Torchbook paper

Let us begin with Myerson and Banfield,[2] two political scientists who analyze an effort to plan public housing in Chicago. At stake were the site locations for and the quantity of housing. In a classic illustration of interest-group conflict and bargaining, the authors describe how the planner's efforts are largely undone or ignored. They note, in the course of the analysis, that "a comprehensive plan as such is almost never the subject of serious political discussion or action," since most city planning comes into public focus in connection with specific "decisions regarding locations . . . budget amounts. . . ."[3]

Of some interest in the present context is the fact that, while illustrating the critical nature of interest-group politics in public decision-making, the authors do not reject rational planning. Banfield's "supplemental note" on concepts actually defines and elaborates a rational planning model. Borrowing from Herbert Simon and from Talcott Parsons, he lists the following as *the characteristics of rationality in planning:*

- ☐ The decision-maker considers all of the alternatives open, within the "conditions of the situation and in the light of the ends he seeks."
- ☐ He identifies and evaluates the consequences of each of the possible alternatives.
- ☐ He selects the alternative with the probable consequence which is "preferable in terms of his most valued ends."[4]

---

edition, 1963); Martin Myerson and Edward C. Banfield, *Politics, Planning and the Public Interest* (Glencoe, Ill.: The Free Press, 1955; New York: paperback edition, 1964); Robert Boguslaw, *The New Utopians* (Englewood Cliffs, N.J.; Prentice-Hall, 1965); Everett E. Hagen, Editor, *Planning Economic Development* (Homewood, Ill.: Richard D. Irwin, 1963); Jan Tinbergen, *Central Planning* (New Haven: Yale University Press, 1964, paperback); Albert Waterston, *Development Planning: Lessons of Experience* (Baltimore: The Johns Hopkins Press, 1965); John Friedman, *Venezuela: From Doctrine to Dialogue* (Syracuse, N.Y.: Syracuse University Press, 1965, paperback); Benjamin Akzin and Yehezkel Dror, *Israel: High-Pressure Planning* (Syracuse, N.Y.: Syracuse University Press, 1966, paperback); Peter Marris and Martin Rein, *Dilemmas of Social Reform* (New York: Atherton Press, 1967); Karl Popper, *The Open Society and Its Enemies* (London: George Routledge and Sons, Ltd., 1952 edition); Karl Mannheim, *Freedom, Power and Democratic Planning* (London: Routledge & Kegan Paul, Ltd., 1951); Kenneth J. Arrow, *Social Choice and Individual Values* (New York: John Wiley & Sons, 1951); Robert Morris and Robert H. Binstock, *Feasible Planning for Social Change* (New York: Columbia University Press, 1966); Charles E. Lindblom, "The Science of 'Muddling Through'," in Meyer N. Zald, Editor, *Social Welfare Institutions* (New York: John Wiley & Sons, 1965) 214–229; Charles E. Lindblom, *The Intelligence of Democracy* (New York: The Free Press, 1968); Ruth P. Mack, *Planning on Uncertainty* (Washington, D.C., and New York: Resources for the Future and Institute of Public Administration, 1969).

[2] *Politics, Planning and the Public Interest, op. cit.*

[3] *Ibid.*, 12, 13.

[4] *Ibid.*, 314, after Herbert Simon, *Administrative Behavior*, and Talcott Parsons, *The Structure of Social Action*.

Rational planning in this sense may be *comprehensive*, indicating the principal acts by which major ends are to be attained, or it may be *partial*, focusing only on some important or subordinate ends. Planners engaged in a course of action do not always make planned decisions: "The execution of any planned course of action involves the making of opportunistic decisions as well as planned ones."[5]

What the Meyerson and Banfield case provides is a richness of material about interest-group politics, which clarifies just how group preferences and actions affect or should affect evaluation of ends, affect or should affect perception of consequences of choices of various alternatives, and affect the balance between planned and opportunistic decision-making. Rather than leading to a rejection of a rational planning model, the political science insights enrich the model by suggesting where the rationality might focus on preferences, values, interests, adequacy of power and sanctions to accomplish partial or comprehensive plans. True rationality, it has been said, allows for the irrational. Indeed, one has here dramatic evidence for the need to review carefully, in a given situation and in advance, the question of whether conditions for planning actually exist.

Banfield, in fact, offers the outlines of a conceptual scheme to aid in such appraisal process, suggesting the following. We paraphrase:

☐ For analysis of the situation, one should differentiate *conditions* which, for one reason or another, the planner must treat as fixed and *limiting conditions*, which restrict his range of action. Where there are no limiting conditions, one may speak of *opportunity* areas.

☐ *End reduction and elaboration* involve specification of all the ends to be served by the course of action, the clarification of the implications of each, the weighing of the values attached to each—and the choice of ends to be sacrificed or compromised in order to advance others. It is helpful to distinguish the features of the goal which are the "focus of interest and activity" (*active elements*) and the important value conditions in the background (*contextual elements*).

☐ The specification of a course of action may be on one of several levels of generality: *developmental* (what we have called the general policy level); *program*; and *operational* (the most detailed). Operational details may be quite rationally elaborated, while the developmental level is irrationally selected—or vice versa.[6]

Planning theory and social science in their points of convergence can contribute much to systematization of the interest-group elements of decision-making at various stages in an overall process. The Banfield beginnings are most helpful. As indicated in the Preface, we have not sought complete-

---

[5] *Ibid.*, 312–313.
[6] *Ibid.*, 315–319.

ness in this area in the present volume. Practice "wisdom," from which more systematic formulation may follow, requires more regular accumulation.

Another case study, focusing on the Ford Foundation projects in education and on the related efforts of the President's Committee on Delinquency and Youth Crime, also provides dramatic illustration of the potency of political and interest-group dynamics and of the importance of what may be referred to as "organizational" factors. Marris and Rein offer a step-by-step history which includes the early stages of the anti-poverty community action programs as well. Again, plans reflected much that could hardly be seen as rational, and actions often ignored the plans and funding proposals. While not denying the usefulness of many of the programs and the potency of some of the conceptual contributions of these programs, the authors point essentially to what one might define as failures in initial planning. Theories were in some instances inadequate, frameworks too narrow, timing unrealistic, resources insufficient, sanctions too weak, governmental coalitions unstable, preferences conflicting. Inadequate attention was directed to the problem of how one is to reconcile the theories and concepts of experts, the preferences of local, deprived, citizens, and broader political and professional interests. Funding agencies may wish to aid localities yet appear to—or need to—impose their own pictures of desired outcomes of planning.

The Marris-Rein conclusion is interesting and relevant: rather than dismiss planning, they would make it better. They concern themselves with how it may be legitimated, where it gets its value guidelines, and how its disinterested rationality may be protected and enhanced.

Dahl and Lindblom, the first a political scientist and the latter an economist, offer an integrated series of political and economic hypotheses about "the conditions under which numerous individuals can maximize the attainment of their goals through the use of social mechanisms." Noting the general agreement as to the need for planning, the authors see the issue as one of technique and they emphasize the universality of technique among socialist and capitalistic countries. Particular choices rest on goals. In the selection, there are major consequences. Techniques are not fixed; indeed the rate of social invention is increasing. Man may be rational or irrational; plans may fail or succeed. Presumably, technique-consciousness and improvement will enhance achievement of valued ends.[7]

---

[7] Dahl and Lindblom, *Politics, Economics and Welfare*; the quotation is from page xxi. The authors note that rational action requires both *calculation* and *control*, and they consider the possible and the desirable.

Major available control devices are the *price system, hierarchy* (leaders control non-

We shall not here pursue the Dahl-Lindblom analysis of rational action mechanisms and strategies or their helpful clarification of welfare economics except to note their emphasis on the problems, in true rational action, of assembling information, achieving communication, coping with many relevant variables, and dealing with the complexity of relations among variables. These factors often impose severe limitations upon rational action. "Solutions" involve improved information and communication systems; efforts to reduce variable complexity by quantification, sampling, or delegation of decisions to leaders- experts- electorate-computers; more comprehensive calculation by science; or calculated risk. Because none of the available *calculation* or *control* mechanisms is completely satisfactory as a basis for comprehensive rationality, the authors suggest the importance of a technique which they believe is in general use and which they call incrementalism.[8]

> Incrementalism is a method of social action that takes existing reality as one alternative and compares the probable gains and losses of closely related alternatives by making relatively small adjustments in existing reality, or making larger adjustments about whose consequences approximately as much is known as about the consequences of existing reality, or both. Where small increments will clearly not achieve desired goals, the consequences of large increments are not fully known, and existing reality is clearly undesirable, incrementalism may have to give way to a calculated risk. Thus scientific methods, incrementalism, and calculated risks are on a *continuum* of policy methods. [*Emphasis added.*]
>
> Why is emphasis on alternatives closely related to existing reality an aid to rational calculation?
>
> First, the consequences of alternatives that bear a remote relation to existing reality are generally more difficult to predict.
>
> Second . . . people cannot accurately foresee their own wants. Even assuming a perfect forecast of events, men cannot rationally choose among alternatives drastically different from present reality; only after they have tested the alternatives by choosing and then experiencing could they know whether they really wanted them. To be sure, they can exclude many unwanted alternatives without actually testing them. Most people do not need to live in a concentration camp, have an accident, get sick, become unemployed, or be disgraced in order to find out they would not like it. But it is much more difficult to know which of the remaining alternatives is preferable when the obviously undesirable alternatives are excluded. Incrementalism is a process of constantly testing one's preferences by experience.
>
> Third, because an individual has many goals, some of which conflict with

---

leaders, as in bureaucracy), *polyarchy* (democracy, with non-leaders in control), and *bargaining* (leaders control each other). These control systems take various forms and often appear in different combinations.

[8] *Ibid.*, Chap. 3.

one another, rational action as we have shown requires a delicate and changing compromise among goals and a constant attention to the points where a marginal adjustment will bring about a gain in goal attainment. This is incrementalism in individul action, and the logic applies equally to social action.

Fourth, incrementalism is an aid to verifying the results of one's choices. This is in keeping with the principle of isolating a single variable. Results after one has acted can be compared with conditions before the change, and the relation of the particular choice to the particular changes is more easily determined.

Fifth, incrementalism helps to insure control. Incremental change gives prescribed superiors an opportunity to issue rather detailed instructions or to check in detail the actions of their subordinates. As a general matter, the larger the increments of change, the more difficult it is for prescribed superiors to check on their subordinates or even to give instructions that are any more than a blank check.

Sixth, incrementalism is reversible. When mistakes are made, they can more easily be repaired.

Seventh, incrementalism permits both the survival and the continual alteration of the operating organization. The attempt to secure abrupt change by prescription usually fails because the operating organization, with its own codes and norms, resists sudden, large-scale change. . . .

Eighth, for all these reasons, incrementalism is an aid to the rationality of the electorate and therefore to polyarchy. Indeed, it is the system of change practiced in all the durable polyarchies of the West.

Incrementalism should not be confused with a simple commitment to the idea that gradual change is always preferable to rapid. . . . The greater the degree of scientific knowledge available about a given instrumental goal, and provided people are reasonably confident about their preferences, the larger is the increment of change that can be rationally made.[9]

Incrementalism has aroused considerable response. It is the subject of the volume by Braybrooke (a philosopher) and Lindblom.[10] How, these authors inquire, may one evaluate and choose policies? If one dismisses the naive and vague criteria of priority methods (announcing generalized values or listing more specific criteria without ranking or weighting), one is left with what the authors call the *rational-deductive ideal* and the *welfare function*. The *former* involves expressing ultimate values quite specifically, so that they may be arranged in priority order and their relevance to given circumstances made clear—and then deriving from such ultimate values inter-

---

[9] Robert A. Dahl and Charles E. Lindblom, *Politics, Economics and Welfare* (New York: Harper & Bros., 1953; Torchbook paper edition, 1963), 82–84.

[10] Braybrooke and Lindblom, *op. cit.*

mediate principles for specific cases. The *welfare function* is the economist's effort to quantify the rational-deductive method. Specific decisions are made about ends and one emerges with numerical values with which to evaluate use of resources. (Under an alternate approach to the welfare function, one does not formulate ends but, rather, preferences among specific social states.)

The helpful expositions of these approaches in the Braybrooke-Lindblom work need not be here reviewed. Immediately relevant is the conclusion that "the rational-deductive ideal and the welfare function are not merely incapable of being *fully* realized (which everyone admits), but are, *in most circumstances and most connections* fruitless and unhelpful as ideals." Social analysts face practical difficulties which the advocates of these approaches seem to ignore.[11] While these methods claim comprehensiveness as logically necessary, they imply "superhuman" control of a large number of variables. Most critical, they treat policy questions as *intellectual*, not *political*, questions ("choose among alternatives after careful and complete study of all possible courses of action and their possible consequences and after an evaluation of those consequences in the light of one's values").[12]

*Disjointed incrementalism* is thus offered as a strategy that copes with difficulties of evaluation and policy choice in a political climate. It may be adapted to situations in which conflicting values are not resolved. It is offered as a widely practiced approach. Its relationship to pragmatism and probable debt to John Dewey are acknowledged. It is justified by particular reference to the interplay of facts and values, said to make separation of study of facts and evaluation impossible as separate phases, and to the fact that information is often not worth its costs.

Disjointed incrementalism focuses on "small changes," a not-too-clear point on a continuum, perhaps signifying non-structural change. Non-incremental, or large, change is not readily accommodated as a planning outcome in democracies based on consensus politics. Cleavage is avoided by building upon consensus and following *remedial, serial,* and *exploratory* policies. For example, one concentrates on states people wish to remedy, not on constructing complete utopias. One seeks consensus on action to be taken, not on ultimate principles. The focus in assembling information and evaluating next steps is on incremental alteration of a defined status quo, not on vague future states. Even consequences of proposals are looked at in a restricted

---

[11] *Ibid.*, 16, emphasis supplied.

[12] *Ibid.*, 40. The authors call the comprehensive method *synoptic*.

sense only—avoiding central values. Only those objectives are considered which are relevant to possibly available means; only those facts are assembled which are not, in the overall picture, too costly. Problems are transformed in their definition, as data and values are explored. An emphasis results on *evils* "to be moved away from" more than on *goals* "toward which to move." Steps in sequence (serial), oriented toward remediation, become cumulative (incremental). Each is realistic, with its potential effectiveness thereby enhanced.[13] One often chooses *sub-optimization,* solution of a lower-level problem, in place of a general attack.[14]

Employing a somewhat different vocabulary, William Peterson notes that deductive and utopian planning often may be comprehensive, but ineffectual. He urges inductive planning, the pragmatic, piecemeal coordination of public policies.[15] John Friedman, emphasizing the latent functions of planning as he experienced it in Venezuela, illustrates the need to assure that the degree of rationality and comprehensiveness is functional for the context. He would follow an optimal model, but adapt it as appropriate.[16] His product would be not a master plan but a "rolling plan," something "like a drifting cloud," a "dialogue," a process of responsible decision-making rather than a doctrine.

What does this suggest for the framework which we have offered? First, it should be noted, Braybrooke and Lindblom do not deny either the limited and unsatisfactory results of some disjointed incrementalism or the *existence* of synoptic evaluation. Others record circumstances in other countries in which, at some times and on some levels, comprehensive, analytic, ambitious planning has been undertaken and has in some measures been effective. Both Hagen and Waterston illustrate many comprehensive as well as partial plans, noting both successes and failures in many parts of the world—as does Tinbergen. Myrdal describes comprehensive economic and social efforts in developing countries. Others note that sub-optimization as a sole strategy accepts non-coordination and may make the whole worse. None among these observers cites the failures to justify discarding efforts at comprehensive rationality, preferring instead the view that the choice of degree of comprehensiveness depends on a total situation. Ruth Mack argues that, to plan on uncertainty, one often must structure the decision situation in the

---

[13] *Ibid.*

[14] Lindblom, "The Science of 'Muddling Through'."

[15] William Peterson, "On Some Meanings of Planning," *Journal of the American Institute of Planners,* XXXII, No. 3 (May, 1966) 130–142.

[16] Friedman, *op. cit.,* 49–55, 71.

broadest sense, so as to comprehend major variables which condition the outcome.[17]

Planning does range in the degree of comprehensiveness which it finds politically feasible and socially acceptable, just as it does in its capacity to assemble all that is relevant to rational decision-making. It must attend to variables of the sort proposed by Meyerson and Banfield, by Dahl and his several collaborators, by Marris and Rein, and others—to decide in a given instance the depth and scope of change to be considered, the items to be defined as contextual, the limiting conditions to accept, the strategies to be considered principal. These, however, are elements of the rationality. They do not constitute a departure from rational to political planning but, rather, *the introduction of political variables among the other variables as relevant to the definition of task, choice of policy, and programming specifics.*

In short, our framework finds most of the detailed illustrations and strategic prescriptions of disjointed incrementalism as congenial. We wonder whether the diverse elements should be termed a "strategy" apart, for we see no evidence that a rational planning approach could not gradually systematize the applications and adaptations assembled by proponents of disjointed incrementalism as enriching components of a more complete planning model. We are throughout on comfortable and familiar ground in reviewing the illustrations of alleged incrementalism, while also recognizing the dangers of steps that are too small, dreams that are too constricted. Using Roland Warren's terminology,[18] we see no need to assume that rational planning takes place in a social vacuum and that, when appropriate, it will not arrive at incremental approaches, whether small or large.

For planning may be allocative or innovative, small- or large-change-oriented, often avoiding social structural issues but sometimes tackling them, frequently nullified by political conflict and bargaining—yet occasionally successful in understanding, capturing, relating to, nullifying, or expressing such forces as well. It can and should occasionally be what Braybrooke and Lindblom would call synoptic, while it frequently is—as most of the illustrations in this volume probably are—what they would prefer to call "focused," an effort based on the imposition of limiting structure derived from judg-

---

[17] See Waterston, Hagen, Tinbergen, in the works already cited. Also Andrew Shonfield, *Modern Capitalism: The Changing Balance of Public and Private Power* (New York: Oxford University Press, 1965); and Gunnar Myrdal, *Asian Drama*, 3 volumes (New York: Twentieth Century Fund and Pantheon Books [paperback edition], 1968). Also, Ruth Mack, *op. cit.*

[18] Roland L. Warren, "The Impact of New Designs of Community Organization," *Child Welfare*, XLIV, No. 9 (November, 1965).

ments of relevance, priority, and feasibility.[19] The distinctions probably signify not absolutes, but points on a continuum.

In a sense, rational planning is like formal organization. Just as the organizational theorist or administrator may, indeed must, relate systematically to informal organization, so must the planner think systematically about and provide for the irrational, the political, the unmanageable. Thus pragmatism is scientific and so-called synoptic techniques are actually pragmatic and not rigidly deductive. The political scientists and philosophers enhance rational frameworks rather than deny them.[20] As numerous social scientists have noted, the fact that experts are often treated as window-dressing and intelligence as ritual does not negate the circumstances in which facts and rationality do count. Both Daniel Bell and Samuel Beer argue that, the *unique* characteristic of our present era, the "post-industrial society," is the extent to which "goals are less and less set by old pressures and pressure groups; more and more by the invitation of pure learning and research knowledge. Information as it accumulates provokes intervention. . . ." Increasingly, theory becomes the point of departure in social and political innovation: "Men now seek to anticipate change, measure the course of its direction and its impact, control it, and even shape it for predetermined ends."[21]

---

[19] Braybrooke and Lindblom, *op. cit.*, 42–45.

[20] See Bertram M. Gross, "Planning as Crisis Management," a Preface to Akzin and Dror, *op. cit.* Also see Melvin Webber, "The Role of Intelligence Systems in Urban-Systems Planning," *Journal of the American Institute of Planners*, XXXI, No. 4 (November, 1965), 289–296.

[21] Samuel Beer, as summarized by Theodore H. White, in *Life*, May 12, 1967; and Daniel Bell, "Notes on the Post-Industrial Society (I)," *The Public Interest*, No. 6 (Winter, 1967), 25.

# INDEX